Deleuze's Philosophical Lineage II

I0807222

Deleuze's Philosophical Lineage II

Edited by Graham Jones and Jon Roffe

EDINBURGH
University Press

Edinburgh University Press is one of the leading university presses in the UK. We publish academic books and journals in our selected subject areas across the humanities and social sciences, combining cutting-edge scholarship with high editorial and production values to produce academic works of lasting importance. For more information visit our website: edinburghuniversitypress.com

© editorial matter and organisation Graham Jones and Jon Roffe, 2019
© the chapters their several authors, 2019

Edinburgh University Press Ltd
The Tun – Holyrood Road
12(2f) Jackson's Entry
Edinburgh EH8 8PJ

Typeset in 11/13 Sabon by
Servis Filmsetting Ltd, Stockport, Cheshire
printed and bound in Great Britain.

A CIP record for this book is available from the British Library

ISBN 978 1 4744 4918 2 (hardback)
ISBN 978 1 4744 4920 5 (webready PDF)
ISBN 978 1 4744 4919 9 (paperback)
ISBN 978 1 4744 4921 2 (epub)

The right of Graham Jones and Jon Roffe to be identified as the editors of this work has been asserted in accordance with the Copyright, Designs and Patents Act 1988, and the Copyright and Related Rights Regulations 2003 (SI No. 2498).

Contents

Acknowledgements

We would like to take this opportunity to thank the immensely long-suffering authors of this volume, the preparation of which distended beyond all reasonable expectation. The fruit of their collective patience is the book itself. Our thanks to all of you for allowing us such a large overdraft on your trust.

Anyone who has worked with Edinburgh University Press – a number of our prospective readers, certainly – will know how decisive the singular Carol Macdonald is in thoughtfully advancing the cause of Continental philosophy. As always, she has been key. In addition to Carol, though, we want to thank a number of other people who were essential to its completion (in all kinds of ways): James Dale, Naomi Farmer, Rebekah Mackenzie and Kirsty Woods. We want to sincerely thank them for their support, patience, good-humour, wisely-timed ill-humour and all-around excellence. Without them all, this book, among numerous others, would simply not exist.

Jon would like to thank the Department of Philosophy at the University of New South Wales, where a significant part of the work done on the book was undertaken. Graham would also like to acknowledge the support of his friends and colleagues during the completion of this odyssey.

List of Abbreviations

AO	*Anti-Oedipus*
AZ	*Deleuze from A to Z*
B	*Bergsonism*
D	*Dialogues*
DI	*Desert Islands and Other Texts*
DR	*Difference and Repetition*
ECC	*Essays Critical and Clinical*
EPS	*Expressionism in Philosophy: Spinoza*
ES	*Empiricism and Subjectivity*
F	*Foucault*
FB	*Francis Bacon: The Logic of Sensation*
FLB	*The Fold: Leibniz and the Baroque*
K	*Kafka: Towards a Minor Literature*
LS	*The Logic of Sense*
M	*Masochism*
MI	*Cinema 1: The Movement Image*
N	*Negotiations*
NP	*Nietzsche and Philosophy*
PI	*Pure Immanence: A Life*
PS	*Proust and Signs*
SPP	*Spinoza's Practical Philosophy*
TI	*Cinema 2: The Time Image*
TP	*A Thousand Plateaus*
TRM	*Two Regimes of Madness and Other Texts*
WP	*What is Philosophy?*

Introduction: The Deleuzean fuscum subnigrum

Graham Jones and Jon Roffe

> This method had many advantages; for the painter had a light ground for the light portions of his work and a dark ground for the shadowed portions. The whole picture was prepared; the artist could work with thin colours in the shadows, and had always an internal light to give value to his tints.
>
> (Goethe, *Theory of Colours*, §905)

A major conceptual resource in Deleuze's philosophy, from the 1960s onwards, is Gottfried Wilhelm Leibniz's expressionist theory of the monad. While the monad is transformed and modified a great deal – first into the intensive individual, and then into the nomad, or at least one version of the nomad – it provides Deleuze with a group of related concepts that his philosophy would, perhaps, be impossible without.

Deleuze's various presentations of the inner reality of the monad in particular – expressive monadic perception – are marked with a genuine passion for what Beckett once called Leibniz's 'splendid little pictures',[1] a relish for Leibniz's dramatic, even demented, metaphysics. Here is how he presents this claim of Leibniz's in *The Fold*:

> Each monad thus expresses the entire world, but obscurely, confusedly, since it is finite and the world is infinite. This is why the depth [*fond*] of the monad is so dark. Since the world does not exist outside the monads that express it, it is included in each monad under the form of perceptions or 'representatives', *infinitely small actual elements*. Once again, since the world does not exist outside the monads, these are minute perceptions without an object, hallucinatory micro-perceptions. The world exists only in its representatives, insofar as they are included in each monad. It is like a lapping of waves, a confused noise, a fog or mist, a dance of dust. It is a state of death or catalepsy, of sleep or drowsiness, a fainting or dizzy spell. It is as if the depth of every monad were constituted by an infinity of small folds (inflections) that are ceaselessly being made and unmade in all directions, such that the spontaneity of the monad is like that of a sleeping person tossing and turning on its bed. The

> micro-perceptions or representatives of the world are these minute folds proliferating in all directions: folds in folds, fold upon folds, folds following folds, like one of Hantaï's paintings or Clérambault's toxic hallucinations. And it is these minute perceptions, which are obscure and confused, that make up our macro-perceptions, our clear and distinct conscious apperceptions: a conscious perception would never appear if it did not integrate an infinite set of minute perceptions that destabilize the preceding macro-perception while preparing for the following one.[2]

At a number of moments in *The Fold*, when describing these dark depths of the monad, Deleuze makes use of a striking Latin phrase: *fuscum subnigrum*. The value in maintaining the Latin in translation reflects the difficulty of conveying each word separately: *fuscum* from *fuscus*, 'dark, swarthy, dusky'; *subnigrum*, from *subniger*, 'blackish, dark, almost black'. Deleuze's extended rendering is to the point: 'very dark, in fact almost decorated in black, "fuscum subnigrum"'.[3]

An illuminating phrase, nevertheless. After cursorily passing over it a few times, a careful reader of Deleuze might try to connect it back to Leibniz's own work, to see where it appears and the range that Leibniz gives it as a characterisation of the inner life of monads. Upon inspecting the footnote that Deleuze himself appends to the passage, a first challenge: it refers not to any work of Leibniz's, but to Goethe's *Theory of Colours*.

Now, Goethe himself never uses the Latin phrase in his text, speaking in the relevant passages of the 'dark grounds [*dunkle Gründe*]'[4] which were 'probably introduced' by Tintoretto (to whom Deleuze also refers), involving a first layer of colour put on the canvas before further work was done. He continues, writing that 'The ground in question was red brown [*rothraun*].'[5]

From where, then, does Deleuze get this specific term? The problem becomes more vexing given the extremely marginal place it holds in Leibniz's work. Its single appearance, to our knowledge, is in a summary document called 'Table de définitions', likely composed in the final years of Leibniz's life, and assembled from various versions and elements by his secretary, Johann Friedrich Hodann. The 'Table' was not published in Leibniz's lifetime, and only saw the light of day when it was excavated from the *massif* of Leibniz's unpublished work by the French mathematician, philosopher and economist Auguste Couturat, who included it in the collection *Opuscules et fragments inédits de Leibniz* in 1903.

The 'Table' begins with definitions of being and existence, the abstract and the concrete, before taking in various shapes, elaborating a detailed but eccentric taxonomy of living things ('Flowers are composed of perfect, imperfect and mixed, where the imperfect consist in flowers that only partly form . . .'[6]) and a number of different groups of 'Varia' (one list includes ink, maps, the tuba and the sword).[7] Under the heading 'Sensibile Qualities', Leibniz includes subheadings devoted to 'Taste', 'Common Mixed Affections', 'Vegetable Affections' and 'Colour'. It is as a member of the latter, a list eclectic enough to give Borges some competition, that the phrase finally appears. Interlacing Latin and German, Leibniz writes '*Ex albo et nigro mistus, ut* cincreus *et similes. ita* fuscum *subnigrum est* dunckelbraun':[8] 'The mixture of white and black, cinereous and the like makes *fuscum subnigrum*, which is dark brown.' The fact that Deleuze refers to Couturat's other published work on Leibniz a number of times in *The Fold*, and once to the *Opuscules*,[9] makes it very likely indeed that it is this obscure remark included within a strange list of colours that is the source of the phrase.

The contrast between the marginal status of the phrase *fuscum subnigrum* and the central context in which Deleuze deploys it is probably clear enough at this point. That Leibniz's remark and Goethe's discussions also fail to share a common German word for the colour in question is the last detail in a strange net of facts that surrounds its apparition in *The Fold*.

We have presented this seemingly arcane investigation here because it illustrates in a particularly clear way the major problem confronting anyone wishing to read Deleuze in anything more than a cursory, mercenary or instrumental fashion. Though it is indeed possible to extract key concepts from Deleuze's works, to read them with an eye to their application and indeed, in some cases, to read them in whatever order you like, what can appear to be the solid kernels of any future 'Deleuzism' quickly show themselves to be nodes in complex conceptual, textual and historical structures that are not the real content of Deleuze's thought, but its implicit, problematising background. It is because this is the nature of Deleuze's work that expository work of the kind found – we hope – in this volume and its precursor are necessary.

*

It has been a decade now since we first began putting together the first volume of *Deleuze's Philosophical Lineage*. In the introduction to the previous book we presented an overview of the field loosely labelled 'Deleuze Studies' and made several observations and criticisms concerning the biases or presuppositions that we saw as driving several dominant interpretative tendencies. Moreover, we pointed out that, despite a number of attempts to 'apply' Deleuze's concepts in a diverse range of fields and contexts, nonetheless much work still remained to be done in identifying and understanding Deleuze's sources and influences (of which Volume 1 of *Deleuze's Philosophical Lineage* was meant to provide an impetus of sorts) and that this would require a concerted effort towards translating a number of works previously unavailable in English. Well, how much difference a decade makes! Recent years have seen the translation of several of Simondon's works, as well as translation of particular texts by Tarde, Klossowski and previously unavailable works by Guattari (not to mention the Lacan and Badiou industries which continue to offer up translations at regular intervals). The last few years have also seen the publication of a number of interpretative commentaries on Deleuze's work that mark a significant preparedness to accept that there may not, in fact, be one homogeneous 'Deleuzian' philosophy (that is, the clichés that have come to stand in place of his ideas) and that there are tensions and elisions in his work that allow for different – even competing – renderings of, or even trajectories derived from, his thought. We will return to this latter situation by way of conclusion below.

Indeed, overcoming the related insularity of previous Anglo readings of Deleuze's oeuvre has been one of the biggest impediments bedevilling the field for a few decades now. The previous volume contributed – in its own small way – to encouraging an interest in these lesser-known thinkers and their respective ideas and approaches. Indeed, since its publication we have seen a plethora of articles appear devoted to discussing some of these figures, both as regards their impact on Deleuze (as well as other Continental philosophers), and as philosophers in their own right. More importantly, recent years have seen the appearance of translations of previously unavailable works by a number of these figures (Maimon, Ruyer and, of course, Simondon, are three specific examples introduced in Volume 1 of *Deleuze's Philosophical Lineage* that immediately spring to mind), allowing many more commentators to explore (and check the relevance and accuracy) of these important works.

It is with these issues in mind that we have prepared this second volume on Deleuze's sources and influences, attempting to push even further than previously by selecting this time lesser-known (and even sometimes quite obscure yet still important) figures. This is – at least from our point of view – more of an advantage than a disadvantage, and what makes this series an attractive and valuable contribution to Deleuze scholarship. In doing so, we hope to be getting down to the philosophical nitty-gritty that often is ignored in discussions of Deleuze's ideas (particularly when they are 'applied' in other domains or disciplines). The principal aim of this series is to introduce readers to those philosophers and artists that influenced the aims and development of Deleuze's oeuvre. That these influences may not already be widely known is irrelevant to their significance or the degree of influence they actually exerted. Moreover, whether they were overtly referred to in Deleuze's own work many times or but a few times is not necessarily an accurate gauge of their actual conceptual significance.

Maldiney and Schelling present two good examples. As Ron Bogue demonstrates, Maldiney's influence should not be underestimated; indeed, his notion of rhythm provides a key means by which Deleuze can account for how intensity is both 'translated' and explicated in a punctiform manner into extensity and qualities, on the one hand, and the emergence of localised times and spaces that accompany the generation of rudimentary points of view (that is, larval selves), on the other. Similarly, in the case of Schelling, we find ourselves in the presence of a philosopher who – from the point of view of a certain orthodox reading of both Deleuze's work and German idealism (given its proximity to Hegel) – might seem to be unrelated to Deleuze's project. But, as Kyla Bruff demonstrates, the two philosophers' shared debt to Spinoza opens up a rich set of connections and questions.

However, all of this being said, and despite the efforts of a decade, *much still remains to be done*: for example, the works of thinkers such as Gueroult and Maldiney still need translating into English so as to make them available to Deleuzian scholars, but also accessible more broadly. Moreover, this ongoing process of excavation and interpretation may well involve in the future returning to and re-examining works that many may feel have already been sufficiently dealt with and clarified, such as those of Bergson and Plato, for we cannot safely make the assumption that the significance of such works for Deleuze has already been adequately understood. Furthermore, there remain many areas of Deleuze's work that still require detailed exploration – to name but two: his changing relation with psychoanalytic ideas over a period of roughly fifteen years, and the largely unnoticed interrelations of his work with some of his contemporaries (such as Lyotard, Châtelet, Derrida and Serres, among others).

In the light of these concerns, we hope that this volume will open yet new lines of research and encourage those interested in Deleuze's ideas to move beyond the more obvious associations which are already well (perhaps even excessively) serviced.

*

We would like to conclude by returning to the thematic of the *fuscum subnigrum*, this time not as a description for the depths of the monad in Leibniz, but for the characteristic status of Deleuze's own philosophy.

Reading Deleuze is never straightforward, and this is primarily because, as we have been saying, he never works on a blank canvas. Unlike his well-known description of a primary destructive work as a prelude to creation in *Francis Bacon*, however, Deleuze's own method of working rarely began with 'a complete *curettage*' (AO 311), a complete bleaching-out of the past and its legacy of possible clichés. Instead, underneath the systematic construction of concepts, a plurivalenced background can be discerned – here heavy, there light – constituting the field in relation to which the construction can take on its own values of light, weight and gravity. As Goethe says, the use of a variegated field 'has many advantages' for the painter, advantages that, however, multiply the difficulties for any attempt at reconstructing Deleuze's philosophical construction.

But it is the dialectical relationship – one that Deleuze insists on – between this distinct–obscure dark background and the clear–confused foreground that is perhaps the perfect emblem for the relationship between the obscure network of Deleuze's influences and their integrations in his published works. We have spoken about the very real progress that Deleuze scholarship has made in recent years. However, this must be balanced not just, as we have said, by the realisation that there is much further to go, but by the fact that there is a dynamic structural limit that differentially constricts how much of Deleuze can be made 'clear–confused' from a given point of view. For instance, the more weight we give to Maimon in our reading of Deleuze, the more obscure the latter's cinema books might appear; similarly, a shift in analytic perspective to, for instance, Jean Wahl's influence on Deleuze might make certain empiricist and pluralist features rise to the surface, while those which indicate his early attachment to psychoanalysis might fall into the background.

Beyond this limit though, we are not necessarily reduced to silence. After all, there remains the imperative, Deleuze's imperative: *create*. But, in this volume at least, we and its other authors instead continue the midwifery of archaeology and explication, each in our furrows, for the benefit, we hope, of the work yet to come.

Notes

1. Samuel Beckett, Letter to Thomas MacGreevy, 5 Dec. 1933, in *The Letters of Samuel Beckett, Volume 1*, ed. George Craig, Martha Dow Fehsenfeld, Dan Gunn and Lois More Overbeck (Cambridge: Cambridge University Press), p. 172.
2. Gilles Deleuze, *Le Pli: Leibniz et le baroque* (Paris: Minuit, 1988), pp. 114–15. We cite the (unfortunately) unpublished translation by Daniel W. Smith.
3. Deleuze, *Le Pli*, p. 44; Smith's translation slightly modified to indicate the adjectival character of the phrase.
4. Johann Wolfgang von Goethe, *Theory of Colours*, trans. Charles Lock Eastlake (Cambridge, MA: MIT Press, 1970), §907. The original German of the *Farbenlehre* is available online at http://sydney.edu.au/intellectual-history/documents/Goethe_zur_Farbenlehre.pdf (last accessed 13/8/2018).
5. Goethe, *Theory of Colours*, §908.
6. Gottfried Wilhelm Leibniz, 'Table de definitions', in *Opuscules et fragments inédits de Leibniz*, ed. Louis Couturat (Paris: Félix Alcan, 1903), pp. 451–2.
7. Leibniz, 'Table de definitions', pp. 470–1.
8. Leibniz, 'Table de definitions', p. 489.
9. The direct reference in *The Fold* to the *Opuscules* appears early on. See Deleuze, *Le Pli*, p. 6 n. 4.

1

Lucretius

Michael J. Bennett

Although there is considerable critical interest in treating Deleuze's work as a brand of philosophical naturalism, 'nature' is not a concept he thematises very often.[1] When Arnaud Villani suggested, in a 1981 interview, that a concept of nature or *phusis* plays a major role in his work, Deleuze agreed but mused that he had been only 'circling around' this theme without considering it directly.[2] The exception to this rule of reticence is Deleuze's relatively early (1961) essay on the Roman poet and Epicurean philosopher Titus Lucretius Carus. 'Lucrèce et le naturalisme', which first appeared in *Études philosophiques*, was subsequently adapted, retitled 'Lucretius and the Simulacrum' and included alongside an essay on Plato in the appendix to *The Logic of Sense* (1969). If Deleuze is best understood as a kind of naturalist, then perhaps this short essay affords an interpretative key for thinking about his mature work, especially the differential philosophy of *Difference and Repetition*. In addition to containing early formulations of key ideas, the Lucretius essay also encapsulates Deleuze's approach to the history of philosophy as the art of 'begetting monsters' (N 5–6). In placing the accent on particular passages, translating concepts in telling language, and implicitly juxtaposing Lucretius and Plato, Deleuze moves beyond the simple explication of Lucretius' poem *De Rerum Natura* into a collaborative enterprise of concept creation.

Nature as the Production of the Diverse

The suspicion that 'Lucrèce et le naturalisme' anticipates some of the core insights of *Difference and Repetition* seems to be vindicated within the first few lines of the essay. Lucretian naturalism aims to think 'the diverse as diverse . . . a difficult task on which, according to Lucretius, all previous philosophies had run aground' (LS 266). To support this judgement Deleuze refers to passages where Lucretius waxes lyrical about the diversity of species of living beings, of the individual members of those species, and of their heterogeneous parts.[3] Seasoned readers of Deleuze, however, will recognise the claim that philosophers have failed to think 'the diverse as diverse' and the following assertion that Lucretius' task is to consider the 'principle of the diverse and its production' (LS 266) as prefigurations of both the critical and positive components of *Difference and Repetition*. In particular, the famous opening words of Chapter Five seem to renew the Lucretian project of discovering the productive principle or condition of the diverse when they announce: 'Difference is not diversity. Diversity is given, but difference is that by which the given is given, that by which the given is given as diverse' (DR 222). Later in that chapter, Deleuze alludes explicitly to one of Lucretius' examples of the diversity of nature: 'no two . . . grains of wheat are identical' (DR 252).[4] His intention here is to block the inference that the field of individuation (of the intensive morphogenetic processes that produce actual, differenciated individuals) is something like a species-form that would be the same for all its members (which would imply that the coming to be of differences presupposes identity). Deleuze says that the absence of such an identity characterises not just actual existent things, like Lucretius' grains of wheat, but also the conditions of their actualisation. In the ontological categories of *Difference and Repetition*, these conditions are the intensive processes that mediate between differential, virtual ideas and actual things with extensive properties. For our purposes, however, this telling allusion and the parallel between Deleuze's ambition and the project he attributes to Lucretius are important for reading Deleuze as a naturalist. The role played by intensity or difference in itself in *Difference and Repetition* is the role played by *nature* in the Lucretius essay: 'Nature must be thought of as the principle of the diverse and its production' (LS 266).

By *natura* Lucretius does indeed mean something profoundly productive. Its creative exuberance is embodied in the fertile figure of the goddess Venus, to whom, the opening lines of the proem say, all living things owe their birth. Lucretius describes *alma* ('bountiful' or 'life-giving') *Venus* inspiring animals with reproductive sexual instinct and directing natural processes like the pilot of a ship.[5] It quickly becomes evident, however, that for Lucretius the teeming bounty of productive nature owes less to divine benevolence than the truth of Epicurean doctrines about the nature of the universe. The influence of Epicurus, who lived in Athens during the late fourth and early third centuries BCE, was considerable in Roman Italy by the time

Lucretius composed his poem in the mid-first century BCE. Lucretius' contemporary Cicero mentions and disputes Epicurean doctrines in *De Fato* and *De Finibus*. The city of Herculaneum, in the shadow of Vesuvius, seems to have been a hub of Epicurean intellectual activity at the time. Fragmentary texts by Epicurus himself and (possibly) Lucretius have been recovered there from carbonised scrolls at the so-called Villa of the Papyri.[6]

In *De Rerum Natura* Lucretius describes Epicurus in grandiose, heroic terms. Epicurus 'wandered in thought and understanding through the immeasurable universe [*omne immensum*]' and brought back 'spoils, namely, knowledge of what can come to be and what cannot, and for what reason the power of each thing is limited [*finita*] and fixed by a deeply buried boundary stone [*alte terminus*]'.[7] For Lucretius, the productivity of nature is explicable on the basis of the principles of Epicurean physics. For example, the axiom that nothing comes to be out of nothing leads to the core atomist insight that the majority of material bodies (all those that are generated by natural processes) are in fact compounds of indestructible particles that Lucretius calls 'first bodies'.[8] Moreover, what we call the destruction of compounds is really only the rearrangement of what Epicurus called 'atoms'.[9] Finally, the movement of compound bodies presupposes that, however solid they seem, they must not be packed solid with atoms but relatively rarefied or porous, veined by empty spaces like caves permeated by water.[10]

As Epicurus said, everything is made of atoms and void. The most ontologically fundamental loot of his cosmic intellectual expedition is the physical system according to which 'what can come to be' are compound bodies or aggregates, and 'what cannot' are the atoms themselves, which are neither created nor destroyed. What about the other 'spoils' Lucretius says Epicurus brought back, the knowledge of what is limited and marked by boundaries? Lucretius repeats the formula about laying down a 'boundary stone' (*terminus*) several times.[11] There is thus good reason to think that he considers one of Epicurus' major accomplishments the differentiation between the immeasurable (*immensum*) universe and what is finite (*finita*) and bounded. Deleuze certainly thinks so: 'The first two books of Lucretius conform to this fundamental object of physics: *to determine what is really infinite and what is not*, and to distinguish the true from the false infinite' (LS 272).

Lucretius traces this distinction carefully. He explains that, for example, although atoms come in a variety of shapes, the number of the shapes is not infinite. If the variety of atomic shapes were unlimited, there would be infinitely large atoms, and the bodies they compose would also be infinitely large. But this is not so, because atomic compounds are enclosed by a 'certain limit' (*certa finis*).[12] In contrast, the number of atoms of each shape *is* infinite, as is the magnitude of the void or space in which they move and accumulate. Lucretius (like Epicurus) argues deductively that this must be so in order for the phenomena such as we know them to be possible. Suppose that space, or the void, were finite. Then, Lucretius says, there would be a centre and a periphery to the universe and because of its weight all matter would accumulate at the centre or the 'bottom' of the closed cosmos, in which case the motion of the celestial bodies, which do not settle in one place, could not occur. Suppose, on the contrary, that the number of atoms were limited in unlimited space. The atoms would be 'dissolved' or permanently disaggregated in the vastness of the void.[13] In either case the dynamic living activity of nature could not have occurred. Therefore, it must be, as Epicurus said, that 'in terms of the number of atoms and the magnitude of the void, the universe is infinite [*apeiron to pan*]'.[14]

From these arguments Deleuze does not pick up any specific conclusions about the existence of atoms and the void. Rather his summary takes the form of a thesis about nature itself: 'Nature as the production of the diverse can only be an infinite sum' (LS 277). The infinite (and therefore creative) universe contrasts sharply with an imagined (but nowhere realised) bounded or closed universe that gathers, in so far as it is bounded, its elements into a whole. Deleuze describes Epicurean nature as 'a sum, but not a whole' (LS 267), by which he means that Lucretian nature does not 'totalise' or universally quantify over its constituents. As Lucretius argued, it is in virtue of this absence of a natural totality that nature produces. Because nature is not a whole, as Deleuze puts it, it 'is a power' (LS 267).

Deleuze's phrase 'somme infinie' probably renders Epicurus' 'pan apeiron' or maybe Lucretius' expression 'omne immensum', which both mean literally 'unlimited all'. If so, then it is noteworthy that *somme* translates the Latin *omnis* or Greek *pan*, rather than their close synonyms, respectively, *totus* and *holos*. Both mean 'all' but the latter are semantically distinct because they express the gathering of parts in a whole. *Totus* and *holos* mean 'all' in the 'collective' sense and *omnis* and *pan* in the non-collective, or 'distributive', sense (LS 267).

Deleuze uses this Epicurean distinction between open and closed universes and the implicit semantic distinction between two senses of 'all' to motivate the following construction of the history of philosophy: 'Lucretius reproached Epicurus' predecessors for having believed in Being, the One and the Whole' (LS 267). Although ostensibly a statement about Lucretius' views, Deleuze's interpretative claim actually goes beyond the text of *De Rerum Natura*. Lucretius does indeed criticise the philosophical errors of Epicurus' predecessors but his point is to discredit rival theories of matter (*materies*).[15] Lucretius focuses on the pluralistic materialism of Empedocles and Anaxagoras, for example, whereas Deleuze makes it sound like Lucretius has Plato or Parmenides in mind. Even the materialist monism singled out by Lucretius, which holds that there is one kind of substance underlying natural diversity, is the fiery cosmology of Heraclitus, hardly a Parmenidean.

Slight interpretative overreaching like this tells us something important about Deleuze's use of Lucretius. By setting the Lucretius paper alongside the essay 'Plato and the Simulacrum' (originally, 'Renverser le platonisme') in the appendix to *The Logic of Sense*, Deleuze establishes 'naturalist' and 'antinaturalist' poles of ancient Greek philosophy and aligns himself with the former. While Deleuze deprecates the way in which the transcendence of the Platonic idea deprives nature of its immanent power by reducing matter to mere appearance, he lionises the immanence of productive power in Lucretian nature. If, by proximity, Lucretius is made to appear to be offering an alternative to Plato (rather than Heraclitus, Empedocles and Anaxagoras), then it licenses the interpretation that the two essays are complementary, and perhaps even stronger, but strictly false, claims such as: 'Lucretius' target is the Platonic-style transcendent turn and the distinction between model and copy such a turn implies'.[16]

As Brooke Holmes has noted, however, Deleuze's arguments against Platonic antinaturalism have overshadowed the arguments in favour of Lucretian naturalism and flavoured their interpretation.[17] We should be cautious not to treat the Lucretius essay as a simple addendum to the one on Plato. A more prudent interpretation of Deleuze's views on Lucretius' reproach to Epicurus' predecessors concludes that, in the Lucretius essay, the problem with the holism implied by a closed universe seems to be that it lacks explanatory power. Identifying the principle of nature with a totality ('One' or 'Whole') is the mistake on which Epicurus' rivals founder because in these cases 'we do not understand diversity and its production'

(LS 267). For Deleuze, relating diversity to a prior identity is a bad explanation masquerading as a good one, precisely because, as Epicurus knew, it fails to account adequately for the production of the diverse. In fact, given the weakness of holistic explanations, it is actually necessary to use diversity and its production to explain the appearance of wholes, not the other way around. Paraphrasing Deleuze's Whiteheadian mantra, natural holism runs afoul of the first principle of empirical philosophy: universals do not explain anything, but must themselves be explained.[18]

Once again, this reading of Lucretius seems to anticipate Deleuze's later arguments in *Difference and Repetition*. For example, the emphasis on the failure of philosophers to explain the production, genesis or coming-to-be of higher-order systems resonates with Deleuze's radicalization of Maimon's critique of Kant and his method of substituting transcendental genetic conditions for extrinsic conditions of possible experience.[19] Lucretius is also looking for genetic explanations. As Ryan Johnson puts it, Deleuze admires Lucretius' 'bottom up' method, where the explanatory stress is laid on how the diversity of natural products comes about, rather than offering quasi-explanations based on the assumption of certain implicit givens.[20]

Infinitesimal Minima and the Swerve

Deleuze's appropriation of the Lucretian *clinamen* or 'swerve' of atoms affords the clearest specific example of the conceptual link between the Lucretius essay and the argument of *Difference and Repetition*. Deleuze treats the Epicurean doctrine of the swerve as a foreshadowing of the determination of quantity characteristic of the differential calculus.

Lucretius, following Epicurus, distinguishes between atoms and what he calls *minima*.[21] Although atoms are physically indivisible, they are *conceptually* resolvable into partless 'extrema' or minimal points. These minima are essentially atomic parts without independent existence (no atom is ever composed of only one minimal part) and they cohere in each atom in a different manner to the aggregation of atoms in compounds. If there weren't such minima, Lucretius argues, a finite body – indeed, every atom – would be composed of infinite parts, a proposition against which 'sound reason protests'.[22] That is, to deny the existence of minima for finite bodies means confusing what really is with what isn't really infinite.

Deleuze notes that in Lucretius the arguments for the existence of minima appear to be arguments by analogy with sensation. Just as it is possible to isolate within an episode of sensation a smallest sensible part (such as a visible patch of a shade of red within the manifold perception of a red book), it is also possible to isolate conceptually (even mathematically) a minimum part of the atom in thought (LS 268).[23] In the appendix to *The Logic of Sense*, Deleuze follows the allusion to the atom/minimum distinction with a sentence that is at first opaque: 'We go from the noetic to the sensible analogue, and conversely, through a series of steps conceived and established according to a process of exhaustion' (LS 268). The reference to the method of exhaustion is no accident. 'Exhaustion' is the modern name for the characteristically Greek geometrical procedure, pioneered by Eudoxus and Archimedes, of finding the area of a shape by inscribing within it a series of other shapes whose areas converge with the area sought, a procedure often thought to anticipate the concept of the limit of a function.[24] By invoking exhaustion, Deleuze signals that there is in Epicurean atomism something analogous to, or which anticipates, the analysis of infinite sums and infinitesimal quantities in the differential calculus. The argument can be boiled down to two claims: first, the Lucretian minimum is something like an infinitesimal (which explains why Epicureanism was so at odds with the orthodox Greek geometry that explicitly excluded infinitesimal quantities), and, second, that the *clinamen*, or atomic swerve, is something like a differential relation.[25]

These claims both become more explicit in *Difference and Repetition* when Deleuze (quite briefly) characterises Epicurean atomism as embodying a physical 'problematic idea' (DR 184), anticipating the approach to problematic ideas characteristic of the infinitesimal calculus – especially what Deleuze cheekily calls its 'barbaric' or 'pre-scientific' expressions (DR 170). The 'problematic' quality of Lucretian atomism reappears in *A Thousand Plateaus* when Deleuze and Guattari place Lucretian physics alongside Archimedean geometry as attestations of the nomad epistemology of 'minor sciences' that exist in a productive tension with the dominant scientific and mathematical epistemology of their time (TP 361–5). Deleuze's claim that there is in Epicurean atomism something like the differential relation depends on a provocative and idiosyncratic interpretation of the swerve, which is without a doubt the key to the analogy between atomism and the calculus.[26]

For an entire tradition, going back to Cicero's *De Fato*, the Epicurean swerve was supposed to be what introduces indeterminacy into physical systems. Cicero presents the swerve as a way for Epicureans to avoid the necessitarian implications of atomism. Lucretius himself depicts the *clinamen* in this light: 'given that all motions are always connected and new motion arises out of old by a stable rule, if atoms didn't initiate motion by swerving thereby breaking the bonds of fate . . . then where would free will [*libera voluntas*] come from . . . ?'[27] Deleuze bucks the interpretative trend. He thinks that what is crucial about the swerve is not the indeterminacy it guarantees to the universe in motion, but rather the intrinsic determination it gives to relations among atoms:

> In this regard, the *clinamen* is by no means a change of direction in the movement of an atom, much less an indetermination testifying to the existence of a physical freedom. It is the original determination of the direction of movement, the synthesis of movement and its direction which relates one atom to another. (DR 184)

Deleuze explicitly relies on Lucretius' other argument for the swerve, which suggests that it is linked to the doctrine of minima:

> When these atoms are being drawn downwards by their own weight straight through the void, at totally uncertain times and in uncertain places they turn aside a little in space, just so much that you could call their motion changed. If they were not accustomed to swerve [*declinare*], everything would fall downwards through the deep void, like drops of rain, no collisions would occur and no blows be effected among the atoms: nature would not have created anything.

Lucretius glosses the infinitesimal degree of declination a few lines later: *nec plus quam minimum*, 'no more than a minimum'.[28]

Deleuze joins this interpretation of the swerve as determination to the conceptual fraternity he detects between Lucretian atomism and the differential calculus. For example, he says in 'Lucretius and the Simulacrum' that the '*clinamen* is the original determination of the direction of the atom . . . a kind of *conatus* – a differential of matter and, by the same token, a differential of thought, based on the model of exhaustion' (LS 269). Similarly, in *Difference and Repetition*: 'there is something analogous in the *clinamen* to a relation of the differentials of atoms in movement' (DR 184). The word 'differential' is significant here. Deleuze means that Lucretius (and Epicurus) anticipated the interpretation of determination as conditioned by 'difference in itself', according to which 'Difference is the state in which one can speak of determination *as such*' (DR 28), of which *dx*, the differential, is the symbol – although they did so in the old imperfect form that links the thought of difference to the existence of infinitesimals (DR 170).

In fact, if the swerve is analogous to the 'relation of differentials', then Deleuze appears to be asserting that the doctrine of the swerve anticipates the 'treasure buried within the old so-called barbaric or pre-scientific interpretations of the differential calculus', namely, the 'reciprocal determination' of differences embodied in the 'differential relation' *dy/dx* (DR 170). By means of this reciprocal determination of differences, Deleuze wagers it is possible to offer an improvement upon Kant's account of the 'problematic Idea' – with its three aspects of being indeterminate, determinable and infinitely determinable. The differential relation promises a preferable account of the transcendental ideas to Kant's, in which, Deleuze says, two of the three aspects (the last two) are merely 'extrinsic' characteristics. Part of Deleuze's ambition in *Difference and Repetition* is to use these conceptual resources from the calculus to improve upon Kant's account of problematic ideas by moving 'beyond Kantian extrinsicism' (DR 180).[29] By defending the notion that there is a conceptual bridge between Epicurean atomism and the differential calculus, Deleuze is saying that, with certain qualifications, Lucretius is already beyond such an 'extrinsic' perspective. Specifically, that's because the swerve, so long an embarrassment for Epicureanism, already embodies the 'reciprocal determination' of differentials (DR 184), in this case, minima or 'differentials of matter' (LS 269).

Deleuze incorporates this reading of the swerve as intrinsic determination into his conception of Epicurean nature as the production of the diverse. Lucretius explains that the production of the diverse could not occur if nature were a whole. Unlike the Stoic cosmos which gathers all causes up into a whole they identify with fate, Epicurean nature means the absence of that whole. This absence of natural totality, however, itself requires an explanation. For Deleuze, the swerve serves just this purpose. As he puts it, the intrinsic determination of causal series is what guarantees their 'irreducible plurality', that is, the fact that they cannot be gathered into one whole (LS 270). In other words, the *clinamen* does not express the absence of determination in natural systems, but their immanent self-determination that need not refer to any order, like a systematic totality, that transcends them.

Simulacra

So far it looks as though Deleuze treats Lucretius and Epicurus as precursors to positions articulated later with more rigour. That does not, however, exhaust his appreciation. Deleuze isolates in Epicurean atomism an idiosyncratic emphasis on *speed*. For example, Lucretius says the movement of atoms is of 'surpassing quickness', and Epicurus describes unimpeded atoms as moving 'as fast as thought' (*hama noêmati*), a phrase which is probably meant to imply that a conceptual minimum of motion across a minimum of space occurs in a minimum of time.[30]

Deleuze also construes the intrinsic determination of diversity in the Epicurean universe in terms of this emphasis on speed. The *clinamen*, he says, 'is tied in a fundamental manner to the Epicurean theory of time' (LS 269). Although atoms move 'as fast as thought', the swerve determines atomic movement by joining speed to direction or giving motion a vector. According to Deleuze, this synthesis of speed and direction is 'necessarily accomplished in a time smaller than the minimum of continuous time' (LS 269). A similar remark appears in *Difference and Repetition* (DR 184). If the argument for minima in Lucretius proceeds by analogy with minimal *sensations*, then, Deleuze reasons, there will be analogous speeds in both cases: the speed of thought and something faster that it presupposes, and the speed of sensation and something faster that it presupposes. In the case of thought, the speed of atoms presupposes the surpassing speed of the swerve; in the case of sensation, the surpassing speed it presupposes is that of what Lucretius calls the *simulacra*. In other words, Deleuze's argument about *simulacra* in the Lucretius paper redoubles the argument about *clinamen* but shifts it from the register of thought (where it is made to do important work in *Difference and Repetition*) to the register of sensation.

Lucretian *simulacra* are films of ultrafine atoms emitted by bodies, which make perception possible without being perceptible themselves. Atomic compounds constantly emit such 'membranes' just as fire produces smoke and cicadas shed their skins.[31] These emissions cause sensations to the extent that they interact with our sense organs and the seat of sensation, spirit (*anima*), and they also cause thought as they interact with the mind or soul (*animus*). Both *anima* and *animus* are material aspects of the body, composed of exceedingly fine, round and mobile atoms distributed throughout its parts.[32] The analogy or continuity between the Epicurean doctrines concerning sensation and thought is well evidenced in Deleuze's source texts. For example, as Deleuze perceptively notes, Epicurus uses the phrase 'as fast as thought' to describe the motions of both solitary atoms and films of simulacra (LS 274).[33]

The use Deleuze makes of this perception–intellection analogy is, however, less well supported. As I said above, the two essays on 'The Simulacrum and Ancient Philosophy' seem to present two dimensions, positive and negative, of one argument. Deleuze seems to be suggesting (without stating it) not only that Lucretian naturalism is a corrective to Platonic 'antinaturalism', but also that the Lucretian *simulacrum* embraces the 'positive power' of the 'copy without model' that, in Deleuze's view, Plato himself mishandled – in a word, that the Epicurean doctrine of the simulacrum goes some way towards accomplishing the wished-for 'reversal of Platonism' (LS 262). As I have also said, however, this conclusion is too hasty. The Plato essay casts a long shadow on the Lucretius essay and it obscures important details. For example, not only do Lucretian and Platonic 'simulacra' play different roles in very different philosophical systems, but, if one looks at the Greek, they do not even seem to be the same word. Lucretius' Latin word *simulacra* translates Epicurus' *eidôla*, 'images', whereas the Platonic word translated 'simulacrum' in the Plato essay seems to be *phantasma*.[34] The point of this observation is not to cavil, but to shed light on Deleuze's approach to using Lucretius. Following Brooke Holmes, we can call this kind of argument by proximity Deleuze's method of 'ingenious juxtaposition'. He juxtaposes what are, in fact, fairly different concepts (like Plato's *phantasma* and Epicurus' *eidôlon*) in order to bring out their resonances with one another and to suggest certain conclusions about the history of philosophy.[35]

This philologically cavalier but nonetheless subtly insightful method is widespread in the Lucretius essay. For example, Deleuze accentuates Lucretius' distinction between two kinds of sensible compounds emitted by bodies, those which are detached from their surfaces and give the forms and colours apprehensible by vision, and those which 'emanate from the depths' and cause the perception of smells, sounds, tastes and changes of temperature (LS 273).[36] In addition, Deleuze says, Lucretius recognises a 'third species' of sensible emissions, distinct from those that come from the surface and the depths: 'These are phantasms, which enjoy a high degree of independence with respect to objects and an extreme mobility, or an extreme inconstancy in the images which they form' (LS 275). In the passage Deleuze refers to, Lucretius does not say 'phantasm' at all: 'Lest you happen to think that the images [*simulacra*] of things which fall away from them are the only ones moving about, there are indeed others that arise spontaneously on their own in the part of the sky we call air.' Lucretius likens the production of such images to the way cumulous clouds sometimes assemble in the forms of giants and wild beasts.[37] This is 'ingenious juxtaposition' in action. Deleuze calls such relatively independent simulacra 'phantasms' not because Lucretius uses that term but because unlike other perceptible emissions these appear to be *images without originals*, copies without models, in a sense that resonates with the essay on Plato.

Demystification

The speed of simulacra and the relative independence possessed by at least some of them are, in Deleuze's estimation, the factors responsible for the all-too-human temptation to superstition and deference to myth. Deleuze introduces the discussion of Lucretian *simulacra* by referring to the close connection between physics and ethics in Epicurean naturalism (LS 272–3). Epicurean physics has a practical goal: demystification. It is the therapy for a 'troubled humanity', terrorised and disturbed in spirit by illusions like the possibility of an infinite capacity for bodily pleasure (that is, the notion that living an infinitely long time would be more pleasurable than living a finite duration), and of a potentially infinite punishment of the soul after death.[38] Both of these illusions depend on the presumption that the soul or personal identity endures infinitely, and thus both arise from the same kind of failure to distinguish correctly between what is and what is not infinite. As Deleuze puts it, 'The false infinite is the principle of the disturbance of spirit' (LS 278). The moral function of Epicurean therapy is to place limits or 'boundary stones', just as in physics. It is necessary to distinguish the infinity of the universe from the finitude of all atomic compounds within it and to correct thereby the unchecked human desires that lead to misery.

Deleuze credits the Epicureans not only with diagnosing such unlimited ambitions and desires as ethical pathologies requiring philosophical therapy, but also with offering an explanation for their pervasiveness. These illusions arise because of the characteristic behaviour of simulacra. The Epicureans know how strange it may sound that simulacra constitute the conditions of perception without being perceptible themselves. Lucretius encourages his readers not to reject on this basis the existence of *simulacra* or their role in perception: we should 'not find it too strange that the *simulacra* that strike our eyes cannot be seen individually, while the things themselves are perceptible'. It is no stranger than the fact we feel the bite of the wind as a continuous sensation rather than the succession of discrete cold particles.[39] The imperceptibility per se of simulacra depends on their incredible speed, faster than the sensible minimum. If the arguments for *clinamen* and *simulacra* are doubles, then, just as the swerve that determines the direction of atoms occurs in a 'time smaller than a minimum thinkable time', the procession of simulacra occurs in a time 'smaller than the minimum sensible time' (LS 274). Just as the *clinamen* is the sub-thinkable condition of thought, the *simulacrum* is the sub-sensible condition of sensation.

According to Deleuze, the implications of the speediness of simulacra are more widespread, and more ethically insidious, than their simple imperceptibility. The gradation of different speeds that Deleuze extracts from Epicurean doctrine also explains why humanity is so susceptible to illusion: 'In virtue of their speed, which causes them to be and to act below the sensible minimum, *simulacra produce the mirage of a false infinite in the images which they form*' (LS 277). The subliminal speed of imperceptible films of fine atoms is responsible for the illusions hindering ethical progress. The chief culprits, Deleuze says, are the 'third and swiftest species' of images, 'phantasms' that arise in the air of their own accord: 'It is particularly with the third and swiftest species, the phantasms, that one witnesses the development of the illusion [of human infinity] and the *myths* that accompany it' (LS 277). The independence of certain simulacra from any 'originals' is not an unambiguously positive result. It also creates the conditions for the kind of major errors that can dominate human existence and calls for caution and vigilance on the part of the naturalist philosopher.

Fast and unmoored simulacra are especially apt to produce illusions when they interact with the *animus* during sleep and conjure up dream images (LS 276). Lucretius often describes how dreams occur as a result of the unexpected combination of simulacra, and in one passage he suggests that such visions have caused humans 'since remote antiquity' to imagine the existence of 'divine figures' and to attribute infinite life to them on account of their constant succession.[40] On Deleuze's reading, this means that the 'belief in gods rests upon simulacra, which seem . . . to represent the infinite' (LS 277). The intimation of unlimited beings nocturnally caused by free simulacra licenses the breakdown of the correct distinction between infinite and finite. It gives the impression that some finite beings are infinite with respect to duration, an impression that is easily transferred to other finite beings, such as the human soul.

Because the existence of the gods supposedly controverts the correct distinction between true and false infinity, Deleuze concludes that the ethical project of Epicurean naturalism in general reduces to *demythologising* philosophy, and *detheologising* it in particular. As he puts it, 'The speculative object and the practical object of philosophy as Naturalism . . . coincide on this point: it is always a matter of denouncing the illusion, the false infinite, the infinity of religion and all of the theologico-erotic-oneiric myths in which it is expressed' (LS 278). The task of demythologising philosophy here seems also to involve de-Platonising it: 'Being, the One and the Whole are the myth of a false philosophy totally impregnated by theology' (LS 279).

This anti-theological reading of Lucretius does not sit well with the text of *De Rerum Natura*, especially not the passage on which Deleuze primarily relies. Although Lucretius is consistently hard on superstition or *religio*, which he depicts as an oppressive weight dragging humanity down,[41] it is not likely that Lucretius wishes to evacuate theology from philosophy. Epicurean orthodoxy exerts pressure in the other direction. Epicurus argued that it is correct to accede to the common impression that gods exist 'because we have clear knowledge of them', but that it is necessary not to attribute to the gods anything alien to their imperturbable blessedness, such as the habit of meddling in human affairs. For Epicurus, the problem is not that the gods exist but that we fear them. Such fear is based on a superstitious misapprehension that scuppers the human potential for the good life.[42] While Epicurus doesn't explain how we have 'clear knowledge' of the gods, it is plausible that we know this, as we know anything else, by the action of simulacra on our *animi*. In fact, it may be preferable to interpret the passage about receiving sensible intimations of divine beings in dreams, on which Deleuze relies to support the opposite conclusion, as implying that simulacra give us clear knowledge of the gods. Despite what Deleuze says, it is not obvious that the dream visions we take for gods are results of the action of the kind of simulacra that arise independent of any original source (what he calls 'phantasms'). That is, they could very well be trustworthy visions that proceed from really existing sensible originals. A similar passage in Book 6 of *De Rerum Natura* is harder to read anti-realistically. Lucretius says: if you imagine (falsely) that the gods are wrathful, 'you will not be strong enough to receive the images [*simulacra*] bearing their divine forms carried from their holy bodies to human minds'.[43]

Additionally, the existence of unperturbed, blessed, fearless beings affords a kind of Epicurean ethical exemplar. Although it is necessary to be vigilant about having the correct idea of what a god is, Epicurus describes the ethical project of Epicureanism as becoming 'god-like among men' (*hôs theos en anthrôpois*), in the sense of undisturbed by fears, blessedly indifferent to, for example, the fear of death.[44] Again, the problem for the Epicureans is not theology as such, but the fear and illusion attendant upon misunderstanding the nature of the gods. Since the gods are a part of the natural world, such misunderstanding is tantamount to having a poor grasp on physics. It is difficult to read a poem that opens with an invocation of Venus as completely anti-theological.

Epicurean theology need not spoil our appreciation of the naturalistic ethic Deleuze draws from Lucretius, so long as we accept the qualification that not all myths, and not all conceptions of the gods, are equally problematic. Not all myths are equivalent to the Parmenidean–Platonic–Stoic ones that are primarily in Deleuze's crosshairs. The specific myths expressed in the concepts of 'Being, One, and Whole' are those that 'deprive Nature of all its positivity' (LS 278). It is not obvious that Epicurean theology involves a myth like these. Unlike the Stoics, the Epicureans don't identify God with the totality of the cosmos, nor, like the Neoplatonists, with the imparticipable One.

Naturalism, as 'the philosophy of affirmation', most radically breaks with myths like these (LS 279). To say so is once again to paraphrase the idea that naturalism involves a genetic explanatory method. Such philosophical myths induce philosophers to seek the identical within or beneath the multiple. To Deleuze's way of thinking, this is to deny the 'multiple qua multiple' its productive power – to say 'no' to multiplicity by relating it to a unity or wholeness putatively at work behind the scenes. Deleuze diagnoses the prestige of such a negative view of nature in the history of philosophy. In this light, naturalism means the countervailing tendency that affirms the 'multiple as multiple', seeks to do justice to its productivity, and attacks the prestige of the negative. Deleuze's point is that, just as Epicurus thought of his philosophy as a therapy for miserable, god-fearing humanity, naturalism in philosophy can be a therapy or corrective for the 'prestige of the negative' and the myths of 'Being, One, and Whole' that deny nature its productivity.

Deleuze thus presents Lucretius as setting the agenda for a whole counter-tradition: 'From Lucretius to Nietzsche, the same end is pursued and attained' (LS 279). The earlier reference to *contatus* suggests that Deleuze would place Spinoza, along with Nietzsche, in this lineage of philosophers who have risen to the ethical challenge of naturalism.[45] What links each of these figures, to Deleuze's mind, is their shared emphasis on denouncing false mythologies that imprison the mind and on producing a free human, liberated from the illusions making her anxious and sad. Naturalism is ethical therapy: 'One of the profound constants of naturalism is to denounce everything that is sadness, everything that is the cause of sadness, and everything that needs sadness to exercise its power.' Correlatively, for the naturalist, 'the diverse as diverse as the object of joy' (LS 279). Similar passages appear in Deleuze's books on Spinoza and Nietzsche in the 1960s. Deleuze places *De Rerum Natura* alongside the *Ethics* and *The Genealogy of Morals* as a complementary critique of theological illusions and a core text for the 'ethic of joy' that Deleuze promotes as practical philosophy (NP 18).

Although Deleuze does not develop the thought in the Lucretius paper, one of the main drawbacks to illusion and 'sadness' is that their jointure is easily exploited. Practical naturalism denounces 'everything that needs sadness to exercise its power' (LS 279). This includes the ascetic priest of Nietzsche's genealogy who 'needs negation to establish his power' (NP 196) and the tyrant of Spinoza's *Tractatus*, who prettifies fear in religious vestments in order to hoodwink the people (SPP 25). Lucretius also denounces the 'terrifying assertions of the soothsayers' aimed at clouding the naturalistic ethical programme with fear based on the illusion of unlimited existence.[46] Lucretius agrees with Spinoza and Nietzsche. Liberation from such exploiters is the aim and the great accomplishment of Epicurean philosophy.[47]

According to Deleuze's reading of Spinoza, such liberation brings joy (*gaudium*), the affect that accompanies bodies entering into the kind of healthy, life-affirming combinations with other bodies that the exploiters of illusion had blocked (SPP 19). In the case of Lucretius, philosophical demystification is accompanied by a slightly different affect. The Epicurean equivalent of the feeling of augmented power and good encounters is what Lucretius calls *suavitas*, sweetness, charm, agreeableness. It is defined in the famous opening lines of Book 2:

> It is sweet [*suave*] to watch from shore another person's great labour during a windstorm on the vast sea, not because that fact of someone being tossed about is a delight or pleasure in itself, but because it is sweet [*suave*] to perceive from what evils you are free.[48]

Suavitas is not just pleasure, defined by Epicurus as the absence of the pain. Rather it arises from the *awareness* of that absence as a consequence of intellectual discipline. It is, therefore, the archetypically critical affect. *Suavitas* accompanies critique and demystification. It is the mood of the critical philosopher, a feeling of freedom from illusion, the cultivation of which is the aim of practical ethics. Far from being related to an easy, spontaneous egoism, the feeling of *suavitas* is an achievement of spiritual discipline, self-scrutiny and critical acumen. In particular, the catalyst for critical liberation is the correct distinction between the infinite and the finite. Physics and ethics dovetail because their speculative and practical objects coincide: in physics, naturalism depends on seeing that the universe is infinite (that is, not a unity or whole) but that any given configuration of atoms is finite; in ethics, naturalism likewise depends on placing boundaries (*termini*) on desire and fear.

Conclusion

There is a lot of evidence to support the suggestion that a brand of critical naturalism characterises Deleuze's philosophical work in the 1960s, that this project has a speculative physical or metaphysical dimension and a practical side, and that both are profoundly influenced by an early close reading of Lucretius' *De Rerum Natura*. On the speculative side, the stamp of Lucretius' impact on Deleuze is evident in the theories of difference in itself and of problematic ideas in *Difference and Repetition* and that book's genetic explanatory method. On the practical side, the critique of mystification and the emphases on the joyful affirmation of diversity without recourse to totalising myths and on counteracting the prestige of the negative, sadness and those who exploit it for power, which is first announced in the Lucretius essay, resounds in Deleuze's longer and more detailed interpretations of Spinoza and Nietzsche.

Deleuze's approach to Lucretius involves not only tracking the Roman poet's arguments and picking up key terms and concepts like *clinamen*, but also the ingenious juxtaposition of concepts from diverse philosophical and intellectual systems. For example, Deleuze interprets Epicurean *minima* and the swerve as prefigurations of the intrinsic determination of quantity characteristic of the differential calculus, which he uses to develop an anti-Kantian theory of problematic ideas. The Epicurean swerve embodies the intrinsic determination of productive nature and also explains why natural systems cannot be subordinated to a transcendent or extrinsic totality. Similarly, Deleuze ingeniously juxtaposes Lucretian *simulacra* with Platonic *phantasmata* on the basis of the freedom at least some of these images enjoy from any model with which they share the form, and then uses this freedom to explain the origin of theological illusions. This juxtaposition motivates his interpretation of Lucretius as offering a naturalistic alternative to the myths of Platonic philosophy.

These examples demonstrate that Deleuze is not interested in simply explicating Lucretius' text or explaining Epicurean concepts, but in making philosophical use of them. In advocating Lucretian naturalism, Deleuze is not just reporting the views of another philosopher but fusing their conceptual horizons together. Like the Lucretian universe, this method of collaborating with the history of philosophy is productive and creative. Deleuze writes his commentary on Lucretius in order to give birth to hybrid conceptual offspring that belong simultaneously to both of them.

Notes

1. See Patrick Hayden, 'Deleuze and Naturalism', *Environmental Ethics* 19.2 (1998), pp. 185–204; Keith Ansell Pearson, 'Affirmative Naturalism', *Cosmos and History* 10.2 (2014), pp. 121–36; and Keith Ansell Pearson and John Protevi, 'Naturalism in the Continental Tradition', in Kelly James Clark (ed.), *The Blackwell Companion to Naturalism* (Malden, MA: Wiley-Blackwell, forthcoming).
2. Arnaud Villani, *La Guêpe et l'orchidée* (Paris: Belin, 1999), p. 129.
3. Lucretius, *De Rerum Natura* (Cambridge, MA: Harvard University Press, 2006), for example, 2. 342–8.
4. Referring to Lucretius, *De Rerum Natura*, 2. 371–3.
5. Lucretius, *De Rerum Natura*, 1. 2–4, 19–21.
6. David Sedley, 'Epicureanism in the Roman Republic', in James Warren (ed.), *The Cambridge Companion to Epicureanism* (New York: Cambridge University Press, 2009), pp. 29–45; Dirk Obbink, 'Lucretius and the Herculaneum Library', in Stuart Gillespie and Philip Hardie (eds), *The Cambridge Companion to Lucretius* (New York: Cambridge University Press, 2007), pp. 33–40.
7. Lucretius, *De Rerum Natura*, 1. 74–6. Translations from Lucretius' Latin are mine.
8. Lucretius, *De Rerum Natura*, 1. 149–50, 171, 268–9, 482–502. Compare Epicurus' *Letter to Herodotus*, 38 and 40–1.
9. Lucretius, *De Rerum Natura*, 1. 262–4, 518–19.
10. Lucretius, *De Rerum Natura*, 1. 229–30, 346–9.
11. Lucretius, *De Rerum Natura*, 1. 594–6, 5. 89–90, 6. 65–6.

12. Lucretius, *De Rerum Natura*, 2. 479–528, especially 512–13.
13. Lucretius, *De Rerum Natura*, 1. 984–97 and 1014–20.
14. Epicurus, *Letter to Herodotus*, 41.
15. Lucretius, *De Rerum Natura*, 1. 635–920.
16. Ryan Johnson, 'Another Use of the Concept of the Simulacrum', *Deleuze Studies* 8:1 (2014), p. 79. For a balanced presentation of Lucretius as the obverse of Plato, and its limitations, see Miguel de Beistegui, 'The Deleuzian Reversal of Platonism', in Daniel W. Smith and Henry Somers-Hall (eds), *The Cambridge Companion to Deleuze* (New York: Cambridge University Press, 2012), especially pp. 63–5.
17. Brooke Holmes, 'Deleuze, Lucretius, and the Simulacrum of Naturalism', in Brooke Holmes and W. H. Shearin (eds), *Dynamic Reading: Studies in the Reception of Epicureanism* (New York: Oxford University Press, 2012), p. 318.
18. Compare D vii and WP 7.
19. On Deleuze, Maimon and Kant, see Daniel W. Smith, 'Deleuze, Hegel, and the Post-Kantian Tradition', *Philosophy Today* 44: supplement (2000), pp. 119–31; and Graham Jones, 'Solomon Maimon', in Graham Jones and Jon Roffe (eds), *Deleuze's Philosophical Lineage* (Edinburgh: Edinburgh University Press, 2009), pp. 104–29.
20. Johnson, 'Another Use of the Concept of the Simulacrum', pp. 73–4.
21. Lucretius, *De Rerum Natura*, 1. 599–614, 746–52, 2. 478–99. Compare Epicurus, *Letter to Herodotus*, 56–9.
22. Lucretius, *De Rerum Natura*, 1. 623.
23. This analogy is evident in Lucretius, *De Rerum Natura*, 1. 749–52 and Epicurus, *Letter to Herodotus*, 58–9.
24. On Eudoxus and Archimedes as predecessors of modern calculus, see Carl Boyer, *The History of the Calculus and Its Conceptual Development* (New York: Dover, 1959), pp. 23–33.
25. For an extended defence of this interpretation of Epicurean minima, and more on Deleuze's analogy between Epicureanism and the calculus of infinitesimals, see my *Deleuze and Ancient Greek Physics* (London: Bloomsbury Academic, forthcoming).
26. In *A Thousand Plateaus* Deleuze and Guattari refer to Michel Serres's *The Birth of Physics* (Manchester: Clinamen Press, 2000), which provides a sustained argument to the effect that Lucretius' poem contains some of the earliest formulations of what will be called the differential and infinitesimal calculus, and that these converge with Archimedean geometry (TP 361, 489). It is hard not to agree with Hanjo Berressem, '*Incerto Tempore Incertisque Locis*', in Niran Abbas (ed.), *Mapping Michel Serres* (Ann Arbor: University of Michigan Press, 2005), p. 54, that Deleuze's essay on Lucretius probably 'paved the way' for Serres's book.
27. Cicero, *On Fate*, in H. Rackham (ed.), *Cicero: On the Orator: Book*

3. *On Fate. Stoic Paradoxes. On the Divisions of Oratory* (Cambridge, MA: Harvard University Press, 1942), pp. 22–3; Lucretius, *De Rerum Natura*, 2. 251–6.
28. Lucretius, *De Rerum Natura*, 2. 217–24, 244.
29. On Deleuze's critique of Kantian Ideas, see Daniela Voss, *Conditions of Thought: Deleuze and the Transcendental Ideas* (Edinburgh: Edinburgh University Press, 2013), especially pp. 179–209.
30. Epicurus, *Letter to Herodotus*, 61; Lucretius, *De Rerum Natura*, 2. 164. For discussion of the crucial role speed plays, often with explicit or implicit reference to Epicureanism, throughout Deleuze's work, see Melinda Cooper, 'Vitesses de l'image, puissances de la pensée: La philosophie épicurienne revue par Deleuze et Guattari', *French Studies* 56:1 (2002), pp. 45–60, and Michael J. Bennett, 'Deleuze and Epicurean Philosophy: Atomic Speed and Swerve Speed', *Journal of French and Francophone Philosophy* 21:2 (2013), pp. 131–57.
31. Lucretius, *De Rerum Natura*, 4. 31–2, 56–8. Cf. Epicurus, *Letter to Herodotus*, 46.
32. Lucretius, *De Rerum Natura*, 3. 180–230.
33. Referring to Epicurus, *Letter to Herodotus*, 48 and 61.
34. Epicurus, *Letter to Herodotus*, 46; Plato, *The Sophist* (Cambridge, MA: Harvard University Press, 1921), 236c. The word *eidôla* does appear in *The Sophist* as the general term for 'images', but the key idea is that images are produced by two different kinds of imitation, one which produces faithful 'likenesses' (*eikones*), and one of which produces 'appearances' (*phantasmata*), representations to some extent liberated from their originals, which therefore introduce the possibilities of falsehood and error: *Sophist* 235c–36c, 265a–b.
35. Holmes, 'Deleuze, Lucretius, and the Simulacrum of Naturalism', p. 333.
36. Lucretius, *De Rerum Natura*, 4. 90–8, 549–50, 617–21.
37. Lucretius, *De Rerum Natura*, 4. 129–40.
38. Epicurus, *Principal Doctrines* 18–20; Lucretius, *De Rerum Natura* 3. 944–9 and 978–1023.
39. Lucretius, *De Rerum Natura*, 4. 256–64.
40. Lucretius, *De Rerum Natura*, 5. 1169–82.
41. For example, at *De Rerum Natura*, 1. 62–5.
42. Epicurus, *Letter to Menoeceus*, 123.
43. Lucretius, *De Rerum Natura*, 6. 76–8.
44. Epicurus, *Letter to Menoeceus*, 135. Compare Lucretius, *De Rerum Natura*, 3. 830ff.
45. On the intimate connection between Deleuze's accounts of Lucretius and Spinoza, see Warren Montag, 'Du *clinamen* au *conatus*: Deleuze, Lucrèce, Spinoza', in Alain Gigandet (ed.), *Lucrèce et la modernité: Le vingtième siècle* (Paris: Armand Colin, 2013). For some discussion of

Lucretius and Nietzsche, see Ansell Pearson, 'Affirmative Naturalism', pp. 121–36.

46. Lucretius, *De Rerum Natura*, 1. 102–3.
47. Lucretius, *De Rerum Natura*, 1. 62–79, 6. 25–42.
48. Lucretius, *De Rerum Natura*, 2. 1–4.

Friedrich Wilhelm Joseph Schelling

Kyla Bruff

The reader of Deleuze and Schelling (1775–1854) encounters a series of hermeneutical challenges and paradoxes in attempting to ascertain their relationship. This difficulty is not in the least due to the radical shifts in Schelling's thinking, the critical turning points on which Schelling scholars cannot agree. On the one side, the Schelling of the 'Identity Philosophy' (beginning in 1801) parallels Deleuze as a thinker of univocity, immanence, affirmation and the quantitative progression of difference. In order to align these thinkers as much as possible, Schelling's Spinozism can be overemphasised, his affinity for the mad and chaotic exaggerated (forgetting that Schelling never abandons rational philosophy), and the transcendent, Christian elements of his middle to late philosophy ignored. Readings of Deleuze that stress the latter's relationship to theophany,[1] supplemented with a reconstruction of the historical lineage linking the two thinkers (that is, the French reception of Schelling through Maine de Biran, Cousin, Ravaisson and Bergson leading up to Deleuze), make it appear that both thinkers espouse very similar immanent philosophies of difference and life, and share a common antipathy to Hegel. However, on the other side, Deleuze does not reference the seemingly most 'Deleuzian' period of Schelling's thought (the Identity Philosophy). Instead, he refers to texts from Schelling's middle period, the earliest being the 1809 *Freedom* essay, in which Schelling presents a personal, transcendent God and stresses the separation of God and things in 'toto genere'.[2] As demonstrated below, the extent to which Schelling remains a Spinozist in and after 1809 is debatable.[3]

But Schelling is not entirely inconsistent in his transition from the Identity Philosophy to the Philosophy of Freedom (his middle period). For example, he develops the Principle of 'absolute indifference' of the Identity Philosophy into the *Ungrund* of the *Freedom* essay. Deleuze praises Schelling's *Ungrund* as 'a problematic being or non-existent, a being implicit in those existences beyond the ground' (DR 190).[4]

I maintain there is an indirect influence of Schelling in Deleuze's work. More specifically, they both share certain analogous, triadic, metaphysical structures, originating from a common historical background in Spinoza. I accordingly examine in this chapter how the triad of indifference–subjectivity–objectivity, present in Schelling's Spinozist-monism of the Identity Philosophy, is transformed into the structure of *Ungrund*–ground–existence in his *Freedom* essay. I then assess the relationship of the evolution of this triad with the triadic treatment of expression presented by Deleuze in *Expressionism in Philosophy*. Subsequently, I demonstrate that Deleuze acknowledges a Principle of Indifference in *The Logic of Sense*, but merges it with productivity in a manner that exemplifies a collapse of Schelling's *Ungrund* and ground into a single term. Although this combination seems to present a case in favour of describing Deleuze's metaphysics as dualist (in dyadic sets such as virtual–actual, pre-personal field–empirical individuations, unconscious–consciousness), I suggest that Deleuze's notion of intensity can serve as a middle term, thus bringing Deleuze close to Schelling's *Ungrund*–ground–existence triad of the *Freedom* essay.

The non-ground, or *Ungrund*, will occupy a significant portion of the investigation at hand, for it is arguably the foundation of Schelling's influence on twentieth-century post-subject-oriented metaphysics, including Deleuze. The *Ungrund* is the inaccessible origin of all, including God; it 'cannot be assimilated into the understanding, remaining a kind of traumatic – and potentially liberating – excess'.[5] Following the theogony of Jacob Böhme, the *Ungrund* contracts and divides into two principles, two eternal beginnings, two wills: the dark and the light, ground and existence. Schelling considers these principles the foundational condition of the possibility of life, love and personality. The *Ungrund*'s closest conceptual precursor in Schelling's own thought is the Principle of Indifference in his Identity Philosophy, but its ultimate source lies in Spinoza, the original thinker of 'unconscious' production and the substance–attributes–modes triad.

Schelling's Life and Career

Schelling was born on 27 January 1775 in Leonberg (Württenberg), close to Stuttgart. His father was a theologian, and Schelling studied Latin and Greek with him as a young child. In any extended introduction to Schelling, one finds a discussion of Schelling's precociousness and his status as a child prodigy – by the age of eleven, his teachers had exhausted all the material they had to teach him.[6] At the age of fifteen, Schelling received special permission to attend the Tübinger Stift (the Protestant seminary in Württenberg) joining Hegel and Hölderlin as their roommate (both five years his senior).[7]

Schelling rose to academic prominence at a time when Hegel was still practically unknown.[8] In 1798 (aged twenty-three), Schelling was called as a professor to Jena and became integrated in the Jena Circle (which included famous Romantics such as Goethe, the Schlegels and Novalis). Hegel arrived in Jena following Schelling's encouragement in 1801, and published a work entitled *The Difference between Fichte's and Schelling's Systems of Philosophy*, which was largely interpreted as a defence of Schelling's philosophy against Fichte's.[9] He and Schelling also began editing and publishing in a journal together, the *Critical Journal of Philosophy*. Their collaboration soon came to a halt as Schelling moved to Würzburg in 1803.[10] Hegel's public, intellectual break with Schelling occurred as he set their friendship ablaze with his description of Schelling's Absolute – at this point, the Principle of Identity, or the A=A, of the Identity Philosophy – as the night 'in which all cows are black'.[11] On Hegel's reading, this Absolute has no difference distinguished within it and is thus separated from 'the full body of articulated cognition'[12]; all concrete difference disappears into the black night. Deleuze explicitly denotes this characterisation as 'unjust' (DR 192).

In 1809 Schelling published his seminal *Freedom* essay, marking the shift from his early period (the *Naturphilosophie* and Identity Philosophy) to his middle period and Philosophy of Freedom.[13] At this point, Schelling was steeped in new concerns[14] and theosophical influences,[15] most notably the influence of Jakob Böhme through Franz von Baader. Baader, a Catholic German philosopher, led Schelling to an intensive exploration of the work of Böhme – a Lutheran German shoemaker turned theosophist, on whom Baader lectured extensively.[16] Hegel called Böhme 'the first German philosopher',[17] and Schelling was reading him during the period at which he wrote the *Freedom* essay.[18] As we will see, in the *Freedom* essay, Schelling merges Böhmean theogony with a new reading of Spinoza's pantheism.

Schelling and Spinoza

In the *Ethics*, Spinoza claims there is only one single, infinite substance in which everything exists,[19] namely God or Nature (*Deus sive*

Natura).[20] Substance, God or nature has an infinite number of attributes that express its essence. However, we know only two of these attributes: thought and extension. Under these attributes, everything else appears in modes. The laws of the universe and finite things are therefore *modes* of substance, that is, 'modifications of substance, or that which exists in, and is conceived through, something other than itself'.[21]

There are two aspects of nature for Spinoza – *natura naturans*, its productive, active dimension (God and his attributes), and *natura naturata* – nature's products or 'all the modes of the attributes of God, in so far as they are considered as things which are in God . . .'.[22] Spinoza's radical thesis of the total immanence of substance, God and nature has sparked great debate throughout the history of philosophy, notably on the subject of pantheism. Perhaps the most important of these debates was the 1785 *Pantheismusstreit* (Pantheism controversy) between Mendelssohn and Jacobi, incited by Lessing's confession of Spinozism on his deathbed and his 'insistence that Spinoza was not a "dead dog"'.[23] At the core of this debate were questions regarding the compatibility of Spinoza's speculative, 'determinist' system with the fact (*Tatsache*) of freedom,[24] that is how to reconcile God or substance or Nature with the idea of God or the 'Absolute' as a free subject. These issues, as we will see, are central for Schelling.

In his early *Naturphilosophie* and Identity Philosophy, Schelling defends different forms of an immanent Spinozist monist metaphysics. But in 1809 a shift occurs, and Schelling states in the *Freedom* essay that 'the concept of immanence is to be set aside completely in so far as thereby a dead containment of things in God is supposed to be expressed'.[25] Schelling nevertheless defends the compatibility of freedom (which here implies divine transcendence) and a Spinozist pantheism ('the doctrine that all things are contained in God'[26]) in this text.[27] He maintains that freedom is concealed in the relation expressed in pantheism between God and things as a complete, divine system of nature.

Spinoza offered the young Schelling an initial path outside of the subjective idealism developed by Fichte. Fichte began with the most certain and unmediated principle: 'I am.' This 'I' was then inflated to the status of an 'Absolute I', which posits itself, thereby limiting itself to knowledge of itself. As a result, nature becomes the other side of that which is limited by the 'I'. In his very early thought (around 1795), Schelling follows Fichte's lead, investigating the emergence of the given in terms of the subject's relation to its finite world. However, he quickly breaks with Fichte in his *Naturphilosophie*, in which he sets out to describe the relation between objective spirit and nature.[28] Schelling here insists on nature's intrinsic logic of expression. Nature expresses the absolute and thus cannot be reduced to the status of a Fichtean 'not-I'.[29] Rather, subjective spirit and objective nature are infinite and immanent to each other.[30] Schelling accordingly claims that the poles of subjectivity and objectivity are distinct only quantitatively, and not qualitatively or in nature. This move is inherently Spinozist, for one and the same being pluralises itself in Spinoza through its attributes (and modes). If Spinoza's extension and thought or Schelling's objectivity and subjectivity were qualitatively or essentially different, they would not be of one and the same essence, and would instead reproduce a Cartesian dualism. However, it should be noted that Schelling does not appropriate Spinoza's claim here that there is an infinite number of attributes. There are only two attributes in the *Naturphilosophie*, the 'natural' world and spirit, which correspond to objectivity and subjectivity.

Spinoza's substance provides the original model for Schelling's Principle of Indifference of the Identity Philosophy, because it is the infinite ground common to both subjectivity and objectivity. Michael Vater clearly explains that Spinoza's substance is the 'inaccessible self-founding and self-cognized absolute' which serves 'as an ontological ground for parallel but mutually exclusive orders of phenomenal elaboration, viz. the subjective and the objective (Spinoza's attributes)'.[31]

The Identity Philosophy has '*its starting point in the indifference between subject and object, and its end in their Identity*'.[32] This 'indifference' has no predicates, and cannot be defined in terms of oppositions (one cannot even say 'Indifference is' or 'Indifference is not').[33] In both the *Freedom* essay and the Identity Philosophy, opposing terms arise precisely 'from the Neither–Nor, or indifference, and *without* indifference, that is, *without* a non-ground, there would be no two-ness of principles'.[34] But the end of the Identity Philosophy is the complete *identity* of subject and object.[35] This aim precludes the possibility of freedom, of personality, and of love, which Schelling defines as a relationship between two beings that *could* exist for themselves but do not. The collapse of real difference into absolute identity is the ground of Hegel's aforementioned allegation that Schelling's Absolute is the night in which all cows are black – a statement criticised by Deleuze (DR 191). Furthermore, in so far as the Identity Philosophy chiefly concerns reason's self-recognition of the absolute identity of subject and object, it can be criticised as a closed system of reason disconnected from real events and being.

Schelling breaks free of the limitations of the Identity Philosophy, returning to his prior aim to provide a genetic account of the real emergence of the finite from the infinite in his 1804 *Philosophy and Religion*. Here, the emergence of the finite is presented as a 'fall' from the divine or the absolute (thus, a deficiency, error or collapse). Schelling instils a duality in a manner that prefigures the distinction between ground and existence in the *Freedom* essay; a final state of *complete* identification of the infinite and the finite is no longer sought. Here we begin to ascribe meaning to events in time, for after the emergence of finitude, that is, in the wake of the Fall, there is no going back. There can, however, be a new type of self-conscious and self-related, personal unity of God and his creation, which Schelling calls love.

From the Principle of Indifference to the *Ungrund*

Despite the shift in Schelling's thinking from the Identity Philosophy to the *Freedom* essay, Schelling nevertheless employs the language of indifference in the latter in 1809 to underscore that the *Ungrund* 'cannot be described as the identity of opposites; it can only be described as the absolute *indifference* [*Indifferenz*] of both'.[36] Furthermore, he clearly explains the relation of indifference (the *Ungrund*) to opposition, specifying that it 'is not a product of opposites, nor are they implicitly contained in it, but rather indifference is its own being separate from opposition, a being against which all opposites ruin themselves, that is nothing else than their very not-Being [*Nichtsein*]'.[37] In short, Schelling once again posits opposing terms grounded in a principle to which they are completely other, and therefore with which they can be neither identified nor opposed.

The triadic structure of the early Schelling thus begins with the Principle of Indifference as the foundation of the opposition of subjectivity and objectivity. Analogously, the distinction between 'ground' and 'existence' has its origin in the significance in the *Freedom* essay: existence emerges from the dark, mad, unconscious ground in God, and the two orders exist independently, such that through existence (including human activity and historical events), God reveals himself. Ground and existence, as they emerge from the *Ungrund*, do not resemble Spinoza's attributes of extension and thought as do the subjective and objective of the Identity Philosophy. Instead, ground and existence are the two Böhmean-influenced principles (see below) that are different from one another and hierarchically ordered as the structural condition of the possibility of divine freedom and personality. These two wills are produced from an unconscious decision or contraction of an *Ungrund* that is 'before all ground, thus, the absolute considered merely in itself'.[38] Schelling's description of the *Ungrund* as the absolute here underscores that Spinoza's substance is the initial origin of this concept, for substance is, as stated above, the 'inaccessible self-founding and self-cognized absolute' grounding opposition.[39]

Schelling's *Ungrund* and the ground are easily conflated, for both can be conceived as a 'deep unconscious', and neither can be described as God himself, although they are not outside of God. However, unlike the *Ungrund*, which has no opposite, the ground of being can be defined in opposition to existence. Opposites must have something in common; for example, as discussed in the *Freedom* essay, good and evil are opposites because they are moral orientations which mutually exclude each other precisely because they occupy the same field of sense. The *Ungrund* accordingly serves as the 'common point of contrast'[40] of ground and existence, while being totally other (but not opposite) to them. It is μὴ ὄν, and thus 'names that which *is* as not having being, the indivisible remainder contesting while supporting all beings'.[41]

Whereas the *Ungrund* has primordial will and drive (*Trieb*), the ground emerging from it serves as the chaotic, unconscious dimension of the divine. Existence, or light, is raised out of 'the darkness into actuality in order to live with God everlastingly, whereas evil should be separated from the good in order to be cast out eternally into non-being'.[42] The dark ground longs at once both to be distinct, but also to engender a self-standing being, and thus to provide a foundation for this existent being, without which it cannot *be*. It is, quite literally, the condition of God's existence.[43]

In summary, the *Ungrund* divides and produces the opposition of ground and existence, which opens the possibility of a real, free relationship between God and the world: the *Ungrund*

> divides itself only so that there may be life and love and personal existence. For love is neither in indifference nor where opposites are linked which require linkage for [their] Being, but rather [love] links such things of which each could exist for itself, yet does not and cannot exist without the other.[44]

Evidently, the triad of the *Ungrund*–ground–existence and indifference–objectivity–subjectivity have an analogous structure. Nevertheless, the independence of and difference between ground and existence, as the condition of divine personality and love, do not resemble the joint positing of subjectivity and objectivity of the Identity Philosophy.

Deleuze and the Triad of Expression

Deleuze's positive references to Schelling concern first and foremost the *Ungrund*, whose derivatives appear in Deleuze as the abyss, the transcendental field, the virtual, the neutrality of sense, the plane of consistency, plane of immanence and plane of life. It is my view that Deleuze directly references the *Ungrund* rather than the Principle of Indifference because only the former is ontologically *expressive* and *productive*. Deleuze argues that expression's 'import is to *free* univocal Being from a state of indifference or neutrality, to make it the object of pure affirmation, which is actually realized in an expressive pantheism or immanence' (EPS 333). Expression is accordingly *the agent of freedom* of indifferent being. This expressive agency is lacking in Schelling's Identity Philosophy. Therefore, Schelling's *Freedom* essay exemplifies a Deleuzian 'expressive pantheism' in its defence of the free affirmation of being as existence, which originates in a dark, a-personal, chaotic domain. Deleuze's use of the language of freedom here challenges 'dead' readings of Spinoza. I will return to the notion of freedom at the end of this chapter.

Deleuze maintains that expression can be directly found in the presentation of substance in Spinoza's *Ethics*, and criticises Schelling and the German Idealists for reducing 'expression' to mean either emanation or explication. He writes:

> Postkantian philosophers would seem to have been well placed to recognize the presence in Spinozism of that genetic movement of self-development for which they sought anticipations everywhere. But the term 'explication' confirmed their view that Spinoza had been no more able to conceive a true evolution of substance, than to think through the transition from infinite to finite. Spinoza's substance seemed to them lifeless, his expression intellectual and abstract, his attributes 'attributed' to substance by an understanding that was itself 'explicative'. (EPS 18)

Deleuze thus reasonably concludes that Schelling's source for ontological expression is Böhme rather than Spinoza (EPS 18). The

Böhmean-inspired breaking forth of the dark and light principles, ground and existence, from the *Ungrund* (indifference) is the basis of Schelling's new 'genetic movement of self-development', of the coming-to-consciousness of God and creation in the *Freedom* essay. The *Ungrund* 'posits and confirms' the distinction of the two principles,[45] thereby positively affirming being. Böhme, a thinker of univocity, can be aligned with Deleuze, since Deleuze engaged with esotericism and the occult.[46] Mark Bonta stresses an analogy between Deleuze's and Böhme's views of the cosmos (chaosmos), suggesting that both 'explore the virtual and emergent properties of the non-linear multiverse'.[47] Furthermore, Peter Hallward defends the resonance of Deleuze's philosophy of creation with theophany by identifying an impersonal absolute common to both. However, Böhme is certainly not a major source in the development of Deleuze's metaphysics, and Deleuze in no way adopts his theogony.[48]

Deleuze explicitly states that expression itself is triadic (EPS 333). He demonstrates this through his explication of two different triads of expression: firstly, a triad of substance, and, secondly, a modal triad. Deleuze summarises these triads as follows: 'Substance expressed itself in attributes, each attribute was an expression, the essence of substance was expressed. Now each attribute expresses itself, the dependent modes are expressions, and a modification is expressed' (ESP 110). The terms of the triad of substance are thus (1) substance, (2) attribute, (3) essence, and the terms of the modal triad are (1) attribute, (2) mode, (3) modification. Deleuze identifies a paradox that '"what is expressed" has no existence outside its expression, yet bears no resemblance to it, but relates essentially to what expresses itself as distinct from the expression itself'. This structure of expression 'bears within it a double movement' (EPS 333). He explains:

> Within the triad of substance God expresses himself in his attributes, the attributes expressing the unlimited qualities that constitute his essence. In the modal triad God re-expresses himself, or the attributes in their turn express themselves: they express themselves in modes, modes expressing modifications as modifications of substance, constituting the same world through every attribute. (ESP 334)

In other words, in the first movement, 'God expresses himself in his attributes' and in the second, these attributes 'in their turn express themselves' for themselves (EPS 334).

In the *Freedom* essay, God or substance expresses itself through ground and existence, which are in turn expressions that had emerged from the *Ungrund*. The first movement of divine expression in Schelling is thus the splitting *Ungrund* as the absolute birth of God into two forms which together 'express unlimited qualities related to God as constituting his essence' (EPS 334). The second movement or 'doubling' is God's decision to create that which exists independent from him. The individual expressive elements of our world (including human freedom and action) express 'the totality of the chosen world, which is related to God as the manifestation of his "glory" or will' (EPS 334). The paradox is that God 'brings the world, rather than [its independent elements] into existence' (EPS 334), yet these elements also express God and totality. For Schelling, this independence of creation and human freedom are necessary for God's love and self-revelation.

The basis of this theory of expression is the *Ungrund*, which 'transforms dualities' and brings us beyond mechanistic causality and representation (EPS 335). Deleuze writes, 'an idea represents an object, and in a way expresses it: but at a deeper level idea and object express something that is at once common to them, and yet belongs to each: a power, or the absolute in two of its powers, those of thinking or knowing, and being or acting' (EPS 335). The power of existing and acting (subjective) and the power of thinking and knowing (objective) are the two 'halves', 'dimensions' and 'powers' of the absolute itself which are always unified (EPS 180). Deleuze discovers this unity in Schelling's 1810 *Stuttgart Seminars*, stating that 'Schelling is a Spinozist when he develops a theory of the absolute, representing God by the symbol "A^3" which comprises the Real and the Ideal as its powers' (EPS 118). A^3 is here the reuniting of the Real and the Ideal, of the ground of God and the world he has created.

Deleuze seems to overlook the specificity of this final unity or reuniting in the middle Schelling. Once ground and existence are separated from one another, they are never unified again in a state of initial identity, only separately in love. Their separation is the necessary condition of free, dynamic, unpredictable life in creation and of God's self-authoring personality. Such love and independence is only possible if God is both free to create and is more than his creation, that is, he must transcend it. This un-Deleuzian element lingering in Schelling's middle philosophy means that 'what is expressed' is not modal for Schelling. We are not merely expressions of the essence of substance, but self-authoring, free beings separate from God. However, the *correspondence* of opposites in the *Ungrund*, which 'was everywhere lacking in Cartesianism' (EPS 335), is common to both thinkers.

Deleuze, Indifference and the *Ungrund*

Deleuze concludes *Expressionism in Philosophy* by emphasising that the 'what is expressed' is also called 'sense' (EPS 335). This notion of sense is further developed in *The Logic of Sense*, in which Deleuze sets out 'to determine an impersonal and pre-individual transcendental field, and which nevertheless is not confused with an undifferentiated depth. This field cannot be determined as that of consciousness' (LS 102). This field is characterised by an indifference of sense, which is necessary for the possibility of multiple determinations. As indifference itself, it can naturally also be compared to Schelling's *Ungrund* and Principle of Indifference. Deleuze writes:

> Neutrality, the impassibility of the event, its indifference to the determinations of the inside and the outside, to the individual and the collective, the particular and the general – all these form a constant without which the event would not have eternal truth and could not be distinguished from temporal actualizations. (LS 100)

To explain the neutrality of sense, Deleuze describes a battle that is 'actualized in diverse manners all at once' and experienced differently by each participant. Diversity is possible because the battle itself is 'neutral in relation to all of its temporal actualizations, neutral and impassive in relation to the victor and the vanquished, the coward and brave . . .' (LS 100).[49] The evolution of this pre-personal field in Deleuze's thought becomes affiliated with the 'virtual' of *Difference and Repetition*, and is later transformed into the plane of consistency, the plane of immanence, and the plane of life. This field is paradoxically transcendental (since it is the condition of the genesis of being), but it is not transcendent. It 'coincides with the *purification* of the notion of the transcendental',[50] which sees it as desirable to 'avoid traps, invent a new understanding of the field of individuation' and to explore the productivity of nature 'along with its differentiation and its power'.[51] Echoing the necessary expressivity of substance in Deleuze's Spinozism, Deleuze suggests in the *Logic of Sense* that this pre-personal neutrality of sense is not only neutral and indifferent, it is also productive (*expressive*).

If we consider Deleuze's dual characterisations of sense as both indifferent and productive and his description of Schelling's ground [*fond*] – *Ungrund* [*profond*] relationship, another key difference between the metaphysical structures of the two thinkers arises: namely, Deleuze appears to merge Schelling's ground with the *Ungrund*. Deleuze states, 'the ground [*fond*] as it appears in a homogeneous extensity is notably a projection of something "deeper" [*profond*]: only the latter may be called *Ungrund* or groundlessness' (DR 229). Jason Wirth therefore describes this relationship between the ground and the *Ungrund* as one of synthesis.[52] In short, although Deleuze upholds the Spinozist-inspired distinction between the virtual (*natura naturans*) and the actual (*natura naturata*), he does not sharply distinguish the *Ungrund* – groundlessness, indifference, predicatelessness, the primordial will that wills nothing – from the ground – unconsciousness, darkness, the mad and unruly. Rather, he fuses them into a single descent into the depths, which serves as the condition of individuation (DR 230–1).

Deleuze explicitly appreciates the middle Schelling's breakthrough to the real, the metaphysical role of his *Ungrund* and the discovery of the role of the chaotic and the problematic in ontological production.[53] This appreciation precludes a direct alignment between Deleuze's metaphysics and Schelling's early, immanent, monist Identity Philosophy. In contrast to Hegel, Deleuze makes the following remarks in reference to the middle Schelling:

> [I]t is Schelling who brings difference out of the night of the Identical, and with finer, more varied and more terrifying flashes of lightning than those of contradiction: with progressivity. Anger and love are powers of the Idea which develop on the basis of a *mē on* – in other words, not from a negative or a non-being [*ouk on*] but from a problematic being or non-existent, a being implicit in those existences beyond the ground. (DR 119)

Despite their similarities, Deleuze's interpretation of the Spinozist triad of substance (substance–attributes–essence) is a different type of triad than the Schellingian *Ungrund*–ground–existence structure. That is not to say the former is inapplicable to Schelling's metaphysics – quite the opposite. The first term of Deleuze's triad of substance, namely substance or God, is implicitly present in each of the three orders of the triad we have identified in the *Freedom* essay. The second term, the attributes understood as expressions themselves, maps on to Schelling's ground and existence dyad and their inherent expressive or productive nature (note that the attribute becomes the first term of Deleuze's *modal* triad, in which the second movement of expression occurs). Finally, the third term of the triad of substance – essence – is finally expressed, in the movement of doubling or counter-actualising, as modifications of substance. In this second, creative, affirmative repetition of expression, free human beings are created.

Deleuze's Schellingian Triad

At first, it appears that Schelling's triad in the *Freedom* essay corresponds to a dyad in Deleuze – the *Ungrund* and the ground are combined into the virtual, pre-personal, transcendental field (*natura naturans*) and *natura naturata* persists for both as existence. However, Deleuze arguably postulates intensity as the third term between these two.[54] Deleuze states, 'Intensity is the determinant in the process of actualisation. It is intensity which *dramatises*' (DR 245). Through difference in intensity, which is not observable but can be felt, extensity *becomes*. In short, 'intensive quantities are individuating factors' between *natura naturans* and *natura naturata* (DR 346).

In Deleuze's Bergsonian language, intensities and intensive processes are the pure differences of the virtual which produce the actual. Both intensity and the will of Schelling's ground are of an 'intermediate nature, as desire or appetite, and [are] most readily comparible to the beautiful urge of a nature in becoming that strives to unfold itself and whose inner movements are involuntary'.[55] Deleuze associates 'intensity' with the terms power, depth, potentiality and, perhaps most importantly, 'unconscious' (DR 244–5) – characteristics which also apply to Schelling's ground. For Deleuze, intensity and depth form 'the strangest alliance': 'Depth is the intensity of being, or vice versa' (DR 231).

Intensity, Deleuze writes, 'includes the unequal in itself. It represents difference in quantity' which persists, and cannot be cancelled, sublated or equalised in depth (DR 232). It is the 'fundamental moment present in every [extensive] quantity' (DR 232), but which is 'covered over by qualities' and empirical extensity (DR 233). Intensity can thus be described as the crux of Deleuze's non-Hegelian theory of difference. Although intensity is 'cancelled' in extensity, '[d]ifference is not negation [and] the constituent disparities or enveloped distances inhabit intensive depth' (DR 235).[56] Any observation that difference plays out through a negative process in extensity is an illusion for Deleuze, as real differences engender problems and are never synthesised. Similarly, for Schelling, the progression of difference in being is quantitative. In his theory of potencies (*Potenzenlehre*), developed throughout his middle to late philosophy, Schelling demonstrates the increasing difference in degree or quantity in being in a manner Deleuze praises.[57]

Interpreting intensity as a middle term opens the possibility of identifying a second triad in Deleuze's metaphysics, consisting of the virtual, intensity and the actual. This triad pushes us to consider the implications of reintroducing a Schellingian-inspired conceptual distinction in the abyssal ground of production (the virtual) in Deleuze. Core differences undeniably persist between Schelling's and Deleuze's metaphysics, notably concerning Schelling's notion of a personal, transcendent God and Deleuze's characterisation of the pre-personal field as 'populated by singularities' (indeed, Deleuze claims that Schelling's 'groundlessness cannot sustain difference' (DR 276)). Despite these differences, the elements of this newly identified 'Deleuzian triad' can be mapped on to Schelling's *Ungrund*, ground and existence structure. As I have demonstrated, although Schelling's ground and existence are never unified in the parallel manner of Spinoza's attributes, the *Freedom* essay has a distinctly Spinozist background and its core metaphysical triad is developed out of the monistic triad of Schelling's Identity Philosophy.

The relationship between Schelling and Deleuze could be thematised in a number of ways that are unfortunately beyond the scope of this chapter. For example, one could investigate the relation of Deleuze's passive synthesis of habit to Schelling's will of the ground, focusing on Deleuze's readings of Bergson and Ravaisson.[58] Doing so would perhaps point towards a type of Jungian collective unconscious that Deleuze arguably shares with Schelling.[59] One could alternatively focus on their common understandings of pre-personal life as mediated by Maine de Biran,[60] or the roles of psychosis and the mad in creative production in the work of both Schelling and Deleuze. Finally, it could be fruitful to expound the ethical and moral consequences of their respective notions of freedom as embedded in the metaphysical contexts presented here. Although I will not perform the latter task right now, it is important to at least note freedom as the crucial point of divergence of our two thinkers.

Schelling's hierarchical separation of ground (dark) and existence (light), the latter which ought to (but need not) be higher or above the former, provides for the possibility of divine freedom and God's authentic self-authoring. This moral, self-production of character is called personality, and it exists for Schelling on the level of the divine and of human beings. The freedom of both God and the individual, as we have seen, is defined by the ability to will good or evil. Divine evil is the ground willing to be independent, and human evil is 'willful unconscious',[61] a will to live selfishly, to stray from the universal in a self-destructive pursuit of desire. Deleuze, on the other hand, follows Spinoza in claiming '[t]here are no evils save the reduction of our power of action and the decomposition of a relation' (EPS 247). Evil is thus 'a bad encounter' (EPS 247) comparable to poison. Accordingly, Deleuze does not discuss freedom in terms of good and evil and the development of personality or moral character (for individuals are modes or degrees of power). Rather, freedom concerns the attainment of agency within the collective, the maximisation of self-interest, the experimental discovery of joys – all explored by Deleuze in ethical and political terms which do not demand a God, transcendence or prescriptive morality.

As Deleuze paraphrases from Spinoza, God did not forbid Adam to eat the forbidden fruit – 'He simply revealed to him that such a fruit was capable of destroying his body and decomposing his relation' (EPS 247–8).[62]

Notes

1. For example, Peter Hallward argues that 'the logic of Deleuze's work tends to proceed broadly in line with a *theophanic* conception of things, whereby every individual process or thing is conceived as a manifestation or expression of God or a conceptual equivalent of God (pure creative potential, force, energy, life . . .)' (*Out of this World: Deleuze and the Philosophy of Creation* [London and New York: Verso, 2006], p. 4).
2. Friedrich Wilhelm Joseph Schelling, *Philosophical Inquiries into the Essence of Human Freedom*, trans. Jeff Love and Johannes Schmidt (Albany: State University of New York Press, 2006), p. 13. Henceforth cited as '*Freedom* essay'.
3. Schelling progressively criticises Spinoza's metaphysics from 1809 onwards. For example, in 1841 he accuses Spinoza of diminishing God by allowing everything to logically emerge or emanate from him. By postulating God as the 'necessary, blind existent', he claims Spinoza exerted a violence (*Gewalt*) 'over many minds who forgot all freedom of spirit when they encountered this system' (*Philosophie der Offenbarung 1841/1842 (Paulus Nachschrift)*, ed. Manfred Frank [Frankfurt am Main: Suhrkamp, 1977], pp. 120–1).
4. Furthermore, arguments have been made by commentators such as Iain Hamilton Grant in support of a single empiricist philosophy of

nature and history running throughout Schelling's entire career. See Iain Hamilton Grant, *Philosophies of Nature after Schelling* (London and New York: Continuum, 2006), p. 5.

5. Jason Wirth, 'Introduction', in Jason Wirth (ed.), *Schelling Now: Contemporary Readings* (Bloomington and Indianapolis: Indiana University Press, 2005), p. 7.
6. Bruce Matthews, *Schelling's Organic Form of Philosophy: Life as the Schema of Freedom* (Albany: State University of New York Press, 2011), p. 41.
7. Hegel, Hölderlin and Schelling quickly bonded at the Protestant Tübingenstift, as they shared an 'antipathy to the Seminary' and 'resolved not to become pastors' (Terry Pinkard, *Hegel: A Biography* [Cambridge: Cambridge University Press, 2000], p. 21). They roomed together and also had a common enthusiasm for the French Revolution (Pinkard, *Hegel*, p. 22).
8. At this point in time, working as a *Hofmeister* (private tutor) in conditions which contributed to 'a serious depression' (Pinkard, *Hegel*, p. 47). Pinkard remarks that, while in Jena, Schelling wrote Hegel 'enthusiastic letters about all the things he had read, was reading, and was thinking about (Kant, Fichte, the nature of self) Hegel could only dejectedly reply to Schelling that he was just getting around to looking at these things, and, despondent about his own lack of progress, note to Schelling that in contrast with Schelling's astounding productivity and early fame, "my works are not worth speaking of"' (Pinkard, *Hegel*, p. 57).
9. Pinkard, *Hegel*, p. 109.
10. Ibid., pp. 113–14.
11. Hegel continues, 'this is cognition naïvely reduced to vacuity' (G. W. F. Hegel, *Phenomenology of Spirit*, trans. A. V. Miller [Oxford: Oxford University Press, 1977], p. 9). Pinkard describes that, from Schelling's response to the *Phenomenology* onwards, he and Hegel 'were to be rivals for the attention of the German public for the rest of Hegel's life . . . their original friendship had been based on what they had taken to be a common project. That common project had been defined at first mostly by Schelling, but as Hegel began to make his own way in the world and to separate his own project from Schelling's, the relationship between the two men also changed' (Pinkard, *Hegel*, p. 257).
12. Hegel, *Phenomenology of Spirit*, p. 9.
13. Schelling's thought tends to be broken into the following stages or 'phases': the *Naturphilosophie* (c.1795–1800), the *Identity Philosophy* (c.1801–9), the *Philosophy of Freedom* or the middle Schelling (c.1809–27) and the *Philosophy of Mythology and Revelation* (c.1827–54). There is some debate regarding the precise dates and number of Schelling's intellectual 'shifts', or, indeed, whether he is consistent in any way throughout his thinking.

14. The turn is also often related to Schelling's intense mourning of the loss of his wife, Caroline Schlegel (who died in 1809).
15. The first theosophical thinker notably present in his thinking is Friedrich Christoph Oetinger, whose influence may have begun from the very beginning of Schelling's career. Although the periods and extent of his influence are debated (it is suggested that it likely came through Philipp Matthäus Hahn; see Bruce Matthews, *Schelling's Organic Form of Philosophy: Life as the Schema of Freedom* [Albany: State University of New York Press, 2012], pp. 39–68, and Sean J. McGrath, *The Dark Ground of Spirit: Schelling and the Unconscious* [London: Routledge, 2012], p. 75n4), Oetinger's post-vitalist, non-mechanistic view of matter would have been attractive to Schelling, notably because it espouses a view of matter irreducible to a mechanistic view of the universe and the revelation of life (McGrath, *The Dark Ground of Spirit*, p. 45). This influence underlines the early importance of the concept of life in Schelling's thought – consciousness cannot be everything, for life in matter is more than consciousness (see, for example, Robert Schneider, *Schellings und Hegels schwäbische Geistesahnen* [Würzburg: Tiltsch, 1938]).
16. Jakob Böhme (1575–1624) was an autodidact. He did not read widely, but is known to have read some texts, such as Paracelsus, the Luther Bible and some German mystics. It is also likely that Böhme had access to ideas such as the Kabbalah (McGrath, *The Dark Ground of Spirit*, p. 48)
17. Andrew Weeks, *Boehme: An Intellectual Biography of the Seventeenth-Century Philosopher and Mystic* (Albany: State University of New York Press, 1991), pp. 2–3.
18. McGrath, *The Dark Ground of Spirit*, p. 48.
19. Benedict de Spinoza, *The Ethics*, trans. R. H. M. Elwes (New York: Dover Publications, 1955), I, p. 15.
20. Spinoza, *The Ethics*, IV Pref.
21. Spinoza, *The Ethics*, ID5.
22. Spinoza, *The Ethics*, IP29S.
23. Jason Wirth, *The Conspiracy of Life: Meditations on Schelling and His Time* (Albany: State University of New York Press, 2003), p. 2.
24. Douglas Hedley, *Coleridge, Philosophy and Religion: Aids to Reflection and the Mirror of the Spirit* (Cambridge: Cambridge University Press, 2004), p. 26.
25. Schelling, *Freedom* essay, p. 28.
26. Ibid., p. 21.
27. Pantheism is here defined as 'a complete identification of God with things; a blending of creator and creative being . . .' (ibid., p. 12).
28. Original text: 'Fichte hatte das Sein auf der Tat ergriffen, im Akte des Selbstbewußtseins; er hatte das Sein da ergriffen, wo es sich sogar

im unmittelbaren Bewußtsein darstellt als ein aus der Potenz hervortretendes' (Schelling, *Philosophie der Offenbarung*, p. 111). The late Schelling nevertheless appreciates Fichte's insight that, in so far as the I can subsist *only in an act*, it contains within itself its own potency or power to act or to 'go over' (*übergehen*) into being. In the act of positing itself, Fichte's I limits itself and becomes its own object. Schelling will not accept the Fichtean definition of the objective or nature, but he maintains that Fichte was only one step away from recognizing the 'essence [*Wesen*] that is the prior condition of all being [*Prius alles Sein*]. One had only to leave aside the limitation [of being] to self-positing [*Sichselbstsetzens*] in order to find the absolute point of evolution [*Entwicklung*].' This absolute point for Schelling is the Principle of Indifference (Schelling, *Philosophie der Offenbarung*, p. 111).

29. Michael Vater explains this transition in terms of Schelling's 'rejection of subjectivism'. He writes, 'Subjectivism means that human intellect can explain only what humans experience, and that merely in a piecemeal fashion. Schelling's rejection of subjectivism leads him to embrace a *Naturphilosophie* which is neither an encyclopedia of scientific discoveries nor an isolated meditation on the methodology of experiment and verification, but a metaphysical proof that "considered in and of itself, nothing is finite", based on the way independent nature comports itself and everywhere surpasses limited shapes and operations' (Michael Vater, 'Reconfiguring Identity in Schelling's *Würzburg System*', in Lore Hühn, Paul Ziche and Philipp Schwab (eds), *Schelling-Studien*, vol. 2, [Freiburg im Breisgau and Munich: Verlag Karl Alber, 2014], p. 139).
30. Schelling famously articulates their relationship by stating 'Nature shall be visible spirit and spirit invisible nature' (Schelling, 'Ideas on a Philosophy of Nature as an Introduction to this Science', p. 202).
31. Vater, 'Reconfiguring Identity', pp. 128–9.
32. Original text: '[Die Identitätsphilosophie] hat davon, daß sie zu ihrem Ausgangspunkt Indifferenz, zu ihrem Ende die Identität von Subjekt und Objekt hatte . . .' (Schelling, *Philosophie der Offenbarung*, p. 111).
33. Schelling, *Freedom* essay, p. 69.
34. Ibid., p. 69.
35. Schelling, *Philosophie der Offenbarung*, p. 111.
36. Schelling, *Freedom* essay, p. 56.
37. Ibid., p. 69.
38. Ibid., p. 70.
39. Vater, 'Reconfiguring Identity', pp. 128–9.
40. Schelling, *Freedom* essay, p. 68.
41. Jason Wirth, *Schelling's Practice of the Wild: Time, Art, Imagination* (Albany: State University of New York Press, 2015), p. 63.
42. Schelling, *Freedom* essay, p. 67.
43. Ibid., p. 66.

44. Ibid., p. 70.
45. Ibid., p. 69.
46. For more on this relationship, see Christian Kerslake, *Deleuze and the Unconscious* (London: Continuum, 2007).
47. Mark Bonta, 'Rhizome of Boehme and Deleuze: Esoteric Precurses of the God of Complexity', *SubStance 121* 39:1 (2010), pp. 62–75.
48. For more on the relationship of Schelling, Deleuze, Spinoza and expressivity, see Jason Wirth, 'Animalization: Schelling and the Problem of Expressivity', in Wirth (ed.), *Schelling Now*, pp. 85–98.
49. Continuing with the thematisation of the battle, Deleuze asks us to imagine a wounded soldier 'who is no longer brave or cowardly, no longer victor or vanquished, but rather so much beyond . . .' (LS 101). Through this example, Deleuze exemplifies the 'impersonal will', a concept strongly present in Schelling. This will is impersonal, shared, existing beyond the individual herself, and so the soldier, emerging from struggle, has a 'pure grasping of the event by means of a "volitional intuition",' that is, 'by means of the will that the event creates in him' (LS 101). Schelling describes the will of the ground and the will of love, both 'of which exists for itself', and which 'become one . . . because they are separate and each acts for itself from the beginning on' (*Freedom* essay, p. 42). The activity of the two wills is also present in individuals as well in their freedom to do good and evil (ibid., p. 47).
50. Pierre Montebello, *Deleuze: La Passion de la pensée* (Paris: Vrin, 2008), p. 98, translation mine. The first thing to note is that it is not the subject that makes the transcendental. But, for Deleuze, it is also not God – it is the impersonal and anonymous real. The a-personal transcendental field is the real itself, and that is what is transcendental. In short, the transcendental field provides the originary condition of all production and requires a critique of the individualized I as the centre of all.
51. Montebello, *Deleuze*, p. 98, translation mine.
52. Wirth, *Schelling's Practice of the Wild*, p. 67.
53. Deleuze refers to Schelling, Böhme and Schopenhauer as philosophers able to make 'the Abyss (Sans-fond) speak and [find] the mystical language of its wrath, its formlessness, and its blindness' (LS 106).
54. This debate concerning whether Deleuze's metaphysics is dualistic or triadic also persists in Deleuzian scholarship independent to Schelling. Peter Hallward identifies intensities with the virtual, whereas John Protevi argues that the intensive has 'its own ontological register' of 'impersonal individuations'. See John Protevi, 'Review: Peter Hallward, Out of this World: Deleuze and the Philosophy of Creation', https://ndpr.nd.edu/news/23058-out-of-this-world-deleuze-and-the-philosophy-of-creation/ (last accessed 19/1/2015). Whether intensity ought to be considered as a continuum between the virtual and actual, or a third term for in its own right, is up for debate. In any case, Deleuze's

development of this concept implies that his metaphysics is not strictly dualist.

55. Schelling, *Freedom* essay, p. 59.
56. Deleuze further clarifies, 'every time we find ourselves confronted with qualified oppositions and in an extensity in which these are distributed, we must not count upon an extensive synthesis which would overcome and resolve them. On the contrary, the constituent disparities or enveloped distances inhabit intensive depth' (DR 235).
57. Deleuze explains: 'A, A2, A3 form the play of pure depotentialisation and potentiality, testifying to the presence in Schelling's philosophy of a differential calculus adequate to the dialectic' (DR 191).
58. To this effect, Alberto Toscono suggests a convergence of Deleuze's and Schelling's thought 'diachronically mediated by the lineage of French "spiritualism" (Maine de Biran, Victor Cousin, Félix Ravaisson and Henry Bergson)' (*The Theatre of Production: Philosophy and Individuation between Kant and Deleuze* [Basingstoke: Palgrave Macmillan, 2006], p. 118). Ravaisson ontologises the concept of habit (stimulated by Maine de Biran), and from there develops the doctrine of movement in matter (immanence of life to matter) and an understanding of the visible universe as the exterior aspect of an underlying reality (see Henri Bergson, *Notice sur la vie et les œuvres de Félix Ravaisson-Mollien* [Paris: Firmin Didot, 1904]). The passive synthesis of habit is arguably one of the pillars of Deleuze's understanding of the unconscious. Furthermore, Ravaisson's conception of the mysterious unity of the real and the ideal, the subjective and the objective, in the pre-individuated was directly influenced by Schelling's *Naturphilosophie* and Identity philosophy (see Dominique Janicaud, *Ravaisson et la métaphysique* [Paris: Vrin, 1997], p. 462, and Sinclair, 'Embodiment: Conceptions of the Lived-Body from Maine de Biran to Bergson', in Alison Stone [ed.], *The Edinburgh Critical History of Nineteenth-Century Philosophy* [Edinburgh: Edinburgh University Press, 2011], p. 194). It is historically noteworthy in investigating this lineage that Ravaisson attended Schelling's lectures in Munich and corresponded with the latter directly. Bergson describes Ravaisson's relationship to Schelling as a 'natural affinity' and a 'cluster of aspiration' (Bergson, *Œuvres* [Paris: Presses universitaires de France, 1991], p. 1458).
59. Consult Christian Kerslake, *Deleuze and the Unconscious* (London: Continuum, 2007) for an in-depth exploration on the relationship of Deleuze and the Jungian unconscious.
60. Following a Schellingian influence, Maine de Biran, Ravaisson and Bergson come together and 'invent a movement of life' in the prepersonal (Montebello, *Deleuze*, p. 132). Deleuze states that Maine de Biran 'discovered beneath the transcendence of effort a life, absolute

and immanent' (PI 390) and could thus be considered the original thinker of the affective yet pre-representational and impersonal real (MI 139–40).

61. McGrath, 'The Psychology of Productive Dissociation', *Comparative and Continental Philosophy* 6:1 (2014), pp. 35–48 (p. 38).
62. I would like to thank Dr Sean McGrath, Dr Peter Trnka and Petr Kocourek for their valuable comments and support regarding this chapter.

Heinrich von Kliest

Kamini Vellodi

Heinrich von Kleist (1777–1810) is one of the outstanding figures of German literature, whose boldly unorthodox plays and novellas are today esteemed for their brilliant eccentricity and their insights into the perplexities and contradictions of their time. In their scattered remarks on Kleist, in *Kafka: Toward a Minor literature*, *Dialogues*, *A Thousand Plateaus*, and *What is Philosophy?* Deleuze and Guattari foreground the way he puts literature to work as a 'war machine', a function by which writing breaks through the regime of information, communication and signification and opens to its 'outside' (ECC lv).[1] They refer both to general traits of Kleist's writing and to specific works including *Penthesilea*, 'On the Theatre of the Marionettes', 'On the Gradual Formation of Ideas in Speech', *The Prince of Homburg* and *Michael Kohlhaas*.

Much of Deleuze and Guattari's analysis of Kleist springs from their views on the task of writing. For them, not everyone who writes is a writer, nor does writing have anything to do with being an author or the creation of any other particular genre. Rather, to write is to create 'lines of flight', movements of thought that liberate language from the structures through which it is made to operate as a medium of power, authority and repression. 'Writing is becoming' and to write is 'to invent a new language within language', a 'stuttering' or foreign language that forces language outside its customary grooves. To write is to express an 'intensified' life, beyond the limits of the personal and the structures of the psychoanalytical, a life 'which traverses both the liveable and the lived'. To write is thus to replace interpretation with experimentation that frees thought from the structures of the same and projects it onto the field of 'pure' difference (ECC 1). Thus, Deleuze and Guattari turn to Kleist, not with an eye to the particular (late Romantic) forms of his writing – the drama, the aphorism, the fragment – nor as a biographical study of his condition as author. Rather, what draws them is Kleist's idiosyncratic practice of writing, and – inseparable from this – his reflections on thinking. We often find Deleuze and Guattari attributing to Kleist's works traits which they also discern in other writers important to their philosophical project: Kafka (himself an admirer of Kleist), Artaud, Woolf, Melville, Lawrence, Lenz, Büchner and Hölderlin; and as such their remarks on Kleist are often interwoven or juxtaposed with remarks on these other figures. It is in *A Thousand Plateaus* that Deleuze and Guattari single out the question that for them distinguishes Kleist's work: 'What is a literature of war?' (TP 240; K 55).[2]

I begin with an introduction to Kleist's life and work, and an outline of three major themes in Deleuze and Guattari's reading of Kleist – exteriority, affect and flight – showing how these play out in the analyses of specific works. I then focus and elaborate on the single crucial concept which Deleuze and Guattari associate with Kleist's works – the 'war machine' – through an analysis of their reading of Kleist's play *Penthesilea* (1808), on the one hand, and through an analysis of their contrasting of Kleist with the 'State' figure of Goethe on the other. Finally, I elaborate on Kleist's critique of Kant, and the importance of this critique for Deleuze and Guattari's own anti-Kantian claims on the relations between writing, the war machine and thought both in Kleist's works and beyond. As there has been surprisingly little secondary commentary on the place of Kleist in Deleuze and Guattari's philosophy[3] my analysis is heavily reliant on primacy sources – namely, Deleuze's writing on Kleist, and Kleist's works and private letters.

The Life-Work of Kleist

Kleist's life is as famed for its eccentricity as his work. Born in 1777 in Frankfurt into an ancient aristocratic Prussian military family that furnished officers to the Prussian army and officials to the State, the young Kleist abandoned his calling to the military to take up writing. His output was modest: he produced only six plays and eight novellas, as well as several unfinished works and a series of essays and aphorisms. Countless works were abandoned or destroyed. At the age of thirty-four he took his own life and that of his friend Henriette Vogel in a double suicide.[4]

Overlooked and criticised by the public and the cultural establishment in his own time, Kleist became, in the century following his death, celebrated as one of the towering figures of German literature. His works, characterised by their violent extremes, emotional excesses, unresolved conflicts, enigmatic plots and stylistic eccentricities, challenged the sober norms of German literature and have been hailed both for giving expression to the tendencies of late German Romanticism and for heralding the onset of a peculiarly modern consciousness – as his laudatory reception by such figures as Heine, Nietzsche, Mann, Wagner, Rilke, Brecht, Gide, Lukács and Kafka affirms.

Deleuze and Guattari's Kleist, too, is a writer of the 'most uncanny modernity', uncomfortably lodged within late German Romanticism (TP 356). For them, he is not a tragic figure but an anarchic experimenter whose dis-identification with his own historical present – including the great classical figures of German literature Goethe and Schiller, but also the philosophical figures of Kant and Hegel – and his anticipation of the future of literature is staged not only through the particular style and thematic motifs of his work – battles, voyages, rootless characters, extreme affects and situations – but also through the interpenetration of his writing with his own life.

Indeed, Kleist's literary output can hardly be understood separately from the peculiar circumstances of his life. However, it is inadequate to see his writing as a reflection or representation of these circumstances. Kleist's works do not express the confessional or the autobiographical (at least in reference to a unique author subject), and even a quick glance through his letters reveals to the reader the exaggerated and dramatised lens through which Kleist experienced the world.[5] His remark that 'that it is not we who know, but rather a certain state of mind in us that knows' might be taken as a motto for his writing, which captured the remarkable features of his life and rendered them strangely impersonal.[6] It appears to be with an intuition of this impersonal reciprocity of life and work that Deleuze and Guattari approach Kleist. Indicating their own conception of 'life' as an impersonal and non-organic power that traverses lived experience, they constantly intertwine reference to the events of Kleist's life – his withdrawal from the military, his treatment by Goethe, his suicide – alongside analyses of his work.

By all accounts, Kleist was a taciturn, sensitive and solitary man, with unprepossessing childish looks, a stammer that increased his unease in company, and a disposition prone to illness. The conventions of the nobility, the military, and the experience of war, marked his early life. Aged fifteen, he was placed in a regiment of guards stationed in Potsdam where he remained for six years. While it is clear from his early letters that military life did not interest him –

the young Kleist spent most of his time reading philosophy and mathematics – the experience ostensibly gave him the awareness of conflictual forces and the absurdity of rules and order that would later be so important in his writing.[7] In 1799, in protest against the 'tyranny' of military life (the officers were no better than drillmasters, he wrote), Kleist resigned his post, much to the dismay of his family.[8] On his release he drew up his first 'life-plan', resolving to dedicate himself to the pursuit of education, reason and the 'realm of knowledge' – particularly theology, mathematics, philosophy and physics.[9] It was the first of many such life-plans, enthusiastically drafted but ultimately aborted.

In 1800 Kleist contemplated a career in the civil service, but finally rejected the idea, describing himself as unsuited to serving the State.[10] The following year was a crucial one: it is in 1801 that Kleist reads Kant and by his own admission suffers a profound crisis. This crisis is founded on his (erroneous) belief that, since Kant holds that we cannot have access to the thing-in-itself, there can be no such thing as absolute truths and principles. Described by one commentator as 'the most notorious emotional crisis in German literary history',[11] this conclusion casts Kleist into a groundlessness that will henceforth mark his life and infiltrate his work. He abandons his life-plan of self-education, breaks off his engagement to a young German woman named Wilhelmine von Zenge and begins writing. The following decade, in which he produces all his major works, is marked by a series of aimless journeys, unsuccessful government appointments, aborted literary projects, and physical and nervous collapse. His works – verse tragedies, comedies and stories —received mixed reception. Only a few of his plays were staged, including one (*The Broken Pitcher* [1806]), disastrously, by Goethe, who was openly critical of the younger writer. In 1811 Kleist rowed into the middle of a lake and shot himself, after first shooting the terminally ill Henriette Vogel.[12]

This was a life marked by tensions and the impossibility of their resolution; in Kleist's own words, a life 'torn by opposing forces'.[13] The conflicts between freedom and rule, plan and spontaneity, duty and desire, fate and accident, reason and sensibility govern his life and dominate his work. But his writing is not the scene for any catharsis, resolution or fulfilment. Rather, it continues and intensifies the lived conflicts of his experience. As such, these are works replete with obscured binaries and irresolution, works capturing, in Kleist's own words, the 'extraordinary difficulties', 'strange circumstances' and 'unfathomable misunderstandings' of his experience.

In *The Marquise of O* (1808), a noblewoman renowned for her virtue finds herself 'inexplicably' with child, and is shocked to discover that the culprit is none other than the Count who had earlier saved her from the abuse of some soldiers and who had proposed to her the very next day. In *The Earthquake in Chile* (1807), it takes a natural catastrophe of epic propositions to reunite two estranged lovers, both of whom had been condemned to death for their adulterous passion, only for them to be cruelly vilified again by their fellow men and finally butchered to death by one of the pair's father on the steps of the town's only remaining cathedral. In *Michael Kohlhaas* (1808) – apparently the only story that Kafka recited publicly – the eponymous 'hero', incensed at the injustice of the law, sets out to seek and attain his own justice, in the process becoming a fanatical, nomadic militant, wreaking war and widespread destruction. The Prince in *The Prince of Homburg* (1809–10) disobeys his superior's orders to lead his men to victory, is charged with the death penalty for his disobedience, granted mercy on the condition that he can claim the sentence to be unjust, accepts the penalty, but is freed at the last minute and crowned with the laurel wreath he had been dreaming of at the play's opening. In *Penthesilea* (1808), the warlike Queen of the Amazons enters into a confused love–hate relation with Achilles, Greek hero of the Trojan War, that cannot be resolved, and which casts both heroes into a flight from their respective race.

In all these stories and plays, individuals change dramatically through the action of incomprehensible forces or accidental events. They are presented as conflicted compounds of extremes – the innocent dishonour of the Marquise, the angelic devil that is her saviour, the heroic cowardice of the Prince of Homberg, the deadly righteousness of Kohlhaas, described by Kleist in the story's opening line as 'one of the most upright and at the same time terrible men of his time'.[14] Kleist breathlessly takes the reader across continents and far-flung places, juxtaposing scenes of intimate domesticity with epic descriptions of wars and bloodshed. Situations and characters constantly change; plots unfold at a feverish space. All this occurs through an eccentric style of writing, involving prolonged exegesis without 'development', unexplained digressions, absurd hiatuses, strange accelerations and abrupt shifts in register – a style which Thomas Mann memorably described as 'totally matter-of-fact yet contorted, twisted, surcharged with matter'.[15]

Deleuze and Guattari's Kleist: Exteriority, Affect and Flight

> Kleist: everything with him, in his writing as in his life, becomes speed and slowness. A succession of catatonic freezes and extreme velocities, fainting spells and shooting arrows. Sleep on your steed, then take off at a gallop. Jump from one assemblage to another, with the aid of a faint, by crossing a void. Kleist multiplies 'life-planes,' but his voids and failures, his leaps, earthquakes and plagues are always included on a single plane. The plane is not a principle of organisation but a means of transportation. No form develops, no subject forms; affects are displaced, becomings catapult forward and combine into blocks, like the becoming-woman of Achilles and the becoming-dog of Penthesilea. (TP 268)

Deleuze and Guattari's reading of Kleist, in part shaped by Mathieu Carrière's 1981 text *For a Literature of War, Kleist*,[16] does not remain with the way Kleist invokes unresolved oppositions, but focuses on his creative solution to irreconcilable dualisms, his overpowering of binaries by lines of flight that provide modes of escape and new creative possibilities. To them, Kleist does not remain a victim of or a reactionary to the oppositions that challenge him, but rather makes himself a warrior-producer, a 'man of war'. Before I turn to the concept of the war machine, I will elucidate three key notions in Deleuze and Guattari's analysis of Kleist: exteriority, affect and flight.

Deleuze and Guattari describe Kleist as 'the first to invent' the impersonal element of 'exteriority' (TP 356). His writing displaces the personal element of interiority, which may in the first instance be understood as self-reflexivity or self-reference. This displacement characterises Deleuze and Guattari's view of writing and literature. As Deleuze states in his essay 'Literature and Life', 'to write is not to recount one's memories and travels, one's loves and griefs, one's dreams and fantasies', 'to write is not a private matter', and is 'not to impose a form (of expression) on the matter of lived experience'. Rather literature exists 'only when it discovers the power of the impersonal', it 'begins only when a third person is born in us that strips us of the power to say "I" (ECC 1–3). To take writing into the element of the exterior demands a practice of writing that does not refer back to a subject who writes. For Deleuze and Guattari, Kleist's works epitomise this practice. His 'personal formula is a succession of flights of madness and catatonic freezes in which no subjective interiority remains' (TP 356). The 'ideal' book, they claim, would be one in which everything is laid out 'on a plane of exteriority . . . on a single page, the same sheet: lived events, historical determinations, concepts, individuals, groups, social formations' (TP 9). Many of Kleist's stories offer this. In *The Earthquake in Chile*, for instance, the reader is confronted by the historical determination of an actual natural disaster (the Santiago earthquake of 1647), the lived events of love affairs, childbirth and death, the concepts of fate, retribution and chance, and a plethora of individuals, groups and social formations brought together in different relations through the twists and turns of the narrative – the nuns of the convent, the group displaced after the earthquake, the aristocratic family that adopts the ill-fated couple, and the Father.

Deleuze and Guattari argue that the distinction between the form of interiority and writing's plane of exteriority is produced at the level of composition. A form of interiority is made up of 'bi-univocal' relations – structural relations between binaries that remain external to each other and supplementary to the system. Chess is an example of this, where all the pieces are separate and distinguishable through their distinct functions and forms. In contrast, Deleuze and Guattari give the example of the ancient Chinese game of Go. Whereas chess pieces are 'coded', and each has 'an internal nature and intrinsic properties from which their movements, situations and confrontations derive', Go pieces are pellets that all look the same and which bear only 'an anonymous, collective or third-person function' with only 'situational' properties. The game of chess is structural, functioning on a 'plane of organisation' and development, but a Go piece operates only on a 'milieu of exteriority' (what Deleuze and Guattari also call 'a plane of consistency' or 'plane of immanence', 'where there are only speeds and slownessess, no development') (TRM 133). Go is fundamentally relational and 'exteriorised' – the function of any given piece is determined by its relations to other stones, in contrast to chess, where each piece has its own fixed identity and law. Both games are battles, but chess is an 'institutionalised, regulated, coded war', whereas Go is 'war without battle lines'. Subjectivity is rethought by Deleuze and Guattari along these lines. Reference to an 'I' upholds a bi-univocal relation, between subject and object, and the 'I' functions as though in a chess game, through structural distinctions and 'interiorised' properties. But on a plane of exteriority, subjectivity does not exist as a supplement to the internal determinations of the plane, and is instead made up only of movements, situations and confrontations, not from or between one point to another, but perpetual, 'without aim or destination, without departure or arrival' (TP 353).

Deleuze and Guattari find 'much of the East in Kleist: the Japanese fighter' (TP 356, 400). Individuals, such as the protagonists of *The Earthquake in Chile*, are shown to be in flux, moving as the situation moves, rather than as characters that transcend their circumstances. In their exteriorised nature, Kleist's texts 'are opposed in every way to the classical or romantic book constituted by the interior of a substance or subject' (TP 9). In place of (classical or Romantic) character development of the interiorised depths of a particular, often idealised, psychology (Goethe's *Werther* being a classic example), Kleist gives us characters, fractured and mobilised as collectives by the forces of movements, situations and extraordinary events. Thus, in *The Earthquake in Chile*, we learn nothing of the character of the two protagonists but rather experience them purely as mobile constructions generated by the violence of their circumstances.

This brings us to Deleuze and Guattari's notion of the affect, which they characterise as violent states or conditions that do not belong to a subject and are distinct from 'feelings'; 'nonhuman becomings of man', 'uprooted from the interiority of a subject', and which 'sweep' away the subject effectuating 'a power of the pack that throws the self into upheaval and makes it reel' (TP 356, 240). 'Affects are projectiles, just like weapons', and 'Kleist is no doubt the author who most wrote with affects, using them like stones or weapons' (TP 400). Indeed, Kleist rarely presents us with 'ordinary' conditions – instead characters are presented in violent swoonings, hysterical spells and accelerated chases. In Deleuze and Guattari's terms, his works give us an impersonal movement of affects in place of subjects with their feelings. They forge 'a broken chain of affects and variable speeds, with accelerations and transformations, always in a relation with the outside'.[17] The opening paragraph of *The Earthquake in Chile* presents this: in one breathless sequence we are given terror, anxiety, intimacy, passion, duty, betrayal, recrimination and penitence. The remainder of the text is indeed what Deleuze and Guattari describe as an unfolding of 'variable speeds' and sudden 'accelerations and transformations'. Just as Jeronimo is about to hang himself 'suddenly, the greater part of the city collapsed with a crash'; just as calm is being restored after the earthquake, the announcement of a Mass in the church leads to hordes of people immediately breaking camp and streaming into the city; just as Josephe and Jeronimo think they are once again safe, having escaped the seething crowd inside the church, they are suddenly attacked and bludgeoned to death by Jeronimo's father.[18]

Deleuze and Guattari distinguish another characteristic of affects: their passage through extremes – both extreme speed and absolute immobility. This involves 'undoing' things, and the decoding of the subject – for instance 'the "not-doing" of the warrior'. We encounter this in Kleist's Prince of Homburg who 'unlearns' the code of the military man – first through his dreams and somnambulism and then through the violence of his affects, which spur him to take military action against the 'battle-plan' of his superiors (TP 400).[19] As Deleuze and Guattari note, Kleist seizes affects 'in becomings of sudden petrification or finite acceleration' (WIP 169), sometimes 'linking the petrification of the act to the precipitation of movement'. Which is to say, immobility and speed, catatonia and acceleration, are combined. After a dream-state that lasts for an entire act, in which he admits to a wandering mind that cannot grasp the orders dictated to him, the Prince of Homburg springs into feverish, decisive action in response to a sudden, unexpected event on the battlefield.

For Deleuze and Guattari a 'line of flight' is a movement of becoming on a plane of exteriority. Flight is 'a sort of delirium', where to be delirious is 'to go off the rails', to depart from established codes and produce something from this movement. Delirium, which has an 'intrinsic relationship to writing' (D 30, 42), is 'not a father-mother affair' grounded on the oedipal signifier – that is, the Freudian decoding and interpretation of the unconscious through the terms of the Oedipus complex. Rather, it is a mobile flux of desire, 'a system of asignifying signs' a nomadic affair not bound to the family but which passes through 'peoples, races and tribes' (ECC 4; D 78). It is in this regard that Deleuze and Guattari refer to Kleist's *Penthesilea* as a figure whose delirious actions cannot be interpreted through reference to her familial relations; indeed, she is a figure with no family, only a tribe.

Deleuze and Guattari also identify this nomadic line of flight with the figure of the puppet in 'On the Theatre of Marionettes' (1810), one of Kleist's most obscure texts. The text is a dialogue between a man and a famous dancer who, when he is not dancing, runs a little marionette theatre in the city's marketplace. Asked by the man why he indulges in this pastime, which ostensibly has little dramatic content, the dancer replies that dancers can learn much from puppetry and their 'extraordinary grace'.[20] He explains this graceful effect by recounting the way the puppeteer moves the puppets

– rather than each individual limb being moved separately, each movement has 'a center of gravity'. The puppeteer controls this point from the centre of the figure, and the limbs follow mechanically from this. Thus, 'each time the center of gravity is moved in a straight line the limbs trace curves; and that often, when merely shaken in a haphazard fashion, the entire mechanism slipped into a kind of rhythmic motion that resembled dance.' The dancer goes on to say that this movement is not simply a mechanical affair, but 'something very mysterious. For it [is] nothing less than the pathway of the dancer's soul.'[21] This is why the machinist (puppeteer) needs a special sensibility, and moreover, needs himself to be a dancer. Effectively, the puppet's movements are of a 'natural disposition' for 'it never strikes an attitude' – for attitude 'arises when the soul (*vis motrix*) finds itself twisted in a motion other than the one prescribed by its center of gravity'. Human dancers are forever invoking contorted, unnatural poses, and this artifice is unavoidable, ever since the Fall of Man in the Garden of Eden. But puppets never move against the laws of gravity – that is, they embody the natural grace of Man that he has lost.[22] To explain this strange proposition that a puppet is more graceful than a man, the dancer narrates two episodes – one, a classic tale of narcissism where a young man, discerning in a mirror his beauty for the first time, falls from innocence, and through vanity loses his beauty; the other, an episode in which the dancer is brought face to face with a fencing bear, who with 'perfect calm' successfully parries all the dancer's thrusts, 'as if he could read [the dancer's] soul'. Thus, the dancer concludes, grace is either a condition of those 'devoid of consciousness' (the puppet/bear) or those with an 'infinite consciousness', who having tasted the fruits of the tree of knowledge fall back into a state of innocence.[23]

Deleuze and Guattari do not ruminate on this Rousseauian invocation of lost and retrieved innocence. They are instead interested in the idea of machinism invoked by the puppeteer: 'The puppeteer does not operate according to movements that already represent the figures to be achieved.' Rather he makes his puppet move according to a 'perfectly abstract line neither figurative nor symbolic', and which constitutes the 'true soul of movement' (TP 268). This is an intensive line of flight, with its own logic, that bears no binary relationship to the actual movements of the puppet. Through the movements of the puppet, abstraction becomes real – conjuring a new inorganic reality (TRM 11–12). The puppet show reveals how 'forms and persons are only appearances' produced by the 'intensive displacement of a center of gravity on an abstract line, and by the conjunction of these lines on a plane of immanence' (TP 268). 'Kleist is fascinated by bears', Deleuze and Guattari claim, as 'they are impossible to fool because their cruel little eyes see through appearances to the true "soul of movement", the *Gemut* or nonsubjective affect' (TP 268).

The lines of flight from the institutions of family, State, marriage, military and the cultural elite that characterise Kleist's stories mark his tortuous biography, too. Deleuze and Guattari acknowledge this: Kleist spent his life 'making programmes for life', where a programme 'is not a manifesto', but 'the means of providing reference points for an experiment that exceeds our capacities to foresee' (D 48). Indeed, Kleist's plans rarely had a declared predestined aim, and in their unveiling to his confidants were often cloaked in mystery. Even his first plan – the plan to acquire knowledge – does not have a declared 'end': he wants to know, but does not know what occupation it will lead to.[24] While he presents this initial life-plan as a definite plan for one's life, one which as 'his duty' no 'accidental or extrinsic circumstances can or will hinder', his subsequent abandonment of this plan and a series of others reveals their susceptibility to the vicissitudes of circumstances. Thus, it seems that a life-plan is not an *idée fixe*, but a dynamic map in ongoing contact with real experience – a seeming commonplace of human life, but which in Kleist's case, causes great turbulence. Following his 'Kant-crisis', Kleist's life-plans becoming increasingly rootless, a series of journeys without rationale, or self-imposed strictures to rein in his inner restlessness.[25] Kleist constantly ungrounds his own 'reference points', and writing erupts from this disruption. Deleuze and Guattari read a consistency in this, one that is distinct from the melancholic longing or tragic resignation associated with the Romantic figure. That is, Kleist:

> multiplies 'life-plans' but his voids and failures, his leaps, earthquakes, and plagues are always included on a single plane. [This] plane is not a principle of organisation but a means of transportation. No form develops, no subject forms: affects are displaced, becomings catapult forward and combine into blocks, like the becoming-woman of Achilles and the becoming-dog of Penthesilea. (TP 268)

Penthesilea and the War Machine

These themes of Deleuze and Guattari's reading of Kleist are brought together in their concept of the war machine: 'all of Kleist's work is traversed by a war machine invoked against the State' (TP 268).

Considering Kleist's abandonment of the military order into which he was born, and the many references to war and the military throughout his work, Deleuze and Guattari's analysis of the Kleistian war machine pitted against an institutionalised military is apposite. Their foregrounding of the importance of war in Kleist's work is influenced by Carrière's understanding of war – a 'climate of affective encounter' between 'multiplicities' – as 'the matrix which determines all of [Kleist's] experiences'.[26]

Deleuze and Guattari's notion of the war machine refers not to writing that takes war as its object but to writing as the putting to work of a revolutionary, artistic milieu that attacks the State apparatus of interpretation, communication, signification and representation. As Deleuze and Guattari clarify, 'machines don't mean anything, they merely work, produce, break down' (DI 221). And 'Kleist put literature into an immediate relation with the war machine'(D 123; TP 268). They identify three examples: firstly, the Prince of Homburg who 'lives only in a dream and stands condemned for having reached victory in disobedience of the law of the State' (TP 355–6); secondly, *Penthesilea*, where the war machine of the Amazons operates between the two states, the Greek and the Trojan, producing the becoming-animal of Penthesilea; and thirdly, *Kohlhaas*, where a war machine is unleashed in the protagonist's nomadic and perpetually thwarted search for an idea of justice.

The concept of the war machine is most thoroughly explicated in *A Thousand Plateaus*, in Chapter 12, 'Treatise on Nomadology: The War Machine', a chapter whose publication as a separate text by Semiotext(e) in 1986 indicates its theoretical importance for Deleuze and Guattari. Here, the 'war machine' and the 'State apparatus' are conceptualised as two poles of any political assemblage. The 'war machine' is distinguished from war as a form that is 'institutionalised, regulated, coded . . . with a front, a rear, battles' (TP 353). The war machine in fact wages war against any regulated and coded apparatus that proceeds by hierarchical dualisms and which forms 'a milieu of interiority' – what Deleuze and Guattari call a 'State apparatus' (that is, the State does not refer only to a political state but to any system that fosters a representational image of thought). When the State wages war it does so by appropriating the war machine in the form of the military institution, and this is the form of war that Kleist repeatedly critiques, from his exposure of the unchivalrous behaviour of soldiers (*Marquise*), to the unreasonable consequences of military laws (*Homburg*).

The war machine is outside the sovereignty of the State apparatus and 'prior to its law' – it is not simply exterior *to* the State but is 'itself a pure form of exteriority' (TP 354), bearing 'witness to another kind of justice, one of incomprehensible cruelty at times', but 'at others of unequalled pity'. One might here refer to how the 'unspeakable cruelty' of the Marquise of O's father, who banishes his 'inexplicably' pregnant daughter and attempts to forcefully separate her from her children, then morphs into 'unequalled pity' with the realisation of his error – which Kleist depicts as a scene of reconciliation between father and daughter that borders on the incestuous: he 'pressed long, ardent and avid kisses on her mouth, just like a lover!'[27] Here we find the emergence of new laws, triggered by exceptional circumstances that defy the State codes of the family.

But it is one Kleist text in particular that Deleuze and Guattari focus on for its expression of the war machine: *Penthesilea*, a work which Kleist had described as containing 'all the filth and radiance of my soul together'.[28] The play opens with the Amazons and the Greeks 'locked in battle like two raging wolves'. The 'rage-intoxicated' Amazons, a state of one-breasted women, in 'frantic inundation of headlong flight' and 'burning with lust for war', are disrupting the Greeks' conquest of Troy. In order to resume their mission, Odysseus and Achilles decide to confront Penthesilea, the Queen of the Amazons. But on seeing Achilles for the first time, Penthesilea is smitten, 'drunk with admiration'.[29] Counter to the urgent needs of the warring armies a mutual chase begins, a 'senseless flight', 'a battle of contesting speeds', a pursuit 'bereft of judgment'[30]. Eventually Achilles, falsely believing that Penthesilea will only be free to love and wed him after she has defeated him on the battlefield, calls her to fight. She, thinking he has betrayed her, captures him and tears him 'from limb to limb' with her pack of dogs. Kleist offers no interpretations of this 'mad desire' for Achilles. Her flight is an action which by the recognisable standards of her tribe is incomprehensible, and which remains so for the reader.

Deleuze and Guattari offer an intriguing reading of Penthesilea's delirium and her 'becoming-woman' through 'senseless' flight. Her actions clarify the sense of a 'line of flight' as something other than a fleeing from life, or a flight into the imaginary or into art: that is, the creation of a life, and the putting to work of a war machine (D 49). *Penthesilea* presents us with two war machines – that of the Amazons, 'a Stateless woman-people whose justice, religion, and loves are organized uniquely in a war mode', and that of Penthesilea herself. Achilles is, from the play's commencement, 'already separated from his power', for the war machine already belongs to the Amazons, who 'spring forth like lightning, "between" the two States', and 'sweep away everything in their path'. In his 'ambiguous struggle' Achilles is 'unable to prevent himself from marrying the war machine, and thus betraying Agamemnon and Ulysses [both men of the State].' Nevertheless, he already belongs sufficiently to the Greek state that Penthesilea cannot enter a 'passional relation of war with him' without 'betraying the collective law of her people . . . that prohibits choosing the enemy and entering into one-to-one relationships or binary distinctions' (TP 355). This betrayal – which she of course enacts – constitutes her own nomadic flight from a tribe that was itself already nomadic. As such, her flight is not undertaken in the name of a people, even a nomadic people – it represents nothing and is impersonal. So while Penthesilea cries, 'Am I so selfish, is it my desires alone that call me back into the field, and not my people?', Kleist indicates that it is not a personal motive that drives her, that her 'eye burns with an *alien* light' and she is compelled by an '*enigmatic* force'.[31] In Deleuze and Guattari's terms, her affects have become 'uprooted from the interiority of a "subject" to be projected violently outward into a milieu of pure exteriority that lends them an incredible velocity, a catapulting force'. Her love and hate are no longer feelings but violent and confused affects: 'I love you, oh so much that if I could, I'd eat you up right here,' she cries to Achilles. Her sister Prothoe tells Penthesilea that 'both joy and grief' are ruining her, and she herself declares how easy it is to mistake a kiss and a bite in the intensity of passion.[32] Swinging between these affective poles, she is declared by her fellow women as incomprehensible, defiled by them for her 'disregard for custom', and labelled 'unnameable'.[33] Her flight belongs to no established order by which it can be recognised.

For Deleuze and Guattari, Penthesilea's confused affects are her weapons of war, and function through a 'velocity of deterritorialisation' (TP 356). She is almost always moving at high velocity: she darts forth 'like lightening' and shoots past 'thrown by her own momentum'.[34] But for Deleuze and Guattari her speed is not simply a question of being fast. Rather to have speed 'is to be caught in a becoming, which is not a development or an evolution, but to be an abstract and broken line, that glides between'. Becoming is to be forever in the middle, rather than starting and finishing – where the middle is not 'a form of moderation' but 'a matter of absolute speed' (D30, 32). Speed is crucial to Penthesilea's becoming-woman, her passage into a becoming that glides between two states, and deterritorialises the state of woman while making woman a 'man of war'. We see here how Deleuze and Guattari's concept of becoming-woman has nothing to do with becoming a 'woman' – for Penthesilea accelerates towards a becoming-dog, a 'becoming-animal of the warrior' (TRM 77).[35] This at once encapsulates the condition of the writer: 'writing to produce speed' 'doesn't mean writing rapidly' but rather 'to be a foreigner in one's own language', to produce a stammering of language within language that makes language burst out from the codes by which it customarily is made to signify (D 32–3). Kleist makes Penthesilea stammer through the frequent interruptions of the prose, sudden accelerations and hiatuses, the abrupt shifts between scenes, the lack of exegesis of crucial moments (such as Penthesilea's first sight of Achilles) and, conversely, the prolonged exegesis of moments without direction (such as the love scene between Penthesilea and Achilles which is sharply terminated). In fact, the entire play is presented as a passage without development, as only the 'comings and goings' of Achilles and Penthesilea as they engage in their mutual chase, characters like the stones in the game of Go – defined relationally, and not by essential character traits.

Kleist, the War Machine versus Goethe, Man of State

For Deleuze and Guattari, the dynamics of a story such as *Penthesilea*, where a line of flight lets loose a war machine against the State, as a barbaric and indecorous unleashing of affects, is replayed in Kleist's own war machine against State thinkers including Goethe (who did not conceal his disdain for Kleist) and Hegel. These men, to many guardians of a high-minded, ideal and noble classicism, 'see Kleist as a monster' (TP 356). They 'hated' his new kind of writing. For them,

> the plan(e) must indissolubly be a harmonious development of Form and a regulated formation of the Subject, personage, or character (the sentimental education, the interior and substantial solidity of the character, the harmony or analogy of the forms and continuity of development, the cult of the State, etc.). Their conception of the plane is completely opposed to that of Kleist . . . Goethe gets to the crux of the matter when he reproaches Kleist for simultaneously setting up a 'pure stationary process' that is like the fixed plane, introducing voids and jumps that prevent any development of a central character, and mobilizing a violence of affects that causes an extreme confusion of feelings. (TP 268–9)

Thomas Mann notes Kleist's 'ambivalent attitude to Goethe, forever oscillating between humility and hatred, admiration and fierce jealousy', his eye fixed on the crown of this Olympian.[36] In 1808 Kleist had sent Goethe a copy of the first edition of his journal *Phöbus*, containing a fragment of *Penthesilea*, offering it 'on the knees of my heart'.[37] The fifty-eight-year-old Goethe was then a living institution, an authority on all matters of art, taste and culture, and founder and director of the Weimar theatre where Kleist wanted his *Penthesilea* to be staged. Goethe's acceptance of Kleist would have secured the latter a place within the cultural and literary institution and instant fame. But Goethe replies to Kleist that he 'has been unable to warm' to the title character, that 'she is of so singular a race, and inhabits so alien a region, that I shall need time to find my way to both', and that he is 'always saddened and troubled when I see a young man of talent and spirit awaiting some theatre yet to come'.[38] A month later Goethe did in fact accept Kleist's *The Broken Jug* for the Weimar stage, but he produced it in a conventional three-act form, to allow the audience an intervals for refreshments. An incensed Kleist had to be restrained from challenging Goethe to a duel. Soon after, Goethe denounced Kleist's drama *Katie of Heilbronn* as 'a bewildering mixture of brilliance and foolishness' and the embodiment of 'accursed perversity'. He admitted that he found *Kohlhaas* 'prettily told' but that he could not comprehend how such a 'singular' case could be presented as having universal value. After Kleist's death, he would pronounce that he 'was always filled with horror and disgust by this writer, as though by a body well intended by nature, but in the grip of an incurable disease'.[39]

In retaliation against this damning reception, Kleist published some of his own scathing articles, referring to Goethe as 'the Weimar reworker of the works of others' who, finding the howling of Penthesilea's pack of dogs too grating, decides to set it to sentimental music.[40] Kleist was incensed at Goethe's sanitisation of violent affects into more classically acceptable feeling. In further retaliation, Kleist penned 'A More Recent and Happier Werther' a satire of Goethe's famous morality tale. In Goethe's *The Sorrows of Young Werther* (1774), we are presented with the 'interiorised' development of Werther's character and his 'sentimental education' to final realisation and honourable death. This was a tale that quickly became part of the national consciousness, acquiring an officially State-sanctioned visibility of which there could be no higher affirmation than Napoleon's resounding praise. But in Kleist's version the attempted suicide of the unnamed 'Werther' character renegades, such that what would 'seem at an end' is 'strangely enough only the beginning'. The husband dies instead, allowing 'Werther' to marry his beloved and live happily ever after. Thus, the striving for the virtues of duty and honour in the original novel backfires, opening a surprising line of flight that takes the tale in an unexpected direction. There is no character development, only the account of a shock that alters circumstances, confuses affects and produces a new reality. In this reworking of a classic of early German Romanticism, Kleist signals a new sensibility, an untimely modernity extracted from the Romantic strata.

The 'Kant Crisis': Onset of Writing as War Machine

The disjunction to which Deleuze and Guattari call attention between Kleist the war machine and the State figure of Goethe acquires further sense in light of Kleist's 'Kant Crisis'. Given their implicitly post-Kantian reading of Kleist, it is perhaps strange that Deleuze and Guattari do not mention this pivotal event of Kleist's encounter with the work of the philosopher who arguably inaugurates the State form of thought as an enterprise of representation (TP 367).

Kleist's writing begins with his shock on reading Kant. Kleist's first life-plan to acquire knowledge and dedicate himself to self-education in the extolling of established Enlightenment virtues of learning, moral perfection and a 'golden dependence on the dictates of Reason' is radically destabilised by his encounter with Kant, which produces a 'deeply shattering effect' that 'wounds his most sacred inner being'.[41] He describes it to Wilhelmine as follows:

> If everyone saw the world through green glasses, they would be forced to judge that everything they saw was green, and could never be sure whether their eyes saw things as they really are, or did not add something of their own to what they saw. And so it is with our intellect. We can never be certain that what we call Truth is really Truth, or whether it does not merely appear so with us. If the latter, then the Truth that we acquire here is not Truth after our death, and it is all a vain striving for a possession that may never follow us into the grave.[42]

Recounting the Kantian distinction between noumena and phenomena, Kleist concludes that all we have access to are subjective manifestations of Truth and the contingency of individual existences, which we have no way of checking against the 'original'. The impact of this realisation for Kleist was clear – 'my one, my highest goal has sunk from sight and I have no other'; 'The very pillar totters that I have clung to in this whirling tide of life . . . my love for the pursuit of knowledge.' Voyaging is the immediate response to this experience. Spurning books and study, and overcome by nausea, Kleist flees 'in inner unrest'. Realising that 'movement on a journey would seem more bearable than this boarding in one place',[43] he begins a journey necessitated by a 'violent pull of circumstances' 'remarkable in the extreme'.[44]

Reaction to Kant, flight and the commencement of writing, as a response to what Kleist called the 'passionately intense drive to do something and yet with no goal', are thus inextricably bound up with one another. Writing becomes the arena for an immanent critique of Kantian philosophy: the impossibility of harmoniously reconciling dualisms (including the dualism of reason and sensibility), the impossibility of doing one's duty (critique of the moral imperative), the critique of institutions (particularly the State), the critique of ideas previously held to be universal and unchanging (justice, faith, fidelity), and the critique of reason and knowledge as values.[45] In place of the ground hitherto provided by reason, writing operates as a production of thought that contrasts with what Deleuze and Guattari call the 'State image of thought'.

The notion of a 'State image of thought' is outlined at the end of Deleuze and Guattari's chapter on Nomadology: 'Ever since philosophy assigned itself the role of ground', namely the ground provided by pure reason, thought has been in conformity with the State, which defines itself as the 'reasonable organization of a community'. Only thought, in the name of reason and common sense (that is, the unity of all the faculties provided by the *Cogito*), is capable of inventing the notion of a universal State. This State philosophy was heralded by the Kantian critique. Kant inaugurates the universality of reason as the ground of common consensus and law and therefore the ground of the functioning of the State. In this modern, rational State, everything revolves around a legislator and a subject who are united in a relation of obedience grounded on pure reason and the presumption of a unifying common sense (DR xvi).

Deleuze and Guattari call for thought to shake off this model of the State and to make itself a war machine: 'Thought should be thrown like a stone by a war machine' (D 31). Such a warlike thought 'would come from a violence suffered by thought'. It 'would not operate in a concordance of the faculties, but, on the contrary, would take each faculty to the limit of its discordance with the others'. It would be open to encounters and would 'always be defined as a function of an Outside'. It 'would not have to struggle against error', and it 'would be defined in the movement of learning' rather than the exercise of knowledge (D 24). This argument replays the critique of Kant that runs through Deleuze's early reclamation of critique from its transcendental frame, and his recasting of it as an immanent project of transcendental empiricism able to account for the genesis of values initiated by the force of extraordinary events in the sensible.

Kleist's writing is born of such a violence. Everything in his work testifies to a jettisoning of the Kantian image of thought and the inauguration of thought as war machine. Concordance and harmony are replaced by discordance and irresolution; familiar scenarios replaced by strange encounters; reason and sensibility estranged. In *Michael Kohlhaas*, for instance, reason and the moral law are exposed as no longer universalising principles that unite men, but unattainable goals and principles of disjunction by which the goodwill of the thinker who seeks the truth, and the good nature of thought which possesses the true by right – an image of thought which Kleist explicitly relates to the State – are destroyed (D 23). Accompanying the critique of the manifestations of the State within the individual stories themselves (the military, the family, the clergy, religion), one finds an ongoing critique of the universality of principles that Kleist felt Kant's work signalled alongside an embrace of 'inverted values' such as error. For instance, the error of the Prince of Homburg, deemed 'stupid' and 'mad' by his military compatriots, emerges as a superior value that brings military victory and a new education to all.[46] Finally, Kleist also presents us with a new idea of a processual learning against the notion of *a priori* knowledge.

With respect to the latter, Deleuze and Guattari turn to Kleist's 'On the Gradual Formulation of Thoughts Whilst Speaking' (1805), which they describe as one of 'two pathetic texts' (the other being Artaud's letters to Jacques Rivière), in the sense that in them 'thought is truly a pathos (an antilogos and an antimythos)' (TP 377–8). Here Kleist advocates the process of speaking as a means of thinking, in place of speaking of matters already understood. He explains how speaking in a confused way to his sister, who does not know the subjects he speaks about, yields thoughts and, 'like a great general', he becomes 'suddenly a degree more capable of my objective'.[47] Thus, he says, 'the lines of thought and expression move abreast', sourced from 'a certain agitation of the mind'.[48]

For Deleuze and Guattari, this short text shows how

> Kleist denounces the central interiority of the concept as a means of control – the control of speech, of language, but also of affects, circumstances and even chance. He distinguishes this from thought as a proceeding and a process, a bizarre anti-Platonic dialogue, an antidialogue between brother and sister where one speaks before knowing while the other relays before having understood: this, Kleist says, is the thought of the *Gemut*, which proceeds like a general in a war machine should, or like a body charged with electricity, with pure intensity. 'I mix inarticulate sounds, lengthen transitional terms, as well as using appositions when they are unnecessary.' . . . The necessity of not having control over language, of being a foreigner in one's own tongue, in order to draw speech to oneself and 'bring something incomprehensible into the world.' Such is the form of exteriority, the relation between brother and sister, the becoming-woman of the thinker, the becoming-thought of the woman: the Gemüt that refuses to be controlled, that forms a war machine. (TP 378)

In the warlike passage of thought between himself and his sister, thought is shown as an interstitial activity forced by an encounter with the outside – just as the affects Kohlhaas unleashes, forced by an unexpected event, do not belong to him, but diffuse through the entire country. But what does Kohlhaas's war machine produce? For Deleuze and Guattari, it 'can no longer be anything more than banditry' – a somewhat peculiar remark given the redemption at the end of Kleist's story (Kohlhaas's arch-enemy is imprisoned, prompting Kohlhaas to declare that he has at last found justice). There is a tension between Deleuze and Guattari's implicit claim in the question 'Is it the destiny of the war machine, when the State triumphs to be caught in this alternative: either to be nothing more than the disciplined, military organ of the State apparatus, or to turn against itself, to become a double suicide machine for a solitary man and a solitary woman' (TP 356) (here referring to Kleist's suicide, with the remark that the struggle of the war machine 'is lost from the start' [TP 355]), and their clam that Kleist gives us a new image of thought, one that survives its historical time.

Conclusion

Kleist's role in Deleuze and Guattari's philosophy concerns the project and task of writing – as a breakthrough of the apparatus of interpretation, signification, communication and representation, and as an act of thinking. This role can be contextualised within and compared to Deleuze and Guattari's analyses of other writers – Kafka and his little machines, Artaud and his thought without image, Büchner and Lenz and their beginning in the middle of things, Melville's voyages and stammerings. As such, the themes that mark Deleuze and Guattari's analyses of Kleist – exteriority and impersonality, line of flight, the affect, becoming, delirium, the stammering of language and its opening to the outside – can be found in their analysis of these, and other, writers. But what singles Kleist out, what is more explicit in his work than any of these other writers, is his preoccupation with the notion of war.

War is the ongoing leitmotif both of Kleist's life and his writing – in its style, its plots and its characters. As an institution aligned with the State, and expressed through the military, war is something to be critiqued. But as a tendency that is governed by affects rather than reason, war is something Kleist seems to commend, or at least be compelled by as an idea. Many of his most notable characters– Homburg, Penthesilea, Kohlhaas – are warlike in this affective way. In so far as this outlook is consistent with his own experience – his unhappy youthful experience of the military as an institution, and the subsequent warlike project of his writing – the details of Kleist's life and work are inextricability interwoven. As such, this chapter has paid equal attention to both. And given the affective character of war in Kleist's works, I have attempted to recreate for the reader the extraordinarily affective atmosphere of Kleist's work, the experience of which is key to any comprehension of the concepts that Deleuze and Guattari extract from and develop through it. Indeed, any discussion of literature in Deleuze and Guattari's philosophical lineage would need to acknowledge their own claim about literature as a thought through affects.

Given his preoccupation with and subtle qualification of war, it is no wonder that Kleist's work is invested by Deleuze and Guattari as a basis for their development of the concept of the 'war machine', the revolutionary force that attacks the State apparatus and produces new creative possibilities. Referring to several of Kleist's fictional and non-fiction works, they attribute this war machine to Kleist's style (its speeds and slowness, contrasts and extremes), Kleist's characters (the militant heroes of his stories and plays, impelled to extreme action by the force of their circumstances), Kleist's plots ('broken chain of affects', often involving battles and wars) and Kleist's life – his complex, constantly aborted and remade life-plans.

With respect to Kleist's life, Deleuze and Guattari focus on two key events, both instances of his collision with the 'State image of thought': Kleist's reading of Kant's philosophy (which precipitates his mistrust of reason, knowledge and the universality of values, alongside his commencement of writing) and his encounter with Goethe (which seemed to act as an, albeit unhappy, confirmation of his status outside the institution). Discord and extremity, the exposure of pure forces as intense experiences unliveable under normal circumstances, the mobilisation of ideas and principles through the fecund impact of affects: through these, Kleist's writing functions as an immanent critique of Kant's philosophy and shows how literature can supply the material for transcendental empiricism. One message here seems to be that writing separated from life becomes banal style – indeed, Deleuze and Guattari are critical of the way Kleist's texts 'have ended up becoming monuments, inspiring a model to be copied – a model far more insidious than the others – for the artificial stammerings and innumerable tracings that claim to be their equal' (TP 378).

The return of Kleistian traits in the works in Woolf, Lawrence, Melville, Kafka, Büchner and Artaud is quite different, and when Deleuze and Guattari write that 'many things in modern art come from Kleist' (TP 356), they refer to a return outside the rational progression of art historical styles. This modernism is distinguished both from the Romanticism (and its 'meta aesthetics of matter and Idea') and the Classicism (and its aesthetics of form) of Kleist's own historical time. For Deleuze, the 'postromantic turning point' is situated at the point when the form–matter relation is replaced by forces and intensities, and Kleist heralds this in his use of writing to capture forces at the liminal edge of the liveable, and unthinkable in themselves (TP 342–3). Overturning abstractions and eternal values, Kleist gives us an aberrant world of forces and singularities, a material of writing charged with the intensity of passage and flight. Deleuze and Guattari's Kleist is an untimely figure of nineteenth-century German literary thought, the warring harbinger of literature's post-Kantian potentials, writing for a time, a literature, and perhaps even – as Goethe laconically remarked, unaware of its full implications – a theatre to come.

Notes

1. Brent Adkins notes that Deleuze first publicly discussed Kleist at a conference in Milan in May 1974, in his chapter 'What is a Literature of War? Kleist, Kant and Nomadology', in Craig Lundy (ed.), *On the Edges of Thought: Deleuze and Post-Kantian Philosophy* (Edinburgh: Edinburgh University Press, 2015), p. 105.
2. In *Kafka*, Deleuze and Guattari are referring to Kleist's influence on Kafka. 'The only one [that Kleist] will take as his master is Kleist, and Kleist also detested masters; but Kleist is a different matter even in the deep influence that he had on Kafka. We have to speak differently about this influence. Kleist's question isn't, "What is a minor literature and further, a political and collective literature?", but rather, "What is a literature of war?". This is not completely alien to Kafka, but it is not exactly his question' (K 55).
3. Cf. Ronald Bogue's analysis in *Deleuze on Literature* (London: Routledge, 2003), pp. 116–26; Adkins, 'What is a Literature of War?', and Anthony Uhlmann, 'Expression and Affect in Kleist, Beckett and Deleuze', in Laura Cull (ed.), *Deleuze and Performance* (Edinburgh: Edinburgh University Press, 2009), pp. 54–70.
4. On the 21 November 1811, Kleist set out for the shores of the Wannsee together with Henriette Vogel, a married woman he had known for some time who was suffering from terminal cancer of the uterus. At her request, he shot her, and then shot himself. Kleist and Vogel left a joint letter addressed to mutual friends: 'Remember us in joy and sadness: two strange mortals about to embark on their great voyage of discovery.'
5. In one of his earliest letters to his aunt, for instance, detailing a journey to Frankfurt with his fellow soldiers, Kleist describes at length a violent encounter with a robber. He does not describe the effect of this encounter on him, nor his feelings about the event – he only describes it in all its shocking and strange force and impact for the group. It is interesting that Kleist switches into the plural voice for this passage and switches back into first person straight after its narration. Letter to Helene von Massow, Mar. 1793, in *An Abyss Deep Enough. Letters of Heinrich von Kleist*, ed. and trans. Philip B. Miller (New York: E. P. Dutton, 1982), pp. 15–16.
6. Kleist, 'On the Gradual Formulation of Thoughts Whilst Speaking', in *Selected Prose of Heinrich von Kleist*, ed. and trans. Peter Wortsman (New York: Archipelago Books, 2010), p. 262.
7. *Heinrich von Kleist. Five Plays*, ed. and trans. Martin Greenberg (New Haven and London: Yale University Press, 1988), p. xv.
8. Kleist, Letter of 18 Mar. 1799, in *An Abyss Deep Enough*, p. 22.
9. Kleist first mentions these plans in a letter to Christian Ernst Martini,

his childhood tutor. 18 Mar. 1799, in *An Abyss Deep Enough*, pp. 19–25.

10. 'I do not wish to accept an official position. I am expected to do what the State asks of me, and yet may not inquire whether what it asks is good. I am to be a mere tool for unknown ends – I cannot be.' *An Abyss Deep Enough*, p. 73.
11. Greenberg, *Five Plays*, p. xvii.
12. Letter to Marie von Kleist, 19 Nov. 1811, in *An Abyss Deep Enough*, pp. 202–3.
13. Letter to Wilhelmine, 5 Sept. 1800, in *An Abyss Deep Enough*, p. 52.
14. Kleist, *Michael Kohlhaas (From an Old Chronicle)*, in *Selected Prose*, p. 143 (my italics).
15. Thomas Mann, 'Kleist and His Stories', Preface to *The Marquise of O- & Other Stories*, ed. Martin Greenberg (London: Faber & Faber, 1960), p. 14.
16. Bogue comments that Deleuze and Guattari make use of this unpublished text 'in virtually all of their comments on Kleist'. *Deleuze and Literature*, p. 119.
17. See also Deleuze in *Negotiations*: 'Kleist and Kafka [write] in affects' (N 137).
18. Kleist, 'Earthquake in Chile', in *Selected Prose*, pp. 16, 26, 31.
19. Kleist, *Prince Friedrich von Homberg*, in *Three Plays. Prince Friedrich von Homberg, The Broken Pitcher, Ordeal by Fire*, trans. Noel Clark (London: Oberon Books), p. 40.
20. 'On the Theatre of Marionettes', in *Selected Prose*, p. 265.
21. Ibid., p. 266.
22. Ibid., p. 268.
23. Ibid., p. 273.
24. Letter to Christian Ernst Martini, 18 Mar. 1799, in *An Abyss Deep Enough*, p. 24.
25. Cf. Letters to Wilhelmine von Zenge, Berlin, 14 Apr. 1801 (p. 99); Adolfine von Werdeck, 29 July 29 (p. 121), and to Henriette von Schilieben, 29 July 1804 (p. 157).
26. Quoted in Bogue, *Deleuze and Literature*, p. 119.
27. Kleist, *The Marquise of O-*, trans. Richard Stokes (London: Hesperus, 2003), p. 44.
28. Letter to Marie von Kleist, 1807, in *An Abyss Deep Enough*, p. 175.
29. Kleist, Heinrich von, *Penthesilea*, trans. J. Agee (New York: HarperCollins, 1998), pp. 5, 7.
30. Ibid., pp. 11, 15, 25.
31. Ibid., pp. 33, 59, 92. My italics.
32. Ibid., pp. 146, 81, 145.
33. Ibid., pp. 104, 124.
34. Ibid., pp. 19, 21.

35. Deleuze refers to Ulrike von Kleist, the writer's androgynous and asexual sister, as a 'woman-machine'.
36. Mann, Preface, p. 11.
37. Kleist, Letter to Goethe, Dresden, 24 Jan. 1808, in *An Abyss Deep Enough*, p. 179.
38. Letter from Goethe to Kleist, 1 Feb. 1808, in *An Abyss Deep Enough*, p. 179.
39. Ibid., p. 177.
40. Ibid., p. 178.
41. Letter to Christian Ernst Martini, Potsdam, 18 Mar. 1799, in *An Abyss Deep Enough*, p. 24. This initial outlook was shaped, at least in part, by his reading of Christoph Martin Wieland (1733–1813), an influential poet of the German Enlightenment, p. 94.
42. Letter to Wilhemine von Zenge, Berlin, 22 Mar. 1801, *An Abyss Deep Enough*, p. 95
43. Ibid., p. 97.
44. See the letters written to Ulrike von Kleist and Wilhemine von Zenge, between February and April 1801, in *An Abyss Deep Enough*, pp. 89–100.
45. 'human knowledge makes us neither better nor happier', Letter to Wilhelmine von Zenge, 15 Aug. 1801, in *An Abyss Deep Enough*, p. 123. There is much scholarship on the impact of the 'Kant crisis' on Kleist. Cf. Tim Mehigan, 'Kleist, Hume, Kant and the "Thing in Itself"', in Bernd Fischer (ed.), *A Companion to the Works of Heinrich von Kleist* (Rochester, NY: Camden House, 2003), p. 166.
46. 'There are certain errors that demand a greater outlay of intellect than the truth itself.' Fragment 1, in *An Abyss Deep Enough*, p. 253.
47. In *Selected Prose*, p. 219.
48. *An Abyss Deep Enough*, pp. 221–2. See also 'On Thinking Things Over: A Paradox', in ibid., p. 217.

Jakob von Uexküll

Carlo Brentari

The aim of this chapter is to provide a critical assessment of the way in which the thought of Jakob von Uexküll (1864–1944) is used by Deleuze (and, in *A Thousand Plateaus*, by Deleuze in collaboration with Guattari) in defining his ontology of becoming. The most pertinent text will therefore be *A Thousand Plateaus* (1980),[1] but in the concluding remarks we will also make a significant reference to Deleuze's book *Spinoza: Practical Philosophy* (1970).[2] In *A Thousand Plateaus* the name of Uexküll recurs three times, and all references (and this is also valid for Deleuze's other books) are to a single book of Uexküll's, *Mondes animaux et monde humain*,[3] which includes the French translation both of *Streifzüge durch die Umwelten von Tieren und Menschen* and of *Bedeutungslehre*[4] (both works are also published together in the cited English edition *A Foray into the Worlds of Animals and Humans*[5]). At one level, it would be superfluous to discuss how a wider knowledge of the author might have led Deleuze to a different view of his theoretical biology, especially regarding the role of the subject in the constitution of the environment. But, as we will see in the final section, this is not quite the case. In order to assess the contribution of Uexküll, it is instead appropriate to begin with a brief exposition of the ontology of becoming developed by Deleuze and Guattari – with the caveat that, in respect to this ontology, I will give privilege to the traits which are best suited for the comparison with Uexküll himself.

Deleuze and Guattari's *A Thousand Plateaus* is a work that admits multiple interpretations: aesthetic, political and literary-critical, among others. Our interpretative strategy will be to read it as an attempt to develop a processual and pluralistic ontology; in particular, the authors' proposal aims at overcoming the traditional view of reality, a view pivoting on substances, subjects and other stable centres of experience, and is deeply bound to the presence of vertical, hierarchical relations of determination between such centres and a multiplicity of qualities, properties and states of things – a verticality that often, but not necessarily, results in metaphysics. In short, *A Thousand Plateaus* can (also) be read as an ontological laboratory in which the authors try to substitute subjects and substances with processes and processual phases (that is, various forms of *becoming*: the folding of strata, the intensification of forces and so on) and hierarchical relationships in mutual *horizontal forms of determination* among beings. In this respect, the text can be associated (among a few others) with Alfred N. Whitehead's *Process and Reality* (1929)[6] and Nicolai Hartmann's *Philosophie der Natur. Abriss der speziellen Kategorienlehre* (1943)[7] as a positive contribution to the renewal of contemporary ontology.

In the introduction to *A Thousand Plateaus*, the system of oppositions on which the work is based is shown through the botanical figure of the rhizome. In botany, a rhizome is a horizontal underground plant stem of a greater diameter than the actual stem, which can produce the shoot and root systems of a new plant; this capacity allows the plant to colonise the surrounding soil, but also to return to germinate after winter. In *A Thousand Plateaus*, the rhizome becomes the model of a horizontal germinal capacity and, as such, is placed in opposition to every vertical model of production and interpretation of reality. In its first appearance, the rhizome model concerns the book itself; *A Thousand Plateaus* is presented as being a work that escapes all traditional – that is, vertical and dichotomous – forms of determination (author and text, subject and object, art and Nature) and exposes instead '[the] working of matters, and the exteriority of their relations' (TP 4). On the same page, however, there is a specification that allows us to affirm the ontological scope of the rhizome model: 'In a book, *as in all things*, there are lines of articulation or segmentarity, strata and territories; but also lines of flight, movements of deterritorialization and destratification' (TP 4, italics added). To be precise, Deleuze and Guattari propose botanical models even for the traditional, vertical structures of order: the figure of the tree and the (specular) system of the roots.

Tree and roots have two features in common – verticality and dichotomy:

> A first type of book is the root-book. The tree is already the image of the world, or the root the image of the world-tree. . . . The book imitates the world, as art imitates nature. . . . The law of the book is the law of reflection, the One that becomes two. . . . One becomes two: whenever we encounter this formula . . . what we have before

> us is the most classical and well reflected, oldest, and weariest kind of thought. (TP 5)

Verticality and dichotomy are explicitly refused in the name of a horizontal circularity: 'Nature doesn't work that way: in nature, roots are taproots with a more multiple, lateral, and circular system of ramification, rather than a dichotomous one' (TP 5). Through the opposition to the tree/root model, the ontological traits of the rhizomatic ontology emerge as follows: reality is multiple, not dichotomous, and in a continuous, diffuse and germinal movement. Rather, it follows a web-model: 'any point of a rhizome can be connected to anything other, and must be' (TP 7).

Although for our purposes the most important parts of *A Thousand Plateaus* are those where Uexküll is explicitly mentioned – '3. 10,000 B.C.: The Geology of Morals (Who Docs the Earth Think It Is?)' and '11: 1837: Of the Refrain' – three of the 'approximate characteristics' (TP 7) of the rhizome that Deleuze and Guattari sketch in the introductory part of the book will be very useful for our comparison with Uexküll. The first of these is the interconnection of semiotics and ontology; moving from a critique of the idea of universal linguistics (Chomsky), Deleuze and Guattari suggest a reality whose heterogeneity is made even greater by the intertwining of *being* and *meaning*: in a rhizome, 'semiotic chains of every nature are connected to very diverse modes of coding (biological, political, economic, and so on) that bring into play not only different regimes of signs but also states of things of differing status' (TP 7). If multiple authors (including those cited above), have already recognised the fluidity and mutual transposability of the regimes of signs, their rhizomatic – that is, germinal – link with the states of things (and vice-versa) is a new and original element of *A Thousand Plateaus*. This is even more true when we consider that in a processual ontology there is no clear distinction between 'things' and 'states of things': every 'thing' is ultimately a processual phase isolated from the whole of becoming – and this prepares and makes possible its transposition in a system of signs, so that 'it is not possible to make a radical break between regimes of signs and their objects' (TP 8, translation modified).[8]

The second relevant trait of the rhizome is the kind of multiplicity it admits. If we look back at the last mentioned quote, we see that the refusal of the hierarchical structure object/sign (although the same refusal concerns many other structures: subject/object, world/book, centre/periphery and so on) is accompanied by the idea of a recursive multiplication of the element of the rhizome, whereby recursivity means that a rhizomatic element is taken up in a new dimension. This can occur an indefinite number of times: the rhizome 'constitutes linear multiplicities with n dimensions having neither subject nor object . . . and from which the One is always subtracted (n – 1). When a multiplicity of this kind changes dimension, it necessarily changes in nature as well, undergoes a metamorphosis' (TP 23). The subtraction of the One from the dimension it seemingly belongs to and its insertion in a different dimension allows for retracing what the authors call an assemblage: 'An assemblage is precisely this increase in the dimensions of a multiplicity that necessarily changes in nature as it expands its connections' (TP 9), and 'wherein the laws of combination therefore increase in number as the multiplicity grows' (TP 9). As we will see, both the Uexküllian Umwelt and the overall complex of the different Umwelten present the same kind of recursive and dimensional multiplicity that Deleuze and Guattari sketch in their rhizomatic ontology. The process of territorialisation, to mention one of the most relevant cases, is a sort of further elaboration of the perceptive and operative Umwelt of a species.

The third trait of the rhizome model that can be useful in our comparison with Uexküll is the recurrent idea that the internal links inside the rhizome bear a machinic character; for instance, a language is made by '*collective assemblages of enunciations* [that] function directly within *machinic assemblages*' (TP 7–8). The aim of this characterisation emerges from the criticism that the authors direct towards contemporary linguistics:

> Our criticism of these linguistic models is not that they are too abstract but, on the contrary, that they are not abstract enough, that they do not reach the *abstract machine* that connects a language to the semantic and pragmatic contents of statements, to collective assemblages of enunciation, to a whole micropolitics of the social field. A rhizome ceaselessly establishes connections between semiotic chains, organizations of power, and circumstances relative to the arts, sciences, and social struggles. (TP 8)

The machinic articulation of the rhizome requires, as its condition, the absence of a subject, because subjects, and even abstract grammatical subjects, spontaneously institute dichotomies: 'you will construct grammatically correct sentences, you will divide each statement into a noun phrase and a verb phrase (first dichotomy . . .)' (TP 8). Deleuze and Guattari's analysis of natural languages suggests that the machinic character of the internal tissues of the rhizome are fully consistent with the aim of a complete negation of the centrality of the subject, which involves even the negation of the concept of organism: 'The enemy is the organism' (TP 175), write Deleuze and Guattari, and as commentator Brett Buchanan rightly observes: 'the organism is considered the enemy precisely because it is traditionally taken for a static (vs. genetic) and organized (vs. rhizomatic) "judgment of God"'.[9]

There is, in the idea of the machinic assemblage that emerges from *A Thousand Plateaus*, a great difference from seventeenth-century 'mechanism', wherein the idea of the mechanical connection among different organs in a body, or among different entities in the world, was constantly accompanied by the assumption of the regulative action of some Great Machinist. 'Puppet strings, as a rhizome or multiplicity' – write Deleuze and Guattari – 'are tied not to the supposed will of an artist or puppeteer but to a multiplicity of nerve fibers, which form another puppet in other dimensions connected to the first' (TP 9). As we will see, this peculiar use of machinic connections marks a first point of detachment not only from the classical philosophical mechanism, but also from Uexküll's philosophy of organism – where, at least for lower animals, a mechanistic approach to physiology and behaviour is seen as positive if accompanied by the knowledge that there is no machine without a machinist (the animal subject) that leads it: 'The biologist' – writes Uexküll – 'takes into account that each and every living thing is a subject that lives in its own world, of which it is the center. It cannot, therefore, be compared to a machine, only to the machine operator who guides the machine.'[10]

Codes and Associated Milieus

After having briefly outlined some features of Deleuze and Guattari's rhizomatic ontology that will help us in our further analysis, let us now consider the passages of *A Thousand Plateaus* where Uexküll appears explicitly. The first occurrence is in one of the most decidedly ontological parts of the Deleuze and Guattari's text, namely the description of how reality can be stratified without being hierarchical. 'Strata' and 'layers' are, in the terminology developed in *A Thousand Plateaus*, 'planes of consistency' that thicken the original flow of becoming – 'the unformed, unorganized, nonstratified, or destratified body and all its flows: subatomic and submolecular particles, pure intensities, prevital and prephysical free singularities' (TP 49) – differentiate it internally, and lead to the formation of (always relative) centres of stability. These centres can be called forms, codes and even substances, though maintaining the knowledge that their identity is fluid and open. This process is 'the "folding" that sets up a stable functional structure', with the awareness, again, that 'the word "structure" may be used to designate the sum of these relations and relationships, but it is an illusion to believe that structure is the earth's last word' (TP 46).

Inside this process, Deleuze and Guattari focus on the formation of the organic stratum, which depends on the multiple organisation in exterior, interior and associated milieus. The external milieu is given by the substratum that furnishes the matter (or better, that acts as matter for a given stratum); once absorbed in the stratum, the matter changes its organisation and becomes an internal milieu. The process is described as follows:

> The materials furnished by the substratum constitute an exterior milieu for the elements and compounds of the stratum under consideration, but they are not exterior *to* the stratum. The elements and compounds constitute an interior of the stratum, just as the materials constitute an exterior *of* the stratum . . . Once again, this exterior and interior are relative; they exist only through their exchanges. (TP 55)

Outlined here is an attempt to describe the origin of life without starting from the formation of vital centres; the authors are not talking of the origin of the organisms but, rather, of the origins of the organic stratum ('the materials furnished by the substrata are an exterior medium constituting the famous prebiotic soup, and catalysts play the role of seed in the formation of interior substantial elements or even compounds' (TP 55–6)). What is particularly striking in the ontology of the organic stratum is the formation of a complex transitional zone between interior and exterior: 'the limit or membrane conveying the formal relations' (TP 56), 'the membrane that regulates the exchanges and transformation in organization (in other words, the distributions interior to the stratum) and that defines all of the stratum's formal relations or traits' (TP 56). The unity of the three substrata is described in terms of a single '*abstract machine*' (TP 56) that organises the interchanges between interior and exterior. It is actually difficult to overestimate the importance in biology of the formation of membranes and transitional tissues and of their metabolic function. Deleuze and Guattari assume that 'there is a whole history on the level of the membrane or limit' (TP 57) and, without trying to exhaust this history, focus on one of its most relevant junctures: the formation of the *annexed* or *associated milieu*. Here is where the contribution of Uexküll becomes crucial.

An associated milieu can be thought of as a limit or membrane that has undergone a significant increase in complexity and functional differentiation. This step occurs when organisms cease to nourish themselves through direct assimilation and, instead, separate food intake from respiration (a process that is defined by the authors as 'the capture of energy source . . . different from alimentary materials' (TP 57)). The differentiation of food intake and respiration and the surplus of energy that this process implies opens the way to a further increase in the functional complexity of the limit between organism and exterior milieu:

> The associated milieu is thus defined by the capture of energy sources (respiration in the most general sense), by the discernment of materials, the sensing of their presence or absence (perception), and by the fabrication or nonfabrication of the corresponding compounds (response, reaction). (TP 57)

It is easy to see that the new functions acquired by the associated milieu not only have a metabolic character, but also display themselves in the sphere of perception and even behaviour. 'The development of the associated milieus' – write the authors – 'culminates in the animal worlds described by von Uexküll, with all their active, perceptive, and energetic characteristics' (TP 57); such worlds are what Uexküll calls Umwelten.

It is important to note that in *A Thousand Plateaus* the term 'Umwelt' appears only once (and without direct connections with Uexküll), and, additionally, there is no reflection on the speculative possibilities offered by this term (the opposition *Welt/Umwelt*, and so on). Buchanan notes:

> in Deleuze and Guattari's discussion of milieus – wherein Uexküll features decisively – the Umwelt is never raised as such. . . . It is as if they purposely eschew a discussion of the most obvious aspect of Uexküll's thought: his theory of the Umwelt.[11]

In our view, however, the problem is mainly of a terminological nature. In the French translation of *Streifzüge durch die Umwelten von Tieren und Menschen*, the original German word 'Umwelt' is not mentioned, except for in the colophon and in the presentation by Philippe Muller; in the text, the term is translated case by case with 'world' and especially with 'milieu'. Consequently, when Deleuze and Guattari speak of the associated milieu of the tick, they are speaking of its Umwelt. As will be evident in our concluding remarks, what they indeed eschew is the reference of the Uexküllian Umwelt to the subject, and this is favoured by the disappearance of the prefix *Um-*, *around*, which immediately raises the question: around whom?[12]

From the examples Uexküll offers in *A Foray into the Worlds of Animals and Humans*, Deleuze and Guattari choose the respective Umwelten of the tick and the spider. The first is useful for showing how even the smallest number of perceptive and operational traits can combine themselves into an associated milieu that mediates between an animal and its external reality:

> the unforgettable associated world of the Tick, defined by its gravitational energy of falling, its olfactory characteristic of perceiving sweat, and its active characteristic of latching on: the tick climbs a branch and drops onto a passing mammal it has recognized by smell, then latches onto its skin (an associated world composed of three factors, and no more). (TP 57)

In their synthetic reconstruction, the authors see the interplay of energetic, perceptive and operative traits that guides the life cycle of the tick as the formative principle of an elementary associated milieu – that is, in their terminology, a folding of the becoming in correspondence with a precise point of the organic stratum, the tick itself.

The second example is of more profound importance. According to the authors the constitution of an animal milieu, such as the spider's, has a high morphogenetic value. The form – in this case, the form of the spider's web – depends on the codes of the relevant environmental elements (that is, the fly) that shall enter the spider's Umwelt at that precise point. As *A Theory of Meaning* makes clear, the notion of code is central in Uexküll's biosemiotics: the code of a biological species is its 'primal image', its (atemporal and immaterial) archetypus. In a way that recalls the action on material reality of the Platonic ideas, the species-specific archetypal codes influence the formation of anatomical, physiological and behavioural traits of the single organisms: 'the spider's web' – writes Uexküll – 'is configured in a fly-like way [*ist fliegenhaft*]' because the spider has taken up certain elements of the fly in its constitution', or 'has taken up certain motifs of the fly melody in its bodily composition'.[13]

Such a process of 'taking up' is thought of by Deleuze and Guattari as a form of transcoding, or mutual 'tuning in' of the codes of two (or more) organisms:

> Jakob von Uexküll has elaborated an admirable theory of transcodings. . . . The spider web implies that there are sequences of the fly's own code in the spider's code; it is as though the spider had a fly in its head, a fly 'motif', a fly 'refrain'. (TP 346)

The central idea is that an associated milieu can coagulate around another associated milieu, or, in other terms, that a code can incorporate another code in its fundamental traits. This interconnection between ontology and semiotics, morphogenesis and codes, is very close to Uexküllian biosemiotics. Where Deleuze and Guattari depart from Uexküll is, instead, in the different assessment of the biological and evolutionary role of the morphogenesis – or, in other terms, in the biophilosophical context in which this process appears. According to Uexküll, the inclusion of the code, or motive, of the fly in the spider's web form is a timeless event, which always and forever organises the relationship between the two species. In Uexküll's harmonic and deeply teleological view of nature, flies do not evolve thanks to an unplanned (one could say, contingent) relationship with the web traits (resistance of the threads, distance between the meshes, etcetera); the same is true for spiders and their extended phenotype, the web. For Uexküll, the presence of the fly code in the web code is not due to the frantic search for resources that, in the Darwinian view, pushes the species to evolve into new forms and behaviours, but rather is the sign of an overabundance of original forms and dynamics. As a consequence of this harmony, the quota of flies that, every year, end up in the webs is already pre-established and does not threaten the species with extinction; and, since no species faces a risk of extinction, each species can afford the loss of individuals in excess to stage the great theatre piece of life. 'It is hardly a matter of the survival of the fittest' – writes Uexküll – 'but rather, of the survival of the normal in the interests of an unchanging further existence of the species.'[14]

Deleuze and Guattari's analysis of the formation of a new associated milieu diverges from the harmonious and teleological framework proposed by Uexküll's philosophy of Nature; it is, in fact, explicitly evolutionistic:

> the form can develop only through intermediary milieus that regulate the speeds and rates of its substances; and it can experience itself only in a milieu of exteriority that measures the comparative advantages of the associated milieus . . . Milieus always act, through selection, on entire organisms, the forms of which depend on codes those milieus sanction indirectly. (TP 58)

In general, the ontology of becoming sketched in *A Thousand Plateaus* – without being a direct transposition of Darwinism into philosophy of Nature – includes decidedly Darwinian or evolutionistic traits. Among the 'fundamental contributions of Darwinism' (TP 58) the authors mention the discovery of 'the code's ability to propagate in the milieu or create for itself a new associated milieu' (TP 59), and even the fact 'that new forms and associated milieus potentially result from a change in the code, a modification of the code' (TP 59).

Deleuze and Guattari are aware that the situation is more complex. The nineteenth-century vitalists could no longer deny the possibility of the emergence of new forms and species, but instead, they inserted it within the framework of an explicitly teleological vision. They rejected explanations based on an unplanned selection, instead favouring the idea of a pre-established evolution, which is directed to an ever greater wealth of the living. As the authors write, though:

> The change is obviously not due to a passage from one preestablished form to another, in other words, a translation from one code to another. As long as the problem was formulated in that fashion, it remained insoluble, and one would have to agree with Cuvier and Baer that established types of forms are irreducible and therefore do not admit of translation or transformation. (TP 59)

The importance of this statement appears with even greater clarity if one considers that Baer was, for Uexküll, an undisputed reference point.[15] But even Deleuze and Guattari's solution is not entirely satisfactory. Their appeal to Darwinism is linked to the goal to increase and 'free' the differentiation of forms and the processes of becoming within the organic layer – in this respect, the random phenotypic variation from which Darwin started his reflection is a better basis than any pre-established or teleological change. But – on the other side – how can you harmonise this intent with the purpose of eliminating the category of organism from biophilosophy?[16] In the Darwinian theory, the organism is not only the bearer of diversity, but is also its possible beneficiary, and it is the ecology of a species that gives a sense of the diversity, determining the positive, negative or neutral value of a variation. Attempts to find subjects of evolution other than organisms and species (and under the level of the organism: codes, forms or even genes, such in Richard Dawkins's case) have proven to be very problematic.

Refrain and Territory

After having used Uexküll's work to account for the formation of associated milieus within the organic layer, the authors again take up his thoughts to describe some forms of more complex organic processes that appear in the behaviour of higher animals, such as the territory, the home, the rhythm. This possibility – that is developed in chapter '1837: of the Refrain' in *A Thousand Plateaus* – is fully justified on the one side by the general 'rhizomatic' trait of recursivity, and on the other by some of the most interesting pages of *A Foray into the Worlds of Animals and Humans*. In addition to describing – in a less thorough way than, for example, in *Theoretical Biology*[17] – the constitution of Umwelten in their perceptive and operative aspects (*Merkmale* and *Wirkmale*, respectively), Uexküll notes that in some species the activity of sense-conferring to the world around them manages to colour with further significance precise parts of the perceptive environment. This is how phenomena arise, such as the formation in the environment of familiar paths, dwellings and territories; the particular importance given to one or more conspecifics; the possibility that the environment can take on a particular 'search tone'; and the emergence of magical, or even hallucinatory, elements or atmospheres.[18]

As this is not the place to discuss exhaustively this part of Uexküll's thought – one of the most significant, even only for the many links that bind it to the nascent ethology – we now turn to the reading Deleuze and Guattari give of the phenomenon of further signification of milieus: that is, territorialisation. Let us begin with the way Deleuze and Guattari describe the formation of territories within the milieus:

> the territory is in fact an act that affects milieus and rhythms, that 'territorializes' them. The territory is the product of a territorialization of milieus and rhythms. . . . A territory borrows from all the milieus; it bites into them, seizes them bodily (although it remains vulnerable to intrusions). It is built from aspects or portions of milieus. (TP 347)

The way in which a territory is established is the acquisition of expressiveness by some perceptive elements of the associated milieu:

'What defines the territory is the emergence of matters of expression (qualities)' (TP 347); these elements coagulate in regular 'motifs' that the authors call refrains: 'In a general sense, we call a refrain any aggregate of matters of expression that draws a territory and develops into territorial motifs and landscapes (there are optical, gestural, motor, etc., refrains)' (TP 356).[19] The regularity and stability in the behaviour of territorial species strikes the human observer as an unexpected emerging quality of the natural world, and Deleuze and Guattari consider this phenomenon as a form of spontaneous expression of the underlying ontological stratum.

In other words, Deleuze and Guattari see the acquisition of expressiveness as an original phenomenon of increasing complexity of the becoming; a phenomenon, in other terms, that is not centred on the single animal or species – to the point that the authors write: 'it amounts to the same thing to ask when milieus and rhythms become territorialized, and what the difference is between a non-territorial animal and a territorial animal' (TP 347). This implies that the biological functions of the phenomenon of territorialisation and of its species-specific procedures adopt a subordinated role. Taking under consideration the example of colour in birds or fishes, the authors state that the colour of a membrane

> remains functional and transitory as long as it is tied to a type of action (sexuality, aggressiveness, flight). It becomes expressive, on the other hand, when it acquires a temporal constancy and a spatial range that make it a territorial, or rather territorializing, mark: a signature. The question is not whether color resumes its functions or fulfills new ones in the territory. It is clear that it does, but this reorganization of functions implies first of all that the component under consideration has become expressive and that its meaning, from this standpoint, is to mark a territory. (TP 347)

And, in a more explicit way: 'Functions in a territory are not primary; they presuppose a territory-producing expressiveness' (TP 348).

The authors use this evaluative line in a critical perspective. Their target is Konrad Lorenz's thesis that the instinct of aggression is the ontogenetic and phylogenetic basis of the territory (see TP 348), but the criticism can be easily extended to Uexküll (even if, obviously, not in its phylogenetic part). Even if we restrict our examination to *A Foray into the Worlds of Animals and Humans*, it appears very clearly that all the elements of the Umwelt – including the territory – are linked to what Uexküll calls the *Funktionskreis*, a circle of functions that arise *from* the subject and *for* the subject. In other texts – and, in particular, in *Theoretical Biology* – the animal subject is also the bearer of a pre-established plan of construction (*Bauplan*), from which the different functional circles (for example nutrition, escape, and, if present, territory and sociability) branch out according to the species-specific ecology.

Although it is evidently the intention of the authors to address the processuality of the living toward higher forms of expressive freedom – always of the territory, they say: 'Can this becoming, this emergence, be called Art? That would make the territory a result of art . . . [T]his constitution, this freeing, of matters of expression in the movement of territoriality [is] the base or ground of art' (TP 348) – it is equally clear that this attempt does not match Uexküll's own thinking on this matter. This is not because Uexküll aims at ontologically separating human and non-human animals (on the contrary, he supports a gradualist vision of the relationship between animal and human Umwelten), but instead, because Umwelt and functional circles, and at a deeper level functional circles and living subject, are inseparable.

Concluding Remarks: Uexküll as Spinozist?

Clearly, Deleuze and Guattari are influenced by Uexküll; however, this influence is highly selective. Their interpretive strategy towards Uexküll's thought can be summarised as an attempt to maintain all of those elements that may account for the increase in complexity of the becoming, but without agreeing with the basic presuppositions of such thinking: the foundational role of the animal subject. Thus, the formation of the associated environments is presented as the result of the 'folding' of ontological strata; the interconnection between semiotics and ontology is seen in the perspective of a morphogenetic autonomy of codes and environmental elements; and, finally, the formation of higher organisational levels in the associated environments (territorialisation) is seen as a kind of spontaneous and radical rearrangement of biological functions, a rearrangement that tends towards expressiveness and art.

The authors' belief that Uexküll's thought could provide a valuable point of support for their de-subjectified ontology arises largely from the fact that they had only a single text available, the French translation of *A Foray into the Worlds of Animals and Humans*. Despite this being one of the richest in documentary material (including the reports of Konrad Lorenz's first experiments), this text deliberately keeps away from overly speculative issues in theoretical biology. In other words, in *A Foray into the Worlds of Animals and Humans* the author tries to avoid giving explicit support to vitalistic and metaphysic theses that would have been perceived as unscientific; however, such theses have always been and are still present in his conceptual background. Moreover, most of these (as they can be found in other Uexküllian texts) are very difficult to reconcile with a rhizomatic and de-verticalised ontology: the idea of the plan of construction (*Bauplan*) as an intangible and supratemporal instance that drives the formation of the anatomy, physiology and behaviour in animals; the limits imposed on the becoming by a teleological conception of Nature; the action of an omnipresent (but empirically unknowable) *Naturfaktor* that harmonises *Bauplan* and environments of the different species and avoids extinctions and imbalances.[20] Even the machinic character of the rhizomatic formations, as we have seen above, finds no support in the thought of Uexküll, who accepts the mechanistic model only on the condition of maintaining, in the machine, the leading presence of a machine operator.

However, the main limitation in the use Deleuze and Guattari made of Uexküll's thought lies in having ignored the foundational role that the Estonian biologist ascribes to the subject in the constitution of the Umwelt. In his theoretical biology, this process is explicitly presented by Uexküll as an extension to biology of the transcendental approach that Kant developed in his *Critique of Pure Reason*:

> The task of biology is to expand the outcome of Kant's research in two directions: i. to take into account the role of our body too, in particular of our sense organs and central nervous system, and ii. to investigate the relationships with the objects of the other subjects (animals).[21]

In a less explicit way, this is reaffirmed even in the popular work *A Foray into the Worlds of Animals and Humans*, in the discussion of the basic coordinates of the perceptive and operative Umwelt:

> Without a living subject, there can be neither space nor time. With this observation, biology has once and for all connected with Kant's philosophy, which biology will now utilize through the natural sciences by emphasizing the decisive role of the subject.[22]

This implies that reality is, in itself, unknowable, and that every living being's experience is the product of a transcendental elaboration of the rough and 'rhapsodic'[23] material given by the sensory receptors – an elaboration that can attain very different levels of complexity, from the elementary Umwelt/experience of a jellyfish to the rich and cognitively articulate experience of mammals and human beings. Thanks to the Kantian heritage, in other terms, the Umwelt is thought of as a transcendental species-specific construction. To this frame of thought (and this is one of his most original contributions), Uexküll adds decidedly semiotic traits.[24]

The extent to which Deleuze's reading of Uexküll departs from the latter's own thought appears in full when you consider the way in which it appears in the text *Spinoza: Practical Philosophy*. The importance of Spinoza as a foundation for Deleuze's thought is difficult to underestimate; Spinoza provides him with a thought pattern in which all entities are neither substances nor subjects, but instead are contingent modes of a single substance/nature (SPP 123–4); each mode 'is a capacity for affecting and being affected', and living beings are no exceptions: 'you will define an animal, or a human being, not by its form, its organs, and its functions, and not as a subject either; you will define it by the affects of which it is capable' (SPP 124).[25] Here Deleuze draws upon Uexküll for the first time, presenting the Umwelt of the tick as an 'animal world with only three affects [a visual, an olfactory and a thermic affection] in the midst of all that goes on in the immense forest' (SPP 124–5).

Obviously, the possibility of reading this in a Spinozian key is linked to those aspects of Uexküll's thought that do not concern the question of the subject, but rather the interaction between different Umwelten. This interaction is described (more than explained) by Uexküll through musical metaphors, such as the counterpoint or the symphonic composition among the Umwelten – as Benoît Goetz rightly points out, 'Deleuze trouve donc chez notre baron zoologiste (dont il fait une lecture plus spinoziste que kantienne) l'idée d'un plan de composition de la Nature'[26] – and is assigned to the harmonising action of a higher subject-nature: 'all these different environments are fostered and borne along by the One that is inaccessible to all environments forever. Forever unknowable behind all of the worlds it produces, the subject – Nature – conceals itself.'[27] Notwithstanding the difficulty in understanding how exactly Uexküll thinks the interconnection occurs among multiple subjective and species-specific centres (the animals) and among their transcendental productions (their Umwelten), it should be noted that many interpreters have seen in this facet of Uexküll's thought more than a Spinozian model, rather than a sort of Leibnizian monadology[28] (in particular, with respect to the existence of a multiplicity of centres of perspective and the vitalist idea of a profound and pre-established harmony in the relations among them[29]).

The Spinozian interpretation of Uexküll's conception of Nature appears as a consequent part of the definition of an ontology without subjects and without organisms – an enterprise in which, as it now seems clear, Uexküll cannot be used if not partially and with some forcing. In this concluding paragraph, however, it should be remembered what the aim of this enterprise is: to get rid of a static or deterministic conception of subjects, substances, organisms and bodies, and switch to a natural ontology pivoting on elementary forces and processes of spontaneity and self-movement. This switch has, for Deleuze and Guattari, a highly freeing and expressive potential:

> what is called *art brut* is not at all pathological or primitive; it is merely this constitution, this freeing, of matters of expression in the movement of territoriality: the base or ground of art. Take anything and make it a matter of expression. (TP 349)

If we imagine this last exhortation as applied to a living subject, or to the meta-subject Nature, we are not so far from the Uexküllian idea of the constitution of an Umwelt made of matter and meaning.

Notes

1. Gilles Deleuze and Félix Guattari, *A Thousand Plateaus. Capitalism and Schizophrenia*, trans. Brian Massumi (London and New York: Continuum, 2004).
2. Gilles Deleuze, *Spinoza: Practical Philosophy*, trans. Robert Hurley (San Francisco: City Lights Book, 1988).
3. Jakob von Uexküll, *Mondes animaux et monde humain, suivi de Théorie de la signification*, trans. Philippe Muller (Paris: Denöel, 1965).
4. Jakob von Uexküll, *Streifzüge durch die Umwelten von Tieren und Menschen: Ein Bilderbuch unsichtbarer Welten. Bedeutungslehre* (Hamburg: Rowohlt, 1956). Before being published jointly in 1956, the two texts had the following first editions: Jakob von Uexküll and Georg Kriszat, *Streifzüge durch die Umwelten von Tieren und Menschen: Ein Bilderbuch unsichtbarer Welten* (Berlin: Verlag von Julius Springer, 1934); Jakob von Uexküll, *Bedeutungslehre* (Leipzig: Verlag von J. A. Barth, 1940).
5. Jakob von Uexküll, *A Foray into the Worlds of Animals and Humans with A Theory of Meaning*, trans. Joseph D. O'Neil (Minneapolis: University of Minneapolis Press, 2010).

6. Alfred N. Whitehead, *Process and Reality* (Toronto: The Macmillan Company, 1929).
7. Nicolai Hartmann, *Philosophie der Natur. Abriss der speziellen Kategorienlehre* (Berlin: de Gruyter, 1950).
8. The English translation used here, which reports 'it is not *im*possible to make . . .' (italics added), has been corrected after a comparison with the original text: 'l'on ne peut pas établir de coupure radicale entre les régimes de signes et leurs objets' (Gilles Deleuze and Félix Guattari, *Milles Plateaux. Capitalisme et schizophrénie* (Paris: Les Éditions de Minuit, 1980), p. 13).
9. Brett Buchanan, *Onto-Ethologies: The Animal Environments of Uexküll, Heidegger, Merleau-Ponty and Deleuze* (Albany: State University of New York Press, 2008), p. 170. Julien Pieron understood this point very well: 'l'adoption généralisée du concept de *machine* est pour Deleuze une façon de se détourner radicalement d'une pensée de l'organisme, . . . non dans le sens du mécanisme cartésien, mais dans celui d'une pragmatique généralisée : la nature comme champ d'agencements divers, . . . qui peuvent tout autant donner lieu à des régimes d'organisation "organiques" qu'a des régimes d'anorganisation potentiellement – mais non nécessairement – créatrice de vie' (Julien Pieron, 'Monadologie et/ou constructivisme? Heidegger, Deleuze, Uexküll', *Bulletin d'analyse phénoménologique* 6:2 [2010], pp. 86–117 [p. 93]).
10. Uexküll, *A Foray into the Worlds of Animals and Humans*, p. 45.
11. Buchanan, *Onto-Ethologies*, pp. 176–7.
12. In fact, the problem is raised in Philippe Muller's presentation of *Mondes animaux et monde humain*, which describes the object of Uexküll's study as the animal's 'milieu concret or vécu (le terme allemand "Umwelt" se traduirait le mieux par "entours", qui ne figure malheureusement pas . . . dans le vocabulaire technique du biologiste' (Philippe Muller, 'Présentation', in Uexküll, *Mondes animaux et monde humain*, p. 7).
13. Jakob von Uexküll, *A Theory of Meaning*, in *A Foray into the Worlds of Animals and Humans*, pp. 190–1.
14. Ibid., p. 185.
15. Cf. ibid., pp. 70, 185, 193.
16. In respect to this point, Deleuze's approach could be efficiently integrated by Nicolai Hartmann's pluralistic ontology of Nature, in which the category of organism does jeopardise the processuality and multiplicity of the real; see Hartmann, *Philosophie der Natur*, pp. 519–35.
17. See Jakob von Uexküll, *Theoretical Biology* (London: Kegan Paul/ Trench, Trübner and Co., 1926); translation by D. L. Mackinnon of the first edition of *Theoretische Biologie* (Berlin: Gebrüder Paetel, 1920), chapters 1, 2, 3 and 4, where Uexküll deals with the basic traits of the

subjective Umwelten: time, space, content-related qualities, presence of unified objects, and so on.

18. See Carlo Brentari, *Jakob von Uexküll: The Discovery of the Umwelt between Biosemiotics and Theoretical Biology*, trans. Catriona Graciet (Dordrecht, Heidelberg, New York and London: Springer, 2015), pp. 149–51.
19. The whole discussion of the formation of milieus and territories is full of musical figures, which, as in Uexküll, constantly tend to overcome their metaphorical use towards a literal use; for this point, see Brentari, *Jakob von Uexküll*, p. 213. It has to be said, however, that in Deleuze this is explicitly allowed by the author's refusal of the status of metaphors for the ontological figures or models used in *A Thousands Plateaus*: 'If we interpret the word "like" as a metaphor, or propose a structural analogy of relations (man-iron = dog-bone), we understand nothing of becoming' (TP 302).
20. The relationship between the notions of *Bauplan* and *Naturfaktor* is one of the most controversial points in Uexküll's theoretical biology, but it can be said that the first is the empirically observable effect of the action of the second (which, in itself, remains unknowable): the plan of construction, writes Uexküll, 'has nothing to do with the actual natural factor [*der wirkliche Naturfaktor*] which forces physical-chemical processes to take a certain course. [This] is the only way we can know the effects of the said natural factor. In itself, the natural factor is completely unknown to us. Driesch, referring to Aristotle, calls it "entelechy", Karl Ernst von Baer calls it "goaldirectedness [*Zielstrebigkeit*]"', Jakob von Uexküll, *Umwelt und Innenwelt der Tiere* (Berlin: Springer 1909), p. 13 (trans. Catriona Graciet).
21. Jakob von Uexküll, *Theoretische Biologie. 2. gänzlich neu bearbeitete Auflage* (Berlin: Springer 1928), p. 3. The question of the subject is central in the whole production of the Estonian biologist; cf. in particular some articles that the Estonian biologist published in *Die neue Rundschau* at the beginning of the 1910s: Jakob von Uexküll, 'Die Umwelt', *Die neue Rundschau* 21 (1910), pp. 638–49; 'Das Subjekt als Träger des Lebens', *Die neue Rundschau* 23 (1912), pp. 99–107; 'Wie gestaltet das Leben ein Subjekt', *Die neue Rundschau* 23 (1912), pp. 1082–91, and 'Wirkungen und Gegenwirkungen im Subjekt', *Die neue Rundschau* 23 (1912), pp. 1399–406 .
22. Uexküll, *A Foray into the Worlds of Animals and Humans*, p. 52.
23. The reference here is to the 'rhapsody of perception' that, in the *Critique of Pure Reason*, furnishes the rough material for the transcendental forms of sensibility, space and time; see Immanuel Kant, *Critique of Pure Reason*, trans. Norman Kemp Smith (London: Macmillan, 1990), A156/B195.
24. Brentari, *Jakob von Uexküll*, pp. 107–14.

25. It is evident that, thanks to his Spinozism, Deleuze's consideration of the animal allows him a greater degree of individuation than does the Uexküllian approach, which remains linked to the idea of the species-specificity of the Umwelten; as noted by Yogi Hale Hendlin, 'while Uexküll recognizes the interiority of nonhumans in a way that both joins imagination and science, he fails to attend the specificity of each member of that species. He begins his analysis not of *this* bee, or *that* dog, but by generalizing the species' possibilities . . . What Deleuze and Guattari give us, as well as the late Derrida of *The Animal that Therefore I am*, is the specificity of the (ontologically decentred) individual. . . . Yet, for their own part, Deleuze and Guattari (as well as Derrida) can be accused of superficiality and lack of scientific rigour' (Yogi H. Hendlin, 'Multiplicity and *Welt*', *Sign Systems Studies* 44:1/2 (2016), pp. 94–110 [pp. 102–3]).
26. 'Deleuze therefore discovers in our baron zoologist (who he reads as more Spinozist than Kantian) the idea of a plan of composition of Nature' (Benoît Goetz, 'L'araignée, le lézard et la tique: Deleuze et Heidegger lecteurs de Uexküll', *Le Portique* 20 [2007]; available at https://leportique.revues.org/1364 [last accessed 8/9/2016]). The possibility to see in the recourse to musical metaphors a relevant point in common between Uexküll and Deleuze has been recently highlighted by Frederick Amrine; cf. Frederick Amrine, 'The Music of the Organism: Uexküll, Merleau-Ponty, Zuckerkandl, and Deleuze as Goethan Ecologist in Search of a New Paradigm', *Goethe Yearbook* 22 (2015), pp. 45–72.
27. Uexküll, *A Foray into the Worlds of Animals and Humans*, p. 135.
28. Cf. the complex evaluation by Konrad Lorenz of the figure of the Estonian biologist: 'Uexküll – die-hard vitalist, staunch idealist, Kantian – actually an enemy of natural science, because "the environment of every man is separate from that of another", a sort of monadology; . . . But, true to the double life that idealist naturalists often lead, he is still the most accurate researcher in physiology' (Konrad Lorenz, 'Referat über J. v. Üxküll' (1948), unpublished transcription by Hilde Fürnsinn of a seminary by K. Lorenz, conserved in the Lorenz-Archive of the KLI Institute for Evolution and Cognition Research of Altenberg, Austria, p. 1); cf. also Pieron, *Monadologie et/ou constructivisme?*, p. 92 and n.
29. In *Der unsterbliche Geist in der Natur*, this pattern of thinking is used to compensate for the charge of solipsism that can be moved to many philosophical theories focused on the subject. In a comparison, the variety of Umwelten that makes up Nature is equated to a multitude of images of the same field that are reflected in the drops of dew: 'Each of these myriads of drops mirrors all the world with the sun, the mountains, the forests and the shrubs, a magical world within itself. Imagine for a moment, in his mind, that each one of these innumerable drops

does not only shine in the diversity of the shimmering colors, but also possesses its own subjective tone, the one that distinguishes all living beings, then you will understand that the theory of the environment has nothing to do with this silly solipsism' (Jakob von Uexküll, *Der unsterbliche Geist in der Natur. Gespräche* [Hamburg: Wegner, 1938], pp. 47–8).

5

Marcel Proust

Graham Jones

> *Life is short, art long, opportunity fleeting, experience treacherous, judgement difficult.*
>
> (Hippocrates)

Despite initial resistance to the idea within Deleuzian commentary across the English-speaking world, it has become increasingly accepted in recent years that Deleuze is a systematic – indeed, a system-building – philosopher. The origins of this intellectual disposition are usually sought in his dissertation *Difference and Repetition* (1968) and its complex and detailed account of a 'transcendental empiricism'. However, it can be traced – with varying degrees of relevance and comprehensiveness – back even earlier to his works on Hume, Nietzsche, Kant, Proust and Bergson.[1] Of these, *Proust and Signs* (1964) proves particularly illuminating – even instructive – because it introduces, foregrounds and synthesises so *many* of the elements that will constitute the thematic weave of Deleuze's subsequent works, particularly *Difference and Repetition*.[2] Reading this slender yet incredibly rich volume alongside his subsequent monographs, I believe, is as useful in understanding many of Deleuze's later concerns and concepts as consulting any of the numerous introductory overviews devoted to his work. Perhaps, in light of this, it is time to rescue *Proust and Signs* from its undeserved obscurity and neglect, and reassess its significance both in regards to the established image of Deleuze's thought in current circulation and within his work as a whole.

Proust and *À la recherche du temps perdu*

> *Thanks to art, instead of seeing one world only, our own, we see that world multiply itself and we have at our disposal as many worlds as there are original artists.*[3]

Valentin Louis Georges Eugène Marcel Proust was born in Auteuil, Paris, on 10 July 1871. He spent much of his childhood in Illiers, which provided the template for 'Combray', one of the important settings for his famous novel, *À la recherche du temps perdu*. He was a sickly child and asthma plagued him throughout his life, to the point where he spent the final years of his life largely bedridden. His father was a distinguished medical specialist and a French Catholic and his mother – who could also speak English – came from a wealthy Jewish family, and this heritage made Proust simultaneously the denizen of different 'worlds'.

It was expected by Proust's family that he would follow in his father's footsteps, and although throughout his life he maintained an interest in science, particularly biology (and the desire in his literary works to find general 'laws' of human behaviour clearly testifies to this), he instead went on to study literature and philosophy. The latter is worth noting because it would be no exaggeration to suggest that Proust's novel, a modernist masterwork – and often regarded as one of the greatest European novels of the twentieth century – is also perhaps one of the most philosophically informed novels ever written. It is hardly surprising, then, that it should be of great interest to Deleuze for whom philosophy (or at least a certain kind of philosophical practice) was *paramount*, and who, moreover, regarded an artist's way of life, of their very being, as a direct manifestation of a specific 'philosophical' perspective, of a way of both grasping and constructing their world.

À la recherche du temps perdu took Proust thirteen years to write, and the final parts were published posthumously because the polishing of the manuscript had not been completed when he died in 1922 at the age of fifty-one. However, it is not clear that it can be said to have ever been truly finished in terms of its form and content as Proust had a tendency to keep revisiting and adding parts to it, and there is evidence to suggest that he would have continued to do so if death had not intervened.

The work itself is quite intimidating in length – almost one and a half million words (consisting of well over three thousand pages and involving more than two thousand characters) – and was originally divided into seven volumes.[4] The basic plot is quite straightforward and akin to a *bildungsroman*: it recounts the life and development of a would-be writer, the novel's narrator (for the most part unnamed but who in at least two places is referred to as Marcel), who aspires to great artistry but also craves the admiration of his peers, alongside entry into the higher reaches of society. After various adventures and misadventures in love along the way, and after many years of failed effort (and seeming resignation) in respect to his vocation and various desires, he eventually comes to realise his artistic ambition.

The novel famously begins with an extended sequence in which the narrator moves in a semi-awakened state through a series of half-remembered events and imaginings, until eventually he alights upon the childhood memory of waiting in bed for his mother's good-night kiss. The novel ends with him, in his dotage, meeting a childhood friend's granddaughter at a reception just after the end of the First World War, and being inspired to finally begin writing his masterpiece (which presumably we are holding in our hands and reading). The entire journey of the novel from beginning to end recounts in incredibly attentive detail all the vagaries of Marcel's development as a social, psychological and aesthetic entity.

Large parts of the work detail the snobbery, hypocrisy, ruthlessness and blatant self-interest that Marcel directly observes in the aristocracy and its bourgeois sycophants, as well as the difficulties faced by the artists whom the upper class and the nouveaux riches patronise in their parlours and salons. Proust is unsparing in his unflattering, and often comic, depictions of these traits in various characters, but he also does not shy away from showing that Marcel is subject to many of them himself as a dilettante romantically yearning to join the influential ranks of higher society. It is a key feature of the novel that it takes Marcel many years, and numerous detours and disappointments, to transcend the limits of his misguided prejudices and ambitions concerning the significance and desirability of social hierarchy and to overcome his need for validation through the opinions and approval of others. This fraught journey towards understanding is, however, already metaphorically established in the first volume which is largely set around Combray, and where Marcel's family go for walks along *two paths* – which lead out of opposite gates but which (towards the novel's end he is surprised to discover) actually intersect – called respectively the 'Méséglise way' (also sometimes 'Swann's Way') and the 'Guermantes way'. Proust's aesthetic design suggests that these respective paths symbolically introduce and establish the two directions that Marcel's own life can take and thus represent the different temptations that he wrestles with on his 'journey' (and which characters such as Charles Swann, Dr Cottard, Brichot, Saint-Loup, Madame Verdurin, Bergotte, Vinteuil, Bichel and Elstir, encapsulate in one way or another, and with relative degrees of 'success' and 'failure'): the first is a conventional life circumscribed by comfortable bourgeois (that is, stereotypical) 'reality' and its seedy, hidden underbelly, and the second a more difficult and idealised life of refined taste and creative hardship (but also subject to great vanity, envy and pretension). Ultimately, both paths prove unsatisfying in and of themselves. However, the final scene of the last volume suggests that Marcel sees in his unexpected encounter with Swann and Odette's granddaughter the hope of a reconciliation between these two paths, and this provides him with the final impetus to begin writing his novel.

Proust and Signs

Unlike contemporaneous French readings of *À la recherché du temps perdu* of the 1950s and early 1960s, Deleuze's approach does not focus upon the novel's autobiographical 'parallels', or analyse its protagonist's complex psychology or the cultural setting of fin-de-siécle France, nor examine its detailed 'phenomenological' rendering of aesthetic experience, but instead emphasises what Deleuze believes is most 'profound' about the work: that it details the *development* of a 'man of letters'.

What is particularly striking – and possibly unique – about Deleuze's approach in *Proust and Signs* is that he finds a degree of systematicity (albeit implicit) within the novel that goes beyond any conventional concern with narrative or symbolic architecture. Deleuze begins his analysis by foregrounding several interrelated aspects of the text which, though perhaps today seem uncontroversial, were somewhat unusual at the time of *Proust and Signs* initial publication: namely, i) the problematising nature and scope of the Search and its transformative qualities; ii) the *signs* which provide the raw material for this process of almost alchemical transmutation; iii) the relationship of both the Search and of signs to the workings of *time*; and finally iv) how all of the these relate to the notions of learning and *apprenticeship*.

The idea of a Search is, of course, already foregrounded in the novel's actual title *À la Recherche du temps perdu*, which translates more accurately as *In Search of Lost Time*, rather than its usual English rendering of *Remembrance of Things Past*. Deleuze takes the title quite literally, insisting that the notion of the Search (always capitalised) is what constitutes the overt theme and goal of the novel's narrative. However, this raises the persistent question of what is the 'lost time' referred to in the title. Is it time wasted on frivolous concerns and infidelities? Events somehow hidden by time's passage, or the true significance of which go unrecognised? Or perhaps even time's own obscured nature? – and, as we shall see, Deleuze's addressing of these questions and their implications is tied to a range of other important concerns. In emphasising these, however, Deleuze deliberately shifts attention away from the one feature that had largely dominated previous *anglophone* readings of the novel: namely, the episodes of involuntary memory for which it is often celebrated and which are seen by many as its artistically defining feature. In fact, Deleuze provides an interpretation that runs directly counter to such readings when he asserts that the work is not *primarily* about memory, in respect to either its workings or significance, for 'memory intervenes as a means of search, of investigation, but not the most profound means; and time past intervenes as a structure of time, but not the most profound structure' (PS 3). Deleuze makes this claim not in order to dismiss the significance of memory and the past – an issue which we will examine in more detail shortly – but in order to relocate them within the broader dynamic schema of the novel. Instead, he argues that the work fundamentally concerns the narrator's Search for 'truth' as it unfolds over the course of his life, an apprenticeship that the narrator gradually undergoes in learning to make sense both of his own world and of how his experience and insights relate to the worlds of others.

But, just as the novel is not directly about memory, nor is it, strictly speaking, primarily *about* time, although every element of its form, content and meaning is suffused with, and made possible by and through, the workings and effects of the temporal. Though life may – as Kierkegaard famously observed – be lived forwards but only understood backwards, Deleuze's interpretation of this contrary movement through the events and implicit Search of Proust's novel demonstrates that time is a much more complex structure (or set of structures) than we usually acknowledge, for if 'time has great importance in the Search, it is because every truth is a truth of time' (PS 94).

Deleuze's opening contention is that the work is primarily about a process of learning in pursuit of truth, and one '*oriented to the future' and not the past* (PS 4). The Search is thus fundamentally 'the narrative of an apprenticeship' that marks the temporal path from ignorance and mere opinion to understanding and wisdom, 'for the Megelise Way and the Guermantes Way are not so much the sources of memory as the raw materials . . . two ways of a formation' (PS 3).

As such, the one who searches for truth undertakes an

apprenticeship (original Latin *apprehendere*: 'to apprehend or learn'; Old French: 'inexperienced or unskilled'; subsequent meaning: 'to abide by or serve under an agreement to take instruction or learn skills or a trade'), a process of learning in which the novice or supplicant attends to a practice with the aim of creatively embracing or replicating its core elements. Deleuze describes such an apprenticeship as a process of *sensitisation* in which the learner acquires a skill or heightened sensibility through a process of scrutiny, differentiation and refinement. But, more importantly it is a process in which the apprentice attends to the nature and functions of 'signs' (not by simply imitating or neutrally observing but, more importantly, by 'participating'), discerning where they may lead, or what they might enable or disclose. Moreover, the Search is, Deleuze insists, essentially a *temporal* apprenticeship to the interpretation of signs and – as we shall see – it is the *signs of art* that ultimately and retrospectively reveal this fundamental truth. It is the protagonist's increasing facility with interpreting different kinds of signs that ultimately enables him to grasp what is most profound, most true, in respect to experience and existence, and it is art that finally reveals to Marcel the true nature of things.

Given their obvious importance, what then *are* signs in Deleuze's interpretation of Proust's work? Perhaps surprisingly, they are neither nominative nor referential in function (that is, they do not simply name or identify the objects of our experience), nor are they the signs (consisting of a conjoined signifier and signified) associated with the Saussurian-inspired 'structuralist linguistics' prominent in the early 1960s. Instead signs here serve as forceful *relays between* subjects and objects, between subjects and other subjects, or even within subjects (in respect to their own faculties), thus bringing them into some kind of relation, inviting or soliciting attention as to their directives and meanings. This is why Deleuze emphasises that signs are differentiated by their various functions – grouping them accordingly – and that these functions relate to how they permit access to or delimit different perspectives, or potentially 'shared' worlds, and common qualities.

Nonetheless, signs do share certain features that can traverse such elements: i) that they have an active dimension (they often *do* something to – both *with* and *within* – the recipient, even if he or she does not comprehend what it is); ii) that they somehow *indicate or even envelop* something other than themselves (this being what makes them signs, rather than simply qualities or objects); and iii) that they bear specific *relations to time*, fundamentally denoting temporal relations, and do so because they either accompany or directly involve various processes of anticipation, association, sympathy, recollection or retrospection.

The most important feature of such signs, however, uniting all of these characteristics, is that they are neither transparent nor readily forthcoming in their presentation – instead they seem to veil or obscure, enigmatically suggesting meanings as yet inaccessible. In this regard, they call for interpretation– thus the apprentice (whom Deleuze likens to an 'Egyptologist') strives to identify or locate this meaning in an attempt at understanding what is being experienced or observed. Ultimately, the 'search for lost time is presented as a system of signs' (PS 84) and these signs are like hieroglyphs, demanding of us their deciphering and interpretation.

Deleuze identifies four main *types* of signs in the novel: these are the signs of worldliness, amorous signs, sensuous signs and, finally, the signs of art. It is Marcel's slow success at traversing and navigating each sign-milieu, from social signs through finally to those of art, that characterises his own apprenticeship, and thus transforms him into an artist (and his life – his experience, learning and understanding – into the raw material for his writing).

The first type of sign concerns 'worldliness' – in both senses of the word: as pertaining to the 'worldly' (to experience and material values), and to the generation of lived 'worlds' (different forms of social existence and social identity). Basically, these are the most material sort of signs because they primarily concern appearances – that is, they suggest something else without actually providing or presenting what they suggest and, in this sense, they take the place of the idea or action itself. Thus, these signs stand – indeed, often substitute – for the things they seemingly designate. At Madame Verdurin's literary salon, for example, the participants provide 'clever' little signals that they are amused without the vulgarity of actual mirth (a nod of the head, a gesture with the hand, or a glance held for but a few seconds by another, serves to acknowledge one's wit and thus one's potential worth). Indeed, Madame Verdurin herself often hides her (possibly immobile) face in her hands as if suggesting her amusement is uncontrollable. These, then, are the 'worldly' signs of social interaction that constitute the social bond, and demarcate social worlds wherein various visible behaviours mark the 'implicit' laws of social etiquette and deference, legitimising and controlling entry to or exclusion from a clique, group, community or class. The signs of worldliness multiply and replace one another with great rapidity, and provide the (ever-changing) rules and fashions, the currency by which individuals may be granted or denied access to specific social situations, or more generally to the shared 'worlds' of other communities. As such the realm of worldly signs is one of passwords, tokens and sigils that grant the bearer power of entry and movement.

Most importantly, though, such signs make *genuine thought seem unnecessary*. Instead, making appropriate noises and engaging in (the semblance of) activity substitutes for authentic contact – for high society and the art world are partitioned realms where being seen to be doing or saying something – is far more important than actually having anything worthwhile to say. The exchanging of such signs is a wasting of time *together* that need not involve thinking but rather the circulation of received thought and emotion: one merely has to know the *right* way to present oneself, the *right* topics to discuss, the *right* things to say and the *right* responses to display, within any given milieu. However, these rules are ultimately arbitrary (in as much as they could have been otherwise, and elsewhere might well be different) and thus require careful and persistent attention in order to grasp their appropriate usage. One small misstep at the wrong time or in the wrong situation risks social humiliation or even ostracism. The risk of success or failure attached to these interactions engenders what Deleuze calls a 'nervous excitation', granting them an almost ritualistic formalism – for how these signs are recognised and utilised is far more important than any content potentially ascribed to them. Ultimately, the implication is that the social bond is fundamentally vapid, and, because such signs are conventional in their origins and significance, that they are tantamount to social stereotypes or communicational clichés. In this sense, then, worldly signs can often appear vacuous or stupid because they denote experiences where authentic thought and action are absent, even irrelevant – and Proust suggests that this is as true of friendship as any other social scenario. Nothing profound occurs therein and yet these signs still constitute a fundamental part of the Search, for they make us increasingly attentive to the mysteries of signs, and educate and sensitise us as to their appropriate employment and interpretation.

The second type of signs are those associated with love. Two characteristics of such signs are particularly striking. First, these signs concern the profound amorous connections we form with a specific individual (usually beginning with one's primary caregiver – for Marcel, his mother – and serially 'repeated' or reiterated thereafter, perhaps in a crush, followed by the first fumblings of love, then a carnal relationship, and so forth, in as much as each subsequent relationship contains thematic threads or residues of the previous ones, whil anticipating those yet to come). The key word here is 'individual' because such amorous or erotic relations require that we first *individuate* someone, that we isolate them from their group or environment and increasingly attend to the singular characteristics that seem to define or set them apart (in Marcel's own case, first Gilberte and then Albertine, and in Swann's, Odette). Indeed, these characteristics usually become compulsive lures that capture and absorb more and more of our time and attention, as through attachment we strive to merge with the 'One' we are besotted with.

Secondly, this foregrounds a concept which Deleuze already introduced in his discussion of the social signs of worldliness but which he now grants even more significance: that our interaction with other human beings suggests 'possible worlds' associated with them (that is, that there exist 'realities' beyond or independent of our own lived existence, which have their own meanings, rules and priorities). In particular, as we individuate the 'beloved' we become aware that he or she inhabits (or is inhabited by) 'worlds' shaped by their own very different meanings and concerns and priorities, and of their relations with others, and we find ourselves trying increasingly to identify and understand these in order to gain access to them.

However, there are two limitations that constrain and even define our relations with the beloved 'other' and his or her worlds: 1) that more by default than design these same worlds often exclude us, only further serving to fuel our desires (because each attempt at understanding an aspect of their existence and thus penetrating further into their interiority merely introduces further contiguous and enigmatic features demanding interpretation), and 2) that homosexuality sets a potential limit to how much we can ultimately feel we 'know' them. These two limitations each evoke an intense feeling of 'jealousy' which accompanies love as its lining, and usually proves more profound than love itself. For jealousy increasingly compels us to seek evidence of infidelity or betrayal in the other's every glance, and expose the potential falsehood in each and every word they say. It continually provokes the imagination, filling the mind with painful fantasies. In this sense, Deleuze suggests that the beloved's statements are always accompanied by the possibility of deception, and anticipating these prospective 'lies' invokes a more intense level of interpretation than does love itself (which complacently promises a misguided harmony) – for jealousy, and the suspicion and suffering it causes, is far richer in signs demanding of interpretation.

Jealousy, that 'mad, sad desire to possess', is particularly provoked by our sense that, in being potentially excluded from the other's world, we are therefore not everything for them even though they are everything for us (that is, we cannot be sure that we really hold a special or central place in their affections and concerns), and as a result we fear that our place could as easily be filled or taken by another. In a sense, we keep asking of the beloved (in search of reassurance): *what am I (if anything) for you?*

Moreover, the mystery posed by another's sexuality can also provoke jealousy – for example, Marcel's anxieties about Albertine's lesbian proclivities which he struggles to understand, and lead him to virtually imprison her.[5] In this sense, homosexuality also marks the extreme limit of potential exclusion from the beloved's world. In respect to this limit Deleuze does not mean that heterosexuality presents some kind of normative standard against which the former is then measured – although we should keep in mind that he is primarily examining Proust's treatment of the subject (which itself reflects Proust's own reputed yet hidden sexual preferences, and his depiction of a sexually prejudiced society) – but instead suggests that jealousy meets its zenith in the fact that we suspect some further 'other' (a third person) can share a bond with the beloved that excludes us because we are fundamentally different from both of them, although they may yet be alike (in respect to their gender and the identification it offers). This otherness testifies to the separation of the sexes – a division Proust represents through the figure of the hermaphrodite in whom both sexes coexist but in a non-reproductive relation, and from whom the two sexes emerge as two lines that never intersect thereafter.[6]

Ultimately, the signs of love – when salted with jealousy – generate an excessive proliferation of interpretation, in which nothing is spared scrutiny. Whereas worldly signs invite attentiveness and the need to 'read' social signs appropriately, amorous signs increase the level of scrutiny and interpretation because we focus our 'intimate' attention with such intensity upon another's way of being. In an important sense, scrutinising them teaches us how to look ever more closely, and thus amorous signs mark yet a further stage in the journey and the ongoing development of the apprentice.

The third kind of signs are those of sensuous impressions, of which the signs of involuntary memory are the most famous and potent examples.[7] The latter seem to suggest an unconscious association of past and present ideas or situations, which many critics have assumed to be the primary focus – indeed, the centrepiece – of the work's thematic concerns, thus suggesting that it is fundamentally Bergsonian in inspiration.[8] The novel is replete with such moments of sensuous evocation that fill the narrator with an intense joy or spiritual ecstasy – hearing the Vinteuil Sonata, the sight of three trees on the horizon, the sound of shoes and wheels on the cobblestones in the street, the texture of a folded napkin, the sound of a spoon against china – and these continually cause Marcel to try (and, until the novel's end, fail) to understand the enigma of their power and seeming contingency. The best-known example, of course, is Marcel's sense of overwhelming joy when he dips a 'petite madeleine' (a kind of sponge-biscuit with scalloped edges) in to his tea and then imbibes the combination:

> No sooner had the warm liquid mixed with the crumbs touched my palate than a shudder ran through me and I stopped, intent upon the extraordinary thing that was happening to me. An exquisite pleasure had invaded my senses, something isolated, detached, with no suggestion of its origin. And at once the vicissitudes of life had become indifferent to me, its disasters innocuous, its brevity illusory – this new sensation having had on me the effect which love has of filling me with a precious essence; or rather this essence was not in me it was me. . . . Whence did it come? What did it mean? How could I seize and apprehend it? . . . And suddenly the memory revealed itself. The taste was that of the little piece of madeleine which on Sunday mornings at Combray (because on those mornings I did not go out before mass), when I went to say good morning to her in her bedroom, my aunt Léonie used to give me, dipping it first in her own cup of tea or tisane. The sight of the little madeleine had recalled nothing to my mind before I tasted it.[9]

In this example, the flavour of the tea conjures through its sensuous infusion the recollection of a similar experience from childhood that overwhelms Marcel with its intensity. It seemingly 'bridges' time, first juxtaposing and then seemingly conflating and purifying two temporally distant moments.[10] Deleuze carefully points out, however, that it is *not* a shared concept that is revealed in the drawing together of the two 'experiences' but in fact 'the identity of a *quality* common to two sensations, or a *sensation* common to two moments, the present and the past' which then *triggers* the recollection and produces a corresponding image (PS 74, italics added). And, moreover, this recollection itself is not of Combray as it was ever empirically experienced in the past but instead felt as an absolute, as the very essence inhabiting and contracting the two experiences (seemingly far removed in time) and giving them a supersaturated significance.

Deleuze does not deny that there is a Bergsonian element at work here, but suggests that its role and significance have been poorly grasped within critical circles.[11] Involuntary memory testifies, he argues, to the ontological nature of the past – of a pure past that has never, in fact, been 'present'. Deleuze establishes an important distinction here that separates the workings of involuntary memory from the efforts of voluntary recollection. The latter consists of the storage of present experiences as 'snapshot'-like images or representations within the mind. When we engage in an act of voluntary remembering we are comparing or associating a current or extant perception with a 'present' perception that we experienced previously (that is, one that is no longer 'now' but which was cognitively registered). However, this generates a confusion in our comprehension of time, for we think of the *past* as simply something that comes after the present, as constituted *after* the fact.

Unlike voluntary recollections, involuntary memories do not directly evoke (or mirror) what actually came before – a previous moment stored as an image within the empirical mind – but instead an essence that bridges two disparate moments in experiential time, an essence that links them both virtually and thematically but which was never experienced in itself *because it constituted a temporality that was never actually 'present' either now or previously.*

In this sense then, involuntary memory does not refer to a 'no longer present' moment but a pure past (in a sense all the iterations of a possible experience) that serves as a transcendental precondition for time's passage, and thus constitutes the very *being* of the past itself. This past does not follow the present that it supposedly was but coexists with it, insisting as an ontological reservoir that allows presents moments to pass without itself passing, subsisting as the coexistence of all moments. This is why the recollection of Combray is imbued with such sublime intensity:

> [It] appears as it could not be experienced: not in reality, but in its truth; not in its external and contingent relations, but in its internalized difference, in its essence. Combray rises up in a pure past, coexisting with the two presents, but out of their reach, out of reach of the present voluntary memory and of the past conscious perception.

> 'A morsel of time in the pure state' . . . is not a simple resemblance between the present and the past, between a present that is immediate and a past that has been present, not even an identity in the two moments, but beyond, *the very being of the past in itself*, deeper than any past that has been, than any present that was. 'A morsel of time, in the pure state,' that is, the localized essence of time.
>
> '*Real without being present, ideal without being abstract.*' This ideal reality, this virtuality, is essence, which is realized or incarnated in involuntary memory. *Here as in art, envelopment or involution remains the superior state of essence.*
> (PS 61, italics added)

Such an essence 'unfolds' a world immanent to the empirical, an underlying reality or truth, but only in the form of a glimpse of something that recedes or withdraws almost as soon as it appears. This essence is an internalised difference dwelling within 'dark regions, [and] not in the temperate zones of the clear and distinct' (PS 100), and which straddles or underlies the two elements in an empirical temporal series, revealing them in fact to be simultaneous and coexistent within the 'ontological' pure time that provides the very condition of experience.

Deleuze aligns such essences with Leibniz's notion of a universe made up of an infinite number of monads each with its own unique perspective upon the same fundamental reality:

> But what is an absolute, ultimate difference? Not an empirical difference between two things or two objects, always extrinsic. Proust gives a first approximation of essence when he says it is something in a subject, something like the presence of a final quality at the heart of a subject: an internal difference, '*a qualitative difference* that there is in the way the world looks to us, a difference that, if there were no such thing as art, would remain the eternal secret of each man' . . . In this regard, Proust is Leibnizian: the essences are veritable monads, each defined by the viewpoint to which it expresses the world, each viewpoint itself referring to an ultimate quality at the heart of the monad. As Leibniz says, they have neither doors nor windows: the viewpoint being the difference itself, viewpoints toward a world supposedly the same are as different as the most remote worlds. This is why friendship never establishes anything but false communications, based on misunderstandings, and frames only false windows. This is why love, more lucid, makes it a principle to renounce all communication. Our only windows, our only doors are entirely spiritual; *there is no intersubjectivity except an artistic one.*
> (PS 41–2, italics added)

However, despite the seemingly spiritual character of such recollections – which crucially suggest the possibility of an eternity transcending experience – their very transience and ephemerality and the tantalising and elusive glimpses they provide (that is, that they contingently and unexpectedly arise and just as quickly subside) suggest that the signs of involuntary memory do not take us far enough, that they do not ensure sufficient necessity to be able to sustain a vision of the absolute.

The issue here is the persistent materiality of the sign, for, although the bridging of two elements is premised in respect to sensuous signs of involuntary memory upon a shared *quality* and the intimation of the underlying essence that it provides, the link still derives from a material connection that obstructs any enduring relationship with the absolute. Such involuntary recollections can only give us the 'image' of eternity, rather than eternity itself. However, the significance for the Search of sensuous signs, and the encounters with involuntary memory that they evoke, resides not in their failure to provide us with eternity but, rather, that the brief and elusive image of it which they provide nonetheless *points to its very existence* – in other words, they testify to a spiritual (that is, virtual) continuity: in short, a realm of ontological coexistence that unites all things. As such, the real connections suggested by sensuous signs persist beyond their actual material qualities, thus presenting yet another stage in the progression of the Search, albeit one that penetrates beyond the more material signs of worldliness and love.

These differential essences glimpsed in respect to such sensuous signs suggest the possibility of immortality, of a mysterious persistence beyond physical decay and death, but it is only with the signs of art – which are capable of uniting, systematising, transmuting and purifying the contributions of the three previous types of signs[12] – that the Search finds its fruition, its *raison d'être*. This implicit unity, and its congruent power of purification, is what distinguishes the signs of art from all the other types of signs – of worldliness, amorous signs and sensuous signs – which are still *tied* to their material 'origins' both in their seeming 'character' and the manner of their unfolding or 'explication' (that is, we are inclined to believe that their truth somehow either resides within or is dependent upon their materiality itself, or otherwise emerges directly from our own subjective associations between a material 'impetus' and a memory). In contrast, the signs of art both transcend this material substrate while contributing to the final revelation that all signs ultimately emerge from (and point towards) an immanent, transcendental realm. Indisputably, in the first instance we perceive in the work of art the material sounds of a beautiful melody or turn our gaze towards the viscous paint on the canvas, but when we are fully receptive to the work of art and its signs we are somehow transported beyond these. The material elements fall away or dissolve as the truth encompassed within the work reveals itself to us. As Deleuze says more than once, signs are half-sheathed in objects but also half-sheathed in something else (PS 27, 36, 39–40), *a realm of immaterial essences that produce meanings* apprehended by (and coiled within and thus constitutive of) the subject. Signs emerge from these essences at work, and testify to their eternal, virtual subsistence such that it 'is essence that is the last word of the apprenticeship or the final revelation' – indeed, 'essence is the birth of Time itself' (PS 38, 45).

The signs of art provide a spiritual communion that enables us to overcome the suffering engendered by the previous types of signs: for worldly signs invariably lead to dissatisfaction once we realise (as does Marcel towards the novel's close) that social discourse (even communication among friends) is a largely futile attempt to hold back the movement of time by filling it with shared 'ideas' and concerns that prove themselves to be nothing more than fads or, worse, a jockeying for meaningless status amid the most banal of entreaties or dismissals; similarly, love is accompanied by disillusionment and the anguish of jealousy, although, perversely, jealousy is itself eventually revealed to be insignificant when one's fascination with the beloved fades and indifference or contempt takes its place; and even the evocations of involuntary memory serve only to intensify our frustration when they refuse to yield their secrets to intellectual reflection.

Marcel suffers all of these disillusionments in his pursuit of social status, of true fidelity, and the overwhelming joy of recollection, and yet more often than not when he receives what he craves he is intensely disappointed (such as when his mother accedes to his demand for a goodnight kiss or his beloved Albertine gives ground to his seduction) and almost immediately begins to lose interest in the objects he has long sought to understand or conquer. Proust's implicit suggestion about such painful misadventures is that suffering in various forms (frustration, disappointment, betrayal) is the necessary precondition of wisdom and self-understanding, and it is a message that Deleuze readily seems to endorse. But for both Proust and Deleuze art finally offers, if not salvation from suffering, then perhaps a form of redemption; not because it avails us of the satisfaction we were previously denied (although it can potentially ameliorate this) but because it grants us final understanding of ourselves and the nature of time. It is only with, and through, the signs of art that suffering can be understood and overcome, for these signs carry us beyond their actuality so that we can see the hidden continuity of things. The self, the empirical ego, is dissolved within this grand vision that Deleuze will refer to (in subsequent works) as a 'chaosmos'.

This is true immortality: the insight that we see how we are part of the entirety of things and the unfolding of difference within the structures of time associated with each of the types of signs – of *worldly signs with wasted time*, *amorous signs with lost time*, *sensuous signs with time recollected*, and finally the *signs of art with time fully regained* and restored in its purity – marks a gradual dematerialisation and increasing journey 'inwards' (if, by the latter, we refer not to the interiority of the personal psyche but rather the immanent interconnectedness of all things). For, in a sense, there never really was anything lost – this was but an illusion or misperception generated by at least one or more stages of the Search. Art finally reveals to us that nothing was ever truly wasted or missing but simply not yet clearly grasped – for the truth of time was there all along waiting to be revealed.

At its end, every part of the Search – all the failures, detours, frustrations and disappointments are revealed to be necessary and imbricated steps in coming to recognise the truth of the Search, the necessity of apprenticeship (hence the contingency of the encounter, on the one hand, and the necessity of what is then revealed, on the other – the conditions of actual experience such that it could not have been otherwise):

> All the stages must issue into art, we must reach the revelation of art; then we review the stages, we integrate them into the work of art itself, we recognize essence in its successive realizations, we give to each degree of realization the place and the meaning it occupies within the work. (PS 66)

This is why the final volume of the novel which deals with the narrator's insights concerning the role and importance of art (and his realisation that all the events, sufferings and epiphanies of his life constitute the raw 'material' of his vocation) is called 'Time Regained', for

> [t]he artistic essence reveals an original time, which surmounts its series and its dimensions. This is a time 'complicated' within essence

> itself, identical to eternity. Hence, when we speak of 'time regained' in the work of art, we are concerned with that primordial time that is in opposition to time deployed and developed – to the successive, 'passing' time, the time generally wasted. (PS 62)

The immaterial signs of art (which transcend understanding while being immanent to experience) finally provide the truth of the Search, because they bear witness to Time's own essence, and give us a genuine intimation of the implicit unity of Time – and the unity provided to us *by* Time – that we cannot otherwise empirically experience (borne as we are within time's own movement).

The Role of Thought

> *There is a Proustian vision of the world. It is defined initially by what it excludes: crude matter, mental deliberation, physics, philosophy.* (PS 91)

In the final chapter (of the original edition) of *Proust and Signs*, Deleuze returns to a theme that recurs throughout: namely, Proust's criticisms of philosophy – indeed, Proust's belief that art is ultimately superior to philosophy because the former is able to provide (and account for) truths that the latter cannot. In part, Proust's critical view of philosophy stems from his scepticism concerning the workings of the intellect (and the faculty of understanding in general). On a number of occasions in *À la recherche du temps perdu*, for example, Proust mocks idle speculation or intellectual generalisation, either by associating these with the most pompous, complacent and self-satisfied of characters, or through revealing their unfortunate consequences when they lead to conclusions that prove misleading or ill-founded. However, as Deleuze notes, these negative depictions usually pertain to the use of the intellect in ways for which it is ill-suited – thus the real target of Proust's contempt is, in fact, not intellect as such but rather the misapplication of understanding when it is employed as a kind of idly speculative or unfounded activity divorced from the exigencies of actual encounters.

It is just such misapplications that lead the narrator to fundamentally misconstrue the nature of many of his experiences, and fall deeper into the trap of what Deleuze calls 'objectivism' and 'subjectivism' (distortions and biases that beset all of the faculties but seem particularly acute in respect to the intellect): in the case of the former, the narrator's mistaken assumption that the truths of signs reside *within the objects* or persons that emit them (and moreover, that such individuals understand these truths themselves), and in the latter his overcompensating movement towards the opposite extreme in concluding that all such truths are but *subjective chains of association* implicit within his own thinking.[13] This is why Deleuze repeatedly emphasises that for Proust the application of the intellect should come *after* rather than before an encounter, because *understanding is a retrospective process* driven and guided by the interpretation of signs.

> In Proust, *thought in general appears in several guises: memory, desire, imagination, intelligence, faculty of essences.* But in the specific case of time wasted, of 'lost time,' it is intelligence and intelligence alone that is capable of supplying the effort of thought, or of interpreting the sign. *It is intelligence that finds — provided that it 'comes after.'* Among all the forms of thought, only the intelligence extracts truths of this order. (PS 23, italics added)

But these tendencies also involve another more fundamental and persistent problem related to the understanding: that its misconceived activities and goals are shaped by related presuppositions about the very nature of thought and truth; presuppositions which provide the dubious foundation for the dominant rationalist tradition of philosophy: that is, that philosophy and its pursuit of knowledge are premised on a presumed affinity with truth.

Deleuze refers to this constellation of presuppositions as an 'image of thought' – a notion he derives from his earlier book *Nietzsche and Philosophy* wherein he sees Nietzsche as objecting to the high opinion that philosophy has of itself, particularly its characterisation of its own endeavours as a noble and upright commitment to the pursuit of knowledge, in which it willingly embraces and exercises the natural capacity for understanding and the desire for truth – the philosophical birthright – purportedly inherent in all men. This is, Nietzsche insists, a self-serving (and self-indulgent) mythology in which nothing is really placed at stake – least of all philosophy's own assumptions.[14]

In contrast to such philosophical hubris, Deleuze sees Nietzsche as advocating an alternative image of thought wherein thinking is 'never the natural exercise of a faculty. Thought never thinks alone and by itself . . . Thinking depends on forces which take hold of thought' (NP 108). Similarly, Deleuze sees Proust's work as offering a different image of thought from that of the philosophical tradition (PS 94);

indeed, one which raises the poet above the philosopher in respect to the pursuit of truth, because it refutes the latter's foundational presuppositions: namely, that the philosopher 'wants the truth' and assumes 'in advance the goodwill of thinking' (a nuptials premised on the unquestioned assumption that there exists a natural affinity or accord between thought and its subject-matter, and between thinker and world).

Rather than bearing an innate affinity with (or desire for) truth, Proust views thought as characterised by an inherent stupor, a complacency that resists the effort of interpretation and which is all too willing to settle for what is recognisable and familiar, such that it often mistakes its own preferences and habits for truth. Instead, it is only when the subject is provoked, forced even, to confront something enigmatic that it can potentially exceed its own banality and narcissism.

This explains, I believe, why Deleuze embraces Proust's account of an apprenticeship to truth presented in terms of a difficult and fraught Search, subject to confusion, tangents, missteps and false starts, and without a predetermined method or outcome, because it opposes one of the most fundamental and influential descriptions of philosophical 'learning' in Western philosophy: namely, Descartes's reasoning exemplified in the 'method of doubt' presented in his *Meditations on First Philosophy*.[15] This method essentially involves Descartes isolating himself from the world at large and then, while alone and inert, *voluntarily* seeking via intellectual means what is indisputably certain and true. Through the application of 'reason', a process he accords to all men in principle, he strips away anything which is illogical or introduces the possibility of ambiguity or doubt: first, by excluding the contributions of the senses because perception presents unreliable data – things can appear to be one way and then turn out to be another (for example, that wax which usually appears solid and without odour when placed close to a flame becomes liquid and develops an intense smell) – and then gradually through a process of subtraction retreating towards what constitutes a logical 'certainty' – that his own capacity to think cannot be refuted (hence, the famous 'cogito'). Through the voluntary application of reason – *choosing a subject at will and then reflecting upon it* – Descartes arrives at the disembodying fantasy *of thought*, thus affirming the deep-seated prejudice against the sensuous within Western philosophy.

Although at first glance Descartes's 'method' seems to evoke the compositional practice of an artist or author – and involve a similar process of 'purification' – the underpinnings of what is presented is, in fact, completely at odds with what Deleuze finds in Proust's novel, where the narrator must continually engage with the world itself, beset by unexpected sensations and the struggle with interpreting signs, subject to painful or joyous encounters that make demands upon him that he cannot understand or even conceive of in advance, and which culminates in profound encounters with the signs of art.

The exercise of such voluntary 'meditations' lacks value for Proust because it is too closely tied to the conventional, to the explicit, to the abstract, and the easily designated. Indeed, the voluntary exercise or application of the understanding in advance of any given situation will invariably fall short of providing any kind of genuine insight, will fail to grasp truth; instead serving only to affirm its own pre-existing ideas and prejudices. This is why Proust sees communication among such like-minded 'thinkers' (even among the closest of friends) as largely vapid and superficial. Nothing profound can come of it. Instead, in Proust's depiction of the apprenticeship and the role of signs, a different way of conceiving of thought is offered up – one in which the contingency of our encounters with the various kinds of signs *violently compels us to think* and to pursue truth: 'The leitmotif of Time regained is the word force: impressions that force us to look, encounters that force us to interpret, expressions that force us to think' (PS 95). This is why the encounter with signs is so crucial to the development of the apprenticeship, for being external to thought they force it beyond its innate stupor. The Proustian apprenticeship and its search for truth thus provides a counter-philosophical (even anti-philosophical) 'image of thought' that does not *know in advance* what it will find (or even perhaps what it is looking for): 'The sign is the object of an encounter, but it is precisely the *contingency of the encounter that guarantees the necessity of what it leads us to think* . . .' (PS 97, italics added).

This, then, is the second fundamental revelation of the Proustian Search (already implicit in the first, concerning the relationship between art and truth and essences and time), that all of these elements discover their own truth in the notion of the *involuntary*. This is why Deleuze insists that Proust's novel is not primarily concerned with the role of involuntary memories but instead *with involuntary encounters* – and all such encounters begin at the level of the sensory, by way of signs, marking social encounters, amorous encounters, and sensuous encounters, before finding their ultimate fulfilment in the signs of art:

> Only the sensibility grasps the sign as such; only intelligence, memory or imagination explicates the meaning, each according to a certain kind of sign; only pure thought discovers essence, is forced to conceive essence as the sufficient reason of the sign and its meaning. (PS 100)

Genuine thought always begins with the involuntary: we are forced to think by something essential that is external to thought (PS 95); for it is only when faced with whatever is fundamentally alien to our expectations or comprehension that we respond in a creative or novel rather than habitual manner.

The involuntary is thus the necessary overcoming of a fundamental limitation that resides within thought's ordinary workings, for thought functions in respect to the different faculties or types of cognitive activity as a means of constructing mental representations (for example, here is an image of what is perceived, here a recollected image of what is no longer perceived, here an imagined image of what was never perceived, and so on). In this sense, thought is not unique to any given faculty but can arise from any and all of them, as long as each faculty contributes to the mediating requirements of representation. Thus, in respect to their voluntary application, the faculties work together in concert, constituting a harmony or general accord in which each contributes to and converges upon the construction of an identifiable and 'recognisable' object (that is, each faculty merely adds information premised on the assumption of representing the same, single 'pre-existing' object of our attention: this is a chair; this is an apple; this is a finger, and so forth). However, genuine or authentic thought (which Deleuze refers to as 'pure thought') emerges in a fundamentally different manner, and in response to foreign priorities – in fact, in defiance of the requirements of representation in general. In the involuntary encounter (which Deleuze likens to Plato's famous description of the mind being compelled to think when confronted by perplexing 'contrary sensations' [PS 100–1]) each faculty is pushed into an unfamiliar exercise that potentially breaks with this convergent accord, initiating a process that generates a thought finally capable of grasping essences. As a result, instead of settling for what is familiar or recognisable, the faculties contribute differentially such that we can no longer automatically presume to know or understand what the object of the encounter is. Each faculty is violently compelled to seek its own truth but does so in a manner also indicative of its own respective nature, and in discovering and attaining 'its own limit, it rises to a transcendent exercise, it understands its own necessity as well as its irreplaceable power' (PS 99). Moreover, like a chain-reaction or a zigzagging lightning bolt, the force of each faculty's own transcendent 'detonation' is transferred to, and triggers that of, the next, and from this movement thought emerges, disjunctively relayed across the various faculties – of sensing, of remembering, of imagining and so on – until it reaches its purity in the grasping of essences, and unmediated contact with difference – for '[c]reation is the *genesis of the act of thinking within thought itself*' (PS 97, italics added).

Genuine thinking only occurs when we are compelled to forgo our reliance upon mental clichés. The involuntary encounter with something external to thought provides this impetus, inducing a vertiginous movement that draws from each faculty something specifically novel and unique to itself but which also resists its automatic subordination within a synthetic act of voluntary mental reflection. Throughout *À la recherché du temps perdu* Marcel confronts just such involuntary encounters in respect to each of the different types of signs that provide the Search with its very dynamism and which finally culminate in the revelatory signs of art:

> The greatness, on the other hand, of true art . . . lay, I had come to see, elsewhere: [through art] we have to rediscover, to reapprehend, to make ourselves fully aware of that reality, remote from our daily preoccupations, from which we separate ourselves by an ever greater gulf as the conventional knowledge which we substitute for it growers thicker and more impermeable . . .[16]

It is only under the compulsion of an involuntary encounter that the understanding is able to escape its complacency; otherwise, when left to its own devices intellectual endeavour degenerates into mere laudanum for the soul. It is only when thinking is forced to its limits under the pain of a necessity that comes from *outside* its own borders – through sensory experience – that it can begin to approach truth and authenticity. For philosophy to be wise, thought must first be made to suffer, and the subject must be forced beyond its own innate inertia wherein it too often settles for that (representation) which presents itself as agreeable to all and sundry, and allows the status quo to go unchallenged.

Ultimately, Deleuze agrees with Proust that art is superior to philosophy in the pursuit of truth; for it is art which provides us with the most profound encounters, capable of shocking even philosophy beyond its tawdry dream of omniscience and confronting it with the truth of the complex metaphysical and 'aesthetic' reality that simultaneously composes and permeates our very existence:

> Our vanity, our passions, our spirit of imitation, our abstract intelligence, our habits have long been at work, and it is the task of art to undo this work of theirs, making us travel back in the direction from which we have come to the depths where what has really existed lies unknown within us.[17]

Notes

1. Throughout this article I refer (and restrict my commentary) to the original edition of *Proust and Signs* (1964) – Gilles Deleuze, *Proust and Signs* (Minneapolis: University of Minnesota Press, 2000). In a subsequent edition published in 1970, a further section – almost equal in length to the first – was added (and amended in a minor manner in 1976). This second section shifts the analysis towards examining the nature of the supposed unity (or rather the lack of a centre) in the novel.
2. In *Proust and Signs* we find Deleuze introducing – if sometimes in a nascent manner – many notions that will subsequently be developed in *Difference and Repetition* (subject to certain revisions): such as the theory of multiple, interconnected temporalities or syntheses (and most importantly of a transcendental or 'pure time'); a new 'model' of learning; a theory of signs and difference; of serial relations in respect to the understanding; a theory of the 'other'; of possible worlds and multiple points of view; of implication and explication (that is, folding and unfolding); of the distinction between virtual and actual; an account of determinability; of repetition as figuring a differential 'theme'; of representation as an image of thought; of a Kantian-informed facultative model; and, most crucially, the belief that all chains of thought begin with unexpected sensual encounters linked in some way to an ontological memory. Moreover, some of these concepts are subsequently developed in other works besides *Difference and Repetition* – for example, the notion of sign-regimes which is reworked in *Anti-Oedipus* and then again in *A Thousand Plateaus* (and which also serve as prototypes of some of the signs described in the two 'Cinema' books).
3. Marcel Proust, 'Time Regained', vol. 6, p. 254. All references in this chapter are to Marcel Proust, *In Search of Lost Time*, 6 vols (London: Vintage, 1996).
4. The titles of these seven volumes are in sequence (and in English translation): 'Swann's Way'; 'In the Shadow of Girls in Flower' (or 'Within a Budding Grove'); 'The Guermantes Way'; 'Sodom and Gomorrah'; 'The

Prisoner'; 'The Fugitive'; and 'Time Regained'. In certain editions 'The Prisoner' and 'The Fugitive' are published together in a single volume. Also, the section in the first volume that deals directly with the life of Charles Swann – whose life and fate serve as a sort of counterpoint to the narrator's (and which, unlike the rest of the novel, is written in the third person) – is sometimes published as a separate volume.

5. Moreover, this leads Proust to suggest that homosexual loves are perhaps more profound than heterosexual ones because of their *clandestine nature*. In fact, in the novel Proust depicts homosexuals as recognising one another by way of secret 'astral signs' which either mystify heterosexuals or to which they are blind.
6. Deleuze seems to anticipate here Lacan's infamous view of the unbridgeable divide between the sexes.
7. Deleuze also claims that there is another kind of sensuous sign that does not conjure involuntary memories, although this qualification often goes unnoticed in commentaries. The second type are what he calls sensuous signs of 'desire and imagination' (among which we might include captivating images – such as the Steeples – or extended flights of fancy) in which a cascade of allusions is born from a sensuous impetus and then serially relayed through successive associations.
8. This is a confusion in part engendered by the translation of the novel's title. Proust himself objected to the rendering of the title in English as *Remembrance of Things Past* (an allusion to Shakespeare's sonnet) rather than the more literal *In Search of Lost Time*. It is difficult not to share Proust's bewilderment as the English version suggests a different thematic focus for the novel – memory and recalling the past – rather than Proust's own explicit priorities concerning Time itself and the search in the present for the possibilities of the future. The title was not, after all, 'In search of lost memories' but 'In search of lost time', thus suggesting a search for the nature of time – but of course it is a search that must be carried out within time, and it is this immersion in and organisation by time that both shapes the contour (and inflects the overall flavour) of the Search.
9. Proust, 'Swann's Way', vol. 1, pp. 51–4.
10. However, Deleuze also notes that if the present moment somehow triumphs over the past evocation within the encounter then the outcome is more likely to be extreme suffering or grief over what is seemingly lost or gone (such as when Marcel in bending over to tie his shoelaces tearfully reminiscences about his grandmother's death).
11. Bergson was, in fact, Proust's cousin by marriage and, although Proust presumably was familiar with Bergson's famous work, he denied any overt influence of the latter's philosophy upon the writing of *À la recherche du temps perdu*.
12. This seems to suggest that Deleuze sees the signs of art as bearing some

relation to Kant's notion of the 'aesthetic idea'. However, this is too complex an issue to explore here.

13. Similarly, this accounts for the narrator's frustration in his repeated attempts at understanding the role of involuntary memory – that is, his misguided belief that such enigmatic evocations can somehow be summoned or translated into readily accessible and familiar concepts if he simply persists in reflecting on them or tries to replicate the mental or psychological conditions under which they first appeared – because he fails to grasp that this marks a limitation internal to the voluntary application of the intellect itself.
14. Gilles Deleuze, *Nietzsche and Philosophy* (London: Athlone Press, 1983). See pp. 103–10 for Nietzsche's discussion of the 'image of thought'.
15. René Descartes, *Meditations and Other Metaphysical Writings* (London: Penguin, 1998).
16. Proust, 'Time Regained', vol. 6, p. 253.
17. Ibid., p. 255.

Charles Péguy

Craig Lundy

Charles Péguy is referred to by Gilles Deleuze on twenty-one occasions, spread across ten books from *Difference and Repetition* (1968) to *What is Philosophy?* (1991). Although Deleuze's usage of Péguy is somewhat narrow, he is employed at significant locations in the analysis of repetition and events, both of which are areas of capital importance to Deleuze's broader philosophy. In this respect, while Deleuze is not a Péguyist and ignores many of Péguy's main contributions to thought, Péguy nevertheless plays a vital role in the formation and explanation of Deleuze's thinking.

I.

Born in 1873, Charles Pierre Péguy was the son of a peasant family from Orleans. His father died the year after his birth, having never fully recovered from traumas sustained in the Franco-Prussian War of 1870–1, and Péguy was raised by his mother and grandmother. From an early age Péguy was a talented student and he won a series of scholarships that eventually led to his admission at the prestigious École normale supérieure (ENS) in 1894. An academic career beckoned, but these aspirations were dashed when he failed his *agrégation* in 1898. Péguy instead pursued a career in publishing, founding the journal *Les Cahiers de la Quinzaine* in 1900. Although the *Cahiers* struggled financially and rarely had more than a thousand subscribers, it was nevertheless a well-known and modestly influential publication, with contributions from notable authors that included Romain Rolland, Anatole France, Georges Sorel, Jean Jaurès, Jean and Jérôme Tharaud, Julien Benda and Henri Bergson (though without his prior knowledge[1]). The *Cahiers* frequently published controversial commentary on contemporary socio-political issues, with Péguy the serial offender, and the journal prided itself on both its independence from political parties and its willingness to publish contrary views.[2] The *Cahiers* also served as Péguy's personal loudspeaker, and in its pages can be found the majority of his prose writings. With the arrival of war in the summer of 1914 the *Cahiers* closed its doors and Péguy volunteered for frontline duty. He would not live much longer, falling at the Battle of the Marne in September – a key battle on the outskirts of Paris that contributed significantly to halting the German blitzkrieg.

To say that Péguy was a complicated and idiosyncratic figure would be an enormous understatement, illustrated by the seemingly contradictory causes that his name is associated with: Péguy was at once a socialist and a Catholic, a Dreyfusard and a supporter of the army, an urban *avant-gardiste* and a peasant of *l'Ancienne France*, a staunch Bergsonian to the end, though only with regard to the philosopher's early works. If viewed from the other direction, we could say that Péguy was none of these things, as they are conventionally understood; rather, he was a specialist in heresy who never shied from decrying the perversions of each cause as and when he perceived them.

Taking the first of these listed causes, it is said that Péguy was introduced to socialism as a teenager by the town blacksmith Boitier, who served as a male mentor for Péguy in the absence of his father.[3] While at the ENS, which was at that time a leftist bastion, these predilections were greatly intensified. Along with fellow classmates such as Léon Blum, the young Péguy was a great admirer of Jean Jaurès and Lucien Herr (the revered socialist librarian of the ENS).[4] Péguy's early work testifies to this socialist commitment: his first literary creation, the dramatic play *Jeanne d'Arc* (1897), was dedicated to all those who had fought for the establishment of 'the universal socialist republic', and his first academic publication was a review essay for the *Revue socialiste*.[5] After quitting academia, Péguy promptly opened a socialist bookshop, investing the entirety of his recently acquired dowry. Although the bookshop was a thriving hub of socialist activity, as a commercial venture it failed completely. To stave off bankruptcy a socialist consortium including Herr and Blum raised new finances and assumed management of the shop. The new arrangement proved short-lived. Aside from operational disagreements (Péguy could not countenance his own essays being subject to review by an editorial board), it soon became clear that Péguy's political and philosophical positions were at odds with the socialist orthodoxy. Things were brought to a head in December 1899, when the first General Congress of French Socialist Organisations banned intraparty debate in order to promote socialist unity. Adhering to such censorship was impossible for Péguy, and by the first week of January he had severed his ties with the party and opened the *Cahiers*.

From the offices of the *Cahiers*, opposite the Sorbonne, Péguy launched a series of scathing critiques against prominent and powerful figures in politics and academia. High on his hit list were the 'parliamentary socialists' whom he had recently separated himself from. According to Péguy, the parliamentary socialists were guilty of betraying the collectivist cause for their own personal political gain. This behaviour, Péguy thought, was clearly exemplified by the manner in which the socialist vanguard handled the Dreyfus Affair and its aftermath. In 1894 Captain Alfred Dreyfus, an officer of Jewish decent, was convicted by military court of selling official secrets to the Germans. Two years later new evidence came to light that strongly suggested the framing of Dreyfus and an attempted cover-up. For the remaining years of the century France was rocked by this scandal and the nation was divided into two camps: the largely republican and socialist Dreyfusards who campaigned for the innocence of Dreyfus, and the anti-Dreyfusards who defended the integrity of the army and generally supported the Church in its disagreements with the young Third Republic. Péguy was the most fervent of Dreyfusards and, with his socialist comrades, readily engaged in street battles. According to Péguy, what they were fighting for was not merely the release of Dreyfus from captivity; to fight for Dreyfus was to fight for justice, which is to say a France that was just. Dreyfus was thus synonymous with justice, and at stake was nothing less than the fate of France, the soul of France, and its legacy as a great and just nation. Péguy's ambition, as such, was to facilitate a collective and public acknowledgement by the nation at large that Dreyfus was innocent, and that this innocence must be defended and proclaimed if France was to prove worthy of herself. In his words: 'Where we were concerned, the question was never whether Dreyfus was innocent or guilty. But whether people would have the courage or not to declare and to know him to be innocent.'[6] Péguy was therefore willing to sacrifice himself for Dreyfus, but this sacrifice, in his eyes, was made in order to save the nation, not just one man. To quote Péguy at greater length:

> And we, what did we say? We said that a single injustice, a single crime, a single illegality, particularly if it were officially confirmed, particularly if it were universally, legally, nationally condoned, a

> single crime is enough to make a breach in the social compact, in the social contract, a single forfeit, a single dishonor is enough to dishonor a people. It becomes a source of infection, a poison that corrupts the whole body. What we defend is not only our honor, not only the honor of a whole people, in the present, but the historical honor of our whole race, the honor of our forefathers and children.[7]

Unfortunately for Péguy, France did not emerge from the Affair with her honour intact. In 1899 Dreyfus was given a second trial and again found guilty. By this time, however, the 'parliamentary socialists' were in a position to procure a presidential pardon for Dreyfus, on condition that he confess to the accused crime. This was a compromise that Dreyfus was willing to accept, but Péguy could not, for it did not deliver the required recognition of innocence. And to make matters worse, Dreyfus's release had been secured by use of a monarchical mechanism. Thus while the Dreyfusards were in one respect victorious, in so far as the freedom of Dreyfus was successfully attained, for Péguy the movement ended in failure. In fact, the Dreyfusards, in the opinion of Péguy, suffered a fate worse than defeat: their cause had been colonised, hijacked from within by paper parliamentarians and redirected towards a new aim – the attainment of political power.

The Dreyfus Affair was without question the seminal event of Péguy's life, and its impact on his thinking cannot be overstated. Indeed, it is through reflecting on this event that Péguy comes to formulate a novel theory of events. At the start of 1910 Péguy published an essay by Daniel Halévy in his *Cahiers* titled 'Apology for our Past'. In this essay, Halévy, who was a friend of Péguy's at the time, offered a *mea culpa* for his Dreyfusard past, roughly on the grounds that their actions had endangered French unity and was thus not in the nation's best interests. Péguy felt compelled to reply and six months later published a response, 'Memories of Youth' (*Notre jeunesse*). One of the reasons Halévy agreed to write his essay was that he figured enough water had passed under the bridge – the Affair, in other words, was now history, and so could be treated as such: historically. But, for Péguy, it was precisely this operation – the conversion of Dreyfusism from a living and breathing movement into a museum piece – that required an explanation and apology. Péguy's response to Halévy thus does not simply consist in providing a different version of events. It most certainly does this, but, more importantly, in doing so Péguy creates new categories for understanding and approaching the event: *mystique* and *politique*.

As noted above, Péguy was extremely bitter about the political compromise that deflated the Affair. The treason committed by the 'parliamentary socialists' was double. Firstly, they betrayed the nation by accepting a 'temporal salvation' of France when it was her 'eternal salvation' that was at stake.[8] Secondly, and perhaps of equal importance to Péguy personally, the 'parliamentarians' betrayed the true Dreyfusards by stealing their name and legacy. In 'Memories of Youth' Péguy is thus desperate to distinguish between the genuine and false Dreyfusards, and he does so by employing the terms *mystique* and *politique*:

> *Appearances* no doubt are on Halévy's side; those who appear are on his side. What I mean is that if one only considers the Dreyfusists who are to the fore, in the public eye, the journalists, publicists, lecturers, candidates, parliamentarians and politicians, all those who talk about chatter and scribble and publish, the immense majority who appear on the scene, almost the whole lot hurried to take part in the Dreyfusist demagogy, and by that I mean the political demagogy that issued from the Dreyfusist *mystique*. But what I contest is that those who *appear* in history (and whom history seizes upon, in return, with such avidity) have a great importance in the depths of reality. At that depth, where the only important realities are found, I maintain that *all* the mystical Dreyfusists remained Dreyfusists, that they remained mystics, and kept their hands clean. What does it matter whether appearances, *phenomena*, whether all the officials, all those out for profit, should have abandoned, denied, betrayed and ridiculed the *mystique* in favor of the *politique*, and of the policies which issued from it, and of political demagogy? *That*, my dear Halévy, as you yourself would say, *is life*. What does it matter if they sneer at us? We alone represent something, and they do not. What does it matter if they turn us to ridicule? They themselves live through us, and only exist by virtue of our existence. Their very vanity would not exist but for us.[9]

In truth, Péguy is not entirely clear in this essay about what he means by *mystique* and *politique* (especially the former term). But as this quote suggests, the terms more or less correlate to the distinction between creation and capture. For Péguy, 'everything begins as a *mystique* and ends as a *politique*'.[10] A *mystique* is furthermore said to be 'organic' and 'alive', in contrast to a *politique* which is 'logical' and 'parasitic'. Taking the example of the Dreyfus Affair, Dreyfusism began life as a *movement* that exuded its own *mystique*. But at a certain point the *mystique* of Dreyfusism became devoured by the *politique* to which it gave birth, it became a political programme, a policy that captured and tamed the *esprit* of Dreyfusism. In time this *politique* claimed the name 'Dreyfusism' for its own, effacing its *mystique* in the process, but this is precisely because a *politique* excels at capturing rather than creating – that is its nature, what it does. As Péguy elaborates:

> It came in to profit, and, like all profiteers, came in afterward. It came in as a parasite, as a follower. It did not come to fight or to found. That is the usual historical error, the common intellectual mistake, where history is concerned: to attribute the shadow cast by the abuses of the profiteers to the virtues of the founders. The founders came first. The profiteers follow on.[11]

The 'intellectual mistake' that is being referring to here is 'the historical optical illusion which consists in constantly transferring the present into the past, the ulterior to the anterior'.[12] By virtue of this illusion, it appears as though the currently recognised and victorious Dreyfusards (the ones that appear in our history books) planned the whole Affair and saw it through to glorious fruition. But these merchants of *politique* feed off the work of others; just like the temporal category of the present, they '[substitute] for the real organic movement of history, with its perpetual movement from past to future, falling on the uneven fringe of the present, a hard angular shadow at each moment thrown by the present on the past, like a shadow of the corner of the wall, of the house or gable which seems to be on the street.'[13] Thus while history may have designated Péguy a traitor to the cause, since he did not support the 'party of Dreyfus', Péguy argues that it is *they* who are the traitors, since they betrayed the *mystique* of Dreyfusism in order to serve their own political and temporal ends. 'All parties live by their *mystique* and die by their *politique*',[14] which is to say that a *mystique* is what one should die for, while a *politique* is what one lives off of.[15]

In setting out his thoughts on the Dreyfus Affair, Péguy is clearly motivated by personal grievances: the 'parliamentary socialists' were extremely late in arriving to the defence of Dreyfus,[16] but they received much of the credit to the detriment of Péguy's own place in history. In reflecting on how this has happened, Péguy concludes that his effacement from history can be explained by a common mistake regarding the appraisal of events – a misconception, moreover, that is 'perhaps the greatest of intellectual illusions': namely, the failure to distinguish between the *mystique* and *politique* of events, and, following, the tendency to confuse a presiding power for that which created it. 'In all those ordeals it is the inward force, the violence of the eruption which constitutes the thing, the historical matter, rather than the matter which constitutes and imposes the ordeal.'[17]

At this point it is necessary to mention two other agendas that are at play in Péguy's theory of events and reflections on the past, one religious and the other intellectual. The term *mystique*, it will have been noted, has overtly religious connotations. This is no accident. Péguy was an industrious writer. However, at the end of 1907 his pen came to rest and he produced almost nothing for two years. During this hiatus Péguy revealed to a friend that he had recovered his faith,[18] and in 1910 Péguy relaunched himself as a Catholic poet – the persona by which he is more widely known today. This makeover was of moderate success. Although he quickly gained a new readership and came to entertain aspirations of winning the prestigious Grand prix littéraire of the Académie française,[19] Péguy quickly alienated his new Catholic friends since he was unwilling to apologise for his Dreyfusard and socialist past. In fact, a good deal of his essay 'Memories of Youth', published shortly after his first major piece of Christian poetry, attempts to reconcile the *mystique* of Dreyfusism with the *mystique* of Christianity. The details of this union are not of great importance here, but it is useful to bear in mind that Péguy's attitude towards Christianity and the Church is coordinate with his appraisal of Dreyfusism and the 'party of Dreyfus': if the Christian faith 'appears' to be antithetical to Dreyfusism and the Republican *mystique*, this is because it has been converted into a *politique* by the clergy. What is required is thus a rejection of Church dogma and a renewal of the Christian *mystique* – the intended purpose of his poetry.[20]

In this task of spiritual renewal Péguy saw himself as following the lead of Henri Bergson. As Péguy succinctly puts it in a letter to Bergson: 'You are the one who has reopened the source of spiritual life in this country.'[21] Péguy first encountered Bergson in 1898 at the ENS, where Bergson briefly worked before his appointment in 1900 to the Chair of Greek and Latin Philosophy at the Collège de France. Péguy was a regular attendee of Bergson's lectures, often in the company of Georges Sorel,[22] and he considered himself to be Bergsonian to the core, going so far as to suggest that he was, 'after Bergson himself, and I would dare say almost with Bergson himself, the only Bergsonian who also knows what he's talking about'.[23] The insights appropriated by Péguy from Bergson are many, but chief among them is the ambition of Bergsonian philosophy to confront reality directly, free of the 'ready-made' and inherited constructions that obscure and confine reality. Taking this lesson to heart, Péguy declares war on all those intermediary parties that inhibit such direct confrontations with reality, which is to say reality in its duration, as *mystique* and movement. From this we can start to see why Péguy's Bergsonism is compatible with his Dreyfusism and Christian faith: it is by following Bergson and his method of intuition that Péguy seeks to elaborate a Dreyfusism and Catholicism free of the institutional powers that dictate dogma and prevent a direct communion with *mystique*.

Despite Péguy's aspirations to become a recognised and successful Catholic poet, the placement of Bergson's work on the Catholic Index in 1914 provoked Péguy to mount a defence of his mentor. Although Péguy was not a great admirer of Bergson's *Creative Evolution* (1908) and had become close friends with the self-proclaimed anti-Bergson Julien Benda, he could not stand for the ingratitude shown to Bergson by his detractors and thus set out to show them just how large their debt was. In the last six months of his life Péguy wrote two 'Notes' on Bergson, the first directed at his intellectual critics (principally Benda) and a second targeting his attackers from the Church. The second Note would go unfinished, stopped mid-sentence on account of Péguy receiving his mobilisation order for the war. In considering these two essays and Péguy's other various engagements with Bergson's philosophy, it cannot be said that Péguy was the most accurate reciter of Bergson. Péguy also had a tendency to extend Bergson's ideas beyond their initial parameters, most notably applying Bergsonian notions to the level of socio-political and cultural collectives. Nonetheless, Péguy's faithfulness to the spirit (if not letter) of Bergsonism cannot be questioned – a 'filial fidelity' that Bergson himself was willing to acknowledge: '[Péguy] knew my most secret thought, such as I had never expressed it.'[24] This Bergsonism would also play a key role in Péguy's other major and longstanding intellectual agenda – his critique of modernity and the 'modern' Republic.

Following her defeat in the war of 1870–1, France understandably engaged in some soul-searching to ascertain what caused the disaster. Among the reasons proffered, it was agreed by members of the young Third Republic that Germany's intellectual superiority could not be ignored as a factor.[25] High on the republican agenda was thus the renovation of France's educational system – a process that had been under way before the war, but was sharply accelerated by its outcome. In the early decades of the Third Republic the Napoleonic *Université* was dismantled and replaced with a new academic regime that favoured positivism, scientism and historicism in the humanities.[26] These transitions, which closely echoed the overhaul of the Prussian educational system following France's victory at Jena in 1806, were not easily achieved and had no shortage of opponents, none more vigorous than Péguy. Péguy was by no means opposed to the widening of educational access – he himself came from a poor family that relied upon external financial support for his education. But what Péguy objected to were the 'modern' values upon which the new system was based and the manner in which they were forcefully and dogmatically implemented by the Republic.

Between 1904 and 1907 Péguy wrote a series of essays that attacked the new 'modern' regime in French academia and politics.[27] Central to these essays is Péguy's critique of the twin ideals of 'progress' and 'science' – or, to be more specific, the belief that modern scientific methods both vindicate and assure the inevitability of human progress. In language strikingly reminiscent of Nietzsche (though curiously unacknowledged by the author), Péguy argues in these essays that the 'modern world', far from delivering 'progress', leads to degradation and ultimately a belief in nothing.[28] But, aside from his dim view of modernity, what further disturbed Péguy was the cosy connection that existed between republican politicians and the new intellectual vanguard – the secular priests of the Sorbonne, as Péguy called them, which included the likes of Durkheim, Lanson, Lavisse, Langlois and Seignobos. Given the frequency of regime change in France since the Revolution, the young Third Republic was naturally eager to effectuate an irreversible break with 'Old France' and ensure its long term survival. To this end, the scientistic and progressive mantra of 'modern' academia was a natural fit for the Republic and could easily be put to political use. As a result, several of the leading 'modern' academics played an active role in formulating government policies that culminated in the sharp separation of Church and State.[29] Surveying this process, Péguy concluded that republicanism, in its desire to be the midwife of the 'modern world', had become a victim to its *politique* – an outcome proven by its virulent repression of Christianity and insistence upon a new scientific image of truth. Péguy's response was typical of the man: 'WE REFUSE TO ACCEPT DOGMAS FORMULATED BY THE TEACHING STATE QUITE AS MUCH AS THE DOGMAS FORMULATED BY THE CHURCH.'[30] Thus, as before, we can see that for Péguy the problem was located not at the level of *mystique* – of republicanism, for instance, as a creative force – but rather in the cynical appropriation of such durational movement and its replacement with a *politique* that was more than willing to use the new version of 'truth' to its advantage: 'One may never know what acts of cowardice have been motivated by the fear of not appearing sufficiently progressive.'[31]

II.

Péguy appears regularly in Deleuze's oeuvre. Aside from important appearances in *Difference and Repetition*, *The Logic of Sense* and *What is Philosophy?*, Péguy is also referred to by Deleuze in his books on *Francis Bacon* and *Foucault*, the two cinema books, the essay 'He Stuttered' (see *Essays Critical and Clinical*), and in two interviews: 'Control and Becoming' (see *Negotiations*), and 'Foucault and Prisons' (see *Two Regimes of Madness*). In all but two minor instances, Deleuze appeals to Péguy within a discussion of either the nature of 'repetition' or the nature of 'events'. Nearly all of these references, furthermore, pertain to Péguy's essay *Clio* – a piece, published posthumously, that encapsulates the various themes discussed above. For the remainder of this chapter I will therefore give a brief introduction to Péguy's *Clio*, after which I will examine the two major uses that Deleuze makes of Péguy.

Péguy wrote two versions of *Clio* between 1910 and 1912. The first version initially appeared under the title *Véronique: Dialogue de l'histoire et de l'âme charnelle*, while the full title of the second version (which is the only one Deleuze draws from) is *Clio: Dialogue de l'histoire et de l'âme païenne*. As these titles spell out, the essay is a dialogue between Clio, who in Greek mythology is the personification of History as a muse, and a 'carnal/pagan soul' – Péguy himself. Although the dialogues ambulate across a number of themes, the critique of modern historiography is a driving concern. As Clio laments in the opening of the first version: 'How times have changed! What has become of me? I no longer recognize myself . . .'[32] French academia, as I noted above, experienced a significant phase of transformation in the late nineteenth and early twentieth century. This was especially true of History, which underwent a process of reinvention whereby its trappings as a literary enterprise were discarded in favour of the 'scientific method'. Such a transition was hardly unprecedented – academic History in Germany, to give the most relevant example, had recently completed their own conversion, and the French hoped to replicate their success.[33] The 'modern' approach to History aimed to minimise the historian's subjective influence in deference to the objective facts. Accordingly, History was conceived as an encyclopedic endeavour in which knowledge of the past is incrementally obtained through the collective effort of impartial specialists that rigorously apply the scientific method to studies of the past, culminating in a unified depository of historical facts – the Book of History, one might call it. My description here is no doubt overly simplistic, but so too was that of many leading proponents of modern historiography. The influential Ernest Renan, for instance, had the confidence to predict in 1890 that 'In another century mankind will pretty well know everything that can be known about its past.'[34] The end of History to such modern enthusiasts thus appeared nigh (roughly coinciding, oddly enough, with the date later suggested by Fukuyama), and this was made possible by, on the one hand, a conceptualisation of the past as ontologically static, and, on the other hand, an elevation of the historians' capabilities via a scientific methodology that afforded access to the static past.

Péguy's retort to the new regime of History in France focuses on these two aspects – the ontology of history and the method for engaging with it.[35] Following Bergson, Péguy argues that the past is never fully done with, but rather forms a durational continuity with the present that unfolds into the future. The image of the past as composed of static and discrete facts is thus a misleading fiction, for it fragments reality into separate pieces that do not correspond with the true nature of reality-in-duration. While 'modern' historians are busy compiling their encyclopedia, the past as a part of synthetic duration continues to move on without them:

> The event follows its course. The event runs like a river, if it is still possible to use this expression, and I [the 'modern' historian] am line fishing. Whatever happens continues to happen. And I continue to be on the wrong page . . . Thus am I, with my index cards, one who runs on foot after an automobile.[36]

Péguy's critique of modern historiography extends to the valorisation of 'manuscripts' and so-called 'primary sources'. Again, the problem pinpointed here by Péguy is the replacement of durational reality with a fixed artifact. When 'modern' historians engage with such manuscripts they commonly consider themselves to be engaging with history itself, but as Péguy notes, such manuscripts are more exactly, and nothing more than, 'the first copy of the first edition for the recording of history'.[37] As Péguy goes on to say:

> Will we ever know how many times and in how many languages and under how many forms the work was played before falling onto the paper, at this time, under this form, in this medium of paper? This time, that you call the first, enters into a series of countless times. It is in no way an origin, it is not a source point, it is not a creation from nothing.[38]

So for Péguy, as we can see, it must be remembered that the coveted manuscripts of modern historiography are not originary; rather, they are the byproduct of a creative process. They may be able to give us a snapshot of a historical event, but for this very reason they are poorly placed to convey the durational life, the *mystique*, of that event. Modern historiography, in its extreme form, is also based on an impossible dream, for it is simply not feasible to provide an exhaustive account of a historical event. If one wishes to say anything about the past, then decisions will need to be made, and they will be made based on incomplete information. The historians' craft, therefore, is one of selection, narrativisation and distilling the whole from a part; from among the brute facts, a story must be woven together that is faithful to the *mystique* of the event. And when these selections and distillations are made, according to Péguy, the historian reveals herself to be an artist. If the historian was merely a transmitter of bald facts about the past, then it would be literally impossible to write a history book, since one would need a day to write the history of a second, a year to write the history of a minute, and so on.[39] But thankfully, so Péguy thinks, proper historians of the grand style, such as Jules Michelet for example, show us another way; they show us an *art form* of listening to the musings of Clio, so as to connect with the vitality of a historical event.

To give us a better idea of what he has in mind, Péguy unsurprisingly offers a literary example: reading. What is it that makes someone a good reader of a literary classic? Take Hugo's *Les Châtiments*. The historicist would have us believe that in order to understand this text one must gain a detailed knowledge of French history since the Revolution, as well as before that, and Roman history while you're at it. A familiarity with Hugo's life and those connected to him would also be required, including what they all ate for breakfast, if that information is available, and so forth. And once this detail is adequately digested, then one may read *Les Châtiments* with confidence (if one is so bold). For Péguy, on the other hand, the good reader of *Les Châtiments* begins by reading *Les Châtiments*, preferably a version with no preface or editorial commentary attached, and aims to stay as close to the text as possible at all times. The good reader allows the text to breathe, to escape the suffocation of history. When this happens, the reader communes with the text, '*enters into it*'.[40] Engagements with the past, so the analogy goes, should occur the same way – one should commune with history and incarnate the past in the same way that a good reader collaborates with the author of a masterwork:

> What a marvelous fate, and almost frightening, that so many great works, so many works of great men and of very great men, find their fulfillment, their completion, their culmination, in us, my poor friend, and our way of reading. What a frightening responsibility lies upon us.[41]

Such subjective tampering by the present would be anathema to the resolute historicist of the modern vintage, but without this communion, Péguy argues, historical events (as well as works of art like *Les Châtiments*) are destined to die. For as Péguy surmises from Bergson, the passing of time – or ageing (*viellissement*), as Péguy terms it – is unceasing and inescapable. A best-case scenario is therefore that a past event (or artwork) is *revived* by the present: the good reader/historian reanimates the past event/work by breathing their own life into it, so as to hear it sing again in new surrounds. And when this happens, it is as if 'Homer is new this morning, and there is nothing perhaps so old as today's newspaper'.[42] The philosophy of history and reading that *Clio* offers is thus not one of revolution or reform, but resurrection; it is a theory of ageing and renewal. This does not mean, it must be noted, that Péguy proposes a cyclical theory of history, and nor does he suffer from the 'historical optical illusion' (of transferring the present into the past). Instead, he gives us a theory that venerates creativity, and more exactly *continual* creativity, since the inescapable fact of ageing demands that yet another effort be made, and then another.

It is this attunement to creativity that attracts the interest of Deleuze. The first and most frequent context in which Deleuze refers to *Clio* concerns repetition, and in two respects: one pertaining to style and the other to ontology. Although he is not widely known today, Péguy's quality as a writer has been celebrated by many esteemed individuals over the years, including André Gide,[43] T. S.

Eliot,[44] Walter Benjamin,[45] Michel Foucault[46] and Bruno Latour, who went so far as to describe Péguy as 'the greatest French prose writer and no doubt the deepest philosopher of time'.[47] Two features of Péguy's writing style bear mentioning for our purposes: duration and repetition. To begin with, Péguy's writing exemplifies the unravelling divergences of a Bergsonian duration. Those familiar with Péguy's oeuvre will concur that his essays have a tendency to veer off course, sometimes abandoning the topic announced in the title to pursue some other interest that has organically emerged. Péguy is also willing to dispense with the conventional form of chronological narration – most notably in *Notre patrie* (1905), where he recounts the events of a few days in the order that the various thoughts cross his mind (rather than the chronological order in which they 'actually' occurred). The aim of Péguy's writing style is thus to install us within a vital flow, a moving train of thought. He does not present the reader with perfectly formed and polished diamonds – the 'ready-made'. Rather, Péguy pulls the reader down into the depths of his thinking, where it is working, so that the reader can experience first-hand its struggle towards the surface.

The predominant linguistic mechanism that Péguy employs to enable this direct confrontation with reality in its duration is repetition. As may have been intimated from the block quotes above, Péguy writes in long sentences that proceed through the repetition and slight variation of a word or phrase. He also frequently interrupts himself mid-sentence and then recommences by repeating what he said before the interruption. As a result, the reader is forced into a position of suspense – of suspending final judgement and holding on to a provisional motif as it is expanded. Furthermore, the repeated words, being privy to the previous iterations as well as the insights of the interruption, find themselves in an increasingly enriched environment that in turn opens up new avenues for exploration and association. This technique could be well described by the terms 'intensification' and 'complexification', but even better would be the term 'condensation', drawing from the Bergsonian example of a condensing cloud,[48] for this notion has the advantage of also conveying the gradual creation of a new form.

And therein lies the significance of Péguy's writing style for Deleuze's thoughts on repetition: it is through the repetition of words and phrases that Péguy opens up a space for experimentation leading to the new. Because Péguy's repetitions operate in duration, in a serial form, they highlight the differences between each iteration within the sequence, as well as what has occurred in the meantime. They also draw attention to the different milieus in which they occur and mark the transition points from one series to the next. Repetition, as such, is used as a means for engendering difference and transformation, or, as Maurice Blanchot puts it, *growth through insistence*.[49] Deleuze makes much the same point but using different terminology. In *Difference and Repetition*, Deleuze describes Péguy's repetitive style as one of 'contiguity', 'in which the step-by-step creation of an internal space within words proceeds by tiny differences' (DR 22), while in his essay 'He Stuttered' Deleuze nominates Péguy's writing style as an example of how to 'grow from the middle' – specifically, through the use of substantives, 'each of which defines a zone of variation until it reaches the neighborhood of another substantive, which determines another zone' (ECC 111).[50] And when raised within the context of *The Logic of Sense*, Deleuze says of Péguy that he was able 'to invent an entire language, among the most pathological and aesthetic that one might dream of, in order to explain how a singularity is prolonged in a line of ordinary points, but also how it begins again in another singularity, how it redistributes itself in another set' (LS 53).

But Deleuze's debt to Péguy on the nature of repetition goes far beyond his writing style. As he remarks in the introduction of *Difference and Repetition*, Péguy 'makes repetition not only a power peculiar to language and thought, a superior pathos and pathology, but also the fundamental category of a philosophy of the future' (DR 5). What does Deleuze mean here by this connection of repetition and the future? In order to show how a philosophy of repetition is at one and the same time a philosophy of the future, of engendering the future, Deleuze's opens *Difference and Repetition* by explaining how repetition, if anything, is not generality. Generality, according to Deleuze, concerns 'the qualitative order of resemblances and the quantitative order of equivalences' (DR 1). In the realm of generality, particular instantiations of a general idea can be exchanged or substituted provided that they satisfy the criteria of resemblance; the particulars resemble one another, or can be said to be equivalent, with respect to the generality that they are particularities of. A repetition, on the other hand, does not merely 'resemble' or 'equal' an original occurrence – it *repeats* it. We might be tempted to say that a repetition is the 'same' as that which it repeats, but there is one crucial difference between the two: only one is a repetition; one is 'older' than the other. For this reason, they each have a singularity that is non-exchangeable and non-substitutable. In Deleuze's words:

'To repeat is to behave in a certain manner, but in relation to something unique or singular which has no equal or equivalent' (DR 1). At this point of his explanation Deleuze makes a crucial shift: thus far repetition has been conceived of and discussed at the level of externalities, but what if such manifest repetition was animated by 'a more profound, internal repetition within the singular' (DR 1)? It is here that Deleuze calls on Péguy, citing two examples from *Clio* of this internal repetition: Federation Day in France (Bastille Day), which commemorates the storming of the Bastille in 1789, and Claude Monet's *Nymphéas*, a series of approximately 250 paintings of water lilies.

The significance of these two examples is found in their ability to illustrate a repetition of the 'unrepeatable'. Each time the French commemorate the falling of the Bastille, it is not as if the Bastille falls all over again, just like the first time. On the contrary, if the fall of the Bastille is celebrated, it is because of the *uniqueness* of this historical event. Similarly, Monet's *Nymphéas* are not simply reproductions of the first painting in the series. Rather, they are repetitions of a singularity, each of which differ in their repetition and in so doing contribute to a 'growth through insistence' and 'creation of an internal space'. This leads Deleuze to say that 'repetition interiorizes and thereby reverses itself', so that it is 'the fall of the Bastille which celebrates and repeats in advance all the Federation Days [and] Monet's first water lily which repeats all the others' (DR 1). But we must be very careful with this statement: the theory being put forward here is not one of reverse causality or retrospective realignment; it is not that the falling of the Bastille has been refashioned by the present to be a repetition in advance of Federation Day. Such an interpretation, as we know, would fall foul of the 'historical optical illusion'. Péguy's point is instead that the falling of the Bastille is an event of such significance that it demands in advance that it be commemorated in the future.[51] Or when Monet creates his first painting of water lilies, there is something about it that calls for further iterations, that calls forth its repetitions in advance – repetitions that do not aim to resemble, equate or clone the initial creation, but pay homage to and revitalise its legacy, like the best contemporary renditions of a jazz standard.[52] In short, there is a power (*puissance*) or *mystique*, internal to the initial event, that produces in advance its repetitions – a repetition raised 'to the "nth" power', or 'repetition as universality of the singular' (DR 1).

A few pages later Deleuze extends his analysis of repetition contra generality by setting out four 'principal propositions'. Péguy is invoked in this passage, but always in parentheses and only where a similarity can be drawn with Nietzsche and Kierkegaard, who are the guiding figures for the propositions. His influence here is thus minimal and ancillary.[53] Deleuze's praise of Péguy is then repeated in Chapter 2 ('Repetition for Itself'), again alongside Kierkegaard, the two of which are referred to as 'the great repeaters' (DR 95). But it is also on this occasion (and only this occasion) that Deleuze finds cause to admonish Péguy. By this stage of Chapter 2, Deleuze has just finished setting out his three syntheses of time (present, past and future). Elaborating this theory is beyond the scope of our current investigation; however, by way of summation Deleuze states that 'in this final synthesis of time, the present and [past] are in turn no more than dimensions of the future: the past as condition, the present as agent' (DR 93).[54] Or, put differently, 'The present is the repeater, the past is repetition itself, but the future is that which is repeated' (DR 94). Péguy fits this picture quite nicely due to his strong link between repetition and the future – his 'reversal' of repetition, in which repetitions call forth and are in aid of an emerging future. The past is a condition for this process and the present is the agent who repeats, who commemorates Bastille Day as it were, but *what* is repeated is the future, in so far as it is the future repetitions of an event that are engendered in advance. Despite this favourable appraisal, however, Deleuze goes on to say that Péguy was ultimately 'not ready to pay the necessary price' (DR 95), and this is because when faced with a pure and passive form of time, Péguy turns away and fills this empty form with his Christian faith. As such, Péguy successfully evades the grounding of time in the repetitions of habit and/or memory, but he subsequently replaces them with a supreme foundation: God, which in turn grounds the self.

> Undoubtedly, faith possesses sufficient force to undo habit and reminiscence, and with them the habitual self and the god of reminiscences, as well as the foundation and the ground of time. However, faith invites us to rediscover *once and for all* God and the self in a common resurrection. (DR 95)

Péguy may mirror Nietzsche in many ways, but he is definitely no anti-Christ.[55] Indeed, a central theme for Péguy's Catholic poetry is the status and meaning of God's incarnation as Christ. As for the inspirational hero of Péguy's dramatic and poetic works, Joan of Arc, her importance derives from the manner in which she communes directly with God, confronts the Church and renews Christian faith.

This tale of spiritual salvation is thus entirely contrary to Nietzsche's conclusive finding: the eternal return, which 'is not a faith, but the truth of faith' (DR 95), and hence a level of repetition far surpassing Péguy's, which eventually rediscovers the self and God (as Péguy did during his 1908–10 hiatus).

This criticism indicates the extent to which Deleuze is willing to follow Péguy's thoughts on repetition. From this point forward, the primary purpose of Péguy for Deleuze will concern the nature of events. Deleuze, to be precise, quotes the same passage from *Clio* on six separate occasions. The first three of these (DR 189; LS 53, 340) occur within extrapolations of the *problematic* nature of events. The passage reads as follows:

> Suddenly, we felt that we were no longer the same convicts. Nothing had happened. Yet a problem in which a whole world collided, a problem without issue, in which no end could be seen, suddenly ceased to exist and we asked ourselves what we had been talking about. Instead of an ordinary solution, a found solution, this problem, this difficulty, this impossibility had just passed what seemed like a physical point of resolution. A crisis point. At the same time, the whole world had passed what seemed like a physical crisis point. There are critical points of the event just as there are critical points of temperature: points of fusion, freezing and boiling points; points of coagulation and crystallization. There are even in the case of events states of superfusion which are precipitated, crystallized or determined only by the introduction of a fragment of some future event.[56]

Péguy is but one of several important sources for Deleuze's 'problematic' philosophy. The primary progenitor for both Péguy and Deleuze, however, is Bergson.[57] According to Bergson, problems do not pre-exist their solutions; rather, the two are co-emergent. This means that the articulation of a solution goes hand in hand with the articulation of the problem. So contrary to the convention of 'finding' solutions to 'ready-made' and inherited problems, Bergson contends that the task of philosophy is to find problems, not solutions, and learn how to *state* them properly, to *invent* them:

> But the truth is that in philosophy and even elsewhere it is a question of *finding* the problem and consequently of *positing* it, even more than of solving it. For a speculative problem is solved as soon as it is properly stated. By that I mean that its solution exists then, although it may remain hidden and, so to speak, covered up: the only thing left to do is *un*cover it. But stating the problem is not simply uncovering, it is inventing. Discovery, or uncovering, has to do with what already

> exists actually or virtually; it was therefore certain to happen sooner or later. Invention gives being to what did not exist; it might never have happened. Already in mathematics and still more in metaphysics, the effort of invention consists most often in raising the problem, in creating the terms in which it will be stated.[58]

To pose a problem properly is thus to solve it, or more accurately *dissolve* it, and this activity is synonymous with the distillation of a problem's distinctive features – the critical and/or remarkable points that comprise a problematic constellation.

Given that Bergson is the explicit source for Péguy's problematic philosophy, it might seem slightly strange that Deleuze prefers to cite Péguy rather than Bergson himself, but the reason for this is that the above passage from *Clio* effectuates a seamless transition from 'the problem' to 'the event'. While the first half of the quote describes the dissolution of a problem and the passing of a crisis point, the second half extends this description to events – like problems, events are composed of distinctive points, or 'singularities'. Péguy's discussion of events in *Clio* also has the added advantage of positing a dualistic ontology of the event. As we've established, a major objective of Péguy's *Clio* is to elaborate a Bergsonian notion of historical duration in contrast to the dominant model of modern historiography. Péguy thus distinguishes two kinds of time, or approaches to time: one of duration, which is rich and has depth, and the flat spatialisation of time that isolates and objectifies discrete elements. When transferred to the realm of history, this dichotomy becomes, on the one hand, the durational movements and generative forces *of* history (*mystique*), and on the other hand that which 'appears' *in* history (*politique*). And in Deleuze's terminology, this distinction in turn becomes 'ideal events' or simply 'the Event', and 'real events' or 'states of affairs'. We can then say that solutions are to problems as 'real events' or 'states of affairs' are to 'ideal events' or 'the Event'. Now, there are clearly differences between these various dichotomies, and not insignificant ones. But at minimum we can agree that Péguy gives voice in *Clio* to features of the (ideal) event that will be absolutely crucial for Deleuze, including its 'problematic' nature, its distinction from and relation to states of affairs, and the manner in which transitions occur via 'critical points' from one series or set of singularities to another.

Several of these features will be at play when Deleuze returns to *Clio* at the end of his career (WP 111–13, 156–7; N 170–1). These later usages, however, also reveal a shift in emphasis and framing. In a 1990 interview with Antonio Negri, Deleuze remarks that he 'became more and more aware of the possibility of distinguishing between becoming and history' (N 170). Other interviews from this period testify to Deleuze's growing interest in the distinction,[59] and it will also feature in his final book with Guattari *What is Philosophy?*. When Deleuze returns to Péguy's *Clio* in that book, it will be in aid of explaining this important dualism. Deleuze previews in his discussion with Negri how he will use Péguy in *What is Philosophy?*. In response to a question about Nietzsche's notion of the Untimely, Deleuze invokes the dualism of history and becoming, after which he says: 'History isn't experimental, it's just the set of more or less negative preconditions that make it possible to experiment with something beyond history' (N 170).[60] It is this remark that precipitates the entrance of Péguy's *Clio* to the conversation. We are now told that, according to Péguy's *Clio*,

> there are two ways of considering events, one being to follow the course of the event, gathering how it comes about historically, how it's prepared and then decomposes in history, while the other way is to go back into the event, to take one's place in it as in a becoming, to grow both young and old in it at once, going through all its components or singularities. (N 170–1)

As with the corresponding section of *What is Philosophy?*, the guiding framework here is *experimentation*. At this stage of *What is Philosophy?* (the conclusion to Part One) Deleuze and Guattari are concerned with reinforcing their views on the experimental nature of philosophy as a practice: 'To think is to experiment, but experimentation is always that which is in the process of coming about – the new, remarkable, and interesting that replace the appearances of truth and are more demanding than it is' (WP 111). Péguy's thoughts on the nature of events have thus been pressed into the service of describing philosophical experimentation as a process, using the dualistic terminology of history and becoming. An inspection of the relevant quotations attests to this altered emphasis. Until this point Deleuze had only ever cited the one page from *Clio*, but he now references with Guattari a five-page section. Added stress is also placed on a line from further down Deleuze's favoured page, which reads: 'nothing happened, and we are in a new people, in a new world, in a new humanity' (WP 111).[61] The focus here, as such, is not so much on the passing or dissolution of a problem, but rather on the facilitation and emergence of new ones – on the 'slight displacements [. . .] which entail, as Péguy says, the modification of a problem' (WP 113).

Deleuze will refer to Péguy one final time in *What is Philosophy?* This reference will reprise earlier engagements and solidify Péguy's place in Deleuze's philosophy as one of the two thinkers, along with Blanchot, 'to have gone the farthest into the event' (WP 156). The surrounding context and usage of Péguy, however, will have slightly changed once again. Unlike Deleuze's previous quotations of *Clio*, on this occasion there is no mention of 'problems', whether it be the problematic nature of events or the processes of transition from one problem to another. Experimentation within the framework of becoming and history is also not explicitly mentioned. Instead, focus is placed on the nature of movements between 'the Event' and 'states of affairs'. As before, the citation of different pages from *Clio* alerts us to this adjustment. Deleuze and Guattari also only paraphrase rather than quote Péguy, effectively translating *Clio* into their own conceptual terminology. Péguy's thoughts on the nature of events are now presented as supporting Deleuze and Guattari's distinction 'between, on the one hand, the state of affairs through which we, ourselves, and our bodies, pass and, on the other hand, the event into which we plunge or return, that which starts again without ever having begun or ended – the immanent aternal [*l'internel*]' (WP 157).

Regrettably, Deleuze and Guattari's discussion in *What is Philosophy?* of Péguy's *internel* is all too brief. The same can be said for its initial treatment in Deleuze's two books on the cinema. On no less than five separate occasions across these two books Deleuze appeals to Péguy, connecting his notion of the *internel* with the films of Dreyer, Fellini and Bresson. As with the use of Péguy in *What is Philosophy?*, Deleuze's aim in these instances is to flesh out a dual philosophy of time and the event, whereby a distinction is drawn between the 'historical state of things' on the one hand, or in other words 'the horizontal succession of presents', and on the other hand the 'vertical line' that unites each of those presents with the past in its entirety – the 'internal' and 'aternal' dimension of an event, with all of its coexisting levels of depth, from within which 'one ascends' to the states of affairs found on the surface (MI 106 and TI 91, 243, 297). Although this gives us some sense of Deleuze's broad objective when deploying Péguy's *internel*, it must be nevertheless admitted that it is not exactly clear to what Deleuze is actually referring, as the term does not appear in the passage of *Clio* that he cites (p. 230), nor in any other passage of Péguy referenced by Deleuze.

It is perhaps revealing that Deleuze's use of Péguy in *What is Philosophy?* largely proceeds by paraphrasing and selective quotation. Péguy, for instance, did not himself advance the dualism of history and becoming in those terms. Moreover, Deleuze and Guattari disregard Péguy's obsession with 'ageing' and the inherent Bergsonism of *Clio* – indeed, in the two paragraphs following their final reference to Péguy, Deleuze and Guattari describe the event as a 'dead time' in contrast to the vitality of Bergsonian duration (WP 157–9).[62] And as one final example of the widening discrepancy, Clio may be aghast by what she has become in the 'modern world', but this does not mean, as Deleuze and Guattari imply, that she sees history as necessarily opposed to experimentation and becoming, or even distinct from it – after all, she *is* history, and a Bergsonian to boot. Rather, Clio is merely against a particular kind of history and in favour of another. This might be a minor distinction from Deleuze and Guattari's depiction, but it is nevertheless an important one, especially as far as Péguy is concerned, given his desire to rescue history from the clutches of modern historiography.[63] Thus, while there are kernels of truth to Deleuze's late implementations of *Clio*, such as the articulation of two forms of and engagements with time, it would be equally accurate to label these uses as experimental and productive misuses of Péguy.

Notes

1. See Anthony Edward Pilkington, *Bergson and His Influence: A Reassessment* (Cambridge: Cambridge University Press, 1976), p. 30.
2. Péguy once remarked that 'a review only continues to have life if each issue annoys at least one-fifth of its readers. Justice lies in seeing that it is not always the same fifth.' Quoted in Roger Kimball, 'Charles Péguy', *The New Criterion*, Nov. 2001, p. 19.
3. Hans A. Schmitt, *Charles Péguy: The Decline of an Idealist* (Baton Rouge: Louisiana State University Press, 1967), p. 69.
4. In time Péguy's admiration for Jaurès would undergo a spectacular reversal, culminating in a thinly veiled incitement for his assassination (an act that was indeed carried out on the eve of the First World War).
5. Charles Péguy, 'Un économiste socialiste, M. Léon Walras', *Revue socialiste* 25 (1897), pp. 174–86.
6. Charles Péguy, 'Memories of Youth' [*Notre jeunesse*], in Charles Péguy, *Temporal and Eternal*, trans. Alexandre Dru (Indianapolis: Liberty Fund, 2001), p. 42.
7. Ibid., pp. 75–6.
8. Ibid., pp. 76–7.
9. Ibid., pp. 36–7.

10. Ibid., p. 17.
11. Ibid., pp. 70–1.
12. Ibid., p. 69.
13. Ibid., pp. 69–70. Péguy's thoughts here are clearly inspired by his reading of Bergson, and his choice of language is extremely similar to Bergson's essay 'The Possible and the Real', which infamously elaborates Bergson's theory of retrospective transference from the present to the past as an intellectual illusion that misrepresents the process of creation. Most interestingly, however, Péguy wrote 'Memories of Youth' ten years prior to Bergson's 'The Possible and the Real' (which was first delivered at Oxford in 1920).
14. Péguy, 'Memories of Youth', p. 33.
15. Ibid., p. 80.
16. Jaurès only became a Dreyfusard in 1898, influenced in part by Péguy, and at the 1899 General Congress of French Socialist Organisations it was agreed to remain neutral on the issue. See Schmitt, *Charles Péguy*, p. 14.
17. Péguy, 'Memories of Youth', p. 72.
18. M. Adereth, *Commitment in Modern French Literature: A Brief Study of 'Littérature Engagée' in the Works of Péguy, Aragon, and Sartre* (London: Victor Gollancz, 1967), p. 68.
19. The jury could not choose between Péguy and Romain Rolland, so no award was given. See Schmitt, *Charles Péguy*, p. 29.
20. See Péguy, 'Memories of Youth', p. 39.
21. Letter from Péguy to Bergson, Mar. 1914, quoted in Sylvie Manuel-Barnay, 'Charles Péguy and Prophecy', in *History of European Ideas* 40:6 (2007), p. 780.
22. Schmitt, *Charles Péguy*, p. 28.
23. Charles Péguy, 'Note conjointe sur M. Descartes et la philosophie cartésienne', in Charles Péguy, *Œuvres en prose complètes*, vol. 3, ed. Robert Burac (Paris: Gallimard, 1992), pp. 1282–3.
24. Cited in Yvonne Servais, *Charles Péguy: The Pursuit of Salvation* (London: Newman Press, 1953), p. 294.
25. William R. Keylor, *Academy and Community: The Foundation of the French Historical Profession* (Cambridge, MA: Harvard University Press, 1975), pp. 42–3.
26. For more detail on this immensely important process, see Keylor, *Academy and Community*, pp. 17–108; see also Pim Den Boer, *History as a Profession: The Study of History in France, 1818–1914* (Princeton: Princeton University Press, 1998), pp. 175–308.
27. The essays to which I am referring are 'Zangwill' (1904), 'Notre Patrie' (1905) and the four 'Situation' essays (1906–7).
28. See, in particular, the fourth 'Situation' essay, 'De la situation faite au parti intellectuel dans le monde modern devant les accidents de

la gloire temporelle', in Charles Péguy, *Œuvres en prose complètes*, vol. 2, ed. Robert Burac (Paris: Gallimard, 1988). See also 'Memories of Youth', where Péguy describes the newly arrived modern world as 'the world of those who believe in nothing, not even in atheism, who devote themselves, who sacrifice themselves to nothing. *More precisely*: the world of those without a *mystique*. And who boast of it' (p. 7).

29. See Keylor, *Academy and Community*, pp. 36–54.
30. Péguy, 'Memories of Youth', p. 50, capitalisation in the original.
31. Charles Péguy, 'Notre patrie', in Péguy, *Œuvres en prose complètes*, vol. 2, p. 42.
32. Charles Péguy, 'Clio I', in Péguy, *Temporal and Eternal*, p. 85. The figure of Clio first appears in Péguy's essay 'À nos amis, à nos abonnés' (1909). Other essays in which Péguy develops his critique of modern historiography include 'Compte rendu de congrès' (1901), 'Zangwill' (1904) and the 'Situation' series (1906–7).
33. See Keylor, *Academy and Community*, pp. 75–89; see also Den Boer, *History as a Profession*, pp. 175–308.
34. Ernest Renan, *The Future of Science: Ideas of 1848*, trans. Albert D. Vandam (London: Chapman & Hall, 1891 [1890]), p. xv.
35. In the first version of the dialogue Clio is criticised by Péguy for what she has become in the 'modern world'; however, in the second version Clio has become a Bergsonian and joins with Péguy in criticising those who view her in a 'modern' light.
36. Charles Péguy, *Clio* (Paris: Gallimard, 1932), p. 190. Translation taken from Glenn H. Roe, *The Passion of Charles Péguy: Literature, Modernity, and the Crisis of Historicism* (Oxford: Oxford University Press, 2014), p. 112.
37. Péguy, *Clio*, p. 135. Translation taken from Roe, *The Passion of Charles Péguy*, p. 107.
38. Péguy, *Clio*, p. 135. Translation taken from Roe, *The Passion of Charles Péguy*, p. 108.
39. Péguy, *Clio*, p. 193.
40. Ibid., p. 19.
41. Ibid., p. 21, translation mine.
42. Charles Péguy, 'Note sur M. Bergson', in Péguy, *Œuvres en prose complètes*, vol. 3, p. 1255.
43. 'Never has [our language] been less Latin, less concise; never has it been freer or at the same time more disciplined; never has it responded more quickly to the slightest breath of the spirit. Here one finds as it was in Rabelais – quite young, in process of formation.' André Gide, Review in *La Nouvelle Revue française*, cited in Margorie Villiers, *Charles Péguy: A Study in Integrity* (New York: Harper & Row, 1965), p. 248.
44. In the opinion of T. S. Eliot, Péguy is 'the man whom I consider the

greatest journalist, in the best sense of the term, of my time.' See T. S. Eliot, 'Views and Reviews: Journalist of Yesterday and Today', *The New English Weekly* (8 Feb. 1940), p. 237.

45. According to Walter Benjamin, '*nothing* written has ever impressed me so very much because of how close it is to me, because of my feeling of oneness with it.' See Walter Benjamin, 'To Gerhard Scholem, Klosters, Sep 15, 1919', in *The Correspondence of Walter Benjamin, 1910–1940*, ed. G. Scholem and T. W. Adorno, trans. M. R. and E. M. Jacobson (Chicago: University of Chicago Press, 1994), p. 147.
46. See Gilles Deleuze, 'Foucault and Prisons', in TRM 281.
47. Bruno Latour, 'Trains of Thought: Piaget, Formalism and the Fifth Dimension', *Common Knowledge* 6:3 (1997), p. 179.
48. See Henri Bergson, *Matter and Memory*, trans. N. M. Paul and W. S. Palmer (Mineola, NY: Dover Publications, 2004), p. 171. See also Henri Bergson, *Creative Evolution*, trans. Arthur Mitchell (Mineola, NY: Dover Publications, 1998), p. 5.
49. According to Blanchot, Péguy's 'repetition is actually the indefinite return of a form that seeks to grow through insistence, through its alliance with duration, through the fact that it imposes itself and, by dint of patience and length, is drawn from something else to become more than itself.' See Maurice Blanchot, 'The Solitude of Péguy', in Maurice Blanchot, *Faux pas* (Stanford: Stanford University Press, 2001), p. 282. Translation taken from Roe, *The Passion of Charles Péguy*, p. 203.
50. As Deleuze goes on to say in that essay: 'In Péguy, stuttering embraces the language so well that it leaves the words intact, complete, and normal, but it uses them as if they were themselves the disjointed and decomposed members of a superhuman stuttering. Péguy is like a thwarted stutterer' (ECC 111).
51. Note that in French history the date of 14 July 1790 is itself known as a singular event: Fête de la Fédération, at which the fall of the Bastille and French unity was celebrated. Péguy takes the point one step further, suggesting that the initial storming of the Bastille was itself a festival, a celebration to mark the *culmination* of a transformation, and thus the first commemorative ceremony and the first anniversary of the storming of the Bastille: 'the taking of the Bastille was the first *Fête de la Fédération*' (see Péguy, *Clio*, pp. 114–15).
52. Péguy rhetorically asks, which of Monet's *Nymphéas* is the best? One might say the last, as by then Monet has perfected his technique and perhaps 'arrived' at what he was driving at. But Péguy nominates the first painting, because it is this one that gave rise to and called forth its repetitions. In this respect, the first one is the best 'because [Monet] was able to do it least well' (Péguy, *Œuvres en prose complètes*, vol. 3, p. 126).
53. Perhaps the most interesting of these references is Deleuze's inclusion of Péguy as someone who develops 'the opposition between the private

thinker, the thinker-comet and bearer of repetitions, and the public professor and doctor of law, whose second-hand discourse proceeds by mediation and finds its moralising source in the generality of concepts (. . . Péguy against the Sorbonne)' (DR 7). As we have seen, the private thinker opposed to the academy who confronts and creates the real by shunning the ready-made and repeating oneself is an apt description of Péguy.

54. Translation modified (the text mistakenly has the word 'future' when it should be 'past').
55. In the opinion of Bruno Latour, Péguy is the equal of Nietzsche and no less deserving of attention. As it happens, Latour attributes their contrasting receptions by academic Philosophy to the influence of Deleuze, who successfully philosophised Nietzsche (in a disciplinary/institutional sense) but on Péguy has 'only been decisive in regard to one matter'. See Bruno Latour, 'Charles Péguy: Time, Space, and le Monde Moderne', *New Literary History* 46:1 (Winter 2015), pp. 43–5.
56. Péguy, *Clio*, p. 269.
57. Deleuze had a competitive advantage over Péguy in their respective readings of Bergson's problematic philosophy, as Deleuze had access to Bergson's 1934 essay 'Stating of the Problems' – the essay, drawn on by Deleuze in *Bergsonism*, that most clearly lays out Bergson's thoughts on the matter.
58. Henri Bergson, 'Introduction II: Stating of the Problems', in *The Creative Mind: An Introduction to Metaphysics*, trans. M. L. Andison (Mineola, NY: Dover Publications, 2007), p. 37. Note that the link between the problem and mathematics, which will feature in Deleuze's problematic philosophy, is already present in Bergson.
59. See 'We Invented the Ritornello' in TRM 377–8 and 'G as in Gauche' (AZ).
60. For a separate but related analysis of how Deleuze employs Nietzsche's notion of the Untimely, see Craig Lundy, 'Deleuze's Untimely: Uses and Abuses in the Appropriation of Nietzsche', in Jeffrey Bell and Claire Colebrook (eds), *Deleuze and History* (Edinburgh: Edinburgh University Press, 2009), pp. 188–205.
61. Original quotation found in Péguy, *Clio*, p. 269. Translation modified by Paul Patton; see Paul Patton, 'Events, Becoming and History', in Bell and Colebrook (eds), *Deleuze and History*, p. 46.
62. For a detailed examination of Péguy's theory of ageing with respect to Deleuze, see James Williams, 'Ageing, Perpetual Perishing and the Event as Pure Novelty: Péguy, Whitehead and Deleuze on Time and History', in Bell and Colebrook (eds), *Deleuze and History*, pp. 142–9.
63. For a full explanation of this point, see Craig Lundy, *History and Becoming: Deleuze's Philosophy of Creativity* (Edinburgh: Edinburgh University Press, 2012).

Wilhelm Worringer

Vlad Ionescu

German art history constituted a solid point of reference in the intellectual milieu of France during the 1970s. While Heinrich Wölfflin's *Principles of Art History* (1915) had been acclaimed all over Europe, the work of Aloïs Riegl and Wilhelm Worringer was translated and commented upon during this period.[1] Gilles Deleuze addresses these three figures in his courses on painting held during the spring of 1981 at Université Paris 8. Their concepts are reshaped within the frameworks of *A Thousand Plateaus* (1980) and *Francis Bacon: The Logic of Sensation* (1981). Yet what is the genealogy of the concepts that Deleuze borrows from Worringer? Throughout his work, Worringer himself appropriates two fundamental intuitions from Riegl: firstly, on an ontological level, Riegl argues that visual arts realise a will-to-art (*Kunstwollen*), a notion that designates the way in which cultures intentionally shape their material environment so that it produces visual pleasure.[2] For Riegl, there is no qualitative progress in the visual arts simply because each age has its own ideal of beauty. Secondly, art history confronts us with a structural problem inherent in visual presentation itself, namely that images originate in the contrast between a *differentiating* outline and an *undifferentiated* background. For example, concretely, the Egyptian relief consists of an outline that emerges from a background and represses the density of the presented objects. In Late Roman art, a colourful background inserts the presented objects in a dynamic relation that accentuates their density. Whereas in the Egyptian relief the outline is *haptic* (or *tactile*) because it depicts the clear material consistency of objects as if they were touched with the fingers, Late Roman art is *optic* because it disintegrates the consistency of objects, presenting them as chromatic variations that are meant for a purely visual perception. Hence, Late Roman art is not a stylistic regression following the Antique period but the logical consequence of a structural problem for all visual arts: the presentation of objects in space.

Abstraction and Empathy: A Typology of Intensities

Worringer takes up the following two elements from Riegl's art theory: the *intensive* justification of visual arts as the realisation of a *drive* and the conception of the artwork as an answer to a structural problem of visual arts. Worringer's *Abstraction and Empathy* (1907), his doctoral dissertation, is introduced as *A Contribution to the Psychology of Style*. Art is approached as a phenomenon that responds to two opposing psychological drives: the drive to abstraction versus the drive to empathy. Abstraction refers to man's original contact with nature when the infinite extension of space is met with an intimidating powerlessness as a 'spiritual dread of space' (*geistigen Raumscheu*).[3] Man's initial reaction towards nature is not assimilation but a problematic confrontation when man divests objects of their arbitrary characteristics, like their movement in space or their temporal becoming. Just as Deleuze argues in *What is Philosophy* (1991), Worringer too considers that art and science originate in a confrontation with chaos (WP 66). Significant here is the common constructivist relation to chaos because Worringer argues – echoing Riegl's *Questions of Style* (1893) – that ornament does not imitate nature but transforms its organic movement into 'the life-denying inorganic, in crystalline, generally speaking, in all abstract regularity and necessity'.[4]

Empathy, on the other hand, is a notion that Worringer borrows from Theodor Lipps's *Ästhetik* (1903–6). Lipps introduced empathy as a notion that founded a theory of symbolism: external forms are primarily meaningful because they correspond to the human 'vital movement' (*Lebensbetätigung*). Vitality is the way the body feels when it freely moves and this euphoric feeling determines the relation to other forms. If I take pleasure in organic forms, it is because the movement that I perceive in these forms is *contiguous* with the human body's own vital feeling. Organic forms are not beautiful because they imitate nature but because they correspond to our own euphoric vitality.[5] Worringer condenses Lipps's aesthetics into the succinct phrase that aesthetic enjoyment is objectified self-enjoyment, meaning that aesthetic pleasure is the result of enjoying my own vitality in a different sensuous object.[6] However, what for Lipps was a generic psychological account of the aesthetic experience becomes for Worringer a specific type of visual arts. The art of empathy, other than the art of abstraction, presupposes a tranquil psychological relation to space:

> The need of empathy can only be the presupposition of the will-to-art there where the will-to-art tends towards the organic-naturalistic, i.e. to naturalism in the higher sense of the term . . . The value of a line, of a form consists for us in the value of the life that it embodies for us. It obtains its beauty only through our vital feeling that we mysteriously discharge into it.[7]

Naturalist art does not concern the *imitation* but the *emulation* of the organic unhindered movement of life. In this sense, Antiquity *and* Renaissance have an identical psychological presupposition, that is, the unhindered contiguity between the organic form of the object and man's own vital feeling.[8]

Equally important is that Worringer equated empathy to 'aesthetics', defined as the realisation of the classical 'artistic feeling' (*Kunstempfind*).[9] The context of the debate is significant because he alludes to both the Romantic and *normative* account of visual arts that idealised the organic forms of antiquity and nineteenth-century *psychological aesthetics* (Gustav Fechner) where experiments proved the objectivity of equally organic forms. Worringer combined his psychological perspective with an 'archaeological' approach, meaning that he questions this normative Classicist aesthetics by confronting it with an analysis of primarily Egyptian and Gothic art. Just like Riegl, his goal is to oppose the 'unscientific' conception of art history in terms of periods of decline.[10] Empathy is a psychological state that Worringer designates as *immanence*, meaning that it characterises epochs when divinity is conceived as active *within* the world. The outcome of this religious view is the 'anthropomorphisation of the world', the unity of God and the world appearing as the unity of man and the world. That is why under the regime of empathy (immanence and classicism), the movement of our own vitality is transferred onto the form of the created objects.[11]

However, the original psychological state (*Urzustand*) is that of anxiety because man is confronted with external phenomena without understanding their perpetual change. Worringer designates this state as *transcendence*, meaning a disproportion between the human finitude and the infinite nature of the universe. This religious view triggers an *instinctual* reaction towards the endogenous organic shapes and the infinitely extending space. Instead of emulating the sensuous movement of things, primitive man divests them of this intimidating liveliness; organic movement is transformed into inorganic and abstract shapes that are infinitely repeated. Hence, the premise of transcendent art is the 'deorganicisation of the organic, i.e. a transformation of the changing and limited into unlimited values of necessity'.[12] Instead of organic and harmonious sensuality, the 'values of necessity' are the invariable geometrical lines and crystalline forms. Hence, prior to the *euphoric* relation to the world that characterises empathy, there is the *dysphoric mood* of abstraction. Both psychological dispositions mediate the world in different types of images. Observe, however, the opposite sense of the terms 'transcendence' and 'immanence' in Worringer compared to Deleuze. In Worringer's essay, while 'transcendence' designates the art of abstraction and instinctive expression, 'immanence' refers to the art of organic and naturalistic presentations.

Without referring to Worringer, Deleuze makes use of a similar idea in *Francis Bacon: The Logic of Sensation*. Here, Deleuze argues that Christianity's belief in an incarnated God who dies on the cross and ascends to heaven allows the introduction of accidents in His visual presentation. When a deity is absolutely transcendent and inaccessible, its presentation is restricted to essences (what Worringer would call 'values of necessity'). When God enters the world, He also emulates the vitality of the human body so that subsequently contingent bodily movements are depicted. The modern regime of art begins with the substitution of essences for 'accidents', as Deleuze calls them (FB 123–4). These accidents are nothing else than the organic sensuality that represented, for Worringer, the aesthetic regime of empathy. The reference to 'accidents' as constitutive elements of visual arts is traceable back to Riegl's *Historical Grammar* where it was argued that monotheism introduces a tension in the realm of visual arts. Whereas polytheism allows for the dissipation of different forces, a perfect divinity cannot be presented through 'accidental secondary appearances of the body' (*zufälligen erscheinungen des Körplichen*). However, Christianity, relying on the idea that God becomes man, permits the embodiment of the spiritually perfect into an imperfect nature: 'Ugly nature is the medium of spiritual beauty.'[13] We will have to return to this notion of the accidental because it explains the transformations of visual forms in the history of art. After all, accidental means both 'not-necessary' (in the sense of opposite to the crystalline forms), but also unfolding in time (as opposite to the eternally stable). Modernity in the visual arts represents, for Riegl, an increasing presentation of 'transient nature' as in the Renaissance, when it was believed that the artist 're-create[d] the accidental'.[14]

The psychological approach of visual arts was not new when Worringer was writing. In *The Origin of Baroque Art in Rome*, the courses that Riegl held between 1901 and 1902, he introduced the notions of *will* and *sensation* (*Empfindung*). On the one hand, under the psychical force of the will, the material unity of the bodies is depicted, clearly differentiating their constitutive parts. On the other hand, sensation designates an internal conflict that dissipates forms in space and presents them as subjective and optical impressions. The polarity haptic versus optic is here too, explained according to psychological principles.[15] In his book *The Dutch Group Portrait* (1902), Riegl also distinguished between three psychological principles that mediate the relation to the world: firstly, the *will* isolates figures from their environment; secondly, *feeling* (*Gefühl*) points to an interior affective life that the Greeks, for instance, presented as suffering; finally, *attention* (*Aufmerksamkeit*) is a form of disinterested contact with the world that Riegl detects in the gazes of the figures presented in the seventeenth-century group portraits that look outside the picture plane and initiate a contact to the viewer.[16] This is a type of intentionality that shows directedness towards the world yet without trying to subordinate it to the will.

Temporality and the Modulation of Forms: Questions of Art

Now, our hypothesis is that the psychological analysis of art interests Deleuze because it provides concepts that explain the artwork in terms of intensive forces. Worringer subordinates the *history* of art to a *typology* of psychological drives of abstraction and empathy. These two concepts reduce the porosity of art as a complex cultural phenomenon to two assemblages of forces. Artistic styles actualise these psychological drives that repeatedly remerge in historical time: the art of antiquity and the Renaissance actualise the drive to empathy just as the Gothic and Expressionism are actualisations of the drive to abstraction. While the first two emulate harmonious forms, testifying to a euphoric and tranquil relation to organic nature, the other two consist of crystalline forms that are infinitely repeated and testify to a dysphonic and disquiet relation to organic nature.

Deleuze's philosophy of art reiterates Worringer's analytic approach to art history: visual arts are accounted for in terms of *intensities* (as opposed to an iconological interpretation), *anonymous* and *spontaneous* expressions that surpass the individual and are repeated in time (as opposed to the artistic intention of the artist). Just as Riegl describes – in the *Late Roman Art Industry* – the Late Roman will-to-art by relating reliefs on the Arch of Constantine to the contemporaneous design of buckles and clothes, Worringer discovers the Gothic will-to-art in the North European ornamental lines, assembled in infinite geometric configurations of ribbed vaults, mullions and traceries. Deleuze's interest in Worringer and Riegl is related to this conception of visual arts as an anonymous migration of sensations throughout history. Following Riegl, Worringer transformed the history of art into the history of forces that are re-actualised in different contexts. The actual artwork realises a virtual structure that can be designated as empathy or abstraction.[17] The history of art becomes a variable that oscillates between two values: the *haptic* reduction of objects to abstract forms on the plane or their *optical* rendering as forms diffused in deep space. In this sense, the polarity refers to intensities that oppose imitation and continuously modulate their object of presentation. Instead of resemblance, the haptic and the optic mode of presentation are relatable to Deleuze's concern for the impulsive repetition of singular powers (DF 15). The instinctive component of the abstract line in particular echoes the conception of movement from the introduction to *Difference and Repetition* (1969). The abstract line is a transgressive force that originates in the soul and directly affects the soul (DF 17). Of course, in this particular book, Worringer is not referred to but the dramatic aspectualisation of repetition as a tranformative movement evokes for the reader the equally theatrical description of abstraction.

The concept of abstraction is a conceptual opportunity for Deleuze to formulate one intuition, namely a dynamic conception of form conceived as an infinite variable that repeatedly realises its potential. The canonical examples are the Gothic line that constitutes the ribbed vaults of medieval architecture, and the Expressionism that represents the same spiritualism. Both styles concern an instinctive relation to nature that destabilises all invariable laws of nature. Deleuze would perhaps have also described the spiritual in art as 'the sum of forces that resist the blind law of nature, the automatic course of events'.[18] Like Worringer, he would have also denoted the transcendent and abstract art as the 'deorganicisation of the organic'. Both authors have a tendency to produce parasynonyms that account for one central idea: against the repetition of generalities, to affirm the dissipation of forces that perpetually transform the organic body or any stable structures. In both cases, the anonymous migration of forces in historical time turns the visual into a plane of immaterial and supersensible intensities. This transposition of concepts from psychology interests Deleuze as a strategy of desubjectivisation. After all, the abstract line represents for Worringer a force that overwhelms the viewer because it is stronger than the vitality of his/her body. The vertical velocity of the Gothic lines intoxicates the viewer who experiences an 'exalted hysteria' and 'internal dissonances'.[19] This literal reference to hysteria returns in Deleuze's account of painting where the sensation has a similar disturbing effect:

> A wave with a variable amplitude flows through the body without organs; it traces zones and levels on this body according to the variations of its amplitude. When the wave encounters external forces at a particular level, a sensation appears. An organ will be determined by this encounter, but it is a *provisional* organ that *endures only as long as the passage of the wave and the action of the force*, and which will be displaced in order to be posited elsewhere. (FB 47, emphasis added)

This passage demonstrates that the affinity that Deleuze finds with Worringer's concept of abstraction has one goal in sight: the modulation of *visual* forms by exposing them to *temporal* transformations. Exposing matter to a force means also that its form registers its metamorphosis in time. Deleuze's vivacious rhetoric of the 'body without organs' (Artaud) and his vexatious cultivation of intensities hide one clear intuition: sensations subordinate the lived body to the modulating force of time. A sensation is a force that makes visual forms subject to the speed of time: that is the case with Deleuze's Figure and Worringer's abstraction. In this sense, the expression 'body without organs' means that the organs are not separate forms that constitute a *static* organism but divergent forms because they are caught in a *variable* movement. The impact of time on matter is also one criterion for the description of the Baroque in *The Fold* (1988) where the 'matter-fold' is described as 'matter-time', a temporal progression in the expansion and retraction of movement (FLB 7). The Baroque is an infinite process whose problem is not the end of a fold but its endless unfolding, the possibility of letting it infinitely rise through the ceiling (FLB 34). Note that the correlation of time and movement applies to different artistic styles: the Gothic line forms ribbons and stripes (FB 182); further, in his courses, Deleuze explains the fold in the terms similar to those Riegl uses to explain the evolution of the relief: in the Egyptian and Greek relief the line is related to an immobile background that becomes dynamic in Late Roman and Byzantine art. He contrasts the 'frozen' relief of the Egyptian garment with the 'harmonic' fold of the Greek, which is more flexible and proportional. While the Egyptian fold follows a crystalline law, the Greek abides by an organic law. Hence, the point is not the sensational deformation of organisms but the sensation as a modulating force that maintains forms in movement, mobile and transformable. We see that Deleuze's approach to the visual arts is specific: the aim of painting is to paint forces (FB 182). However, the impact of these forces on matter appears as an index of temporal transformation.

The indeterminacy of forms as the potential of matter also has another aim, namely the connivance between artistic forms and life. For Worringer, art, if it is not anthropomorphic, remains anthropocentric because it is essentially a product of mankind. For Deleuze art is approached within the broader context of life, and in *What is Philosophy?* (1991) he and Guattari are quite clear that art begins with animals that delimit their territory, like the Australian tooth-billed bowerbird that creates a 'stage' on which it performs (WP 184). Just as the force of the Gothic line, sensations, percepts and affects overcome the historical limitation of the artists that created them. Deleuze develops the potential that the concepts of Riegl and Worringer entail, namely that art concerns variable forces whose actual assemblages survive their historically delimited place and time. The abstract line, for instance, overcomes the spatial and temporal limitations of the Gothic and the Expressionist style considered separately.

Haptic and Optic: Questions of Orientation

The notion of abstraction is related to the notion of the haptic that Worringer borrows from Riegl. In *Francis Bacon: The Logic of Sensation*, Deleuze evokes Riegl for whom the haptic designated a linear presentation where forms are kept close to the plane (as opposed to their diffusion in deep space). However, despite his close reading of Riegl, Deleuze transforms the original sense of the haptic line. With this notion, Riegl showed that vision has a *tactile* sensitive dimension in addition to the *optical* identification of objects in space.[20] Yet, while Riegl correlated these two senses with their specific functions in order to explain the 'logic' of visual arts, Deleuze dramatises them and transforms their correlation into a real tension. In this sense, the haptic 'resists' the direct subordination of the hand to the eye (FB 155) and this tactile function disturbs the stability of forms. The haptic becomes in Deleuze an agency of insubordination that resists the restriction of forces in an organic whole. Hence, it is the variability of the Gothic line that Deleuze has in mind when he reads Riegl because he is not interested in the iconic but in the indexical values of the haptic. Instead of creating icons (like in the Egyptian relief), the haptic becomes a transgressive force that destabilises visual structures by relating them to a different sense: the haptic represents a direct contact that resists the optic distance. The hand is an organ that can apply pressure to the surface of the painting without considering its optical clarity, such that the maintenance of forms is a continuous forms *polymorphous state*. In order to affect the body, painting resists all mediation and is perceived as pure presence. Only through touch can the eye transcend its analytic function, like the perspectival eye of the Renaissance which organises space from a distance.

Yet is a moment of euphoric rest conceivable in Deleuze's conception of painting as 'vitalised geometry' (FB 182)? Here is the point where Deleuze differs from Worringer who described the abstract forms as 'the only and the highest ones in which man can *find rest* from the confusing image of the world' (emphasis added). Ironically, the following sentence is absent from the English translation of *Abstraction and Empathy*: 'Then again, the regularity of this inorganic world is reflected in the regularity of that organ with which we overcome our sensuous subjection, namely our human understanding.'[21] According to Worringer, the psychic tension that justifies abstraction aims at a moment of rest. Moreover, he correlates abstraction and understanding as generating similar regular structures. This momentary euphoric rest and the regularity of the abstract forms disappear in Deleuze's culture of intensities that maintain the body in a perpetual modulation.

Nevertheless, a different extrapolation of the haptic line appears in *A Thousand Plateaus*, in a chapter dedicated to the distinction between smooth and striated space. The section concerns the orientation of modern man in a world that is organised according to different spatial principles. *Striated* space maps out the world as a *differentiated* structure, so that distinct points in space mediate the direction of movement. Examples are the grid of streets that determine the movement from one point to another or the maps of geographers. The *smooth* (haptic) space is an *undifferentiated* extension where movement is intuitive rather than calculated, following intensities rather than distinct points in space.[22] The space of the Eskimos, the Sahara Desert, the steppe and the oceans are all realisations of smooth space. Within the context of this chapter, the haptic describes a type of experience that corresponds to a type of space.

The experience of walking through the desert is that of an *extension* that is not felt as an *expansion* in depth: the bodily experience is that of a maximum proximity or absolute contiguity with an extension (because one does advance) that lacks any determinate orientation points (because horizons are interchangeable).

This type of experience corresponds to the movement on a plane rather than in a structured space. Even deep space is felt as haptic if it lacks points of orientation: for example, walking in the dark immediately precipitates that tactile sense. Deleuze and Guattari address various realisations of these two spatial models, from music to physics, mathematics and visual arts. And in this context the continuous and spontaneous movement that constitutes an orientation within the smooth space is described in the terms of Worringer's haptic–close space. This notion has thus two relatable functions within Deleuze's work. On the one hand, in *Francis Bacon*, the haptic accounted for the *temporal modulation* of visual forms, the infinite unfolding of forms that resists organic formations. On the other hand, in *A Thousand Plateaux*, the haptic accounts for *spatial modulations* of the moving body, namely the experience of a continuous movement on an undifferentiated planar extension.

Yet the correlation of the haptic with the close space originates in Riegl's *Historical Grammar*: the *optic* corresponds to the distant space because the eye organises the proportional relations between objects as they extend in deep space. The *haptic* corresponds to the close space, a plane surface that represses all density and on which a clear outline encompasses the material unity of each and every object. Late Roman and Byzantine reliefs represent a shift in the visual arts because they gradually transform the immobile Egyptian background into a mobile background. Hence, the presentation of deep space evolves over time and includes the enclosed space of the Renaissance and the infinite space of the Baroque. In the words of Riegl, there is an evolution from the 'tactile apprehension in the close view' (*die taktische Aufnahme in der Nahsicht*) that isolates forms and makes them clear for the 'optical apprehension in the distant view' (*die optische Aufnahme in der Fernsicht*) where forms are connected and adjusted to one another.[23] The third solution is the abstract line that, for Worringer, no longer *delineates* an organic form but follows its own intensive course.

Deleuze and Guattari object here to Worringer because he conceives the abstract line as the rectilinear Egyptian form that evolves into the nomadic, intensive and spontaneous Gothic line. The problem is that for Worringer – as has already been pointed out – the haptic line does produce regular structures, as in the Egyptian relief. For Deleuze and Guattari, however, the abstract line moves between points and contours while it designates an *infinite* force (as opposed to a *finite* organism):

> Consequently, we do not understand the motivation for the abstract line in the same way, or its identity with the beginning of art. Whereas the rectilinear (or 'regularly' rounded) Egyptian line is negatively motivated by anxiety in the face of all that passes, flows, or varies, and erects the constancy and eternity of an In-Itself, the nomad line is abstract in an entirely different sense, precisely because it has a multiple orientation and passes *between* points, figures and contours; it is positively motivated by the smooth space it draws, not by the striation it might perform to ward off anxiety and subordinate the smooth. (TP 496–7)

The first reason for this 'misunderstanding' is that, for Worringer, the drive to abstraction, the anxiety of organic movement, motivates both the haptic rectilinear line of the Egyptians and the Gothic (nomadic) line. And the second is that Deleuze and Guattari question Worringer concerning the claim that the anxiety of 'primitive' man finds a moment of mental repose in these geometric shapes, a state of repose that would contradict the infinite excitation of the nomad line. The vocabulary of Worringer is clear: the erratic movement of the haptic line has an 'abstract dead regularity'; its shapes constitute points of rest and 'necessary values' (*Notwendigkeitswerte*).[24] Hence, there is an implied *purposefulness* in the haptic line for Worringer that Deleuze and Guattari cannot accept because its erratic movement – the anarchic nomadism that its represents *for them* – weaves up into the striated space. In other words, the deterriorisation of the smooth space 'agglutinates with' the terrirorialisation of the striated space. Maybe we should point to Hegel's *Aesthetics* in order to understand that the term Deleuze and Guattari need here is not 'conformity to the law' (*Gesetzmäßigkeit*), a higher stage of abstract proportional relations, but 'regularity' (*Regelmäßigkeit*), a repetition of the same form. Pure intensity and smooth spaces repeat the *singularity* of a movement – 'conformity to the law' is already a repetition of a *generality*.[25] What Worringer has in mind when he uses the term *Gesetzmäßigkeit* is an *instinctual* repetition that generates *regular* structures. Needless to say, it is precisely this structural aspect that Deleuze and Guattari would consistently resist because they are interested exclusively in the intensity of the movement itself.

On the one hand, Worringer sketches an evolutionary history (*Entwicklungsgeschichte*) of art where intensities constitute forms. In this evolution, understanding replaces instinct and, later, science offers to the educated man the same 'assurance' that abstract art offered to primitive man.[26] Organic beauty is the resolution of a 'crisis' when instinct is 'calmed' (*beruhigt wurde*) by science. Later art becomes separated from science and the emerging classical sensibility tames intensities. On the other hand, for Deleuze and Guattari intensities constitute an absolute criterion. As a result, they emphasise the process but not the structuring of forms that have stable meanings. They are not interested in art historical *styles* but in morphological *gestures* because what they argue in *A Thousand Plateaus* about the Gothic line also applies to what Deleuze consistently argued in *The Fold*: 'the problem is not how *finish* a fold' – the form that falls on itself and constitutes a whole – 'but how to *continue* it' (FLB 34).

Jacques Derrida questioned the absolute value that the notion of touch received in Deleuze and Guattary when he argued that the absolute proximity of the smooth space is a 'continuistic postulation' but not a given experience. All experience of touch implies discontinuities; there are always minimal protuberances that mediate the *form* of what is sensed with the hand or the fingertips.[27] Indeed, already for Riegl and Worringer, the haptic is a type of visuality where the two sensory modes interact in the visible mediation of the world. The absolute continuity of the haptic (as opposed to the discontinuity of the optical) perception repeats the 'difference' of presence and absence. Deleuze would exclude a dialectical approach to the senses as the task of visual arts because, in his view, the latter realise an intensity that resists the conformity to a law. His entire philosophy of art, like Jean François Lyotard's, is founded on the principle that the intensity of a force opposes the generality of the law. Yet the potential of visual art to explore a force without abiding to a rule is a modernist principle. Deleuze (and Guattari) exploit it programmatically but also quite consistently: *form is matter modulating inherent forces* and *visual arts are practices that capture, correlate and manipulate these forces* (FB 56ff.). It is at the level of this conception of form in terms of forces that Deleuze finds an ally in Worringer: the haptic line explains art in terms of anonymous forces. Essentially, while for Worringer the haptic line concerns a drive that justifies a psychological typology of art,[28] for Deleuze the absolute continuity of the haptic turns visual arts in to a theatre of forces.

Conclusion: Which Gothic Line?

Besides his various references to Jean-François Lyotard, Henri Maldiney or Gilbert Simondon, Deleuze's philosophy of art relies heavily on modern art history, especially the work of Wilhelm Worringer, Heinrich Wölfflin and Aloïs Riegl. The appropriation of the concepts of these latter thinkers remains, however, idiosyncratic. Generally, these three art historians have been associated with a phenomenological model of the image.[29] Konrad Fiedler initiated this model when he designated the pertinent object of visual arts as 'pure visibility' (*reine Sichtbarkeit*). The central intuition is that the image is an appearance distinct from its medium, with an internal visual structure that appeals to a specific type of consciousness. On the other hand, Deleuze's appropriation of the polarities that Worringer and Riegl designed follows a different strategy. Two radical differences have to be mentioned: *firstly*, the two polarities of the optic versus the haptic and the closed versus the open space help Deleuze to conceive visual forms in terms of intensities. As a result, the history of art no longer constitutes a story but a continuous modulation of a few elements: the relation between touch and sight, the flat plane and the deep space, the euphoric empathy and the dysphoric abstraction. Whereas this was already the case for Worringer, his analyses integrated this psychological typology into the cultural context where artists worked. Deleuze appropriates the polarities but undermines the function that they had for Worringer, namely an explanation of the past as a homogeneous entity. This stability of the sense of a culture is the evolutionist presupposition – positivistic and *not* Hegelian – that is implied both in Riegl's and Worringer's works.

Secondly, Worringer's concepts are introduced as a 'psychology' of art history. They account for a typology of drives, so they constitute an ideal ally in Deleuze's philosophy of intensities. While Deleuze and Guatarri express little criticism of Worringer's simple (if not simplistic) typology, when they do criticise him it is because his model does not fit their own: the abstract line cannot just generate a striated space and has to be conceived as a continuous nomadic movement (TP 486–7). The Gothic line represents this type of perpetual linear movement for Worringer, yet Deleuze and Guattari do not question the reductive way in which Worringer conceives this art historical style. After all, is the Gothic a linear style? For Deleuze, the Gothic line actualises an immanent force, yet this line originated in a philosophical culture of transcendence. Despite his critics, Erwin Panofsky interpreted the architecture of the basilica of Saint-Denis as the realisation of Abbot Suger's Neoplatonic beliefs.[30] For Panofsky, the Gothic represents the architecture of light and symbolises the emanation of the divine light that descends from heaven and envelops the interior of the church. Besides this complexification of the medieval sensibility where light plays a central role (Panofsky), Worringer takes the abstract character of scholasticism as a correlate of the Gothic line's abstract character. For Worringer, though, the Gothic line is a sign of absolute transcendentalism.[31]

Hence, the Gothic is not just a line but also colour, and both line and colour were not designed as self-referential abstractions but as analogues of the good. Despite the complexity of the style, Deleuze and Guattari are only interested in the constructivist tendency of the Gothic line, just as Worringer was when he described its 'spiritualising tendency' as 'a non-representational mania for construction' (*eine gegenstandslose Konstruktionswut*).[32] Yet whereas this constructivist approach is highly productive in the practice of architectural design, from an art historical perspective such reductionisms entail the risk of falling into generalities. The risk is that the concept of the haptic line may substitute a Hegelian generality for the equally general psychological forces. Is the relationship of philosophy to art history not reductive *ex vi termini*? Deleuze's answer is predictable: these forces are not invariable structures but variable repetitions. Nevertheless, the balance between art historical rigour and philosophical speculation remains an imperative if we want to learn how to design by means of intensities and to think by means of concepts.

Notes

1. All the translations are mine unless otherwise indicated. Worringer's *Abstraction and Empathy* (1907) appeared in French in 1978, two years before the publication of *A Thousand Plateaus*. The equally influential *Gothic Art* (1911) was translated in 1941. Aloïs Riegl's posthumously published courses, edited as *Historical Grammar of Visual Arts* (1966), were published in French in 1978. Wölfflin's *Principles of Art History* (1915) and *Renaissance and Baroque* (1888) – the books that influence Deleuze's understanding of Mannerism and the Baroque – had already been available since 1952 and 1964, respectively. More importantly, the founding figures of modern art history were widely discussed in France. Henri Zerner introduces Riegl's thought in 'L'histoire de l'art d'Aloïs Riegl. Un formalisme tactique' published in *Critique* (Aug.–Sept. 1975, pp. 941–52). Henri Maldiney, the colleague of Deleuze at

the University of Lyon, used Aloïs Riegl's art theory in order to develop a phenomenology of the visual arts on the basis of the rhythm emerging between outline and background. He continued with a phenomenology of form as the rhythmic articulation of the potential and resistances of matter. See, especially, Henri Maldiney's 'L'esthétique des rythmes' and 'L'art et les pouvoir du fond', both published in *Regard, parole, espace* (Lausanne: L'Âge d'homme, 1973). For the influence of Maldiney on Deleuze, see Jean-Christophe Goddard, 'Henri Maldiney et Gilles Deleuze. La station rythmique et l'œuvre d'art', *Revista filósofica de Coimbra* 33 (2008), pp. 109–24.

2. The will-to-art is defined as the 'most pleasurable presentation of things for the eyes by means of visual arts' (*die Dinge mittels der bildenden Kunst möglichst wohlgefällig vor Augen zu stellen*). See Aloïs Riegl, *Spätrömische Kunstindustrie* (Vienna: Österreichische Staatsdruckerei, 1927), p. 401. Worringer refers to Riegl's will-to-art at various points in *Abstraction and Empathy* and emulates entirely his ontological conception of art as the realisation of the *willed* or intentionally desired visual forms (as opposed to the *ability* or technical potential of a culture, the position that the followers of the materialist conception of Gottfried Semper in the nineteenth century supported). See *Abstraktion und Einfühlung. Ein Beitrag zur Stilpsychologie* (Munich: Fink, 2007), pp. 76–7, 167.
3. Worringer, *Abstraktion und Einführung*, pp. 82–3.
4. The original reads: 'im lebensverneinenden Anorganischen, im Kristallinischen, allgemein gesprochen, in aller abstrakten Gesetzmäßigkeit und Notwendigkeit' (Worringer, *Abstraktion und Einfühlung*, p. 73).
5. Theodor Lipps, *Ästhetik. Psychologie des Schönen und der Kunst* (Hamburg: Voss, 1903), p. 102.
6. Worringer, *Abstraktion und Einfühlung*, p. 73. Observe how Worringer appropriates Lipps's definition of empathy: 'the feeling of a positive vital movement that I experience in a sensuous object is the feeling of affirmation of the self or of life' (*das Gefühl der positiven Lebensbetätigung, die ich in einem Sinnlich Objekt erlebe, es ist das objektivierende Gefühl der Selbst- oder Lebensbejahung*) (Lipps, *Ästhetik*, p. 140).
7. The original reads: 'Das Einfühlungsbedürfnis kann als Voraussetzung des Kunstwollens nur da angesehen werden, wo das Kunstwollen dem Organisch-Lebenswahren, d.h. dem Naturalismus im höheren Sinne, zuneigt. . . . Der Wert einer Linie, einer Form besteht für uns in dem Werte des Lebens, das sie für uns enthält. Sie erhält ihre Schönheit nur durch unser Vitalgefühl, das wir dunkel in sie hineinversenken' (Worringer, *Abstraktion und Einfühlung*, pp. 80–1).
8. Ibid., p. 95.

9. See the essay entitled 'Transcendence and Immanence in Art', first published in Max Dessoir's *Zeitschrift für Ästhetik und allgemeine Kunstwissenschaft*, 3rd edn, 1911, in Worringer, *Abstraktion und Einfühlung*, pp. 166. The same idea is repeated in 'Kritische Gedanken zur Neuen Kunst' [1919], in *Wilhelm Worringer: Fragen und Gegenfragen. Schriften zum Kunstproblem*, ed. Erich Fidder (Munich: Piper, 1956), pp. 86–7.
10. Worringer, Abstraktion und Einfühlung, p. 167.
11. Ibid., p. 170.
12. The original reads: 'Entorganisierung des Organischen, d.h. auf eine Übersetzung des Wechselnden und Bedingten in unbedingte Notwendigkeitswerte' (ibid., p. 174).
13. The original reads: '. . . die hässliche Natur als Trägerin geistiger Schönheit'. Aloïs Riegl, *Historische Grammatik der bildenden Künste. Vorlesungen von 1897–1899*, ed. Karl M. Swoboda und Otto Pächt (Cologne: Böhlaus, 1966), p. 39.
14. Ibid., pp. 40, 105.
15. Aloïs Riegl, *Die Entstehung der Barockkunst in Rom. Vorlesungen aus 1901–1902*, ed. A. Burda und M. Dvořák (Vienna: Kunstverlag Anton Schroll, 1923), p. 2.
16. Aloïs Riegl, *Das Holländische Gruppenporträt* (Vienna: Druck und Verlag der Österreichischen Staatsdrukerei, 1931), pp. 13–15.
17. See Vlad Ionescu, 'The Rigorous and the Vague: Aesthetics and Art History in Riegl, Wölfflin and Worringer', *Journal of Art Historiography* 9:9 (8 Dec. 2013), pp. 1–24.
18. The original reads: 'die Summe der Kräfte, die ich der blinden Naturgesetzlichkeit, den automatischen Selbstablauf des Geschehens entgegenstemmen' (Worringer, 'Spätgotisches und Expressionistisches Formsystem' (1925), in *Fragen und Gegenfragen*, p. 93).
19. Worringer, *Formprobleme der Gotik*, p. 50.
20. The correspondence between senses has its own tradition in aesthetics and epistemology, especially throughout the seventeenth and the eighteenth century. In *Plastik* (1778), Herder called for a 'philosophical lexicon' that related a word to the senses and then to the mind. Locke, in his *An Essay on Human Understanding* (1689) argued that touched mediated the impenetrability of things, and Berkeley, in his *New Theory of Vision* (1709), emphasised the primacy of touch in the constitution of space.
21. The original reads: 'die einzigen und höchsten, in denen der Mensch angesichts der Verworrenheit des Weltbildes ausruhen kann. Anderseits spiegelt sich die Gesetzmäßigkeit dieser anorganischen Welt in der Gesetzmäßigkeit jenes Organs, mit dem wir unsere sinnliche Abhängigkeit überwinden, nämlich unseres menschlichen Verstandes' (Worringer, *Abstraktion und Einfühlung*, p. 175). For the English

translation, see Wilhelm Worringer, *Abstraction and Empathy: A Contribution to the Psychology of Style*, trans. Michael Bullock (New York: International Universities Press, 1953), p. 134.

22. The distinction echoes Guy Débord's culture of 'dérives' from the late 1950s, the spontaneous variation of directions in the city, in search of ambiances. The city is the correlate of a 'possible rendezvous', an opportunity for psychological and geographic encounters.
23. Riegl, Historische Grammatik der bildenden Künste, p. 291.
24. Worringer, Abstraktion und Einfühlung, p. 16.
25. The distinction between regularity, conformity to the law (or uniformity) and harmony is addressed in the chapter 'The Beauty of Abstract Form' of Hegel's *Vorlesungen über die Ästhetik*. See Georg Wilhelm Friedrich Hegel, *Ästhetik*, intro. G. Lukács (Berlin: Aufbau Verlag, 1955), pp. 165–70.
26. Worringer, Abtraktion und Einfühlung, p. 174.
27. Jacques Derrida, *Le Toucher. Jean-Luc Nancy* (Paris: Galilée, 2000), pp. 143ff.
28. Jung's polarity introvert versus extrovert repeats Worringer's polarity of abstraction versus empathy. Like empathy, the extrovert is directed towards the object that is assimilated. The introvert moves away from the object that is 'crystallised and fixated into the rigid forms of law, the universal, the typical'. Carl Gustav Jung, *Collected Papers on Analytical Psychology*, trans. Constance E. Long (London: Baillière, Tindall & Co., 1916), p. 293.
29. Lambert Wiesing reinterpreted Konrad Fielder, Heinrich Wölfflin and Aloïs Riegl from this phenomenological perspective in his *Die Sichtbarkeit des Bildes. Geschichte und Perspektiven der formalen Ästhetik* (Reinbek: Rowohlt Taschenbuch, 1997).
30. Erwin Panofsky, 'Abbot Suger of Saint Denis', in *Meaning in the Visual Arts* (Garden City, NY: Doubleday Anchor Books),1955, pp. 126–31. Andreas Speer has shown the lack of a consistent relation between Suger's architecture of light and the philosophy of Pseudo-Dionysius. Speer shows how much of Suger's thoughts on architecture have been read from a Romantic aesthetic perspective and that they miss the complexity of a practice where architecture was inherently related to its liturgical function. See Andreas Speer, 'Beyond Art and Beauty: In Search of the Object of Philosophical Aesthetics', *International Journal of Philosophical Studies* 8:1 (2000), pp. 74–88 and 'Medieval Aesthetics', in John Marenbon (ed.), *The Oxford Handbook of Medieval Philosophy* (Oxford: Oxford University Press, 2012), pp. 661–84.
31. Worringer, *Formprobleme der Gotik*, p. 117.
32. Ibid., p. 70.

Melanie Klein

Piotrek Świątkowski

Readers of *Anti-Oedipus* (1972) are familiar with the vehemence of Deleuze and Guattari's critique of psychoanalysis. Key elements of the theory and practice of Freud, Lacan and Klein are presented therein as a contemporary technique of power that represses the creative and critical potential of desire. As such 'psychoanalysis' produces narcissistic and docile subjects, who wilfully participate in a society dominated by the capitalist mode of production. This ferocious attack on certain premises of psychoanalysis in the books co-written with Guattari had an unwanted consequence for the reception of their work. Despite some recent contrary examples,[1] interpreters have frequently underestimated the importance of psychoanalysis in Deleuze's work. The relation is complicated and can never be characterised as a complete rejection of psychoanalysis in general. Drawing a general conclusion about the relation between the work of Deleuze on desire and psychoanalysis is an impossible task. The diversity of the texts and the degree of their complexity is also far too extensive to provide a clear and nuanced analysis of possible points of intersection and difference. Therefore in the following text, instead of providing such an all-embracing analysis, I will focus on the specific analysis of desire in *The Logic of Sense*, particularly the sections on the so-called 'dynamic genesis of sense', found in the final chapters of the book. The analysis of the dynamic genesis is fundamental as it provides us with a highly systematic analysis of human desire, language and our capacity for thought. It is, moreover, an intervention into psychoanalytic discourse in which Deleuze builds upon the work of Melanie Klein, one of the key figures of British psychoanalysis.[2]

Deleuze's interest in the work of Klein appears to be of crucial importance for the development of his own theory about the nature of desire and psychosexual development, as following Klein's theory allowed Deleuze to construct a viable alternative to the psychoanalysis of Jacques Lacan.[3] In *The Logic of Sense* Deleuze is particularly critical of the transcendental status awarded to the symbolic order within Lacan's account. Although Lacan claimed that his own reliance on structure was not the same as that found in structuralism, for Deleuze the former's theory nonetheless takes a pre-given and fixed structure as a point of departure for its analysis of the unconscious. Lacan's symbolic order is a fixed and unalterable structure imposed upon the unconscious. The main aim of *The Logic of Sense* is to show that, although structures exist in the unconscious, they do not necessarily form an unchanging universal order. Deleuze's sense is innately unstable and always submitted to alteration. It displays the characteristics of an event (*événement*) and emerges out of the direct interactions of bodies with their surroundings.[4] The process that leads to the production of sense is individuation.[5] The properties of a separate entity cannot be determined by a movement from the most general level of sense to the most particular or by an application of form to matter, as is the case in Aristotelian hylomorphism. For Deleuze, each entity emerges in a process of genesis.[6] As such it always carries the capacity to transcend its given material circumstances. A living entity functions within a problematic or virtual field and does not act solely according to the fixed, actualised patterns, analysed by structuralism. During the process of individuation it develops partial solutions to the problems encountered. In short, an individual actualises the virtual. By realising the immaterial events it escapes complete determination by the actual.[7]

In order to reveal the dynamic nature of sense Deleuze emphasises the role played by the body during the very production of sense. The body is not an empty container that receives complete determination from the already established structures but rather produces signs while interacting with external objects. The necessary conceptual elements that allow Deleuze to discuss the genesis of sense and an original production of signs by the body are found in the work of Melanie Klein. At first glance the interest in her work appears to be incidental. Klein, one of the founding members of the object relations theory, was mainly known for her innovative work with young children and her theories concerning the development of an infant. She became a recognised figure for her disagreement with Freud regarding the key importance of the mother rather than the father in the stable development of a child. Following the later work of Freud she also stressed the importance of the destructive drives, seeing the individual's life as a continuous struggle between Eros and Thanatos, between a striving towards pleasure and aggression. The significance of this struggle was particularly visible in her analysis of the two positions that determine the structure of psychic life: namely, the paranoid-schizoid and manic-depressive positions. According to Klein, the first involves a continuous struggle against our own destructive urges. This position consists of continuous interactions with partial objects, such as the breast, that are never part of a complete and organised totality and which randomly generate states of pleasure and distress. The analysis of the second position allows her to show how a partial victory over the destructive urges is made possible due to the protection offered by a 'good' complete object, that is, the mother. Only this object allows a child to overcome the chaotic and fearful experiences of the early life and forges a more organised experience.

Deleuze's interest in the work of Klein particularly relates to her understanding of the nature of early psychic life. He is fascinated by her idea that a child interacts with phantasy objects, that is, objects that accompany the direct physical states of pleasure and distress. Deleuze focuses on the idea that a child's internal psychic life develops out of continuous interactions with the outside world, involving both continuous introjections – that is, inserting positive experiences into one's own body – and projections – rejecting negative experiences and instead placing them outside of one's own body.

This interest in Klein also relates to Lacan's occasional critique of her understating of early psychic life.[8] Lacan had tried to show that Klein overemphasised imaginary relations and thus lacked an understanding of the working of the symbolic order and that she exaggerated the importance of the mother for the child while underestimating the fundamental importance of the father.[9] This critique is evident in Lacan's examination of the case study of a young patient of Klein's, named 'Little Dick'. The boy 'Little Dick' entered analysis with Klein because he was unable to develop meaningful relations with his surroundings. Indeed, 'Little Dick' was slightly autistic. He lived in a world where people do not differ much from toys and other objects. After several therapeutic sessions Klein established a relationship with the child and helped him to increasingly establish contact with the surrounding world. Klein herself was convinced that her therapy had been successful because she was able to explore and change the vulnerable, internal phantasmatic world of the child.[10] As a result he learned to deal with his aggression which, according to Klein, was the primary cause of his predicament. 'Little Dick' developed the internal phantasm of a complete and good object. Due to continuous interactions with Klein, he developed a sense of confidence in the good nature of his environment and developed a sense that a good entity was protecting him from possible misfortune and aggression.

Lacan was nevertheless convinced that Klein entirely misunderstood the cause of the success of her own approach towards the boy. She did not reach into the hidden bodily phantasmatic life of her patient, but rather played the role of what Lacan calls the 'symbolic father'. This meant that, rather than developing a sense of trust towards his environment, the boy was simply helped in comprehending his own behaviour. His actions and experiences became meaningful. He was made aware of the existence of an external structure of sense and gained an understanding of his position within the 'Oedipal triangle'. He successfully accepted the authority of the symbolic father and as such learned to understand the boundaries within which he could move and act.

In a comparably hypothetical analysis of the 'Little Dick' case Deleuze would have likely taken the side of Melanie Klein. On the one hand, he would have criticised the use of such Oedipal terminology, while, on the other hand, he would have been fascinated by the analysis of the process of individuation of the child.[11] Given Deleuze's own ideas concerning psychosexual development (which we will examine shortly) he would have viewed Klein's intervention in this process as allowing the child to develop new bodily phantasms. Indeed, in *The Logic of Sense* Deleuze is interested in the importance of the body during the process of construction of sense and in all the forms of self-organisation of desire described by Klein. In the remaining sections of this article I will show how Deleuze uses and revises Klein's analysis of various forms of such self-organisation, called by her 'positions', in order to develop his own account of the working of human desire. I will discuss in detail the characteristics of the schizoid, depressive and sexual positions and their relation to the theory of Klein. As we will see, the analysis differs greatly from the structuralist one. I will nevertheless also explain Deleuze's modifications to the Kleinian scheme. As we will see, he extends Klein's theory with a profound analysis of both narcissism and non-narcissistic forms of desire.

Dynamic Genesis – Schizoid Position

The dynamic genesis of sense, analysed in *The Logic of Sense*, is a process of development of the topological dimensions that organise desire. It is an analysis of an 'entire geography and geometry of living dimensions', states Deleuze (LS 188).[12] The term 'position', crucial for this analysis, does not refer to a historical moment when a particular erotogenic zone dominates experience, as is the case for Freud. Instead, for both Deleuze and Klein, a position is the systematic manner in which the ego relates and orients itself in respect to the surrounding world.[13] Its interactions are mediated by various phantasmatic constructions, called 'internal' objects, that change from one position to the next. Deleuze in *The Logic of Sense* also speaks here of various dimensions that characterise each of the various positions. He speaks of depth, height and two surfaces: the physical surface of the body, and the metaphysical surface of thought.

The first of the two positions detailed in Klein's account is the paranoid-schizoid position. The initial experiences of a new-born child are similar to the states of tension endured by an embryo. The child experiences pleasant excitations. It enjoys them but also sometimes experiences stress and anxiety.[14] The child must, for example, learn to tolerate either the potential overabundance or absence of food. It must slowly learn to control both the yearning accompanying its anticipation and reception of food, on the one hand, and the stress accompanying its possible privation, on the other. The nature of the received stimuli in this position is nevertheless still limited. The child perceives only parts of the objects in its environment and never the objects in their totality. It relates to the breast as a partial object and not the mother as the whole object. From the perspective of the child, the objects are moreover not submitted to any 'law'. The child lives in a world of disorganised impressions which are often felt as persecutory and generate a state of ongoing insecurity. The temporary states of pleasure quickly change into either over-excitation or into tension and subsequently anxiety.[15] The feelings of satisfaction and pleasure, caused by the sheer presence and warmth of the body of a parent, are quickly overshadowed by the subsequent states of fear, tension and aggression generally generated by the absence of the parents' bodies or ministrations.

For Melanie Klein, these experiences are accompanied by the first mental constructions.[16] The child starts to mentally differentiate between what she terms good and bad partial objects. The good partial object accompanies the experiences of pleasure while the bad partial object relates to feelings of tension and fear. Melanie Klein speaks, for example, of the good and bad breast as the first internal representations.[17] Klein extends her analysis also by pointing to the role of the death drive expressed as aggression, which is already present in all the early experiences.[18] This inner aggression first of all aggravates the states of tension and fear. Klein notices, however, that these early states of fear and aggression are also accompanied by initial attempts at restoration, a topic that will be of importance to Deleuze in his own analysis of desire. The child is fearful of the destruction of the mother's body which it fantasises its own aggression will somehow cause. Moreover, it is frightened that it will be treated with reciprocal aggression and thus engages in attempts at a placatory reparation. In doing so, it projects not only the bad objects, but also the good ones, into the outside world. For instance, food that is thrown up may be experienced as a gift to the mother. A person with a dominant paranoid-schizoid position may, for example, continuously offer presents to others in order to ameliorate the damage he thinks he has caused them. According to this account of the paranoid-schizoid position, however, a successful attempt at restoration is ultimately impossible as there is no principle present that enables it to determine which of its reparative attempts is actually successful; a complete and undivided object, a condition for successful restoration, does not exist as yet.

Each of the different positions analysed by Deleuze (building upon Klein in his own account) is characterised by distinct phantasmatic constructions. To help clarify the nature of the phantasy proper to the schizoid position, Deleuze introduces the concept of the *simulacrum*. There is a clear philosophical reason for this choice. A child in the schizoid position is not aware of the existence of an external order. It does not yet realise that it will be submitted to external laws of the world dominated by fundamental differences and oppositions (LS 188). The psychic representations of its initial experience – the simulacra – arise irrespective of any external order. The child experiences only various excitations which are experienced as different degrees of intensity. For example, the words it hears are not experienced as carriers of pre-established meaning; they are merely noises that vary only in intensity.

The picture of desire in the paranoid-schizoid position is bleak as the paranoid-schizoid person lives in a vicious circle.[19] The compulsive pursuits of pleasure and of striving to fulfil the demands of the self-preservative drive provoke aggression and fear. According to Deleuze, however, it is not necessary to progress towards the manic-depressive position (which we will examine shortly) in order to relieve or gain control over such schizoid suffering.[20] The schizoid fears can be controlled from within the schizoid position itself and not only by means of the continuous introjections of good partial objects. The experience of menacing tension can be overcome not only by the continuous incorporation or assimilation of external object such as food but also by the establishing of a sense of unity that cannot be found in the outside world. This sense will be accompanied by a specific simulacrum, the 'body without organs'. In order to understand the workings of the simulacrum, Deleuze slightly amends the description of the paranoid-schizoid position. According to him, the negative tension is permanently present and cannot be overcome by the introjection of objects. Every partial object that produces pleasure axiomatically contains threatening parts. Partial object food can never be trusted as such. It might contain threatening and poisonous parts that are not easily detected and can menace and destroy the interior of the body. A good object, Deleuze says, must be free from such reservations and cannot contain any threatening parts. Such certainty however, can only be provided by an object that does not possess any separate parts. It can be provided only by an object that is complete (LS 188). The dynamic of the schizoid position is hence determined not by an opposition between good and bad partial objects but by two competing depths. The ego of the schizoid position oscillates between the partial objects and the body without organs (LS 189). This depth of the partial objects is as Deleuze characterises it full of whirling and exploding bits and pieces. The depth of the body without organs, on the other hand, is one of a complete and uncorrupted body. It is a depth in which the threatening interaction with the outside world, the continuous introjections and projections of objects, have been given up. The second depth is hence first of all one of a catatonic, lifeless body. However, Deleuze does not seem to be satisfied with merely offering a destructive solution to the problems of the schizoid position. He tries to argue and prove that a complete rejection of the outside world is not the only method by means of which the consoling experience of the body without organs can be accomplished. He insists that the body without organs can also be established by soldering the partial objects into a unity. The sense of rest that neutralises the various tensions and states of fear can be accomplished in the experience of a fluid mixture, a fluid whole (LS 189). Deleuze speaks here of a principle of liquidity. In order to come closer to an understanding of the nature of this principle alluded to here we can turn to the depiction of water in art. The image of water has traditionally been associated with a state of rest and reconciliation. Water generates a state in which all tension is abolished. One has only to think, for example, of the crucial role water plays in the films of Tarkovsky. But we can also think of the experience of a football supporter during a game in a large stadium or of a political protester during a political rally. Both can go through an experience during which their ego melts within a higher ecstatic and fluid unity of like-minded and ecstatic people.

Manic-depressive Position

The second position described by Deleuze builds upon Klein's account of the manic-depressive position. According to Klein, the two positions develop during the different developmental phases of a child's life.[21] The paranoid-schizoid position fully determines the experience during the first half year of life, but its influence diminishes when new cognitive developments occur. With the passage of time, the child is able to see objects from a greater distance and to tolerate greater degrees of ambivalence, so that it need not *automatically* split and evacuate objects as a means of coping with unbearable states of tension. It is quickly able to differentiate between familiar and unfamiliar faces. The separate parts of a body, such as the breast, hand or face, become part of a complete object, such as the mother. The developing sense of hearing allows for the transformation of noise heard by a child into separate sounds and subsequently into voices. These changes have a tremendous impact on the child's emotional life. The dominant experiences of fear and tension slowly fade away, and the child is able to integrate many of its earlier feelings and impressions into meaningful syntheses. For example, the prior libidinal fixation on partial objects is instead replaced by fixation on complete objects, such as the mother.[22] The child starts to identify with these complete objects and becomes dependent upon them. It becomes more and more aware of the fact that on its own it lacks power. The complete good objects exceeds the child in all respects. The complete object is subsequently slowly incorporated into the internal world of the child and starts to protect its ego against the attacks of 'bad' partial objects. The ego that possesses the complete good object assumes that it has more powers. It feels special and elevated above the others. The introjected good object, the inner core of goodness, is unreachable for all vicious attacks by bad objects. At the same time the ego that introjected the good object does not terminate the relations with the external objects. It continually re-projects the internal good object on to objects in the outside world. First, the parents, but later in life a loved one, a boss or a political leader receive the attributed characteristics of the internal complete good object. These figures appear to be necessary in order to secure the existence of the internal good object. As such they help to protect the ego against hostile attacks from bad partial objects.[23] The most important cause of psychic suffering proper to the fully developed manic-depressive position is hence the fear of losing this object, and the guilt and depression which this generates leads to the individual striving to empathise with the loved object. The ego continually struggles to protect it against the attacks of the external bad partial objects. Essentially, the idealised objects are continually protected against any critique uttered by others.

Deleuze amends the account of the manic-depressive position but does so only in a limited way. What he calls the depressive position is characterised by a new topological dimension: height. The complete good object of the schizoid position starts to belong to this new dimension from the moment the child starts to understand its limited influence on its surroundings. From that moment onwards, the complete good object of the height starts to protect the ego (LS 190). Looking up towards the heights changes the relation of the ego towards the depths. Indeed, the identification of the ego with the good object allows the ego to liberate itself from the depths (LS 190). As such the ego does not sublimate schizoid desire but is rather able to distance itself from the chaos and tensions of the depths, for height provides it with the promise of both order and the disappearance of tension. The ego can now, for example, in the name of a religious belief or social norms, distance itself from direct bodily pleasures. It is strong enough to live what is considered to be a decent, moral life and work exceptionally hard towards a higher position in society. However, this does not mean that identification with the good object of the heights is complete. According to Deleuze, the ego still secretly identifies with the partial objects and suffers during their struggle against the commandments coming from the heights. The ego cannot distance itself completely from the id (LS 190). Climbing the ladder of the social hierarchy will, for example, need to be accompanied by provisional yet successive states of pleasure that are able to compensate for initial sacrifices.

The second difference from Klein's account is that, for Deleuze, the good object as such is unreachable and withdrawn in to the heights (LS 191). Klein does not go as far as Deleuze does, in this respect. For her a person with a dominant manic-depressive position is afraid of losing an object that is, in fact, already internalised. Moreover, according to Klein, the manic-depressive person is always afraid that the aggressive attacks will transform the good object into a bad one and will subsequently lead to its loss. She equally conceives of strategies that can minimise the risk of losing the good object. For Deleuze, in contrast, the good object is never actually possessed. It is always already lost. Hence, the depressive position as such is dominated by the experience of lack and a corresponding state of insurmountable frustration (LS 192). No single existing object can eliminate this state.

In his books written in collaboration with Guattari, Deleuze was always very critical of the importance assigned to this experience in Jacques Lacan's psychoanalytic account. They claimed that lack can never be the starting point for the analysis of desire.[24] Deleuze's earlier view in *The Logic of Sense* is not far removed from this later perspective. Lack is in no sense the main point of departure for the analysis of desire. It has a role to play but it is important *only* in the depressive position and is virtually unknown within the others. Secondly, even within the depressive position, lack is productive rather than alienating. The analysis of a person with strong depressive tendencies will not terminate in a state of cognitive recognition of the unfulfillable nature of desire. It should rather lead to a specific kind of productive relation towards objects. A clinical and literary example given in *The Logic of Sense* is alcoholism (LS 193). According to Deleuze, an alcoholic has to learn to live within the particular time-structure proper to the depressive position. Alcoholism also appears to be a solution to particular problems. The orientation towards the object of the heights allows the alcoholic to replace the schizophrenic principle of liquidity (*principe mouillé*) and overcome the hegemony of the unbreakable present. The depressive position allows the alcoholic to live in a world in which two separate moments, the present and the past, are intertwined.[25] He can experience the present in relation to the past. This is visible in the way an alcoholic might speak about a love relationship. He does not say 'I love her' but 'I have loved'. He lives the two moments at once. It is exactly this mutual relation of both moments that allows him to live what he considers to be a life worth living. He identifies with the objects from the past while engaging in a negative relationship with the objects of the present. According to Deleuze, the alcoholic does not enjoy the harshness of the present as such but is rather interested in something that emerges in the relation of the present to the past.

The Sexual-perverse Position

The final position discussed by Deleuze is the sexual (sexual-perverse) position. The position itself is subdivided into three different phases: the pre-genital, genital and post-castration phases. Klein herself never distinguishes a separate position that can follow on from the manic-depressive one, but Deleuze nevertheless introduces a successive position, building upon certain important facets of her work in constructing his own account of it.[26] The arrival of the sexual-perverse position is characterised by the emergence of a new dimension that complements the depth and the height: the surface of the body (LS 196). Deleuze seems to be inspired here more by the Freud of the *Three Essays on the Theory of Sexuality* than by Klein herself, and speaks of a surface that consists of various erotogenic zones that correspond to isolated yet identifiable areas of the body. Just like Freud, he speaks of zones that develop in the vicinity of orifices marked by mucous membranes – zones that respond to certain kinds of stimuli (LS 197). One of the most important characteristics of this new position is nevertheless directly inspired by Klein's theory. In the sexual position the libido is liberated from the destructive drives which are no longer projected on to external objects. Instead the external objects are experienced as pure sources of pleasure or satisfaction, experienced by means of the various erogenous zones. This new experience is accompanied by a new psychic construction: what Deleuze calls an 'image'.

The emergence of the surface of the body as a separate dimension is a consequence of the process of genesis. It emerges mainly because the height allows the ego to distance itself from the depths. The possible subsequent liberation of the libido from destructive drives can be conceived of only from within the Kleinian framework (LS 352). According to Klein, the main goal of the super-ego, which emerges shortly after birth out of most of the interactions of the child with its environment, is not primarily the suppression of the libido. Its main aim is the limiting of the aggressive and destructive death drive and the strengthening of the libido instead. For Klein only a strong libido enables the ego to engage in trustworthy and loving relations with others. It enables the ego to minimise both the prevailing states of tension and the feelings of guilt or fear, all fuelled by the destructive drives. Within the Kleinian theoretical framework the struggle between the libido and the death drive is nevertheless ultimately insurmountable. The victory of the fragile libido over the destructive drives will always be temporary.[27] Deleuze moves one step beyond Klein. The sexual position is a position on its own and is made possible by a complete liberation of the libido from both the destructive and self-preservative drives. The libido of the surface is hence entirely different from the libido of the depths (LS 199). The libido no longer leans on the self-preservative drive. It thus ceases to produce imaginary substitutes for the objects that guarantee the self-preservation of the organism. The states of pleasure within the sexual position are now separated from the survival strategies of the body. For example, the sucking of the thumb is a state of pleasure that no longer serves as a substitute for the sucking of the nipple. Secondly, the libido also ceases to lean on the destructive drive. This means that the libido is no longer oriented towards sudden elimination of the states of tension. It no longer aims at a state of discharge. The desire organised within the sexual position loses its interest in an idyllic state of rest. The libido of the surface engages in what Deleuze calls the productive work of the surface. It aims at various states of intensification of pleasure and their modulation. Practices developed under the current economic mode of production such as tasting of food, wine, beer and coffee form first examples of such non-orgasmic form of desire. The joy brought about by listening to or practising music as well as dance are other examples and similarly do not rely on the orgasmic nature of desire.[28]

Genital Phase of the Sexual Position

The next development within the sexual position is the genital phase. This phase marks an end to the relative disintegration of the pregenital phase and introduces a form of unified experience. The full integration of the partial erotogenic zones into a unified experience is furnished by the image of the 'phallus', projected on to the genital zone. Here again, Deleuze develops an alternative to Freud's and Lacan's theories about the Oedipus complex by building upon the work of Klein. The image of the phallus that is crucial for the emergence of the unified experience is not the structural mark of sexual difference as is the case in Lacanian psychoanalysis. It is not a symbol of power, nor a major signifier structuring the symbolic order, nor a signifier of lack or loss. Instead this image allows the ego to start to believe in its own restorative capacities, a Kleinian topic mentioned earlier. Here the image of the phallus is that of a reparative organ, projected on to the body's genital zone. For Deleuze, the projection of this image occurs in the case of both boys and girls (LS 200). The image of the phallus allows the ego to undo the shattering and fragmentation it continually perceives in its environment. It is an image of an organ capable of healing and unifying. As such, the image of the phallus can take on the role of a reparative organ only if we consider the previous steps of the genesis (LS 200).[29] The existence of the good complete object is of fundamental importance here. It allows for the transformation of the role of the genital zone. The genital experience is no longer accompanied by the simulacrum of a bad partial object and is instead transformed into an experience of a good object.[30] In the genital phase of the sexual position both girls and boys project the qualities of the good object of the height on to the genital zone. Possession of these good qualities allows them to believe in their own reparative capacities. It equips both boys and girls with a sense of pride and empowerment. They are now convinced that they have found a way to undo the harm and damage attributed to the outside world. The genital phase of the sexual position furnishes their egos with what Deleuze calls a belief in good intentions.

The Post-castration Phase of the Sexual Position

The most profound modification of Klein's theory within Deleuze's analysis of dynamic genesis can be found in his analysis of the Oedipus complex and of the subsequent post-castration phase. As we have seen, the Oedipal desire that emerges in the sexual position does not initially lead to the emergence of any fear or guilt as is usually postulated within psychoanalytic accounts (LS 201). Here, instead, Oedipus is in a sense a peacemaker. However, the good intentions of the ego are nevertheless very fragile and run a high risk of being shattered in a confrontation with the events of daily life. They are almost immediately challenged and the ego is threatened with castration. In *The Logic of Sense* Deleuze discusses two reasons for the disappearance of good intentions. The first one is found in Melanie Klein's own account. The surface is merely a delicate veil that covers the self-preservative drive and the destructive drives of the depths. Any event in life can cause these drives to regain strength and subsequently destroy the fragile surface of the body. As a consequence of minor events, a gentle and considerate life partner can quickly transform into a possessive enemy devoted to control rather than support. Loss of good intentions in such cases will directly lead to a regression towards the depressive or schizoid position. What Klein calls the phantasmatic attempt at healing of the wounded body of the mother can in this case turn into schizoid acts of aggression. The partner who was cared for will be transformed into a threatening partial object that must be controlled at all costs before it causes too much damage. This fear overshadows and destroys all previously existing reparative attempts. In the case of a regression to the depressive position the same partner will replace the reparative acts with attempts to render present some idealised object of the heights. He or she can force the partner to confirm to the rules of idealised married life. This ideal will be protected in a possibly violent manner against all possible deviations that challenge the status of the idealised married life as object of the heights.

According to Deleuze, the danger of regression to previous positions is of fundamental importance, but is also not the only significant challenge faced by the narcissistic ego. Kleinian inspiration reaches its limit here. Castration does not have to lead to a direct return to a state where the libido and the death drive are intertwined. Castration can also lead to the discovery that the world is fundamentally lacking any definite order (LS 205). The ego can come to realise that the splintered body of the mother can never be unified into a complete object. The actions of the ego can appear to it as having merely destructive results. The world will remain shattered, just as it was before the reparative activities of the ego. According to Deleuze, this discovery must necessarily lead to the loss of good intentions. The ego is disenchanted by the discovery of the existence of such an unalterable reality and its incapacity to modify it according to its own wishes. Stated in psychoanalytic terminology, the child is now threatened by the discovery that the phallus can only be the property of the father.

Deleuze's analysis of the consequences of this discovery nevertheless differs greatly from the one developed by Lacan in his early seminars. Deleuze discusses two different responses to the demise of good intentions. Castration can first of all lead to the acceptance of the authority of the symbolic father and what Deleuze calls a subsequent resignation. The ego can come to realise that it has gone too far by fully appropriating the image of the phallus. It becomes aware of the fact that it should have been more prudent in its own actions. It should have been aware of the limits of its own reparative endeavour. It can thus attempt to restore its good intentions. It can make new attempts at restoration and unification of the world by continuing its struggle against the death drive and disintegration. This is a solution that perfectly fits within the psychoanalytic worldview of Melanie Klein.

However, Deleuze is not satisfied with this solution and as a result considers the possibility of yet a further step in the development of the ego.[31] Just like in *Anti-Oedipus*, he wants to conceive of desire such that it can overcome narcissistic good intentions, a form of desire that is crucial to each society organized according to the laws of the capitalist mode of production. Good intentions and narcissism are not inevitable and can be challenged by means other than through simple regression to previous positions. Instead, Deleuze envisages the replacement of good intentions by the development of a proper form of the phantasm and by the construction of sense. Resignation and cognitive acceptance of one's own limitations, central to Lacanian structuralist psychoanalysis, cannot be the sole purpose of the analysis of desire. For Deleuze, in the final phase of the genesis, the architecture of the psyche becomes extended with a new topological dimension, the 'metaphysical surface'. Only on this surface thought is liberated from the body. Only here thought ceases to sublimate the bodily desires and develops its own capacity to symbolise and to produce sense. The symbols developed on the metaphysical surface allow the ego to relate to its environment in a complex and intricate manner. Thought ceases to produce mere responses to what is given. It critically redefines the encountered problems and searches for proper solutions. Deleuze's aim in those passages is to show how such dynamic construction of sense challenges and transforms its organisation in relation to pre-existing external social structures.

The capacity to construct sense is made possible by two factors. The first is the discussed physical experience of castration, characterising the post-castration phase. This is the experience of a limit to one's own reparative capacities, the recognition that the world cannot be redeemed and unified by means of one's own actions. The second factor belongs to the nature of thought itself. Thought is confronted by a similar limit. It cannot comprehend the world and construct an overarching, unified worldview. In the final instance, thought will always need to confront a crack (*fêlure*) that distorts its unity and coherence. Thought is continually disrupted by non-sense that continually tears it apart. The ego must acknowledge that its capacity to think is riven by paradoxes and inconsistencies.

In one of the final moments of the analysis of the dynamic genesis Deleuze underscores the danger pertaining to the moment in which the crack disrupting the metaphysical surface starts to correspond with the castration that destroys the surface of the body. At this moment the ego risks disappearing into the depths or heights. The ego can again lose its capacity to construct sense. It can lose its relation to thought in the schizoid abyss or search for a false refuge in an unfounded order provided by an idealised object of the heights. However, this moment is also one full of possibilities and can reinvigorate production of sense. The confrontation can produce a new relationship between the ego and its environment, by means of a phantasm in its proper form. This phantasm is no longer only bodily in nature, as was the case for the simulacra, idol or the good object of the heights and the images. It is a phantasm that is a proper response to a broader set of problems encountered by the ego in its environment. Such phantasms are discussed by Deleuze not only in *The Logic of Sense* but primarily in his later work with Guattari, albeit under other names. We can think here of the analysis of the various forms of becoming such as becoming-animal or becoming-minoritarian. These phantasms allow the ego to cease perceiving itself as the centre of its own world. They facilitate a continuous switching of positions within a broader set of social relations and the problematisation of its role within its environment. The same phantasms can, for example, allow the ego to switch from the position of a victim to perpetrator.

However, analysis of such phantasms leads us further away from the Manichean world of Melanie Klein. In the end for Deleuze the struggle between the good, loving libido and the bad and aggressive death drive is not eternal. It can be overcome in the constructivist relation of the ego towards its environment, in an opening towards what he calls 'events'. By a strengthening of the process of constructing phantasms even psychoanalysis can facilitate an opening of the ego towards events. Contrary to Klein, for Deleuze the good intentions that are supported by the image of the phallus are never enough. In order to achieve mental health and emotional stability an anorexic patient, for example, needs to pass through the process of becoming-woman. Only such a phantasm can facilitate constructive resistance towards the environment and alleviate the high degree of psychic suffering.[32] Indeed, such a phantasm might enable a meaningful relation towards the continuous flow of goods and could allow for an escape route from the demands imposed upon women by society. This kind of more precise vision of the political nature of individual desire is in the end absent from the work of Melanie Klein.

Notes

1. See, for example, the recent collection of essays edited by Boštjan Nedoh and Andreja Zevnik, *Deleuze and Lacan: A Disjunctive Synthesis* (Edinburgh: Edinburgh University Press, 2017).
2. Until recently almost no philosophical and psychoanalytic literature about the relationship between the work of Melanie Klein and Gilles Deleuze existed. In psychoanalytic literature a supporting analysis can be found in Jean Bégoin, 'L'Anti-Œdipe ou la destruction envieuse du sein', in Édouard Privat (ed.), *Les Chemins de l'anti-œdipe* (Toulouse: Bibliothèque de Psychologie Clinique, 1974), pp. 139–59, where the initial influence of Klein on his work is greatly admired. The situation has begun to change in recent years. The work of Nathan Widder, 'From Negation to Disjunction in a World of Simulacra: Deleuze and Melanie Klein', *Deleuze Studies* 3:2 (2009), pp. 207–31; Joanna Bednarek, 'Logika sensu – najbardziej lacanowska z książek Deleuze'a?', *Praktyka Teoretyczna* 5 (2012), pp. 49–68; Sean Bowden, *The Priority of Events: Deleuze's Logic of Sense* (Edinburgh: Edinburgh University Press, 2011); and, more recently, by Piotrek Świątkowski, *Deleuze and Desire* (Leuven: Leuven University Press, 2015), Aaron Schuster, *The Trouble with Pleasure* (Cambridge, MA: The MIT Press, 2016) and Guillaume Collett, *Psychoanalysis of Sense* (Edinburgh: Edinburgh University Press, 2016), testify to this. This increased attention to the analysis of dynamic genesis is not surprising, certainly given the fact that Michel Foucault, for example, considers it to be of vital importance for understanding the whole of Deleuze's philosophical project and is particularly impressed by the analysis of the phantasm. Cf. Michel Foucault, 'Theatrum Philosophicum', *Critique* 282 (1970), pp. 885–908.
3. Deleuze's critical engagement with structuralism is evident in the article : 'À quoi reconnaît-on le structuralisme', in François Châtelet (ed.), *Histoire de la philosophie VIII. Le XXe siècle* (Paris: Hachette, 1973; pbk edn: Pluriel, 2000). For an analysis of the relation between the work of Lacan of the 1950s and structuralism, see Markos Zafiropoulos, *Lacan et Lévi-Straus, ou le retour à Freud 1951–1957* (Paris: Presses universitaires de France, 2003). For an introduction to the work of Lacan, refer to the analysis of his famous text *Subversion du sujet et dialectique du désir dans l'inconscient freudien*, in Philippe Van Haute, *Against Adaptation: Lacan's Subversion of the Subject* (New York: Other Press, 2001). We must nevertheless remember here that Deleuze's critique is oriented mainly towards Lacan's earlier work.
4. I concur here with the interpretation of the concept of sense offered by Alain Badiou, *Logiques des mondes* (Paris: Seuil, 2006), p. 403. Badiou points to the connection of sense with the notion of the virtual and the event.

5. For an analysis of the theme of individuation in the works of Deleuze, refer to Alberto Toscano, *The Theatre of Production: Philosophy and Individuation between Kant and Deleuze* (London: Palgrave, 2006).
6. For a critique of Aristotelian hylomorphism, see Gilbert Simondon, *L'Individu et sa genèse physico-biologique* (Paris: Presses universitaires de France, 1964). For secondary literature on this topic, consult also Toscano, *The Theatre of Production*, p. 14 and Bowden, *The Priority of Events*, pp. 117–18.
7. Deleuze discusses the problematic nature of sense – for example in the 'Ninth Series of Problematic', in *The Logic of Sense* (LS 52–7). We nevertheless have to acknowledge that for Deleuze the possibility of the production of sense occurring during individuation is not self-evident. The meanings of words or social roles are prescribed by society. An individual generally acts in accordance with the existing actual structures and its capacity to express events is very limited as a result. Deleuze's understanding of sense in *The Logic of Sense* is, in this respect, not entirely different from that of Alain Badiou, who is equally interested in the notion of the event. Cf. Badiou, *Logiques des mondes*, p. 403.
8. The texts of Lacan from the 1950s may, to a significant degree, be seen as a response to the appearance in 1952 of *Développements de la psychanalyse* of Klein and her adherents. See, for example, the text 'Fonction et champ de la parole et du langage en psychanalyse', in *Écrits* (Paris: Seuil, 1966), p. 235 and Lacan's first seminar, '1953–1954, *Le Séminaire I*', in *Le Séminaire,* vol. 1: *Les Écrits techniques de Freud* (Paris: Seuil, 1998). For an analysis of the reasons why Lacan misinterprets the ideas of Klein about the body, refer to Phillipe Van Haute, 'Lacan Reads Klein: Some Remarks on the Body in Psychoanalytic Thought', *Philosophy Today* (2008), pp. 54–62.
9. See, *inter alios*, Jacques Lacan, *Écrits* (Paris: Seuil, 1966), pp. 728–9 and the seminar of Lacan (1956–7), 'La relation d'objet', '12 December 1956', in *Le Séminaire*, vol. 4: *La Relation d'objet*, vol. 1 (Paris: Seuil, 1998), p. 47. Jacques Lacan, 'Some Reflections on the Ego', *International Journal of Psycho-Analysis* 34 (1953), p. 11.
10. For the analysis of the case, see Melanie Klein, *The Psychoanalysis of Children* (London: Vintage, 1997).
11. This aspect of Klein's work is criticised later in Gilles Deleuze and Félix Guattari, 'L'interprétation des énoncés', in *Deux régimes de fous* (Paris: Les Éditions de Minuit, 2003), p. 92 (TRM 89).
12. I will provide here only a schematic overview of the various positions. An extensive analysis of this topic can be found in Piotrek Świątkowski, *Deleuze and Desire* (Leuven: Leuven University Press, 2015).
13. The idea of the 'position' is proposed by Klein in 'A Contribution to the Psychogenesis of Manic-depressive States' [1935], in *The Selected*

Melanie Klein, ed. Juliet Mitchell (New York: The Free Press, 1986), pp. 115–45.

14. Klein analyses the characteristics of this position in 'Notes on some Schizoid Mechanisms?' [1947], in Juliet Mitchell (ed.), *The Selected Melanie Klein* (New York: The Free Press, 1986), pp. 175–200.
15. See ibid., p. 180.
16. For an outstanding analysis of the primary psychic experiences of a child, see Susan Isaacs, 'The Nature and Function of Phantasy', in Melanie Klein et al. (eds), *Developments in Psycho-analysis* (London: Hogarth Press, 1952), pp. 67–121.
17. See also Klein, 'A Contribution to the Psychogenesis of Manic-depressive States'.
18. Klein builds upon the work of Freud, from *Beyond the Pleasure Principle* (1920) onwards. Aggression or the death drive is, according to both Klein and Freud, the most powerful drive. They are the root cause of the continual disruptions in the life of the child. The analysis of the role of the death drive in life of a child can be found, among others, in Tomas Geyskens and Philippe Van Haute, *From Death Instinct to Attachment Theory: The Primacy of the Child in Freud, Klein, and Hermann* (New York: Other Press, 2007).
19. See Klein, 'A Contribution to the Psychogenesis of Manic-depressive States', p. 119.
20. See Klein 'Notes on some Schizoid Mechanisms?', p. 189.
21. It must be noted that for Klein the individual tends to move back and forth between the two positions. This happens in accordance with the vicissitudes of everyday experience. This possibility of changing the position differentiates Klein's account of 'positions' from Freud's more linear and evolutionary account of psychosexual development as a succession of 'stages'.
22. Klein, 'A Contribution to the Psychogenesis of Manic-depressive States', p. 141.
23. Klein points to the fact that the introjection of the complete object into the psyche during the manic-depressive position is less physical in nature than in the paranoid-schizoid position. The introjection is made possible by extended interactions with the complete objects in the outside world. See Klein, 'A Contribution to the Psychogenesis of Manic-depressive States', p. 119.
24. In *Anti-Oedipus*, Deleuze and Guattari assert: '*Le désir ne manque de rien, il ne manque pas de son objet*' (AO 26).
25. Deleuze discusses the problematic of alcoholism in one of the most famous passages of *The Logic of Sense*, in the 'Twenty-Second series – Porcelain and Volcano' (LS 158).
26. For a more explicit analysis of the account of the sexual position, see Świątkowski, *Deleuze and Desire*.

27. Klein, *The Psychoanalysis of Children*, p. 281.
28. Deleuze and Guattari make a similar point later in *A Thousand Plateaus*, claiming that orgasm should not serve as a model for sexual experience. They, for example, discuss various sexual practices that are not oriented towards a discharge. According to them, Chinese sexual practices are exemplary in this respect. See ATP 157.
29. To a certain extent, Deleuze follows Melanie Klein here. He remarks: 'C'est de tous ces points de vue que Mélanie Klein montre que les positions schizoïde et dépressive fournissent les éléments précoces du complexe d'Œdipe' (*Logique du sens*, p. 233).
30. See Klein, *The Psychoanalysis of Children*, p. 252. For a slightly different discussion of Klein's account of female sexuality, see Julia Kristeva, *Melanie Klein*, trans. Ross Guberman (New York: Cambridge University Press, 2001).
31. Due to the relative distance of this topic from the work of Klein, I discuss it only very briefly here. For a more extensive analysis, see Świątkowski, *Deleuze and Desire*, p. 177.
32. For a critical analysis of Deleuze and anorexia, see Monique David-Ménard, *Deleuze et la psychoanalyse* (Paris: Presses universitaires de France, 2005).

Jean Wahl

Sean Bowden

Jean Wahl was born on 25 May 1888 in Marseille, where his father was a professor of English. His family was Jewish, although they no longer observed their religious traditions. A gifted student, Wahl entered the École normale supérieure in 1907 and received his *agrégation* in 1910, coming first in his year in front of his good friend, Gabriel Marcel. He subsequently taught at *lycées* in Saint-Quentin, Nantes, Tours and Le Mans before successfully defending his two doctoral theses in 1920. His primary and secondary theses – *Les Philosophies pluralistes d'Angleterre et d'Amérique* and *Du rôle de l'idée d'instant dans la philosophie de Descartes* – were published that same year by Alcan.

Over the next decade and a half Wahl taught at Besançon, Nancy and Lyon before taking up the Chair of Philosophy at the Sorbonne in 1936. He would hold this position until 1967, despite several interruptions during the Second World War. The first of these interruptions coincided with the Paris exodus in 1940, when Wahl found himself for a brief period of time in Bayonne before being recalled to the Sorbonne. Being of Jewish origin, he was then forced to retire from his university post, although he continued to teach students from a room in the Hôtel de Nice, rue des Beaux-Arts. Finally, in July 1941, he was arrested by the Gestapo and interrogated and tortured at La Santé prison. He was held there for more than a month before being sent to the Drancy deportation camp. Obtaining a fortunate release, he then travelled to the United States where he taught from 1942 to 1945 at the New School for Social Research in New York and Mount Holyoke and Smith Colleges.

Returning to France and the Sorbonne after the war, Wahl became a significant and influential figure. In the words of Levinas, he was 'the life force of the academic, extra-academic and even, to a degree, anti-academic philosophy necessary to a great culture'.[1] As a teacher at the Sorbonne for over thirty years, he taught, supervised or examined many of France's best-known contemporary thinkers.

Those who credit Wahl with an influence upon their thinking include Claude Lévi-Strauss, Michel Foucault, Jacques Derrida, Michel Butor and Gilles Deleuze.[2] Alongside his original philosophical work and his more classical texts in the history of philosophy – on Plato and Descartes, for example – Wahl introduced to the French philosophical scene both little-studied and newly emerging figures in Anglo-American and German philosophy. His studies of Heidegger, James and Whitehead were highly influential, as was his work on Hegel[3] and Kierkegaard.[4] He was founder of the Collège philosophique and the *Deucalion* journal (1946), director of the *Revue de métaphysique et de morale* (1950–74), president of the Société française de philosophie after the death of Gaston Berger in 1960, and president of the Société française d'études nietzschéennes (1963). He was also a member of Acéphale, contributing to the journal of the same name, and an active participant at meetings of the famous Collège de sociologie. Finally, it should be noted that Wahl became known, not only as a philosopher, but also as a poet, publishing several volumes. Indeed, for Wahl, there is an intimate connection between poetry and philosophy, or poetry and metaphysics.[5] As Deleuze would later put it, Wahl 'tore down the boundaries between philosophy and poetry . . . [and] emerges like a philosopher-poet who cannot be reduced to philosophy.'[6]

Jean Wahl died in 1974 at the age of eighty-six. He had been blind for some time before his death, but continued to dictate texts to his wife up to two months before his passing.[7]

Deleuze's Encounter with Wahl

As a student at the Sorbonne from 1944 to 1948, Deleuze followed Wahl's classes on pre-phenomenological existentialism and Anglo-American philosophy.[8] The significance of this early exposure to Wahl's teaching and research interests is evident in Deleuze's later remark in *Dialogues* that, 'apart from Sartre . . . the most important philosopher in France was Jean Wahl. He not only introduced us to an encounter with English and American thought, but had the ability to make us think, in French, things which were very new' (D 57–8). It also appears that, while an assistant professor in the history of philosophy at the Sorbonne (1957–60), Deleuze gave a course in 1957–8 that addressed the core themes of Wahl's work on pluralism and empiricism.[9] I will examine in more detail in the following section the debt that Deleuze's published oeuvre owes to Wahl's work on the pluralist philosophies of England and America. Before doing so, however, it is appropriate to mention some of the other ways in which the encounter with Wahl was decisive for Deleuze's philosophical trajectory.

Dosse speculates that it was almost certainly Wahl who convinced Deleuze to write on Hume, given that Wahl was the figure primarily responsible for the introduction and dissemination of British philosophy in France.[10] It is also highly likely that Wahl, through his publications and teaching, played an important role for Deleuze in rehabilitating Bergson's philosophy.[11] More significantly, it appears that Wahl was a key influence with regard to Deleuze's turn to, and abiding philosophical interest in, Nietzsche. It is true that Deleuze cites Wahl only in passing in *Nietzsche and Philosophy* (he references Wahl's *La Malheur de la conscience dans la philosophie de Hegel* in the context of a discussion of the death of God and its meaning in Hegel – see NP 217, n. 12).[12] Nevertheless, it is noteworthy that the intellectual climate in which Deleuze wrote and published *Nietzsche and Philosophy* – a climate characterised by significant and renewed interest in Nietzsche – was developed, in no small part, through Wahl's efforts. Indeed, in 'Nomadic Thought', Deleuze recognises Wahl's early efforts, along with fellow contributors to the journal *Acéphale*, to expose how Nietzsche had been 'used, twisted, and completely distorted by the fascists' (DI 256). Deleuze was also an active member of the society of which Wahl would eventually become president – the Société française d'études nietzschéennes – which had as its mission to retrieve Nietzsche's work 'from the level of tendentious propaganda to that of thorough-going objectivity and informed critique'.[13] Moreover, as Le Rider notes, Wahl was one of the first academic philosophers to treat Nietzsche with the same seriousness as a Hegel or a Kierkegaard, publishing in 1959 and 1961 the notes from two courses that he gave on Nietzsche at the Sorbonne in 1958–9 and 1960–1.[14] But now it also appears that, in his role at the time as an assistant professor in the history of philosophy at the Sorbonne, Deleuze produced for Wahl's 1958–9 lectures a series of commentaries that would eventually lead to his 1962 monograph, *Nietzsche and Philosophy*.[15] A year later, as is well known, Wahl published a lengthy review of this latter work, full of praise and admiration but also expressing some doubts about Deleuze's account of Hegel and Nietzsche's distance from him.[16] Finally, in 1964, Wahl was an important contributor to the colloquium on Nietzsche that Deleuze organised at Royaumont Abbey.[17] While a detailed study of the relation between Deleuze's and Wahl's Nietzsche remains to be undertaken, it is clear that the importance that Nietzsche assumed for Deleuze owes much to the philosophical and professional efforts of Jean Wahl.

But Wahl's importance for Deleuze is due not only to his teaching and the role he played in French intellectual life. Wahl's published philosophical oeuvre also had an influence on Deleuze. In the following section, I shall explore one of the key philosophical 'debts' that Deleuze owes to Wahl, which relates to Deleuze's understanding of pluralism and empiricism, as well as the work of William James.

Pluralism and Empiricism in Wahl's James and Deleuze

As is well known, in the Preface to the English-language edition of *Dialogues*, Deleuze declares that he always felt that he was 'an empiricist, that is, a pluralist' (D vii). What I wish to do here is examine what Deleuze's pluralism and empiricism owe to his reading of Wahl's *Pluralist Philosophies* and, in particular, Wahl's study of William James in this book.

What does the term 'pluralism' signify in Wahl's work? Abstractly, and negatively, pluralism is opposed to monism, or to the idea of totality. As Wahl puts it, pre-empting Deleuze's later equation of pluralism and empiricism, pluralism is 'a new name given to empiricism, since empiricism is above all a philosophy of the parts in contrast with a philosophy of the whole'.[18] There are, however, many kinds of pluralisms in Anglo-American philosophical thought. Indeed, Wahl identified a plurality of pluralisms: metaphysical pluralism, noetic or epistemological pluralism, moral pluralism, teleological pluralism, political pluralism, religious pluralism and even logical pluralism. Two of the more philosophically interesting kinds of pluralism that Wahl finds in James are metaphysical and epistemological (or noetic) pluralism. Metaphysical pluralism affirms that there is not, metaphysically speaking, one overarching entity. What there is, is essentially diverse or incomplete. As James famously put it, 'something always escapes'.

> Things are 'with' one another in many ways, but nothing includes everything, or dominates over everything. The word 'and' trails along after every sentence. Something always escapes. 'Ever not quite' has to be said of the best attempts made anywhere in the universe at attaining all-inclusiveness.[19]

Epistemological or noetic pluralism, in turn, affirms that there is no all-inclusive explanation of the world. In other words, there is more than one true or correct account of how things are. As Wahl puts it, quoting James:

> [I]nstead of speaking of truth in the singular we must speak of *truths* . . . There is a multiplicity of 'knowers'. There is no omniscient mind, the world is known but partially, by particular subjects, and we are led to what James calls a 'noetic pluralism' . . . '[T]he facts and worths of life need many cognizers to take them in. There is no point of view absolutely public and universal.'[20]

[It is these two kinds of pluralism – metaphysical and noetic – that Deleuze celebrates when he writes that the 'pluralist idea that a thing has many senses, the idea that there are many things and one thing can be seen as "this and then that" is philosophy's greatest achievement' (NP 4).]

One can, however, be a pluralist in many different ways, as Wahl's *Pluralist Philosophies* shows. So how exactly should we understand Deleuze's pluralism? In the Preface to the English-language edition of *Dialogues*, as has been said, Deleuze equates pluralism with empiricism. Moreover, he understands this equivalence to derive from two things: (1) the need to explain the abstract, as opposed to having the abstract explain the concrete; and (2) the aim to find the conditions under which something new is produced, as opposed to discovering the eternal or universal (see D vii).[21] It would seem that Deleuze is here asserting a type of metaphysical pluralism. It is a pluralism that, first of all, denies monism by denying that abstract and totalising categories such as the One, the Whole or the Subject explain the nature of the concrete by, for example, being somehow realised in the concrete. Secondly, Deleuze's metaphysical pluralism is one that understands reality as something necessarily incomplete or, temporally speaking, something not-yet; and in this connection between pluralism and a certain 'temporalism' we find the conditions for the production of novelty.

In what follows, I intend to show the strong parallels between a number of the key elements of Deleuze's pluralistic empiricism and Wahl's account of James's pluralism, and to argue that Deleuze has indeed drawn on Wahl's *Pluralist Philosophies* in developing these particular elements of his pluralism. I will focus on five pluralistic theses or positions that one finds both in Deleuze and in Wahl's James: (1) the thesis that relations are external to their terms; (2) the idea that a pluralist metaphysics entails a radical (or transcendental) empiricism; (3) a critique of monism and, in particular, Hegelian monism; (4) the idea that reality is distributive, or a patchwork of 'plural facts'; and (5) the affirmation of a relation between pluralism, temporalism and the production of novelty. This is not an attempt to provide an exhaustive and systematic explication of Deleuze's pluralistic empiricism, but rather a more restricted exercise. For the most part, I will proceed in a chronological fashion through Deleuze's oeuvre and make explicit at the level of Deleuze's texts those points at which he appears to owe a philosophical debt to Wahl's study of James's pluralism. I aim to show that when the above-mentioned features of pluralism are discussed in Deleuze's work, one tends to find an explicit or implicit reference to James, and more particularly to Wahl's work on James.

Relations are external to their terms

Starting with *Empiricism and Subjectivity*, there is good reason to believe that one of the central empiricist and pluralistic theses in this book – the idea that relations are external to their terms – comes directly from Wahl's study of James. This is the thesis, we can recall, that the relations between terms are determined neither by the nature of the relata themselves, nor by the nature of the contingent ensembles they will form together. In other words, the idea that relations are external to their terms is the idea that there is a multiplicity inherent in reality that persists even when elements of this multiplicity enter into relations and form temporary unities.[22] This is metaphysical pluralism itself, in its opposition to monism. As James puts it, 'pluralism or the doctrine that it is many means only that the sundry parts of reality *may be externally related*. Everything you can think of, however vast or inclusive, has on the pluralistic view a genuinely "external" environment of some sort or amount.'[23] The connections between terms or actualities are thus, for Wahl's James, extrinsic, provisional, numerous and variable.[24] Or again, as will be seen, for James and for Deleuze in *Difference and Repetition*, they are a matter of contingent empirical events.[25] For Deleuze's Hume in *Empiricism and Subjectivity*, these connections are a matter of association which is itself only a habitual tendency, constituted in the given (ES x, 98–101).

There is evidence to suggest that Deleuze's reading of Hume on this point owes something to Wahl's *Pluralist Philosophies*. In the middle of his main discussion of the doctrine of external relations in

Hume, Deleuze writes: 'relations are external to their terms . . . When James calls himself a pluralist, he does not say, in principle, anything else. This is also the case when Russell calls himself a realist' (ES 99). While this passage appears offhand, and while Wahl is not mentioned at all, it in fact reveals something of Deleuze's philosophical debt to Wahl. Indeed, Wahl's *Pluralist Philosophies* explores in detail the thesis of the 'externality of relations to their terms', not only in James, but also in Russell, and the different kinds of pluralism this entails.[26] Moreover, Wahl explicitly connects the pluralism of James and the realism of Russell with regard to the doctrine of external relations, precisely as Deleuze does in *Empiricism and Subjectivity*. Wahl writes:

> the theory of the externality of relations is seen very clearly in the writings of James. Radical empiricism is partly the affirmation of relations without internal foundations in the terms. It was natural that the pluralism of James, the more it unfolded its presuppositions, should prove to be fairly similar to the realism of Russell.[27]

But now, if we put this evidence together with Deleuze's well-known acknowledgement of Wahl as the primary disseminator of Anglo-American philosophy in France (D 58), it appears almost certain that it was through Wahl that Deleuze first encountered the importance of the notion of external relations in Anglo-American pluralist empiricism in general.[28]

Radical empiricism. Transcendental empiricism

This brings us to the second point, which is that both Deleuze and Wahl's James understand metaphysical pluralism to entail, not only a doctrine of external relations, but also a radical empiricism; or, as Deleuze will call it, a transcendental empiricism.[29] It is just such an empiricism that can account for the production of the actual 'identities' we experience, without making reference to an abstract and totalising whole within which things are internally related, as per the monistic thesis. Without wanting to collapse the differences between James's radical empiricism and Deleuze's transcendental empiricism, we can observe that they both entail two broad commitments.[30] The first commitment is to the existence of what Deleuze calls an impersonal and pre-individual field which is shot through with virtual relations and which is ontologically prior to determined individuals and persons (DR 246; LS 102–3). As commentators such as Lapoujade have noted, this field bears a striking resemblance to what James calls 'pure experience' or 'the immediate flux of life'. This 'primal stuff or material' is 'a *that* which is not yet any definite *what*, tho' ready to be all sorts of whats': subjects and objects, thoughts and things, and so forth.[31] What is important to note is that, for both thinkers, it is from this prior field that concrete psychic and physical reality will be produced. And this bring us to the second empiricist commitment that James and Deleuze share. For both thinkers, concrete terms and their relations will emerge from the field of pure experience *by means of an experience*: for James, the direct experience of relations, and for Deleuze, an encounter with intensive difference.

James's and Deleuze's empiricism is thus opposed, not only to monism, but also to the 'atomistic' empiricism that takes the objects of experience to be simply disconnected bits of sense-data that 'rattle against their neighbours as drily as if they were dice in box',[32] and must be related together by operations of the mind (see also DI 163). Their form of empiricism is the affirmation that the relations between experiences require no 'transexperiential agents of unification', for they are themselves experiences of a certain kind.[33] As James puts it,

> the relations between things, conjunctive as well as disjunctive, are just as much matters of direct particular experience, neither more so nor less so, than the things themselves . . . [T]he parts of experience hold together from next to next by relations that are themselves parts of experience. The directly apprehended universe needs, in short, no extraneous trans-empirical connective support, but possesses in its own right a concatenated or continuous structure.[34]

Deleuze's transcendental empiricism, of course, also affirms a thesis of this kind. As he writes in *Difference and Repetition*: 'Empiricism truly becomes transcendental . . . only when we apprehend directly in the sensible . . . the very being *of* the sensible: difference, potential difference and difference in intensity as the reason behind qualitative diversity' (DR 56–7). This intensive difference is, for Deleuze, precisely that which relates the different to the different (DR 117). In other words, for Deleuze, the conditions of the experience of different and determinate actual things depend first of all on a contingent encounter with intensive difference, which determines the virtual relations of the pre-individual field (or virtual Idea) to be incarnated in actual relations (DR 144–5, 245–6).

But now, beyond these general parallels, there is evidence to suggest that Deleuze has indeed drawn on Wahl's reading of James's radical empiricism in formulating his own transcendental empiricism.

In *Difference and Repetition*, in the paragraph following Deleuze's discussion of the conditions of a transcendental empiricism (quoted above), Deleuze cites the poet Paul Benjamin Blood, who, he says, expresses transcendental empiricism's 'profession of faith':

> Nature is contingent, excessive and mystical essentially . . . [T]he universe is wild . . . The same returns not, save to bring the different. The slow round of the engraver's lathe gains but the breadth of a hair, but the difference is distributed back over the whole curve, never an instant true – ever not quite. (DR 57)

What we should notice about this quotation is that it is not taken directly from Blood's *The Anaesthetic Revelation*. It is rather taken from Wahl's translation of James's own quotation of Blood's work in the last text James wrote for publication, 'A Pluralistic Mystic' (1910). Blood expresses the 'profession of faith' of transcendental empiricism, in so far as he, as Wahl indicates, is at once a 'realist' who recognises only empirically given facts, but also a 'mystic' who maintains that that by which facts are given both transcends facts and is part and parcel of the facts themselves.[35] Moreover, in the note to this quotation in *Difference and Repetition*, Deleuze indicates a connection between his own 'transcendental empiricism' and Wahl's work on James's 'radical empiricism', along with the corresponding pluralistic critique of Hegelian monism and its doctrine of purely internal relations. Deleuze writes:

> All Jean Wahl's work is a profound meditation on difference: on the possibilities within empiricism for expressing its poetic, free and wild nature; on the irreducibility of difference to the simple negative; on the *non-Hegelian* relations between affirmation and negation. (DR 311, n. 18)[36]

Opposition to Hegelian monism

This takes us directly to our third point: the pluralistic opposition to Hegelian monism that is in some sense shared by Deleuze and Wahl's James.[37] As Wahl writes, 'Pluralism sets itself over against monism. The pluralist theory begins with a refutation of monism.'[38] And the monism of James's time was the British Hegelianism of Green and Bradley, found throughout American universities at the turn of the twentieth century and especially in the work of Royce. We can see James's hostility to Hegelianism reflected in Deleuze's work, not only in the above-mentioned note about Wahl from *Difference and*

Repetition, but also in Deleuze's essay 'Michel Tournier and the World without Others', first published in 1967, and then again as an appendix to *The Logic of Sense*. Deleuze here alludes to James's pluralistic opposition to Hegel's absolute 'block-universe', which James describes as 'the pure plethora of necessary being with the oxygen of possibility all suffocated out of its lungs'.[39] Deleuze here takes James's longing for the 'oxygen of possibility' to be the invocation of an 'a priori Other structure' – or as Wahl might say, the invocation of a kind of noetic and metaphysical pluralism – which accounts for the manner in which a plurality of 'concrete others [*autruis-ci*]' appear as the expressions of a plurality of different possible worlds (LS 318). Now, while Deleuze here cites neither James nor Wahl directly, Wahl's *Pluralist Philosophies* does contain a discussion of James on this point. Wahl writes: 'The world of the Hegelian appears to us as a world devoid of possibility, deprived, as James expresses it, of the oxygen of possibility.'[40] What makes it highly probable that Deleuze takes this point about James from Wahl's work is Deleuze's tendency to quote from Wahl's *Pluralist Philosophies* whenever a reference to James is called for – whether this be with regard to James's work on the poet Blood, as we've just seen, or, as we shall soon see, when Deleuze discusses James's 'mosaic philosophy' in 'Bartleby; or, The Formula', in *Essays Critical and Clinical*.

A distributive conception of reality: mosaics and patchworks

Before coming to this latter text, we can note that another reference to James, this time in Deleuze's *The Fold*, also arguably bears the mark of Wahl's study of James's pluralism. In *Pluralist Philosophies*, Wahl had explained how, for James, the pluralistic conception of reality is 'distributive' as opposed to 'collective'.[41] In other words, for James, whereas Hegelian monism affirms that the whole is the only genuine and existing unity with all parts ontologically depending on it as such, pluralism asserts that the parts themselves are genuine and existing 'distributive unities' that must be taken both as 'eaches' – each on its own account – and as 'strung-along' or 'additive', always in possible, mediated or actual connection.[42] Indeed, this distributive conception of reality is a correlate of the pluralistic thesis that there are relations external to their terms. For to assert by contrast that relations are uniquely internal to their terms is to affirm a collective conception of reality, which is to say, a single, great totality within which things are necessarily connected or internally related. For

James, then, distributive reality is a reality of 'plural facts', and the so-called 'whole' is only their resultant. These plural facts, as James says, 'lean on each other, but the whole of them, if such a whole there be, leans on nothing'.[43]

Deleuze argues in *The Fold* that the Leibnizian world of monads exists distributively in this Jamesian sense (FLB 100). Each Leibnizian monad must be taken both on its own account and together with the others, just as, for Wahl's James, 'any fragment of the universe asserts itself as independent of all the rest [and] at the same time . . . asserts itself as inextricably one with all the rest'.[44] The 'whole', however – the world – is not an actual substantial thing, or a pre-existing and independent totality in its own right. On the one hand, as Deleuze explains, each existing monad is a distributive unity that 'mirrors' the world on its own account, independently of the others. For Leibniz, the world is actual only in the form of the particular predicates 'included' in the concept of each existing monad, each monad expressing or mirroring the entire world from a particular point of view (FLB 104). On the other hand, the world that is mirrored by each monad, in so far as this world is to be distinguished from the monad, must be understood to be the common horizon of all the monads taken together. The world as a common horizon of all the 'eaches' is thus said by Deleuze to be, not actual, but rather a 'virtuality' that each monad actualises in particular but related ways, and through which what is included in the concept of each monad is connected to what is included in the concepts of the other monads (FLB 23). A monad's predicates are thus relations or events, that is, in so far as each predicate is a relation to existence and to time: to the entire world of monads that each monad mirrors in its own way (FLB 52). It might be objected at this point that the Leibnizian account of 'inclusion' here amounts to a doctrine of internal relations, contrary to the pluralist doctrine. However, while it is true that, for Leibniz, predicates (or relations or events) are *internal* to each monad, it is the world as the common, virtual horizon of the monads taken together that functions as the *external* law of predication, where this means that the 'sufficient reason' for predication cannot be localised in any particular monad, but could only be determined through an 'infinite analysis' of the series of related elements constituting the movement of the world (FLB 51–2, 74).

But now it is this distributive conception of reality – this 'mosaic philosophy' or 'philosophy of plural facts'[45] – that Deleuze celebrates once again in *Essays Critical and Clinical*. In 'Bartleby; or, The

Formula', Deleuze argues that it is Melville who sketches out the traits of what would become Jamesian pragmatism. What is crucial, though, for Deleuze, is that this pragmatism

> is first of all the affirmation of a world in *process*, an *archipelago*. Not even a puzzle, whose pieces when fitted together would constitute a whole, but rather a wall of loose, uncemented stones, where every element has value in itself but also in relation to others: isolated and floating relations, islands and straits . . . a Harlequin's coat . . . an infinite patchwork with multiple joinings. (ECC 86)

James's distributive conception of reality is here clearly recognisable.[46] We recognise as well in these pages James's pluralist pragmatism – a pragmatism that, like Bartleby, 'will fight ceaselessly . . . against the Universal or the Whole' (ECC 87). But, what is more, we see here once again the importance for Deleuze of Wahl's work on James. Deleuze continues in a note that the themes of

> this world-as-archipelago or this patchwork experiment . . . are to be found throughout Pragmatism, and notably among William James's most beautiful pages: the world as 'shot point blank with a pistol' [*le monde comme 'tiré à bout portant d'un pistolet'*]. (ECC 193, n. 21)

What should be noted here is that when Deleuze places inverted commas around 'shot point blank with a pistol', he is quoting Wahl, not James. James never uses the expression 'point blank'; and nor does Loÿs Moulin's 1916 standard French translation of James's essay 'On Some Hegelisms' use the expression *à bout portant*.[47] Wahl, on the other hand, adds this expression in his rather free translation of James, and Deleuze repeats it.[48] Arguably, then, this constitutes good textual evidence for Deleuze's reliance on Wahl's work for his understanding of James and the articulation and re-articulation of various aspects of Deleuze's own pluralism, including his affirmation of a 'distributive' conception of reality.

Pluralism, temporalism and the production of novelty

We come now to the final point of philosophical affinity between Deleuze and Wahl's James: the affirmation of a relation between pluralism, temporalism and the production of novelty. Wahl calls the connection between pluralism and temporalism the 'central fact in the metaphysics of James'.[49] Moreover, Wahl's exposition of this point links this connection between pluralism and temporalism to the other aspects of James's pluralist empiricism examined above: his opposition to monism, his distributive conception of reality, his affirmation of a doctrine of external relations and his radical empiricism.[50]

Wahl first of all draws attention to the way in which James's linking of pluralism and temporalism goes hand in hand with his opposition to monism. The monist believes in eternity, or the existence of a universe made all of a piece and within which everything is necessarily connected. The pluralist, by contrast, holds that the universe is not determined beforehand. It 'grows by its edges'. 'One moment of it proliferates into the next by transitions which, whether conjunctive or disjunctive, continue the experiential tissue.'[51] As Wahl puts it, imperfectly quoting James,

> [the] affirmation of time is essentially the affirmation that the world is not all made, that it is ever making itself . . . 'The thing of deepest – comparatively – significance in life', says James, 'does seem to be its character of *progress*, or that strange sense of reality with ideal novelty which it continues from one moment to another to offer.' 'Ever the edition of the world – or rather editions – are being completed or amended, they are never "eternal".'[52]

This is also, of course, the affirmation of a distributive as opposed to a collective conception of reality. The world is dispersed and parcelled out, 'strung-along' and 'additive', incomplete but completing itself here and there. As James puts it, the distributive 'each-form' is not only the form of reality, but also the form of its temporal appearance.[53]

Wahl also notes that, for James, the pluralistic idea of external relations essentially implies the idea of the existence of time. For Wahl's James, changes in relations between things are movements in a 'fluid duration'.[54] But we also see here the connection between pluralism, temporalism and James's radical empiricism. As has been said, changes in the relations between things are not due to anything trans-empirical – they are themselves experiences that offer themselves to us in a temporal fashion, one by one. It is a series of experiences in the plural that time modifies, but experience itself, as James puts it, 'has ways of *boiling over*, and making us correct our present formulas'.[55] Taking into consideration the radical empiricist conception of pure experience, Wahl then explains that, for James,

> reality is plasticity, indifference. This plasticity, this indifference, is a possibility of change. 'Change that takes place' is one of our first felt experiences; we have the feeling of genuine experiences succeeding one another. Time sets going the world of radical empiricism which

> we had hitherto regarded as static, and makes a really multiple world of it.[56]

Now, to my knowledge, we do not find in Deleuze a discussion of the relation between pluralism, temporalism and the production of novelty that references, or even alludes to, Wahl or James. Nevertheless, given that Deleuze appears to have been significantly influenced by Wahl's study of James's affirmation of external relations, radical empiricism and a distributive conception of reality, we should not be surprised to find that Deleuze similarly understands these pluralistic propositions to go hand in hand with a thesis about the relation between real plurality, time and the production of the new.

While it is not possible here to give a detailed account of Deleuze's conception (or perhaps conception*s*) of time, we can note that Deleuze has always been concerned to understand the conditions of the new in terms of a relation between real multiplicity and time. We see this even in his earliest works in the history of philosophy (especially on Nietzsche and Bergson), but more particularly in a work such as *Difference and Repetition*. In chapter 4 of this latter text, Deleuze develops a conception of a virtual multiplicity (also called a 'problematic Idea') which is comprised of purely differential but reciprocally determined elements and relations, to which correspond distributions of singular points or 'potentials' (DR 183). While not 'actual', this multiplicity is nevertheless real. The reality of this virtual multiplicity is that of a determined structure that will be incarnated in actual terms and relations (DR 209). Moreover, for Deleuze, this multiplicity is the condition for novelty, in the sense that the 'actualisation' of this purely differential multiplicity is, quite precisely, the production of the new (as opposed to a repetition of some pre-existing identity). Crucially, for our purposes here, Deleuze then designates the agent of this actualisation as a 'spatio-temporal dynamism' (DR 214). Or again, as Deleuze will elaborate in the fifth chapter, it is the 'intensive difference' expressed in the spatio-temporal dynamism which 'determines an "indistinct" differential relation in the Idea [virtual multiplicity] to incarnate itself in a distinct quality and a distinguished extensity' (DR 245). And this, of course, as we have already seen, is Deleuze's transcendental empiricism in a nutshell, which we could very well redescribe by paraphrasing the above quote from Wahl: The virtual multiplicity or problematic Idea is the potential for change or novelty. 'Change that takes place' is one of our first encounters. The intensive differences expressed by such spatio-temporal dynamisms set going the world of transcendental empiricism which we had hitherto regarded as a static virtual multiplicity, and makes a multiple and new actual world of it.

Wahl: *passim*

The foregoing section has given us good reason to believe that Deleuze has been oriented in a general way by Wahl's work on James in developing five aspects of his pluralist empiricism: the affirmation that relations are external to their terms; the affirmation of a 'superior' empiricism; an opposition to (Hegelian) monism; a view of reality as essentially multiple and 'distributive'; and the affirmation of a relation between pluralism, temporalism and the production of the new.

It is noteworthy, however, that although *Pluralist Philosophies* is the only one of Wahl's works explicitly referenced in *Difference and Repetition*, Deleuze nevertheless recorded '*passim*' next to Wahl's name in its bibliography (DR 343), indicating thereby that 'the themes of difference and repetition are really present through all [his] work' (DR 334). It is an open question what Deleuze had in mind here, given the lack of engagement with Wahl's particular and persistent philosophical concerns with 'the concrete' and its relation to thought in his wider philosophical oeuvre. In the remainder of this article, then, I will address this question by briefly examining a number of points at which Deleuze's philosophical proximity to Wahl seems evident.

The first thing to be noted is Wahl's philosophical method. Much of Wahl's work tends to be about the thought of others. He is not, however, simply an interpreter of the history of philosophy. Rather, his exploration of the works of others is his primary method for advancing his own philosophical views. His colleague Ferdinand Alquié variously described Wahl's method as a kind of 'pointillism', a 'method of juxtaposition' and a 'philosophy of the "and"', whereby he presents his own thought through the constant 'adjunction' of reflections on the thoughts of others, each of which comes to enrich and correct the overall position.[57] From one end of his oeuvre to another, we thus find Wahl simultaneously engaged both in sympathetic and nuanced readings of various aspects of the work of Hegel, Kierkegaard, Nietzsche, James, Heidegger and so on, and in the indirect presentation of his own philosophical concerns. The resonance of Wahl's 'method of juxtaposition' with Deleuze's own predilection for 'free indirect discourse' is, of course, evident, even if this is unacknowledged by Deleuze.[58]

But now, what of Wahl's particular philosophical concerns? In what follows I will touch upon three of the major and persistent themes of Wahl's 'philosophy of the concrete': the 'thickness' of concrete experience, the simultaneous transcendence and immanence of thought in relation to the concrete, and the inevitability of an existential dialectic brought about by thought's confrontation with the concrete. I will then draw out some of the parallels between these themes and several of Deleuze's key claims in *Difference and Repetition* in order to try to explain the recording of '*passim*' next to Wahl's name in the bibliography to this work.

Wahl's philosophy of the concrete is best introduced with reference to the philosophical orientations it opposes. From the opening paragraph of the famous Preface to *Toward the Concrete*, Wahl takes aim at idealist treatments of concrete experience: in Hegel, but also in the epistemological idealism of Brunschvicg and others. The concrete, for Wahl, has a reality of its own, outside of the work of the intelligence, and it is towards this reality that our thought, language and science are directed. He thus affirms 'a certain realism',[59] and his wish, contrary to the idealistic tendencies of his contemporaries, was to give back to the immediate its value and its role in thought, and to help us better understand the point of departure for thought. However, as discussed above, Wahl's concrete should not be considered 'atomic', as the British empiricists would have it. For Wahl, these empiricists' notion of the element or atom of experience – the sense-data or objects that we are directly aware of in perception – is just as abstract as the idealist's whole. He argues that the atom or element of experience is, as it were, carved out from a complex situation – a situation which can never be reconstituted by the juxtaposition of such elements through the synthetic activity of the mind. For Wahl, the elements of experience are themselves concrete particulars, defined by their contingent and actual interrelations with other beings, rather than isolated atoms of sense-data. Or, as Wahl puts it in the Preface to *Toward the Concrete*, the empiricism that he valorises *can* be considered an empiricism of atomic forms, but only as long as we understand by this atomism an atomism of complex and thick 'configurations' – configurations that an artificial division into discrete elements disfigures. What the empiricists in whom Wahl is interested – especially Bergson, James and Whitehead – take to be grasped in experience are blocks of duration, spatial volumes, events which interpenetrate one another, generalities understood as felt relations, syntheses without the synthetic activity of the mind, particulars taken as totalities, and so on.[60]

Wahl is also an opponent of what he calls, following Whitehead, the Cartesian bifurcation, whose conception illegitimately takes us to be separated from the concrete. For Wahl, thought is in some sense immanent to the real. At the same time, however, Wahl will also claim that the real can only appear to the thought that attempts to grasp it as something transcending thought.[61] The concrete is a single reality, without bifurcation, but the mind can know this reality only by opposing it to itself. In other words, thought's relation to the concrete involves both immanence and transcendence.

> Transcendence is the idea of a beyond by means of which knowledge has a direction, toward which it directs itself, from which it draws its nourishment. Immanence is the idea of this compact density in which no element is absolutely transcendent in relation to any other.[62]

Our existence, then, is both fusion with the world and distance from the world,[63] and 'the world presents itself first of all as something external, to which we are, so to speak, internal'.[64]

But we should also note that, for Wahl, the relation of transcendence that characterises our relation to the concrete has two directions.[65] We move towards the concrete as towards something external that transcends thought, but this very movement is itself an internal transcendence: thought's going beyond itself.[66] In 'Subjectivity and Transcendence',[67] Wahl likewise speaks of a trans-descendance and a trans-ascendance: a trans-descendance towards the concrete which is 'below' thought, but at the same time a trans-ascendance in which thought takes the concrete as a kind of 'paradise lost' that one can only attempt to regain by thought's self-transcendence – in the ecstasy of poetry or, arguably, in the ongoing metamorphosis of philosophical conceptions that Wahl valorises.[68]

Finally, for Wahl, this movement between the below and the beyond – or, as he also puts it, between two kinds of silences (the silence of felt experience 'below' thought and the silence of ecstasy 'beyond' thought) – is defined by a dialectic.[69] Evidently, this won't be a Hegelian dialectic through which Spirit returns to itself by overcoming the series of contradictions it discovered when it initially sought the truth outside of itself (or in sense-certainty). It is rather a dialectic that, according to Wahl, maintains the tension between the opposing terms of which it is comprised.[70] This dialectic initially takes shape with thought's encounter with the ineffable real – an encounter that gives rise to contradictory ideas. To put it in the terms of Wahl's two transcendences, the emergence of contradictory ideas in philosophy results from the thought's confrontation with the trans-descendent concrete in all its thickness and ineffability. But, at the same time, it is through the tense oscillation of these contradictory ideas that philosophy attempts to trans-ascend itself in order to re-arrive at its point of departure. As he puts it, the 'succession of battling ideas is explained by what is below them, by this non-relational ground which [these contradictory ideas] try to make explicit but which will always preserve its implicit character.'[71] Wahl's conception of the dialectic thus entails realism, albeit a realism conceived 'not as a doctrine but as an effort . . . The concrete will never be something given to the philosopher. It will [always] be what is being pursued . . . The real is the limit of the dialectic; the real is its origin; the real is its end, its explanation and its destruction.'[72] So, as in the title of Wahl's book, *Toward the Concrete*, the 'toward' needs to be emphasised just as much as the 'concrete'. The concrete – the real – cannot be separated from the dialectical path that is both engendered by it and that philosophical thinking travels on in its very attempt to pass beyond it.

These three themes, arguably, are reflected in some of Deleuze's key positions in *Difference and Repetition*. Firstly, like Wahl, Deleuze treats the sensible world of experience as comprised, not of atomic forms, but of 'thick' configurations which interpenetrate one another. For Deleuze, the sensible world of experience is a mobile field comprised of enveloping and enveloped intensities or implicated differences, out of which 'metastable' individuals emerge and develop in series of 'passive syntheses' (see generally on this, DR chapters 2 and 5).

Secondly, Deleuze, like Wahl, considers thought's relation to the concrete to involve both immanence and transcendence. Thought, for Deleuze, is immanent to sensible experience in that, like everything else, it is an intensive process. Both the sensibility and cognition of the thinking subject emerge from the intensive world of experience (DR 144–5, 151–3). At the same time, however, Deleuze understands thought's relation to the intensive and differential world of concrete experience to involve what Wahl calls relations of trans-descendance and trans-ascendance. On the one hand, the sensible world trans-descends thought, in so far as it is primarily encountered as something which troubles the subject's sensory-motor and cognitive capacities. On the other hand, thought trans-ascends itself in trying to grasp this sensible reality. For Deleuze, the empirical encounter with an unrecognisable intensive difference – something that does not fit habitual schema – constrains thought's various capacities to 'go beyond' what they are currently capable of in the very act of making sense of this difference (DR 139–48).[73] Indeed, this is the meaning of Deleuze's 'transcendental empiricism', which was characterised above as the apprehension in the sensible of the differential conditions of real experience.

Finally, we arguably see in this claim about thought's self-transcendence in the direction of the intensive difference that gave rise to it a Deleuzian version of what Wahl calls an 'existential' and 'non-Hegelian' dialectic. Deleuze explicitly claims that the differential problems which both engender and are expressed in the movement of thought are dialectical in nature (DR 157, 164, 179). The dialectical movement of thought can also be said to be existential, in so far as it begins with an experience of disruption to habitual ways of perceiving and conceiving the world, and involves a painstaking and experimental process of learning and apprenticeship (DR 139, 164–7). Finally, this dialectic is also clearly a non-Hegelian one, in so far as its motor is the 'unthinkable', sub-representative and purely differential genetic element of thought which underpins and subsists in *all* attempts to explicitly represent it – *including* in the negative form of the series of contradictory representations which Hegel takes to be the motor of the dialectic (DR 161–2, 164, 178, 268). Again, then, the general resonance between some of the key claims in *Difference and Repetition* and the positions found throughout Wahl's wider philosophical oeuvre is unmistakable.

To briefly conclude, however, it is worth emphasising that it would be deeply misleading to claim that Deleuze has straightforwardly appropriated and reworked the general outlines of Wahl's pluralist and empiricist philosophy of the concrete. As the chapters in this volume show, the sources of and influences on Deleuze's philosophical trajectory are many and varied. Nevertheless, what should be clear is that the philosophy of Jean Wahl, as much as the person, should not be overlooked in our efforts to clarify Deleuze's intellectual biography.

Notes

1. Emmanuel Levinas, *Outside the Subject* (Stanford: Stanford University Press, 1993), p. 67.
2. See Alan D. Schrift, *Twentieth-century French Philosophy: Key Themes and Thinkers* (Malden, MA: Wiley-Blackwell, 2006), p. 185.
3. See Bruce Baugh, *French Hegel: From Surrealism to Postmodernism* (New York and London: Routledge, 2003), pp. 1–7 and 19–24.
4. Much of Wahl's work has yet to be translated into English. See, however, Wahl's *Human Existence and Transcendence*, trans. and ed. William C. Hackett (Notre Dame: University of Notre Dame Press, 2016), and the anthology *Transcendence and the Concrete: Selected Writings*, ed. Alan D. Schrift and Ian Alexander Moore (New York: Fordham University Press, 2017).
5. See Jean Wahl, 'Poetry and Metaphysics', in *Transcendence and the Concrete*, pp. 220–36.
6. Gilles Deleuze, cited in François Dosse, *Gilles Deleuze and Félix Guattari: Intersecting Lives*, trans. Deborah Glassman (New York: Columbia University Press, 2010), p. 110.
7. For further biographical details, see Ian Alexander Moore and Alan D. Schrift, 'Existence, Experience and Transcendence: An Introduction to Jean Wahl', in Wahl, *Transcendence and the Concrete*, pp. 1–31; Maurice de Gandillac, 'Jean Wahl', *Annuaire de l'Association des anciens élèves de l'École normale supérieure* (Paris, 1975), pp. 38–45; and Jeanne Hersch (ed.), *Jean Wahl et Gabriel Marcel* (Paris: Beauchesne, 1976), pp. 89–92. I thank Alan Schrift for clarifying several aspects of Wahl's biography in an earlier version of this chapter.
8. Dosse, *Gilles Deleuze and Félix Guattari*, p. 97.
9. Ibid., p. 117.
10. Ibid., p. 110.
11. Ibid. On Wahl's relation to Bergson, see also Giuseppe Bianco, *Après Bergson. Portrait de groupe avec philosophe* (Paris: Presses universitaires de France, 2015), pp. 29–31.
12. There is also an argument to be made that Wahl's *Pluralist Philosophies of England and America*, though not referenced, informed Deleuze's remarks about Nietzsche's pluralism and empiricism (see, for example, NP 4). See also Bianco, *Après Bergson*, p. 306.
13. 'Prospectus de la Société française d'études nietzschéennes', cited in Jacques Le Rider, *Nietzsche en France: De la fin du XIXe siècle au temps présent* (Paris: Presses universitaires de France, 1999), p. 185 (cited in Dosse, *Gilles Deleuze and Félix Guattari*, p. 129).
14. Jean Wahl, *La Pensée philosophique de Nietzsche des années 1885–1888* (Paris: Centre de documentation universitaire, 1959) and *L'Avant-dernière pensée de Nietzsche* (Paris: Centre de documentation

universitaire, 1961). See Le Rider, *Nietzsche en France*, pp. 183–5, cited in Mary F. Zamberlin, *Rhizosphere: Gilles Deleuze and the 'Minor' American Writings of William James, W. E. B. Du Bois, Gertrude Stein, Jean Toomer, and William Faulkner* (New York and London: Routledge, 2006), pp. 54–5. See also Guiseppe Bianco, 'Trous et mouvement: sur le dandysme deleuzien. Les cours en Sorbonne 1957–1960', in Stéphan Leclerc (ed.), *Aux sources de la pensée de Gilles Deleuze* (Mons: Sils Maria, 2005), n. 32.

15. See Bianco, *Après Bergson*, p. 306.
16. See Jean Wahl, 'Nietzsche et la philosophie', *Revue de métaphysique et de morale* 68:3 (1963), p. 353.
17. See Jean Wahl, 'Order and Disorder in Nietzsche's Thought', in *Transcendence and the Concrete*, pp. 237–55. For Deleuze's concluding, synthetic address, see DI 117–27.
18. Jean Wahl, *The Pluralist Philosophies of England and America*, trans. Fred Rothwell (London: Open Court, 1925), p. 153.
19. William James, *A Pluralistic Universe* (Cambridge, MA, and London: Harvard University Press, 1977), p. 145. See also Wahl, *Pluralist Philosophies*, p. 144.
20. Wahl, *Pluralist Philosophies*, pp. 155–6. See also William James, *Talks to Teachers on Psychology, and to Students on Some of Life's Ideals* (New York: Henry Holt and Company, 1899), p. v.
21. Deleuze claims, in fact, that these two characteristics are those with which Whitehead defined empiricism. We should note, however, that Deleuze's understanding of Whitehead was also filtered through Wahl's work. Indeed, Wahl was responsible for introducing Whitehead's philosophy onto the French scene. See, in particular, his *Vers le concret* (Paris: Vrin, 1932), which contains chapters on both James and Whitehead, and is referenced by Deleuze in *The Fold* as a guide to 'the totality of Whitehead's philosophy' (FLB 153, n. 2). On this, see also Williams, James, 'A. N. Whitehead', in Graham Jones and Jon Roffe (eds), *Deleuze's Philosophical Lineage* (Edinburgh: Edinburgh University Press, 2009), pp. 282–99.
22. See also on this, Stéphane Madelrieux, 'Pluralism without Pragmatism: Deleuze and the Ambiguities of the French Reception of James', in Sean Bowden, Simone Bignall and Paul Patton (eds), *Deleuze and Pragmatism* (New York and London: Routledge, 2015), pp. 92–3.
23. James, *A Pluralistic Universe*, p. 145. See also Wahl, *Pluralist Philosophies*, p. 144.
24. Wahl, *Pluralist Philosophies*, pp. 142–3.
25. See also on this Bruce Baugh, 'Transcendental Empiricism: Deleuze's Response to Hegel', *Man and World* 25 (1992), pp. 136–7.
26. Wahl, *Pluralist Philosophies*, pp. 134–5, 243–67.
27. Ibid., p. 255.

28. In 'Trous et mouvement', Bianco discusses the unpublished notes to a course that Deleuze taught at the Sorbonne on Hume's *A Treatise of Human Nature*, discovered in the archives of the École normale supérieure de lettres et sciences humaines de Lyon. We see in these notes the influence of Wahl's work on Deleuze's reading of Hume when Deleuze writes: 'The starting point [of Hume] is *diversity*. We cannot conceive empiricism without a lived reality understood as diverse, theme of a patchwork reality (cf. the pluralists James etc. reality conceived as "Harlequin's cloak"; or Jean Wahl: cf. the commentary given by Mr Alquié on the psychology of Jean Wahl: a philosophy of the "and"). Irreducibility of the diverse' (my translation).
29. There is an argument to be made that Deleuze initially found the phrase 'transcendental empiricism' in Wahl's *Existence humaine et transcendance*. Wahl writes (connecting, as Deleuze later will, transcendental empiricism with the search for the conditions of real as opposed to possible experience): 'There may be, and Schelling has shown it, a transcendental empiricism, seeking the conditions under which experience is, we will not say possible, but real; and this realism will be founded on the critique of the idea of the possible, and on the reality of contingency' (p. 18, my translation). My thanks to Joe Hughes for alerting me to this reference. See his 'Ground, Transcendence and Method in Deleuze's Fichte', in Craig Lundy and Daniela Voss (eds), *At the Edges of Thought: Deleuze and Post-Kantian Philosophy* (Edinburgh: Edinburgh University Press, 2015), pp. 156–7.
30. For a critical view of the relation between James and Deleuze, see Jon Roffe, 'Error, Illusion, Deception: Deleuze against James', in Bowden, Bignall and Patton (eds), *Deleuze and Pragmatism*, pp. 73–88.
31. See William James, *The Writings of William James: A Comprehensive Edition*, ed. John J. McDermott (Chicago and London: The University of Chicago Press, 1977), pp. 170, 215. Wahl, *Pluralist Philosophies*, pp. 138–9. On the comparison between James's pure experience and Deleuze's pre-individual field, see David Lapoujade, 'From Transcendental Empiricism to Worker Nomadism: William James', *Pli* 9 (2000), pp. 190–9. Deleuze and Guattari also draw a connection between their notion of a 'plane of immanence' and James's radical empiricist conception of pure experience when they write: 'When immanence is no longer immanent to something other than itself it is possible to speak of a plane of immanence. Such a plane is, perhaps, a radical empiricism' (see WP 47).
32. James, cited in Wahl, *Pluralist Philosophies*, p. 123.
33. See James, *Writings*, p. 196. James here lists a number of these 'transexperiential agents of unification': 'substances, intellectual categories and powers, . . . Selves'.
34. See the important passage on 'radical empiricism' in James's *The*

Meaning of Truth, reprinted in *Writings*, p. 136. See also Wahl, *Pluralist Philosophies*, pp. 139–40.

35. See Wahl, *Pluralist Philosophies*, pp. 126, 133.
36. In the thesis outline for what would eventually become *Difference and Repetition*, several references to James – almost certainly Wahl's James – can be found. Deleuze writes: 'Essential link of empiricism and pluralism: the taste for and game of diversity as opposed to the work of identification. Admirable description of diversity in James . . . Pure affirmation is a philosophy of difference (James and Nietzsche). The symbolism of Dionysus but also Harlequin's cloak' (cited in Madelrieux, 'Pluralism without Pragmatism', p. 91). This thesis outline was found by Guiseppe Bianco in the Jean Hyppolite archives and is quoted in his unpublished paper 'Philosophies du ET. Que se passe-t-il entre (Wahl et Deleuze)?'. See http://www.diffusion.ens.fr/index.php?res=conf&idconf=685.
37. It may be objected here that James and Deleuze fail to do justice to Hegel. My aim, however, is not so much to defend a particular reading of Hegel as to show a parallel between James's treatment of Hegel as a monist, and Deleuze's treatment of him as a thinker who subordinates the 'free and wild' nature of difference to identity.
38. Wahl, *Pluralist Philosophies*, p. 134.
39. William James, *The Will to Believe and Other Essays in Popular Philosophy* (New York and London: Longmans, Green, 1907), p. 292.
40. Wahl, *Pluralist Philosophies*, p. 151.
41. Ibid., pp. 139, 165–7.
42. See James, *Writings*, pp. 258–9, 457–9, 807–9.
43. See James, *Writings*, p. 457. Wahl, *Pluralist Philosophies*, p. 139.
44. Wahl, *Pluralist Philosophies*, p. 142.
45. James, *Writings*, p. 195. Wahl, *Pluralist Philosophies*, p. 139.
46. James's radical empiricism is also in the background. Consider this passage from *Essays in Radical Empiricism*: 'At the outset of my essay, I called [my philosophy of pure experience] a mosaic philosophy. In actual mosaics the pieces are held together by their bedding, for which bedding the Substances, transcendental Egos, or Absolutes of other philosophies may be taken to stand. In radical empiricism there is no bedding; it is as if the pieces clung together by their edges, the transitions experienced between them forming their cement.' See James, *Writings*, p. 212.
47. In 'On Some Hegelisms', James writes that the 'parts [of the real] seem . . . to be shot out of a pistol at us'. See William James, *The Will to Believe*, p. 264. This appears in the standard French translation as 'il semble que [les] parties [du reel] . . . viennent nous frapper comme des balles de pistolet'. See William James, *La Volonté de croire*, trans. Loÿs Moulin (Paris: Flammarion, 1916), p. 275.

48. 'The parts of the universe are, as it were, fired point-blank.' See Wahl, *Pluralist Philosophies*, p. 141. In the French edition, Wahl writes: 'les parties de l'univers sont comme tirées d'un pistolet – à bout portant'. See Jean Wahl, *Les Philosophies pluralistes d'Angleterre et d'Amérique* (Paris: Alcan, 1920), p. 124.
49. Wahl, *Pluralist Philosophies*, p. 165.
50. See, generally, ibid., pp. 162–9.
51. James, *Writings*, p. 212.
52. Wahl, *Pluralist Philosophies*, p. 164. See James, *Writings*, p. 657.
53. James, *Writings*, p. 808.
54. Wahl, *Pluralist Philosophies*, p. 143.
55. James, *Writings*, p. 438.
56. Wahl, *Pluralist Philosophies*, pp. 162–3.
57. See Ferdinand Alquié, 'Jean Wahl et la philosophie', *Critique* 10 (1954), pp. 519–23; and 'Jean Wahl', *Les Études philosophiques* 1 (1975), p. 81.
58. On 'free indirect discourse', see TP 80 and François Zourabichvili, *Deleuze: A Philosophy of the Event, together with The Vocabulary of Deleuze*, trans. Kieran Aarons (Edinburgh: Edinburgh University Press, 2012), pp. 133–4.
59. Ibid., p. 264.
60. Ibid., pp. 37–8, 257–8, 259–60.
61. Ibid., p. 40.
62. Ibid.
63. Ibid., p. 267.
64. Ibid., p. 264.
65. Ibid., p. 267.
66. Ibid., p. 268.
67. Ibid., p. 157.
68. Ibid., p. 258.
69. Ibid., p. 271.
70. Ibid., pp. 51–2, 266.
71. Ibid., p. 50.
72. Ibid., p. 51.
73. On this, see Sean Bowden, 'An Anti-Positivist Conception of Problems: Deleuze, Bergson and the French Epistemological Tradition', *Angelaki* 23:2 (2018), pp. 57–9.

Martial Gueroult

Knox Peden

In an homage to Deleuze first published in 1972 Clément Rosset relays the impression of a reader of *Difference and Repetition* who remarked: 'It's like eating a biscuit that's missing butter. It's excellent, but dry.' In Rosset's view, 'Deleuze's Dryness' – as the title of his brief homage has it – is a distinctive feature of his work, akin to its coldness, or *froideur*. Disconcerting, this dryness is nevertheless a virtue because it leads us to appreciate all the things Deleuze spares his reader – 'no tears, no emotion, no metaphysical thrills' – thereby allowing a clearer view of the philosophy itself. Rosset speaks of a lack of enthusiasm in Deleuze's writing and one wonders if he's being ironic, given Deleuze's affinity for Spinoza, alternately the prince or Christ of philosophers for Deleuze, and not coincidentally the supreme instance of *Schwärmerei* run amok for critical philosophy. But Rosset's point is that Deleuze gives us a vision of philosophy in which the criteria by which it can be judged are entirely internal to it. There is no enthusiasm because there is no end goal, no purpose for which the task of philosophy is well suited or fashioned. Deleuze is a master of precision. But such is the 'paradox of Deleuze . . . : precision for nothing'.[1]

The jocosity of Rosset's take is to the point. Deleuze once observed a propos Foucault that ontological seriousness requires a diabolical humour (F 111). Rosset's writing merits the same description. Broadly Nietzschean and even more Schopenhauerian in inspiration, Rosset's work has taken the form of a series of belletristic essays seeking joy in the univocity of being, which is to say, in the absence of all alternatives to existence as it is here and now in any given instance.[2] Though he taught for years at Nice, Rosset's writing career has been decidedly extra-academic. This adds pungency to his take on Deleuze's relationship to the academy and the figure with whom he thinks Deleuze shares the most traits:

> [With Deleuze] we don't know if a philosophy is pretty, if it's true, or 'sounds good.' We want first of all to see how it's made, to locate

> its mode of construction, to determine the solidity of its assemblage [*agencement*]. This is a method that is unmistakably academic and scholarly. In fact, Deleuze often seems strangely close to Martial Gueroult. But there's a small difference. Deleuze's method borrows the university's rigor, but it strives for a thought that is neither scholarly nor academic, precisely insofar as it is not in the service of *any* thought, any objective, or any particular themes.[3]

Again, 'precision for nothing'. Deleuze's method brings us towards the singular. And if the singular is truly singular, unique, then it must be incomparable and in some sense unintelligible. The perversity is complete. Rosset sees Deleuze striving for unintelligibility and lauds him for it.

Martial Gueroult pursued the opposite goal. His magisterial volumes in the history of philosophy – on Berkeley, Leibniz, Malebranche, Fichte, Maimon and, above all, Descartes and Spinoza – strove for total intelligibility.[4] Each line of each book was written to make clear the overarching rationality that structured a philosophical oeuvre. Gueroult attempted to explicate his method, which he termed a *dianoématique* (a study of doctrines), in a series of books that were published only posthumously.[5] Various shorter pieces dealt with the same themes, most notably his inaugural lesson at the Collège de France in 1951 and one of his few essays translated into English: 'The History of Philosophy as a Philosophical Problem' (both to be discussed below).[6] But the greatest monument to Gueroult's method are the works themselves. In 2007 Jean-Marie Beyssade described Gueroult's two-volume work on Descartes's *Meditations*, published in 1953, as a *PanzerCartesianer*. Tad Schmaltz expounds Beyssade's Prussian allusion as follows:

> These *Panzer*-type virtues of granite thought, inflexible will, and complete certainty are revealed in particular by Descartes's unwavering adherence to the strict 'order of reasons' found in his *Meditations*. According to Gueroult, this order requires the arrangement of truths in such a way that knowledge of those that precede are necessary conditions of those that follow. In this way, Descartes's system forms a whole in which 'no single truth of the system can be correctly interpreted without reference to the place it occupies in the order.'[7]

This method was deployed in force in the final work of Gueroult's career, a multi-volume study of Spinoza's *Ethics* that remained unfinished at the time of his death in 1976, with two volumes, on books 1 and 2 of the *Ethics*, published in 1968 and 1974, respectively. In

1969 Deleuze praised Gueroult's *Spinoza, I: Dieu* in a prominent review in the *Revue de la métaphysique et de la morale* for being the work in which Gueroult's method found its 'most adequate, most saturated, most exhaustive end or object'. In Deleuze's judgement, 'the book founds the genuine scientific study of Spinozism' (DI 216).

When it comes to Gueroult and Deleuze and the comparison Rosset sets up for us, it's tempting to say *les extremes se touchent* and leave it at that. At some point maximum intelligibility tips over into its opposite: total unintelligibility. But that seems glib, not to mention far too close to a dialectical conception of philosophical interaction that was anathema to both Deleuze and Gueroult. The onus is on us, then, to determine the validity of Rosset's comparison and the significance of it for coming to terms with Deleuze's philosophy and its place in the field of twentieth-century French thought. We'll begin with a brief look at method, then focus on the commonalities between Gueroult's and Deleuze's Spinozas. We will conclude with a broader consideration of Gueroult as a figure whose views on the history of philosophy mattered to Deleuze.

Method

Concerning method, the point of departure must be the internalism that is common to both Gueroult's and Deleuze's work in the history of philosophy. Whether it's Gueroult's books on Spinoza or Deleuze's, you'll find no real reference to philosophical context in the main text (grudging allusions to exteriority find their way into the notes), much less historical or political context. For each reader, the oeuvre of a philosopher is a singular construction, one whose operative animus can be gleaned only by attending to the logic of that construction itself. This is the substance of Gueroult's 'structural-genetic' method as Deleuze presents it: 'A structure is defined by an *order of reasons*, reasons being the differential and generative elements of a corresponding system, genuine philosophemes that exist only in their relation to each other' (DI 202). This description of Gueroult's method bears comparison with the diagnostic that Deleuze offered three years later in 'How Do We Recognise Structuralism?' Here he writes:

> Any structure is a multiplicity . . . Symbolic elements are incarnated in the beings and real objects of the domain under consideration; differential relations are actualized in the real relations between these beings; singularities are just so many places in the structure, which

> distribute the roles or imaginary attitudes of the beings and objects which come to occupy them. (DI 247)

In Gueroult's method, Deleuze stresses the relationship between the order of simple reasons for knowing (*simples raisons de connaître*) and genuine reasons for being (*véritables raisons d'être*), and describes this as a relation between an analytic order and a synthetic order. The analytic order of reasons for knowing aligns with what goes by the name of the symbolic in Deleuze's assessment of structuralism. But by tracking the differential structure of this order, we alight on those sites where thought mirrors or grasps the productive or generative nature of the object of this thought, whatever the object happens to be. What is thought is truly synthetic, the creation of the new, when the reasons for it are identical to the causes of it. The relation of Gueroult's work to Spinoza's – in which Gueroult's effort is the symbolic one, taking Spinoza's philosophy as the 'corresponding system' it seeks to explicate – is functionally analogous to the relation between Spinoza's work and the object that comprises its 'corresponding system', that is reality. When the object of thought is reality or existence as such – a theoretical practice conventionally described as metaphysics – the stakes are high.

The wager of Gueroult's *Spinoza* is that the '*Ethics* is intended to exhibit the structure of nature; it is a rigorous deduction mirroring the immanent necessity of nature.'[8] This image of thought is one that appeals to Deleuze in certain ways. 'Image of thought' suggests something representational, as does Aaron Garrett's apt description of Gueroult's take on the *Ethics* as a kind of mirror of nature. But what Gueroult proffers has nothing in common with the representational thought taken to task in the central chapter of *Difference and Repetition*. In this vision, 'difference becomes an object of representation always in relation to a conceived identity, a judged analogy, an imagined opposition or a perceived similitude' (DR 138). Gueroult's *Spinoza* is not about finding the same in the different or seeking those comforts of recognition that so irritate Deleuze in his key work of metaphysics. The goal is to mirror – or perhaps the better word is mimic – precisely those differential elements that disrupt identity and that forestall recognition.[9] The new can only be recognised as new if it is not recognisable at all.

The broad resonances between Gueroult's method and aspects of Deleuze's own are recognisable, amounting to what might be described not only as an internalism but a non-representational internalism. Yet Deleuze also finds in Gueroult's reading several ideas that will be equally important to his own engagement with Spinoza. Before pursuing further what it is in Gueroult's method that appeals to Deleuze, let's look at Spinoza specifically.

SPINOZA

The first point of contact between the two interpretations is a vision of Spinozism that conceives of God or nature not in substantial terms (despite what is denoted by the concept 'substance') but as a power, a kind of operational differentiation ad infinitum.[10] One of the most controversial elements of Gueroult's reading was his insistence that the first eight propositions of the *Ethics* established an infinity of attributes each of which was in some sense substantial in itself – in other words, infinite substances each constituted by a single attribute.[11] This was not an 'anhypothetical' gesture designed to show the absurdity of such a view. Rather, the aim was to show that the substantial differentiation among the attributes put paid to any idea of quantitative distinction in substance or the applicability of number to an understanding of God or substance tout court. Deleuze writes in his review:

> Spinoza is not satisfied to derive a unicity of constituted substance from a unity of constitutive substances. On the contrary, he invokes the infinitely infinite power of an *Ens realissimum*, and its necessary unicity as substance, in order to arrive at the unity of substances which constitute without losing any of their preceding properties. (DI 211)

The paradoxical result is that the real distinction of the attributes becomes the guarantor of their formal correspondence and ontological identity.

This leads to the second aspect of Gueroult's reading that is essential for Deleuze. Real distinction guarantees ontological identity – what *Difference and Repetition* calls 'the univocity of being' – by grounding the two genetic series of attributes in the self-caused, or *causa sui*. Disavowing exteriority from the outset, Spinoza cannot locate the cause of substance anywhere except in substance itself, which means that all events within substance are ontologically identical, even if (or especially if) they sustain different descriptions according to which attribute appears to be in play.[12] This peculiar monism is an engine of infinite differentiation that forestalls all dialectical contradiction and reconciliation. Such is metaphysically impossible in light of the essences of Thought and Extension, which are really distinct; such is temporally unintelligible in light of the unity of action at play in the *causa sui* – there is no reconciliation to come because there is no causal divergence to begin with. When Deleuze writes, 'The *causa sui* animates the whole theme of power' (DI 213/153), we need to hear the philosophical provenance of the verb *animer*, its connection with Aristotle's animus, the motor, the operational quality that inheres in any driven thing. For Aristotle, animus was linked to telos. Spinoza gives us animus without telos, power that serves itself. And the self-serving self in question comprises infinite differentiation.

A portion of Deleuze's 'Spinoza and the General Method of Martial Gueroult' is devoted to the formal symmetry of this method and its object. What start out as reasons for knowing lead us into reasons for being. Something that appears purely analytic at the outset of the work – interlocking logics and reasons – eventually gains a synthetic traction on things as they are. This leads us to suspect that neither method, neither Deleuze's nor Gueroult's, is arbitrary. The disavowal of context and external factors is not scholastic hubris. It is a principled exercise that finds its warrant in the conviction that the world is exhausted by what is and that there is no possibility, no 'beyond' or otherwise that might serve to justify it. If Fichte or Malebranche or Spinoza must be judged according to systems developed and erected by Fichte and Malebranche and Spinoza, this is because each is in some sense sui generis. And thinking the sui generis is the only kind of thinking there is when it comes to the world as such. 'Absolute rationalism, imposing the total intelligibility of God, key to the total intelligibility of things, is Spinozism's first article of faith' (DI 216).

It is this commitment to the principle of sufficient reason – no event without a cause or reason – that distinguishes Gueroult's approach to the history of philosophy and that accounts for his significance in Deleuze's philosophical lineage. We know Deleuze was committed to the creation of the new; but this should not be mistaken for a commitment to creation *ex nihilo*, anathema to Spinozism. We also know of Deleuze's fondness for rationalist metaphysics; it is the feature that sets him apart from what used to be called poststructuralism. We know finally of his commitment to figures of intensity and the maximal, his penchant for the exhausted, which is not to say the exhaustive. All of this aligns Deleuze with Gueroult in the ways Rosset suggested. But the fact remains that Deleuze also had a penchant for the elusive and ephemeral; not the clear and distinct, but the distinct-obscure. The myriad instances of the Sense-Event in *Logic of Sense* all speak to a kind of instance that grounds intelligibility even as it totally escapes it.

This latter aspect of Deleuze's thought finds no place in Gueroult's work, and certainly not in Gueroult's Spinoza. The beginning of *Spinoza, I: Dieu* lauds Spinoza for giving us a 'mystique without mystery, founded on the double transparency of man to himself and of God to man'.[13] There's no place here for the distinct-obscure. I've argued elsewhere that Deleuze draws sustenance for a vision of the distinct-obscure from Gueroult's (academic) nemesis, Ferdinand Alquié. The claim is only plausible in terms of the Gueroult–Alquié relation and their place in the history of philosophy.[14] Deleuze's preferences and aversions are drawn from an infinite array of sources. But as we position Deleuze in the history of philosophy in France, it's important to recognise the limitations of Gueroult's work from his point of view as well as its virtues. Deleuze found in Gueroult a set of methodological principles, as well as a certain orientation towards German Idealism and its legacy, which might be well summarised if caricatured as anti-Hegelianism. But Deleuze had a fondness for Bergson, who was anathema to Gueroult. And he also was more receptive to the arrival of phenomenology in France and the ontological problematic that it introduced. Gueroult lacked the curiosities that Alquié and a host of others shared. He was from a different generation, a historical figure of sorts in Deleuze's own lifetime.

DIANOÉMATIQUE

Born in 1891, Gueroult was a product of the Third Republic, and he remained a convinced and principled republican throughout his life, such that his sympathies ran Gaullist at a moment when younger colleagues were finding revolutionary resources in Spinozism. He served in the First World War and was injured by a gunshot wound to the head. He resumed his philosophical career after the war and Léon Brunschvicg was the predominant influence on his thought. Esteemed for his sweeping overviews of philosophical history, Brunschvicg more than anyone else worked to naturalise Kant in French terms as an epistemologist whose work was consistent with the positivism of natural and social science.[15] He despised Hegel and German Romanticism in the broadest sense. Such antipathy played a key role in the reaction formation of the interwar years that manifested itself in *normalien* enthusiasm for German existentialism and phenomenology.

Gueroult was immune to all this. His doctoral works were published in 1929 and 1930. The first was his minor thesis on Maimon's transcendental philosophy. The second was the major thesis on Fichte's doctrine of science. Both of these figure heavily in Deleuze's research base. Typically, when you find Deleuze discussing either philosopher, a note to Gueroult's studies is not far away. The significance of these works lies in a certain post-Brunschvicgian take on the legacy of German Idealism, encapsulated best in Jules Vuillemin's study *L'Héritage kantien et la revolution copernicienne* (Paris: Presses universitaires de France, 1954). Common to Vuillemin and Gueroult was a concern for the legacy of the transcendental method found in Kant's critical philosophy. For both, the method bore a certain paradox. It was a means to have done with metaphysics of a classical sort, but the historical outcome was to reorient and rejuvenate metaphysics. The longer-term effect was a more pronounced subjectivism that proceeded via existentialism and found its twentieth-century expression in Heidegger. Gueroult's focus on Maimon and Fichte is not accidental or coincidental, to the extent that it is fuelled by a desire to combat the subjectivist legacy of Kantianism in twentieth-century phenomenology.[16] Both idealists sought to reclaim some kind of contact with the absolute in the wake of critique. In broad strokes, we can say both tried to pursue something like Spinoza's project in Kant's wake.

After these studies, Gueroult published work on other thinkers in early modern philosophy, notably Malebranche, Berkeley and Leibniz. In 1951 he was elected to the Collège de France and he devoted his chair to the 'History and Technology of Philosophical Systems'. The method he outlined in his inaugural lesson and developed further in 'The History of Philosophy as a Philosophical Problem' lay at the core of his studies of Descartes and Spinoza.

Both of these documents address the peculiar status of the history of philosophy as an intellectual practice that is neither history nor philosophy. Philosophy disdains history, Gueroult suggests. 'History is temporality, fact, data, chance, and determinism according to external causes.' By contrast, philosophy 'presents itself as eternally valid for itself, non-temporal, in no way concerned with facts or data, because documents are the only facts'.[17] Gueroult pursues a narrow path here. He maintains that historical truth must be distinguished from scientific truth. The facts of history are contingently true. Once known, we also know things could have been otherwise.

But nevertheless what we know about the past, we know truly. Scientific truths, once known, contain a necessity within them (setting aside whether we're talking about metaphysical necessity or logical necessity). The truths disclosed by science aspire to being true in all instances; they could not have not been true. Philosophy repudiates history; its truths aren't contingent. But neither is philosophy science. The analogy that Gueroult recurrently turns to presents philosophy as sharing features with art.

Coming to understand and know works of philosophy as 'monuments' is not unlike learning to appreciate a work of art. The difference, in Gueroult's view, is that the scholar of art can come to appreciate the artwork without technical mastery of the competences required to generate it. By contrast, to understand a work of philosophy requires a restaging of its order of reasons, its genesis as a work – not its extrinsically determined genesis, but its internal construction as a system. This is why he calls for a 'technology of systems' in the study of the history of philosophy and why he later terms his approach a *dianoématique* or 'study of doctrines'.

In 'The History of Philosophy as a Philosophical Problem', Gueroult puts a finer point on this. As in his inaugural lesson, he presents an antinomy history deals in contingency, philosophy deals in necessity. How can these approaches be reconciled without collapsing into either pole? To treat the history of philosophy as a matter of contingent facts is to collapse into what we might call today a sociological approach to the past, or something akin to Cambridge School contextualism.[18] Gueroult's concern here is that in this vision philosophy becomes an epiphenomenon, explicable only in terms of other historical events and processes. But the opposing pole is no more congenial. If one subsumes the entirety of the history of philosophy to philosophy, one ends up in Hegelianism. This is untenable because it denies the reality – what he describes as 'the presence of a certain real substance'[19] – that lay at the heart of past philosophical systems. Given this antinomy, Gueroult concedes that what counts as a work of philosophy is not something that can be decided upon or known in advance. And he acknowledges that the problem the historian of a philosophy faces is one of a priori conditions.

With gestures like this, we can understand why François Dosse placed Gueroult at the heart of French structuralism, seeing resonances between his work and Foucault's.[20] The aim is to develop a method that would be unique to the history of philosophy, starting with clarity about its objects of concern. Gueroult writes:

> This search for a transcendental nature leads to the idea of a *dianoematic* which would be, with respect to philosophical monuments, the equivalent of an *aesthetic* or transcendental theory of the possibility of works of art as possible objects for art history. There is a certain parallelism between dianoematic and aesthetic. Philosophies stand as monuments of thought having their own value, which is impervious to history; they are as much eternal objects for mediation as artistic monuments are eternal objects for contemplation and emotion. Their paradoxical permanence does not lie in their representative truth, defined as *adaequatio rei et intellectus*; indeed on the contrary it is through it that they appear to be frail, contradicting one another, and running counter to the science of today and tomorrow. It is due to their intrinsic truth, that is, to the concept that they enclose something real (*sui generis*), born of their systematic and architectonic constitution. Now, what constitutes the immortal substance of all works of art is precisely an intrinsic truth, *veritas in re*, which is heterogeneous with all truths of judgment.[21]

Gueroult's appeal to a set of scholastic distinctions shouldn't distract us from the essential point here. Philosophical truth, like artistic truth, does not result from a relationship of correspondence to an external reality. It is not representational. But if the truth art presents comes via 'eternal objects for contemplation and emotion', philosophy presents 'eternal objects of mediation'. The idea here is not mediation in a Hegelian or even a Marxist sense. Rather, Gueroult treats philosophical systems as so many means for apprehending or coming to terms with reality. Philosophy mediates our relationship to reality as such (whatever that is) by presenting us with a specific reality disclosed in the system itself. This is where the language of technology comes in. Philosophical systems are tools for mediating our relationship to reality, for making our way in the world.

This tendency toward the visionary, the exhaustive system that presents us with a certain reality is in full effect in Deleuze's works in the history of philosophy. One of the major ironies here is that Gueroult had nothing but disdain for Bergson. Indeed, Bergson and Étienne Gilson come in for extensive criticism in his inaugural lesson. But Deleuze's book *Bergsonism* is an instance of Gueroult's method deployed towards non-academic ends, taking a non-systematic oeuvre and detecting the system in it. By contrast, Deleuze's book on Kant takes the architectonic of critical philosophy and illuminates it in terms of a singular experience at the core of Kant's thought of a reasoning impervious to constraints erected to contain it. It's no wonder that this least Gueroultian of Deleuze's works is dedicated to Ferdinand Alquié (a detail omitted from the English translation). Rather than seeing a plurality of systems in the history of philosophy, Alquié viewed philosophy as perennially arriving at a confrontation with the gap distinguishing our effort to know the world from the world itself.[22]

Gueroult's slogan was that the historian of philosophy had to be sceptical as a historian, but dogmatic as a philosopher.[23] In this we see a kind of disjunctive synthesis, a holding together of incompatible stances that is nonetheless generative. Coming to understand the reality at the heart of anterior philosophical systems was a matter of decoupling human intelligence from the illusions of subjectivism. In his most extensive defence of the *dianoématique*, Gueroult wrote that 'no doubt the cost of [philosophical] doctrines resides to some extent in the fact that circumstances permitted, in each of them, *the realisation of one of the virtualities of human intelligence*, a realisation that can only be grasped there'. Past philosophies aren't instances of 'a vain ingenuity, but a power of the intellect. The prestige of these realisations comes above all from the fact that, once they are excluded by the movement of philosophical and scientific ideas, they are not totally annihilated, but remain *virtual solutions*.'[24]

This pluralised view of the history of philosophy, this principled anti-Hegelianism, and this commitment to the capacity of different efforts of thought to realise new realities – to present virtual solutions – all of this accounts for Gueroult's significance in Deleuze's philosophical lineage, beyond the common interpretations of aspects of Spinoza's metaphysics. There is much in Deleuze that cannot be traced to Gueroult, not least the commitment to the distinct-obscure and a marked sympathy for philosophies of life that was foreign to Gueroult's inclinations. But this only accentuates Gueroult's significance for Deleuze's metaphysical adventures. His role was as one differential element among others, a philosophical reality that was singular in its own right and no less crucial for the vision of the history of philosophy that Deleuze would pass on to others in his own name.

Notes

1. Clément Rosset, 'Sécheresse de Deleuze', *L'Arc* 49 (1972), reprinted in Catherine Clément (ed.), *Gilles Deleuze* (Paris: Éditions Inculte, 2005), pp. 219–25.

2. See, *inter alia*, Clément Rosset, *Le Réel: Traité de l'idiotie* (Paris: Minuit, 1977); *L'Objet singulier* (Paris: Minuit, 1989).
3. Rosset, 'Sécheresse de Deleuze', p. 224.
4. Martial Gueroult, *La Philosophie transcendantale de Salomon Maimon* (Paris: Alcan 1929); *L'Évolution et la structure de la doctrine de la science chez Fichte* (Paris: Les Belles Lettres, 1930); *Dynamique et métaphysique leibniziennes* (Paris: Les Belles Lettres, 1934); *Étendue et psychologie chez Malebranche* (Paris: Les Belles Lettres, 1939); *Descartes selon l'ordres des raisons*, 2 vols (Paris: Aubier, 1953), trans. Roger Ariew as *Descartes' Philosophy According to the Order of Reasons*, 2 vols (Minneapolis: University of Minnesota Press, 1984/1985); *Malebranche*, 3 vols (Paris: Aubier-Montaigne, 1955/1959); *Berkeley, quatre études sur la perception et sur Dieu* (Paris: Aubier-Montaigne, 1956); *Spinoza, I: Dieu* (Paris: Aubier-Montaigne, 1968); *Spinoza, II: L'âme* (Paris: Aubier-Montaigne, 1974).
5. Martial Gueroult, *Dianoématique, II: Philosophie de l'histoire de la philosophie* (Paris: Aubier-Montaigne, 1979); *Dianoématique, I: Histoire de la histoire de la philosophie*, 3 vols (Paris: Aubier-Montaigne, 1984/1988).
6. Martial Gueroult, *Leçon inaugurale, faite le 4 décembre 1951, Collège de France, chaire d'histoire et de technologie des systèmes philosophiques* (Nogent-le-Rotrou: Daupeley-Gourverneur, 1952); Martial Gueroult, 'The History of Philosophy as a Philosophical Problem', *The Monist* 53:4 (1969), pp. 563–87.
7. Tad M. Schmaltz, '*PanzerCartesianer*: The Descartes of Martial Gueroult's *Descartes selon l'ordre des raisons*', *Journal of the History of Philosophy* 52:1 (2014), p. 2.
8. Aaron V. Garrett, *Meaning in Spinoza's Method* (Cambridge: Cambridge University Press, 2003), p. 101.
9. This notion of a non-reflective mirror or mimicry that forestalls dialectical recapture also accounts for 'a certain proximity' between François Laruelle's method and Gueroult's. See François Laruelle, *En tant qu'un* (Paris: Aubier, 1991), p. 17. Compare Ray Brassier, *Nihil Unbound: Enlightenment and Extinction* (Basingstoke: Palgrave MacMillan, 2007), pp. 118–49.
10. See, especially, Part II of EPS, 'Parallelism and Immanence', 99–186.
11. A. D. Smith, 'Spinoza, Gueroult, and Substance', *Philosophy and Phenomenological Research* 88:3 (May 2014), pp. 655–88.
12. This position is not unlike the 'anomalous monism' advanced by Donald Davidson. Davidson noted the affinities (and differences) between his position and Spinoza's in 'Mental Events' [1970], in Donald Davidson, *Essays on Actions and Events*, 2nd edn (Oxford: Oxford University Press, 2001) and 'Spinoza's Causal Theory of Affects' [1999] in Donald Davidson, *Truth, Language, and History* (Oxford: Oxford University

Press, 2005). See also Knox Peden, 'Donald Davidson's "Spinozistic Extravagance"', *Critical Horizons* 18 (2017), pp. 347–58.

13. Gueroult, *Spinoza, I: Dieu*, 9.
14. Knox Peden, *Spinoza Contra Phenomenology: French Rationalism from Cavaillès to Deleuze* (Stanford: Stanford University Press, 2014). See, especially, chapter 2, 'Spinoza Contra Descartes: Martial Gueroult versus Ferdinand Alquié', pp. 65–93. On Deleuze's debt, see pp. 191–8. The indispensable monograph on Gueroult's work is Christophe Giolito, *Histoires de la philosophie avec Martial Gueroult* (Paris: L'Harmattan, 1999).
15. Léon Brunschvicg, *Les Étapes de la philosophie mathématique* [1912] (Paris: Blanchard, 1981); *L'Expérience humaine et la causalité physique* (Paris: Alcan, 1922); *Le Progrès de la conscience dans la philosophie occidentale*, 2 vols (Paris: Presses universitaires de France, 1928).
16. On subjectivism, see Gueroult *Dianoématique, II: Philosophie de l'histoire de la philosophie*, especially pp. 43–71.
17. Gueroult, *Leçon inaugurale*, p. 9.
18. Compare Quentin Skinner, *Visions of Politics, I: Regarding Method* (Cambridge: Cambridge University Press, 2002).
19. Gueroult, *Leçon inaugurale*, p. 17.
20. See chapter 12, 'An Epistemic Exigency', in François Dosse, *History of Structuralism, Vol. 1: The Rising Sign, 1945–1966*, trans. Deborah Glassman (Minneapolis: University of Minnesota Press, 1997), pp. 79–83.
21. Gueroult, 'The History of Philosophy as a Philosophical Problem', pp. 584–5.
22. See the exchange between Deleuze and Alquié in 'The Method of Dramatization', in DI 147–50.
23. Gueroult, *Leçon inaugurale*, pp. 16–17; Gueroult, 'The History of Philosophy as a Philosophical Problem', p. 573.
24. Gueroult, *Dianoématique, II*, p. 56.

Antonin Artaud

Edward Scheer[1]

> Appréciera-t-on, jugera-t-on, justifiera-t-on le combat?
> Non.
> Le dénommera-t-on?
> Non plus,
> nommer la bataille, c'est tuer le néant, peut-être.
>
> Mais surtout arrêter la vie . . .
> On n' arrêtera jamais la vie.
>
> (Will combat be assessed, judged, justified? No. Will it be designated? Not even that, to name the battle is to kill nothingness, perhaps. But certainly to stop life . . . And life will never be stopped).
> (Antonin Artaud, Letter to Peter Watson, dated Paris, 27 July 1946; OC XII 236)[2]

Avatars of the Last Judgement: Deleuze and Artaud's System of Cruelty

The deployment of Artaud in the work of Deleuze and Guattari is essentially dramaturgical. Artaud is their avatar in a whole series of performative encounters; the schizophrenic against the clinic, the poet against the critic, the radical against the bureaucrat, the dissident against the normative structure (family, society), the body without organs against the organic body. Their manner of proceeding approximates Artaud's own proliferation of protagonists.[3] Throughout the two volumes of *Capitalisme et schizophrénie*: *L'anti-Oedipe* and its sequel *Mille plateaux*, Deleuze and Guattari celebrate Artaud's extravagantly performative style as a radical experiment in thought. They recognise that he is not simply describing things but acting them out in a language that demonstrates the schizophrenic production of reality. Artaud, they say,

> deliberately scrambles all the codes, by quickly shifting from one to another, according to the questions asked him, never giving the

> same explanation from one day to the next, never invoking the same genealogy, never recording the same event in the same way. (AO 15)

Deleuze and Guattari use this same device themselves in playing with the language of psychoanalysis for the purpose of depotentiating it, rendering it as an intellectual readymade, a toy for artists and philosophers. Yet while there are a number of structural analogies between their work and that of Artaud, they are not reducible to one another. For one thing, Artaud is an artist, not a philosopher. His area of production includes writing but also drawing, making radio pieces and public performances. In these works, the flak of fragments and scraps rescued from states of extreme dissociation, he is acting out more than thought experiments but actual experiences of what Foucault termed 'unreason'.

It is an experience which Deleuze describes in the earlier solo work *The Logic of Sense* (1969) as

> a pure becoming without measure, a veritable becoming-mad, which never rests. It moves in both directions at once. It always eludes the present, causing future and past, more and less, too much and not enough to coincide in the simultaneity of a rebellious matter. (LS 1–2)

The shifting and elusive quality of this 'rebellious matter' provides an apt image for Artaud's oeuvre but the point is that, whether understood as the radical suspension of the 'frame-setting message' (Bateson) or the complete absence of any metanarrative, Artaud's 'madness' is, as Derrida says, 'simultaneously more and less than a strategy'.[4] It is a resource he uses throughout his oeuvre and, for Deleuze and Guattari, is fundamental to it.

Appropriately, they rehearse some of Artaud's most colourful scenarios throughout their own work, not as evidence of a generic schizophrenia, but in what Foucault describes in his preface to *Anti-Oedipus* as a 'mobile arrangement' of those ideas. It is an arrangement around which an entire set of experimental practices can be elaborated but one scene in particular seems to arise with a certain intensity, especially in the later works of Artaud and Deleuze. It is the scene of the Last Judgement which Artaud staged in his radio piece *Pour en finir avec le jugement de dieu*. In this abortive radiophonic experiment of 1947, Artaud explored judgement in terms of the state, the church, the text and the body, and re-performs these instances by recalling to them their own motifs, their own terms, in a production which features the intermittent beating of drums in a manner which recalls simultaneously the rhythms of music and the judge's gavel. Deleuze appropriated this title in a late essay, published under the title of 'Pour en finir avec le jugement'.[5]

In this essay Deleuze identifies a more or less coherent set of contestatory practices in Artaud which he calls the 'système de la cruauté' (system of cruelty) and which is pitted against 'la doctrine du jugement' (PFJ 160). This 'system' manifests five characteristic scenes of opposition:

1. immanent critique in opposition to the transcendent modes of thought which give rise to judgement
2. vitality against organisation
3. intoxication or meditation opposed to dreaming
4. the will to power versus the will to dominate
5. combat against war.

In what follows, I will try to elaborate on this system in Deleuze's own terms to identify common cause between them.

Immanent Critique against Transcendent Judgement

In his essay Deleuze describes the process by which the Judaeo-Christian tradition invented a new power for itself, the *pouvoir du juger* (power of judgement), which thereby differentiated human fate (the demonic/geographic division of heaven versus hell) and hypostasised judgement in terms of its 'dernière instance' (PFJ 159). This inaugurated the figure of the priest as judge. But judgement itself was not subject to the differentiations of human destiny since it was and is precisely the act of differentiation taken to the nth degree, to the infinite in a literal sense, which 'makes judgement possible' (PFJ 159). Judgement is based on the assumption of a transcendent position. The judge claims the right to speak from a position beyond contingency, while in fact speaking from a historically determined place. Judgement presupposes a 'relation between existence and the infinite in the *order* of time' (PFJ 159). Every judgement is apodictic in the sense that it 'envelopes an infinity of space, of time and of experience which determines the existence of phenomena in space and time' (PFJ 159). This is the familiar structuralist's paradox since the centre is not part of the very structure which it claims to determine.

Artaud describes this circularity in a manuscript written at the end of 1946: 'in order to judge you must have time and time only exists from the fact of judgement. Without judgement there is no time' (OC

XIV** 205). I could edit the text at this point and create the illusion that Artaud is making a perfectly reasonable point here, but he goes on, and so must we: 'And judgement comes from CEREBRAL ACTIVITY, a piece of carbon installed at the summit of the peak of the point, at the centre-point of the coiled snake' (OC XIV** 205). This is the sort of extreme language that Deleuze in *The Logic of Sense* might have marked down as the language of schizophrenia, 'an entirely different language' which 'we recognise' with 'horror' (LS 84). While not reaching the heights of unintelligiblity that Artaud reached in his adaptation of Lewis Carroll's 'Jabberwocky' (Deleuze's subject in this earlier essay), the sudden emergence of the figure of a coiled snake might cause some readers alarm. But if we read it as metaphor and not symptom, we might see that, through the figure of the end tip of the snake which when coiled becomes its centre, Artaud offers a parodic solution to the structuralist dilemma, the centre thereby entering the structure, while evoking an appropriately abject image for those who dispose themselves of judgement.

In Deleuze and Guattari this is the point where 'state thought' imposes itself and where judgement takes root, where part of the structure rises up to claim control over the entirety. This is the point which must be opposed through ongoing creative critical activity of the sort Deleuze regularly advocated. In this respect the two volumes of *Capitalism and Schizophrenia* can both be read, not just as Foucault suggests in *Anti-Oedipus*, as an introduction to the anti-fascist life, but more specifically as guide books in the struggle against judgement. The themes of resistance are inevitably linked, as in Foucault's work, to the exploration of limits, the process of identifying all limits as 'relative' and therefore potential sites of trespass. The absolute transcendence of limits often seems to be the preferred method for Deleuze and Guattari with their references to *lines of flight* and *becoming imperceptible*, but this does not do justice to the insistence with which they pose the necessity of immanent critique and struggle. They affirm the value of the skewed trajectory, the *dérive*, the schizo stroll, over the apodicticisms of metaphysical departure. As Foucault's work also illustrates, transgressive activity is never based on a univocal transaction with judgement. It is never simply oppositional, and it can fail.

In Foucault the parameters for action are articulated around the theme of the fold: either to fold (*plier*) the forms of judgement so as to make them liveable but to constantly transgress them so as to construct a zone in which to think otherwise, or submit to the judgement (*se plier à*), to return to the fold or be folded (*plié*). In Deleuze the operations of the fold are productive of smooth space, where Artaud's body without organs slips through 'the invading discharges of matter' unseen,[6] where sites of contestation multiply but where the possibility of reversal (botching the body without organs) to a stratified position (fascist thinking) is always present. Both Foucault and Deleuze also employ Nietzschean techniques of resistance, activating the *will to power* and affirming that the conditions of judgement are historically constituted, emerging from what Nietzsche describes as 'the consciousness of being in debt to divinity'.[7] Deleuze elaborates on this, adding that it is not just the fact of the debt but its scope: 'the adventure of debt in so far as it becomes itself *infinite*, therefore unpayable' (PFJ 158). This establishes an economy of guilt in which 'Man does not appeal to judgement, he is only judgeable and only judge in as much as his existence is subjected to an infinite debt: the infinity of the debt and the immortality of existence reflect each other in constituting "the doctrine of judgement"' (PFJ 158–9).

In this context Artaud appears as a force of delimitation of the infinite debt. He is, along with Nietzsche, D. H. Lawrence and Kafka, considered by Deleuze as one of Baruch Spinoza's *grands disciples* in the critique of the Judaeo-Christian tradition. Deleuze's reading of Artaud as a disciple of Spinoza comes more clearly into focus in his book on Spinoza in which Deleuze delineates a devastating account of the world after Spinoza:

> a humanity bent on self destruction, multiplying the cults of death, bringing about the union of the tyrant and the slave, the priest, the judge and the soldier, always busy running life into the ground, mutilating it, killing it outright or by degrees, overlaying it or suffocating it with laws, properties, duties, empires – this is what Spinoza diagnoses in the world, this betrayal; of the universe and of mankind. (SPP 12)

This passage suggests that the basis for the relation between Spinoza and Artaud is that both perceived and sought to counter the global death wish which Artaud labelled 'the judgement of god'.

Deleuze saw that Artaud had suffered 'the most severe form of judgement, the terrible expertise of psychiatry' (PFJ 158). Yet Artaud 'would never cease to oppose to the infinite, the operation of having done with the judgement of God' (PFJ 159). This is a telling observation since it links the ongoing nature of combat in Artaud, as in the production of the body without organs and the sustained vitalism of the theatre of cruelty, with the forces that Artaud saw everywhere under the sign of the judgement of God: the requirement to live an inauthentic life, to 'represent' something or to speak or write in a language that must always be second-hand.

For Deleuze, the principle of immanence is coterminous with Artaudian 'cruelty', which involves, as Artaud specifies in his theatre writings, a cruel – rigorous, implacable, necessary and sustained – contestation of values. Deleuze opposes this cruelty to the 'supplice infini' (infinite torture) of the doctrine of judgement which he illustrates through reference to a number of texts from Greek tragedy in which the gods were said to assign to men their 'lot' in life which then predetermined lives in terms of their natural 'organic' ends or appropriate forms. This system resulted in two modes of judgement: the false judgement of hubris which resulted from men overestimating their gifts, and the redistributive judgement of the gods. This bifurcation was subsequently internalised as the judgement of the self by the self. A significant example in Deleuze is of course Sophocles' Oedipus tragedies, the texts which gave to psychoanalysis so much of its language and logic and remains a key site of the normative exercise of judgement.

Vitality against Organisation

Artaud's work operates as a challenge to normative judgement from its very inception in his famous correspondence with the editor of *La Nouvelle Revue française*, Jacques Rivière. This correspondence with Artaud was published rather than the poems which he had originally submitted, although one or two were included as examples of the 'central loss of thought' which Artaud claimed to suffer. In fact, the logic implied by this publication is clear in Riviere's very first letter to Artaud (dated 1 May 1923):

> (Sir,
>
> I regret that I am unable to publish your poems in *La Nouvelle Revue française*. But I am interested enough in them to want to make the acquaintance of their author. If it were possible for you to stop by the review some Friday between four and six, I would be happy to see you.
>
> Cordially yours,
>
> Jacques Rivière).
>
> (OC I 19)

This development which led to the exchange of letters and their publication is what Maurice Blanchot describes as something that is 'more than the work itself, it is certainly the experience of the work, the movement that leads up to it, that Jacques Rivière is interested in, and in the anonymous and obscure trace that it maladroitly represents.'[8] It is Artaud's commentary on that movement, like 'un heurt indescriptible d'avortements' (an indescribable collision of abortions) (OC I 73), as Artaud phrases it, which for Blanchot, becomes the work itself.

Deleuze also reads Artaud's works as active and vital, a 'writing of blood and of life which is opposed to the writing of a book, like justice opposes judgement, and carries out a real inversion of the sign' (PFJ 160). This 'système physique de la cruauté' consists of the non-organic vitality of the body without organs and the 'affective athleticism' of the theatre of cruelty versus the logic of organisms and masterpieces. In the Rivière scenario Deleuze and Guattari see Artaud as an active thinker,

> explaining that thought operates on the basis of a *central breakdown*, that it lives solely by its own incapacity to take on form, bringing into relief only traits of expression in a material, developing peripherally, in a pure milieu of exteriority, as a function of singularities impossible to universalize, of circumstances impossible to interiorize. (TP 378)

They describe such thinking as 'event-thought' or 'problem-thought' as opposed to Rivière's 'essence-thought'. Only event-thought is capable of emerging into the work as into a foreign country, and it is these vital, uncanny works which Deleuze and Guattari valorise, as Artaud did, over the organised, doctrinaire work: 'The necessity of not having control over language, of being a foreigner in one's own tongue, in order to draw speech to oneself and 'bring something incomprehensible into the world' (TP 378).

For Deleuze, as for Artaud, it is not a work unless it is at the same time a new mode of existence and no new modes of existence are possible without cruelty. Such works threaten the doctrine of judgement since they vitally bring themselves into being whereas judgement insists on repetition, as Artaud's entire critical trajectory illustrates, and on a priori criteria which are infinitely applicable. Deleuze and Guattari's plot summary of the Rivière scenario is as follows:

> Is it by chance that whenever a 'thinker' shoots an arrow, there is a man of the State, a shadow or an image of a man of the State, that

> counsels and admonishes him, and wants to assign him a target or 'aim'? Jacques Rivière does not hesitate to respond to Artaud: work at it, keep on working, things will come out all right, you will succeed in finding a method and in learning to express clearly what you think in essence (*cogitatio universalis*). Rivière is not a head of State, but he would not be the last in the *Nouvelle Revue Française* to mistake himself for the secret prince in a republic of letters or the gray eminence in a State of right. (TP 378)

Much later Artaud would recall that the 'abominable splittings of the personality' that he described in the letters to Rivière were only 'une connaissance perceptive' (a perceptual knowledge) compared with 'des affres' (the torments) he suffered as a result of the controversial electroshock treatments he was subjected to at Rodez (OC XI 13). Artaud indicates that in the Rivière letters he was assuming roles that played out positions, abreacting the symptoms of mental anguish as a good writer would do: 'What is a poet if not a man who visualises and concretises his ideas and images more intensely and with more justifiable delight and liveliness than other men and who, through the rhythmic word, gives them a factual character' (OC XI 11). The point he is making is that he has always used this dramaturgical technique which his critics have always misunderstood from the very beginning. Instead of reading his work as the elaborate dramaturgy of a writer, critics from Rivière all the way through to the clinicians at Rodez twenty years later, tell him he is doing fine and will sort it all out one fine day when he is more himself. But this theatre of judgement has a less humorous side . . .

In a series of heartrending letters to his doctors at the asylum of Rodez, Ferdière and Latrémolière, especially the latter who was directly responsible for administering the treatment, and particularly in the letter dated 6 January 1945, Artaud asserts his right to be treated as a writer and artist rather than a madman. Artaud begs Latrémolière to stop the shock therapy and appeals to his awareness that 'this was not a treatment I should have to undergo, and that a man like myself need not be treated but on the contrary helped in his work' (OC XI 12, 13). In the midst of the life-threatening experience that was the electroshock therapy, Artaud continues to denounce the judgement underlying it, that gives rise to it, with a staggering lucidity and courage:

> I am disgusted with living, Mr. Latrémolière, because I perceive that we are in a world where *nothing lasts*, and where anything may be

> held up to ridicule and accused of unreason according to the state of mind at that moment or on that hour and the unconscious of the accuser, of which he himself, who takes himself to be judge, is totally unaware. (OC XI 12)

The immense pathos generated in the letters of this period would be interchanged at times with a more ludic tone such as in the letters to André Breton. This latter relation was always an ambiguous one. Breton repeatedly emphasised the necessarily literary or theatrical aspects of Artaud's work in an attempt to eclipse the shadow of insanity which, for Breton, hovered over Artaud and always obscured the truly artistic, which in its 'convulsive beauty' was always constituted as such more by the doctor applying the electrodes than by the suffering patient. Of course, this interpretation of Artaud's work serves to return its radically skewed trajectory too quickly to the categories of the aesthetic, those very categories which Artaud worked so hard to multiply beyond functionality. These correspondences all manifest the argument between a mode of judgement which fetishises pure categories (is Artaud mad or a man of the theatre?) over complex vital arrangements (he is neither). Artaud and Deleuze would both argue that such thinking does not allow for the existence of the new; it does not permit its emergence or even its perception. But the relation between Breton, the administrator of Surrealism, and Artaud, its most dangerous exponent, is also an example of Deleuze's third avatar of resistance to judgement.

Intoxication versus Dreaming

Deleuze asserts that 'the world of judgement installs itself like in a dream' (PFJ 162). The problem with dreams is that there is no resistance to judgements in terms of 'a milieu' which would 'subject them to the exigencies of knowledge and experience' (PFJ 162). For Deleuze the first question of judgement is to inquire 'whether or not one is dreaming' (PFJ 162). This is why Apollo is as much the god of dreams as the god of judgement: 'it is Apollo who judges, imposes limits and encloses us within the organic form, it is the dream which encloses life in these forms in the names of which we judge it' (ibid.). Those faithful to Apollo (it is in the Nietzschean sense that Deleuze invokes the name), such as Rivière, Latrémolière and Breton, affirm the sublimated and individuated values of the aesthetic, while those such as Artaud embody the anti-aesthetic, the

Dionysian revolt against the judgement of Apollo. The voluntaristic and the de-sublimated are in opposition to the dream because: 'The dream builds walls, feeds on death and incites shadows, shadows of all things and of the world, shadows of ourselves' (PFJ 162). In his texts on the cinema and in his later writings Artaud would denounce dreams in the same terms which Deleuze uses, for being an immobilised state, 'too directed, too governed' (PFJ 162).

In various texts from *Suppôts et Suppliciations* Artaud negates the value of sleep and the dream precisely because of this shadowing of the self that transpires in sleep: 'In slumber you sleep: there is no self and nobody but ghosts' (OC XIV* 16), ghosts which cannot prevent the theft of life-blood from the body while it sleeps, paralysing it: 'Endormi, le sommeil, le coma' (Asleep, slumber, coma) (OC XIV** 133). These ghosts are too *tamisé* (too 'watered down' or 'insubstantial') for Artaud, playthings for God, 'Le vampire à barbe' (the bearded vampire) (OC XIV** 199). Through the nocturnal interference of these demonological figures of ontogeny, of derived life, the body is drained of 'life', of its true life. But the false life maintains itself through 'the quotidian death of Artaud, from his slumber each night; during which it recharges itself right up a little more each night from everything that makes up life' (OC XIV** 131).

Sleep is a 'quotidian death' and must be resisted through the intervention of an active intoxication (opium) or sleepless vigil (insomnia) the value of which for Artaud is perhaps as much the time he gains, brings into being through refusing sleep, as the symbolic resistance of the organism's programme. Emil Cioran puts this case for insomnia: 'During my insomnia I tell myself . . . that these hours I am so conscious of, I am wresting from nothingness, and that if I were asleep they would never have belonged to me, they would never even have existed.'[9] To abreact 'time's it was', the judgement of the temporal, this also is why 'Artaud ne dort jamais' (Artaud never sleeps) (OC XIV** 130).

In his Surrealist years Artaud affirmed the power of the unconscious in dreams in terms of its capacity to disorganise the world, but he never insisted, as the exponents of *écriture automatique* had done, that this process was untrammelled by the social nor that it was an end in itself: 'Out of the correct use of dreams could be born a new way of guiding one's thought, a new way of relating to the world of appearances' (OC I 288). In later years, after the asylums, dreams would lose their critical value and become, for Artaud as for Deleuze, the social productions of sleep. Dreams became representations of a banal theatre which was not the creation of the sleeper but had been placed there 'by other beings – awoken at that very moment' (OC IV * 16). Having implanted the dream material they proceed to draw it out again from the powerless body, 'Each dream is a piece of suffering torn out of us by other beings' (ibid. 17). This is why for Artaud the dream became a state of consciousness which exacerbates the condition of *impuissance*, that condition which defines human being in general as the absence of creative power and vital energy.

The Surrealists could not hide their impotence in the face of 'the hopeless limitations of matter' (OC I 287). In Artaud's critique of the Surrealists, written shortly after his expulsion, he argues that this impotence explains their resorting to the bad faith of *fatalité*, surrendering to the judgement of God in the form of the Parti communiste français: 'This fundamental bad faith is basic to their machinations' (OC I 285). As far as Artaud was concerned, this bad faith had rendered them an official organ, an institution, like any other; superficial, insincere and inclined to making judgements: 'Talk to them of Logic and they will answer you with Illogic, but talk to them of Illogic, Disorder, Incoherence, Freedom, and they will answer you with Necessity, Law, Obligations, Strictness' (OC I 285).

Deleuze also recognises this tendency in Breton's organisation: 'Groups who interest themselves so much in the dream, psychoanalysis or surrealism, are also quick in reality to form tribunals which judge and punish' (PFJ 162). Artaud's expulsion by Breton constitutes the most visible example, but throughout the entire history of the relation between the two men Breton's function is to judge and to delimit the excess of Artaud. In *Anti-Oedipus*, he is referred to as a defender of the 'Oedipal form of literature', the 'commodity form' which stands in opposition to the schizophrenic literature of Artaud: 'There will always be a Breton against Artaud . . . in order to superegoize literature and to tell us: Careful, go no further!' (AO 134).

Breton was always quick to remind Artaud that his anti-aesthetic interventions, such as his Vieux Colombier recital in 1947, were easily recuperable as aesthetic productions and that Artaud was still *un homme de théâtre* despite his attempts at creating life on stage. In answer to Breton's taunt, Artaud replied: 'no *homme de théâtre*, in the entire history of the theatre, has previously taken the attitude which I had that night on stage at the Vieux Colombier . . . with the visible intention of exploding its framework . . . from inside.'[10] For Artaud this was simply more evidence that Breton had never really lived the experiences of Surrealism, that he had loved their beautiful dreams but had failed to give birth to 'astonishing Realities'.[11] Artaud's conception of the theatre had been related to his early idea of dreams, that the purpose of the use of both forms was to extend them to their limit and beyond, to connect with their essential energies and to create the advent of forms to come. Deleuze refracts these extended conceptions of sleep and dreams as states of Dionysiac intoxication which are modes of escaping judgement.

The Will to Power versus the Will to Dominate

Artaud's last letters to Breton turn around the themes of revolution as self-creation and individual will. In all of Artaud's writings about creation it is striking that it is largely potential power, intransitive power without objects, that he describes. Artaud is not interested in exercising power against others, in dominating others, but in breeching the codes of others in so far as they are restrictive of the free play of creative power in general. This is of course remarkably close to Nietzsche's understanding of the *will to power* with which Artaud's theatre texts have a specific affinity, since cruelty for Nietzsche was linked to the uninhibited exercise of power, and creative power for Artaud was precisely the work of cruelty.[12] It is the cruelty of a kind of rigorous self-discipline that Artaud invokes in these texts, a theatre obsessively dedicated to achieving its own ends. But these ends are not directed at an externally localised object; even the audience in Artaud is an aspect of the entire mise en scène. Artaud's *will to power* is, as Deleuze describes in his own writing on Nietzsche, necessarily directed against the extant theatre/body/self on behalf of that which is to come. To make a body without organs 'was already Nietzsche's project: to define the body to come, in intensity, as the power to affect or to be affected, that is to say, the *Will to power*' (PFJ 164). It is not a will to dominate but a will to explore the limit as the 'centre de métamorphose' (PFJ 167).

What Deleuze discovers in Artaud's theatre writings is a symbol of the *will to power* which crystallises this concept in Artaud and also describes Artaud's use of symbol in the general sense of 'an intensive composite which vibrates and extends itself, which doesn't mean anything, but makes us whirl around in all directions until we pick up the maximum possible forces, of which each receives a new meaning in relation with the others' (PFJ 167–8). Artaud's cruel imagery in *Le Théâtre et son double*, his allegories of plague and alchemy, of incest and cosmic disturbances, of revitalised culture and metaphysics, of affective athleticism and hieroglyphic language, of oriental dance and incantation, are symbols in precisely this sense. They are not attempts to appropriate or subjugate the forms of otherness, for example the practice of the Balinese dancers into Western theatre styles, but on the contrary to fracture their mutually exclusive identities in order to release a transfiguring force in which 'each of two forces intensifies and relaunches the other' (PFJ 168). In his earlier work with Guattari this would have been described as *deterritorialisation* or *destratification*, the lateral metastasis of the *rhizome*, but here it is more simply the basis of the struggle against judgement. For Deleuze, Nietzsche's aphorisms display a similar tendency to 'multiplier et enrichir les forces' (multiply and enrich forces) through analogic association, which is in Nietzsche one of the effects of the active will to power (PFJ 168). But this will is itself neither 'a judgment nor the organic consequence of a judgement' since it 'spurts vitally from a turbulence of forces which carries us into combat' (PFJ 168).

Combat against War

Deleuze opposes the struggle against judgement to the *will to destruction* of the apparatus of war. War always has the judgement of God on side to justify its causes. Its relation to other forces is not mutually enhancing, as in the *will to power*, but internecine. War is the *will to dominate* whereas 'Combat, on the contrary, is that powerful non-organic vitality which complements force with force, and enriches that which it seizes' (PFJ 167). Combat is related to the symbol through this conception of power as 'une idiosyncrasie de forces' (PFJ 167). The symbol is the site of combat. This is why Artaud's theatre texts oppose judgement so effectively, since in launching volley after volley of symbols they multiply the sites of contestation and thereby deny the judgement its proper objects.

At the beginning of *Pour en finir avec le jugement de dieu*, Artaud describes the preparations for war in America as the most naked expression of the logic of social production linking the mass accumulation of infantile sperm with a project of artificial insemination for the production of soldiers,

> in view of all the planetary wars which might ultimately take place, and which would be destined to *demonstrate* by the crushing efficacity of force, the super-excellence of American products . . . And long live war, right? . . . To defend this insane machining against all the competition which won't fail to appear on all sides. (OC XIII 72–3)

In the final section of this piece Artaud contrasts this properly American 'warlike imperialism' with the indigenous Indian civilisation 'based on the exclusive principle of cruelty' (OC XIII 101–2). The contrast of cruelty as opposed to war as read by Deleuze indicates that 'combat *does not pass* that way' (PFJ 167). Combat/cruelty does not repeat judgement but replaces it with the figure of the combatant, the one who engages against the characters and instances of judgement and between the subjugating forces and those that are subjugated (PFJ 165). It is both a *combat-contre* (combat-against) the Other and a *combat-entre* (combat-between) the poles of the Self and which 'determines the composition of the forces in the combatant' (PFJ 165).

These bifurcations are especially in evidence in the case of Artaud's work right from the Rivière letters, which embody the struggle with internalised judgements, what he calls 'the psycho-lubricious thrust of heaven' (OC XII 115). The always anticipated always engaged struggle with and against the symbolic in language, representation and social institutions.

Deleuze lists the essential moves of this *combat-contre* as comprised of gestures of defence and attack, of evasion and bombastic parade and of 'anticipations of a blow that doesn't always arrive'.[13] The movements of *combat-entre*, on the other hand, are visible in the positive becomings: woman, child, animal or, in Artaud, the becomings of his written protagonists: Heliogabalus, Van Gogh, Lautréamont, and, later, Artaud le Mômo. It is through these protagonists, these allies, that Artaud's combat against the judgement of God renews itself, acquires its potency and assumes its different avatars. The man without organs, or *l'homme arbre* (the tree-man), appears in a late letter along with Baudelaire, Poe, Nietzsche and Nerval as such an ally in the combat against the judgement of God, with its invention of *l'homme né* (man-born), which for Artaud represents the inanity of fake humanity, 'Animals without will or thought of their own.'[14]

At the end of this letter Artaud predicts a revolution in which the men of pure will, or the authentic *vivants*, will rise up against the animals, profiteers of falsification, the oedipalised, socialised, digestive humans, with a renewed vigour, not to transfer power but to transform the world. Artaud's allies are pure becomings, unadulterated embodiments of the *will to power*, and as such they are true revolutionaries who will join him in the combat to come:

> This is why I believe that the conflict between America and Russia, even if it were reinforced with atomic bombs, is not much compared to and opposed to this other conflict which will suddenly *ignite* between the maintainers of a digestive humanity on the one hand, and on the other, the man of pure will and his adepts and followers, who are few but have everlasting power on their side. (OC XII 115)

For Deleuze, 'combat is not a judgement of god, but the manner of having done with god and with judgement' (PFJ 168). No judgement is adequate to the advent, that which is always to come; this is why the combat which Artaud delineates above, poses a point of departure from judgement and therefore gestures towards the revolution which Breton could neither conceive nor permit but which Deleuze, both in his work with Guattari and, in later works, on his own, has never despaired of realising in some form. Perhaps what Artaud wanted to achieve in his theatre is just this combat, this intensification of energies operating on and in between extant forms in order to maintain a vitality and to keep alive the concept of the new and the authentic.[15] Perhaps in this sense Artaud is Deleuze's best chance of having done with judgement: 'et la bataille commença et elle n'est pas finie' (OC XIV** 126).

Notes

1. Parts of this text have appeared previously in Edward Scheer, 'I Artaud BWO: The Uses of Artaud's "To Have Done with the Judgement of God"', in Laura Cull, *Deleuze and Performance* (Edinburgh: Edinburgh University Press, 2009), pp. 37–53.
2. References to the following texts of Artaud's *Œuvres complètes* [OC] will be made using the following abbreviations: *Suppôts et suppliciations* (comprises volume 14 of the OC in two parts: XIV* and XIV**); 'Pour en finir avec le jugement de dieu' (OC XIII 65–104); *Héliogabale ou l'anarchiste couronné* (OC VII 13–137); *Ci-gît* (OC XII 75–100); *Le Théâtre et son double* (OC IV).
3. Jane Goodall also makes this point in her excellent study *Artaud and the Gnostic Drama* (Oxford: Clarendon, 1994), arguing that what distinguishes it as a body of writing is its dramaturgy, its manipulation of the textual personae in which Artaud continually reinvents protagonists for and of himself. Texts written about historical figures such as Heliogabalus and Van Gogh are especially significant in the light of this observation in which the extravagance of the Artaudian appropriation of those characters is their dominant feature. In her final chapter she connects the intensified proliferation of identities in

Artaud's later works with the renewed vigour of Artaud's 'struggle against God' (Goodall, *Artaud*, p. 200).

4. Jacques Derrida, 'La Parole soufflée', in *L'Écriture et la différence* (Paris: Seuil, 1967), p. 291.
5. Gilles Deleuze, 'Pour en finir avec le jugement', in *Critique et clinique* (Paris: Minuit, 1993), pp. 158–69. This text will be referred to throughout as PFJ.
6. This phrase comes from the Mary Beach and Lawrence Ferlinghetti translation of the Van Gogh essay where Artaud describes 'les décharges envahissantes' (OC XIII 34; *Artaud Anthology*, p. 146). The translation renders surplus detail but is useful in my own context here.
7. Friedrich Nietzsche, from the *Genealogy of Morals*, cited at PFJ 158.
8. Maurice Blanchot, *Le Livre à venir* (Paris: Gallimard, 1959), p. 50.
9. Emile Cioran, *The New Gods*, trans. Richard Howard (New York: Quadrangle, 1974), p. 106; translation of *Le Mauvais Démiurge* (Paris: Gallimard, 1969).
10. Antonin Artaud, Letters to André Breton on and around 28 Feb. 1947 in *L'Ephémère* 8 (1968), pp. 3–25 (pp. 4, 20).
11. Antonin Artaud, Letter to André Breton, 30 July 1937, just before Artaud left for Ireland. In OC VII 242.
12. Artaud's use of the word is significant for his larger opus in ways which Nietzsche's is not, although, in his *Genealogy of Morals*, Nietzsche does refer to 'this artist's cruelty, this delight in imposing a form upon oneself as a hard, recalcitrant, suffering material, and in burning a will, a critique, a contradiction, a contempt, a "No" into it, this uncanny, dreadfully joyous labour of a soul voluntarily at odds with itself . . . as the womb of all ideal and imaginative phenomena, also brought to life an abundance of strange new beauty and affirmation, and perhaps beauty itself.' The rigorous, conflict driven auto-generative aspects of Artaudian cruelty are all evident in this formulation. Friedrich Nietzsche, *Genealogy of Morals*, trans. Walter Kauffmann (New York: Viking, 1967), pp. 87, 88.
13. PFJ 165. This list is applied in the context to the work of Kafka but it describes equally well one of the essential phases of Artaud's technique.
14. Antonin Artaud, Letter to Pierre Loeb, 23 Apr. 1947, *Les Lettres nouvelles* 59 (Apr. 1958), pp. 481–6 (p. 483). I have made use of Helen Weaver's translation of this text in Susan Sontag (ed.), *Antonin Artaud: Selected Writings* (Berkeley: University of California Press, 1976), pp. 515–19.

Georges Dumézil

Ronald Bogue

Georges Dumézil does not figure prominently in the writings of Deleuze. Aside from a paragraph summarising Dumézil's method in 'How Do We Recognize Structuralism?' (DI 180–1) and a one-sentence reference to Dumézil in *Dialogues* (D 141), Deleuze makes serious use of Dumézil only in *A Thousand Plateaus*, primarily in Plateaus 12 and 13.[1] But that use is crucial, for it helps establish fundamental elements of Deleuze and Guattari's politics and social theory. Deleuze and Guattari open both these plateaus with discussions of Dumézil, in Plateau 12, '1227: Treatise on Nomadology – The War Machine', focusing on Dumézil's opposition of the sovereign and the warrior, and in Plateau 13, '7000 B.C.: Apparatus of Capture', on Dumézil's assertion of the dual nature of sovereignty, as represented by the magician-king and the jurist-priest. They cite Dumézil's studies as 'definitive [*décisives*] analyses of Indo-European mythology' (TP 351), a claim with which Dumézil's many critics would take issue. But if not definitive, they would certainly concur that his analyses are voluminous – 'some 17,000 published pages', N. J. Allen estimates[2] – and that they treat in great detail the mythologies of an impressive number of Indo-European cultures. Hence, in referencing Dumézil, Deleuze and Guattari bring to bear a considerable body of mythological, social and cultural evidence in support of their hypotheses regarding the fundamental opposition between the state and the war machine and the bipartite nature of the state apparatus.

In 'How Do We Recognize Structuralism?' (1972), Deleuze treats Dumézil as a structuralist – a common designation of Dumézil at the time – praising his work as exemplary in the way it 'differenciates the species and parts, the beings and functions in which the structure is actualized . . . no one has better analyzed the generic and specific differences between religions, and also the differences in parts and functions between the gods of a particular, single religion' (DI 180).[3] Dumézil, however, did not consider himself a structuralist, and in

1973 he explicitly rejected any connection with the movement.[4] As he told Didier Éribon, it was only by chance that he settled on 'structure' as a key term in his analyses. In his first book, he spoke of a mythic 'cycle'. But

> [t]he infelicitous word 'cycle' soon disappeared from my vocabulary. I replaced it with 'system', and often, I regret that I didn't stick with that term. I gave in to an objection of Victor Goldschmidt, the future exegete of Plato, who was an auditor of mine at the École pratique des hautes études: 'system', he told me, implies consciousness, will, calculation; but the mythic capital of a society is, for each member of that society, a given element independent of his will; better thus to use the word 'structure'. In fact, Goldschmidt was wrong: 'structure' simply says in Latin what 'system' says in Greek. And when one speaks on one hand of the solar system, of the nervous system, and on the other, of molecular structures, the two substantives are synonymous. But I accepted his suggestion and abandoned 'system' for 'structure'. Which had the unintended consequence, a bit later, of promoting me to the unmerited rank of precursor, indeed, of first theoretician of structuralism.[5]

Dumézil made no use of Saussure in developing his notion of structure, nor did he see himself as employing a specifically 'Dumézilian' method. His claim was that an empirical, comparative examination of a large body of Indo-European philological, mythological and cultural data made evident the existence of a single structure – a trifunctional division of society into sovereign-priests, warriors and herders-cultivators – throughout the civilisations whose languages are of Indo-European descent. Only after several years of research did Dumézil come to realise the existence of this trifunctional structure, and, once having done so, he spent the rest of his long career detailing the ways in which the three functions are manifest in diverse Indo-European cultures.[6]

Dumézil

Dumézil was born in Paris on 4 March 1898. Dumézil early showed his gift for languages – he would eventually learn some thirty ancient and modern languages[7] – reading the *Aeneid* in the original by the age of nine. Besides studying Greek and Latin in school, he began studying German with his father at the age of seven or eight, using as a textbook a bilingual German–French account of the labours of Hercules and the voyage of the Argonauts.[8] This text instilled in

Dumézil a fascination with mythology that was to stay with him the rest of his life.

By the time Dumézil was admitted to the École pratique des hautes études in 1916, he had mastered Greek, Latin, German, Sanskrit and Arabic. His studies were soon interrupted, however, when in 1917 he was mobilised as an artillery regiment officer. He saw serious combat duty in 1918, which he found terrifying.[9] He returned to the École pratique des hautes études in 1919 and received his *agrégation* that same year. Upon graduation, he was assigned a teaching position at the *lycée* of Beauvais, a post he disliked and left after six months. He returned to Paris in 1920 to complete his doctorate, living with his parents and surviving on fees from tutorials and temporary editing jobs. In 1924 Dumézil completed his thesis, *Le Festin d'immortalité. Étude de mythologie comparée*, which was published in the *Annales du musée Guimet*. Dumézil's thesis director, Meillet, noting Dumézil's interest in mythology, had suggested that he examine words relating to myth and religion in different Indo-European languages. Dumézil observed that the Sanskrit *amrta* and ancient Greek *ambrosia* both meant 'nondeath' and designated beverages of immortality, and he argued that a 'cycle' of myths of immortal drinks could be discerned across several Indo-European cultures.

In extending his study in comparative linguistics to comparative mythology, Dumézil had entered dangerous territory. The nineteenth century had seen great success in applying a comparative method to reconstruct from diverse Indo-European languages the components of a Proto-Indo-European language, a hypothetical tongue spoken by a group or groups of people situated in central Asia, and some researchers had attempted to broaden the study of Proto-Indo-European culture by using the same comparative methods to reconstitute a Proto-Indo-European mythology. Chief among these was Friedrich Max Müller (1823–1900), who proposed a 'naturalistic' explanation for all myths, the various deities representing the sun, moon, thunder, dawn, sunset and so on. The work of Müller and other 'naturalists' came under intense attack, and by the 1920s the naturalistic approach to Indo-European mythology had been discredited, and along with it the field of comparative mythology as a whole. Dumézil did not adopt the naturalistic explanations of Müller in *Le Festin*, but articulated his analysis in terms of the fertility rites analysed in Sir James Frazer's *The Golden Bough*, a framework Dumézil would later reject.

In 1925, after having vainly sought a position at the École pratique des hautes études, Dumézil accepted a post in Istanbul, where he taught until 1931. While in Turkey, he published his second book, *Le Problème des centaures* (1929), a work in the same Frazerian vein as *Le Festin*, which argued for a common mythos of fertility behind the figures of the Iranian Gandareva, the Indic Gandharva, the Roman Faunus and Februus and the Greek *kentauroi*. During his stay in Istanbul, Dumézil came in contact with several Caucasian exiles, and soon learned to speak Circassian, Chechen, Abkhaz and Ubykh, thinking that he might be able to find a place for himself in France as an expert in Caucasian languages.[10] He also sought out speakers of Ossetic, the sole Indo-European language spoken by inhabitants of the Caucasus Mountains. Descendants of the Scythians, the Ossetians maintained a rich mythic tradition, which Dumézil was able to absorb once he made contact with an Ossetian community in Istanbul and learned their language. His 1930 book, *Légendes sur les Nartes*, was his first treatment of the myths of the Ossetians, which eventually assumed a key position in his account of Indo-European mythology.

In 1931 Dumézil accepted a post in Sweden at the University of Uppsala, where he remained until 1933. Here, he was able to enrich his knowledge of ancient Germanic and Scandinavian cultures and languages. In 1933 the great Indologist Sylvain Lévi (1863–1935) secured a part-time position for Dumézil at the École pratique des hautes études, which became a full-time post in 1935 when he was named the École's director of studies. In 1934 he published *Ouranos-Varuna* and in 1935 *Flāmen-Brahman*, both Frazerian in approach, the one drawing parallels between the Greek and Indian gods Uranus and Varuna, the other between Roman and Indian priests. In 1936 he began work on *Mythes et dieux des Germains*, but before publishing the book he made the discovery that transformed his studies and established the course of all his subsequent research. Dumézil relates that while preparing his lectures in 1938, which included sessions devoted to the Indian castes of the priestly *brāmana*, the warrior *ksatriya* and the cultivator *vaiśya*,

> I was suddenly struck by the fact that the oldest Roman theology, before the Etruscan period, united in a hierarchical triad the god of the sacred par excellence, Jupiter, the warrior god, Mars, and a certain Quirinus, who is, as analysis of his name indicates (*coi-uir-ī-no-*), the god of the masses, of the whole of the people organised in the curiae (*co-uir-ia-*).[11]

Recognising this parallel between the Indian *brāhmana–ksatryia–vaiśya* and the Roman Jupiter–Mars–Quirinus led him to see comparable triads in other Indo-European myths and cultures. Soon these insights coalesced in his 'trifunctional theory', according to which most, if not all, ancient Indo-European societies were organised through a hierarchical class structure of priests, warriors and herder-cultivators, the three classes respectively fulfilling the basic social functions of sovereignty, military force and productivity. Although the tripartite division of social classes disappeared early in some Indo-European cultures, a common ideology, or set of collective representations, nonetheless continued to manifest itself in most Indo-European myths, legends and religious beliefs.

In his trifunctional theory, Dumézil was able to abandon naturalistic and Frazerian models and adopt a sociological approach to myths, treating them as representations of significant social realities specific to given collectivities. This discovery of Indo-European trifunctionality was aided by two complementary realisations. The first was that Greek mythology, far from being representative of Indo-European ideology, reflected a hybrid culture, whose Aegean elements had obscured and displaced much of its Indo-European heritage, and that the Indo-European tripartite ideology was most clearly preserved in the eastern and western extremes of the Indo-European world – the Indic and Iranian cultures to the east and the Scandinavian, Celtic and Italic cultures to the west. The second was that the Romans expressed their fundamental beliefs less in their tales of the gods than in their legendary accounts of Rome's early history. Dumézil argued, for example, that the figures of Rome's founding king, Romulus, and his successor, Numa, represent the two poles of the sovereign function, and that the battle of the Horatii and the Curatii dramatises the ethics of the warrior function.

After this breakthrough, Dumézil was able to modify *Mythes et dieux des Germains* to reflect his discovery before its publication in 1939. The first work composed according to the newfound trifunctional theory was *Mitra-Varuna: Éssai sur deux représentations indo-européennes de la souveraineté* (1940). This was followed by a spate of publications over the next nine years: a four-volume series titled *Jupiter Mars Quirinus* (*Essai sur la conception indo-européenne de la société et sur les origines de Rome* [1941]; *Naissance de Rome* [1944]; *Naissance d'archanges: Essai sur la formation de la théologie zoroastrienne* [1945]; *Explication de textes indiens et latins* [1948]), a second series, *Mythes romains* (*Horace et les Curiaces* [1941];

Servius et la Fortune [1943]; *Tarpeia* [1947]), and the volumes *Loki* (1948), *L'Héritage indo-européen à Rome* (1949) and *Le Troisième Souverain* (1949).

In 1949 Dumézil was elected to the prestigious Collège de France, the chief advocate of his candidacy being the linguist Émile Benveniste. Thereafter, until his retirement in 1968, Dumézil presented weekly lectures at the Collège de France while maintaining his duties at the École pratique des hautes études. In 1952 Dumézil spent six months in Cuzco, Peru, where he pursued a longstanding interest in learning Quechua, the end result of his stay being a series of articles published between 1954 and 1957 arguing for similarities between Quechua and Turkish. From 1954 to 1972 he spent his summers in Turkey maintaining his research in Caucasian languages. Throughout the 1950s and 1960s he continued to publish at the same prodigious pace, issuing books on Roman and Vedic rituals and myths, on tales and legends of the Ubykh, Ossetians, Laz and other Caucasian peoples, and on the warrior function in Indo-European cultures. During this period Dumézil also wrote two volumes summarising his research, *Les Dieux indo-européens* (1952), and *L'Idéologie tripartie des Indo-Européens* (1958). In the latter Dumézil provides perhaps the most succinct statement of his life's project:

> This investigation is not predicated on any preconceived system of explanation, but utilises the techniques of sociology and ethnography as much as it has recourse to the linguistic analysis of concepts. It has only two postulates: it holds that every theological and mythological system signifies something, that it aids the society which practices it to understand itself, to accept itself, to be proud of its past, confident in its present and in its future. It also holds that the Indo-European linguistic community implied a substantial measure of common ideology the nature of which can be determined by an appropriate application of the comparative method.[12]

In 1966 Dumézil entered what he called his 'balance sheet phase' (*phase de bilan*), his intention being to provide syntheses of his previous work rather than offer new contributions. The results, however, were far from mere recapitulations.[13] Chief among the 'balance sheet' works are the two-volume *La Religion romaine archaïque* (1966), the three-volume *Mythe et épopée* (1968, 1971, 1973), *Heur et malheur du guerrier* (translated as *The Destiny of the Warrior*) (1969), and *Les Dieux souverains des Indo-Européens* (1977).

After retiring, Dumézil spent the academic year 1968–9 at Princeton's Institute for Advanced Studies, and the next three years teaching first at UCLA and then at the University of Chicago. In 1978 he received France's highest academic honour, election to the Académie française, with Claude Lévi-Strauss delivering the welcoming address. Unfortunately, the few remaining years of Dumézil's life were not entirely pleasant. In 1983 Arnaldo Momigliano, an eminent historian of Rome and long-time critic of Dumézil, wrote an essay containing an insinuation that the closing paragraphs of Dumézil's 1939 *Mythes et dieux des Germains* showed clear sympathies with Nazi culture. Momigliano's student Carlo Ginzburg reiterated this charge in a 1984 article, elaborating on Momigliano's insinuation by pointing out Dumézil's association with the right-wing nationalist André Maurras in the 1920s and with his secretary at that time, Pierre Gaxotte, who remained one of Dumézil's close friends until Gaxotte's death in 1982. Dumézil responded to Momigliano and Ginzburg, but Ginzburg and others continued the attacks, some arguing that the entire trifunctional schema is imbued with a fascist and possibly racist mentality. Dumézil died in the midst of this ongoing controversy on 11 October 1986. In *Faut-il brûler Dumézil?* (1992), Didier Éribon mounted a lengthy defence of Dumézil, demonstrating that Dumézil's political leanings, while decidedly rightist in the 1920s and 1930s, were never anti-Semitic or pro-German and that only a tendentious reading of Dumézil's scholarship could support the view that his research is fascist in inspiration and orientation.[14]

Dumézil, Deleuze and Guattari

Dumézil posits an ancient Indo-European tripartite division of society into sovereigns, warriors and herders-cultivators, with each fulfilling a corresponding function – politico-religious administration, deployment of military force, and assurance of abundance and fecundity. Deleuze and Guattari's interest is only in the figures of the first two functions, the sovereign and the warrior. At the opening of Plateau 12: 'On Nomadology', they correctly state that for Dumézil 'political sovereignty, or domination, has two heads', which they identify as

> the magician-king and the jurist-priest. Rex and flamen, raj and Brahman, Romulus and Numa, Varuna and Mitra, the despot and the legislator, the binder and the organizer. Undoubtedly, these two poles stand in opposition term by term, as the obscure and the clear, the violent and the calm, the quick and the weighty, the fearsome and the regulated, the 'bond' and the 'pact', etc. (TP 351)

But this opposition is only relative, they say, and they cite Dumézil to clarify this relation: '"At once antithetical and complementary, necessary to one another and consequently without hostility ... The two together exhaust the field of the function"' (TP 351–2). For Dumézil, Deleuze and Guattari accurately remark, the warrior function, by contrast, is in genuine opposition to both poles of the sovereign function.

In the opening paragraph of Plateau 13: 'Apparatus of Capture', Deleuze and Guattari offer a second synopsis of Dumézil's views, reiterating the same points:

> Let us return to Dumézil's theses: (1) Political sovereignty has two poles, the fearsome magician-emperor, operating by capture, bonds, knots and nets, and the jurist-priest-king, proceeding by treaties, pacts, contracts (the couples Varuna–Mitra, Odin–Tyr, Wotan–Tiwaz, Uranus–Zeus, Romulus–Numa ...); (2) the war function is exterior to political sovereignty and is equally distinct from both its poles (Indra or Thor or Tullus Hostilius ...). (TP 242)

The two poles of sovereignty Deleuze and Guattari identify as 'the principal elements of a State apparatus'. Using terms developed in Plateau 3: 'The Geology of Morals', Deleuze and Guattari assert that the State apparatus forms a 'milieu of interiority' and that the 'double articulation' of the two poles 'makes the State apparatus into a *stratum*' (TP 352). Opposed to this State milieu of interiority is the 'war machine', the embodiment of the war function, which is not simply exterior to the State but 'itself a pure form of exteriority' (TP 354). Deleuze and Guattari caution, however, that 'the exteriority of the war machine is difficult to conceptualize', since the 'extrinsic power of the war machine tends, under certain circumstances, to become confused with one of the two heads of the State apparatus' (TP 354).

Dumézil's analysis of the relationship between war and the figures of the sovereign and warrior is complex, at times offering evidence in support of Deleuze and Guattari's qualitative separation of the sovereign and the warrior, at others not. In *Mitra-Varuna*, Deleuze and Guattari's main source for their synopsis of Dumézil's theses, Dumézil introduces the two poles of sovereignty by comparing the Indian Vedic gods Varuna and Mitra with the first two Roman kings, Romulus and Numa. Of the Vedic gods, Dumézil says, 'Mitra is the sovereign under his reasoning aspect, luminous, ordered, calm, benevolent, priestly; Varuna is the sovereign under his attacking aspect, dark, inspired, violent, terrible, warlike [*guerrier*].'[15] Dumézil finds a version of this antithesis in Romulus and Numa. Romulus is impetuous and violent, murdering his twin brother, abducting the Sabine women, governing in such a way as to offend the elder *patres* and *senatores*. 'Everything Romulus does is warlike [*guerrière*]; even his posthumous advice to the Romans is to cultivate the art of war.'[16] Numa, by contrast, is a calm elder – forty years old when he reluctantly accepts the kingship – a bringer of peace, architect of alliances, dispenser of law and founder of sacerdotal rites. If Mitra and Numa represent the priestly dimension of sovereignty, *brahman* and *flamen*, Varuna and Romulus represent its more explicitly political dimension, that of *rāj* and *rex*.

The unruly nature of Varuna and Romulus is accentuated by their association with groups of wild and disruptive youths. Varuna is the patron of the Gandharva, 'a band of supernatural beings, somewhat divine and somewhat demonic in character, . . . beings with horses' heads and men's torsos',[17] creatures given to excesses in drink and sexuality. Romulus, for his part, has as constant companions the Luperci, a band of disorderly young fighters who carouse, quarrel and join Romulus in the abduction of the Sabine women. The Gandharva and Luperci are associated with speed – Romulus renames his followers 'Celeres', 'the swift ones' – which suggests an opposition of Varuna–Mitra and Romulus–Numa in terms of *celeritas* and *gravitas*. That the Gandharva and Luperci are young indicates a further contrast in the poles of sovereignty between *iuvenes* and *seniores*. The libidinous activities of the Gandharva and Luperci, finally, point to a connection between these groups and fecundity and creation, whereas their counterparts, the *flamines* and *brahmans*, serve the principles of nurture and conservation. 'Flamens and Luperci, brahmans and Gandharva, all share equally in the task of securing the life and fecundity of society.'[18] The *flamines* and *brahmans* ensure the sustenance of life through the orderly performance of rituals executed with mature *gravitas*. The creation or restoration of fecundity, however, must come from the Luperci and Gandharva, the disorderly youths possessed of *celeritas*, that rhythm 'most suited to the activity of violent, improvisational, creative societies'.[19] The Luperci and Gandharva are excessive, the *flamines* and *brahmans* orderly, and 'It is precisely because they are "excessive" that the Gandharva and the Luperci are able to create; whereas the flamines and brahmans, because they are merely "correct", can only maintain.'[20]

It would seem that the two poles of sovereignty represented in the opposition of Varuna–Mitra, Gandharva–*brahmans*, Romulus–Numa and Luperci–*flamines* blur the distinction between the sovereign and the warrior. Varuna and Romulus are warlike, and the Luperci and Gandharva behave like bands of warriors. The ancient complementary pair of *rāj* and *brahman*, Dumézil notes early in *Mitra-Varuna*, 'became the eponyms of the two highest castes . . . the *brāhmana* (members of the priestly caste) and the *rājanya* (or *ksatriya*, member of the warrior caste)'. The line between sovereign and warrior seems further blurred when Dumézil extends his analysis beyond India and Rome to identify in the Scandinavian gods Odhinn and Tyr, and the Germanic gods *Wōdhanaz and *Tîwaz, figures parallel in function to those of Varuna and Mitra. Odhinn and *Wōdhanaz are warlike, and they are patrons of the ferocious bands of warrior *berserkir*.

Yet Dumézil insists that the warrior is unlike the sovereign in fundamental ways. In India, the warrior god is Indra, not Varuna, however warlike the latter may be. Varuna is 'the binder', a god who entraps his enemies in magic bonds. Mitra, his sovereign counterpart, does not literally bind, but he is the god of the contract, the bond of an orderly exchange or proper sacrifice to the gods. Hence, we glimpse here 'a collaboration between Mitra and Varuna, the former presiding benevolently over correctly executed exchanges, the latter "binding" any defaulters'.[21] The god who unbinds Varuna's bonds is Indra, a terrifying war god but one capable of mercy. Dumézil finds a Roman parallel to this theme of binding and unbinding in the relation between Romulus and Numa and in the ancient legal distinction in creditor–debtor agreements between *nexum* and *mutuum*, the former being a bond (*nexus*) in which the debtor stakes his freedom as collateral, the latter being a contract based on mutual trust. Romulus, Dumézil shows, is associated with binding, and Numa with contracts. Although the third Roman king, Tullus Hostilius, represents the warrior function, according to Dumézil, ancient texts do not explicitly identify the merciful suspension of the *nexum* with any specific individual, but with the military in general, as Dumézil sees represented in a legend recounted in Livy II, 23–4, in which those under the bond of the *nexum* are allowed to enlist in the army and thereby be absolved of their debt.[22]

In Dumézil's view, the opposition between Varuna and Indra, the binder and the unbinder, represents a difference in the morality of the sovereign and that of the warrior hero:

> the warrior and the sorcerer alike or, on another level, the soldier and the policeman, make inroads when necessary on the life and liberty of their fellow man, but each operates in accordance with procedures that the other finds repugnant. And the warrior especially, because he is either on the fringe of or even above the code, regards himself as having the right to clemency; the right to break, among other things, the mandates of 'strict justice'; the right, in short, to introduce into the terrible determinism of human relations that miracle: humanity.[23]

The code of the warrior is upheld by the *Männerbunde*, the '"men-only-societies"' (*sociétés de l'homme*) whose 'feral and brutal brotherhood' is characterised by 'disguises, initiations and extraordinary magical powers', societies 'that merit, at least in part, the description "secret"'.[24] These are 'the Marut, the Indo-Iranian "society of warriors"'[25] who follow Indra, and the *berserkir* of German and Norse mythology. They are indifferent to laws of moderation and propriety, but above all they are defined by what the ancient Germans called *Wut* and the Romans *furor*, 'a transfiguring fury', 'a frenzy in which man goes beyond himself to the point of changing his behavior, at times his form', becoming 'a sort of indefatigable monster, insensate or even invulnerable. His triumphant appearance on the battlefield is a sort of demonophany: only to see him, only to hear his cry, and the adversary is penetrated with terror, paralyzed, petrified.' When the German warrior 'puts on the "furor of the *berserkr*", he truly exchanges his nature for that of a wildcat, a bear or a bull, wolf or dog'. He 'runs in all direction on the battlefield with a speed that would make the son of Peleus jealous, and massacres the enemy or his friend'.[26]

'There are many ways of being a war god,'[27] says Dumézil, and only those whose element is physical force are gods of the second function. The true warrior gods and heroes are Indra, Mars, *Thunraz, Thôrr, Tullus Hostilius and Heracles. The terrible sovereigns – Varuna, Jupiter, *Wôdhanaz, Odhinn – are involved in war, but rather than physically enter the fight they use their magical powers to affect the battle, ensuring that force leads to order. Even the jurist sovereign may have a share in war, as is the case with *Tîwaz (Tyr), but he is the god of the assembly and the protocols of war etiquette, and hence 'the jurist of war'.[28] Yet for Dumézil the relation between the terrible sovereign and the warrior is not one of strict opposition. *Wôdhanaz/Odhinn is the 'patron of the band of men-beasts, the *Berserkir* or the *Ulfhedhnir*, the "bear-coats" or "wolf-skins" (as Varuna is of the half-man, half-horse Gandharva, as Romulus is of the feral band of

Luperci)'.[29] In the case of German and Norse mythology, the defining traits of the warrior *berserkir* derive from *Wôdhanaz/Odhinn. He has several magical 'gifts', and he 'communicates his own gifts to [the *berserkir*]: the power of metamorphosis, *furor* (*ôdhr*!), invulnerability, certainty of aim, and, above all, a paralyzing power by which the enemy is immobilised, blinded, deafened, disarmed and brought to its knees before it has even begun to fight'.[30]

The differentiation of sovereign and warrior is no less uncertain in Dumézil's account of the one-eyed/one-handed motif he associates with the two poles of sovereignty. Dumézil observes that Odhinn, the terrible sovereign, is one-eyed, and his paralysing gaze is associated with his disability. (In some accounts, it is said that he surrendered an eye in exchange for magic wisdom.) Tyr, the jurist sovereign, is missing a hand, which he lost in an effort to bind the young wolf Fenrir, who was fated to be the scourge of the gods. The gods playfully invited Fenrir to allow himself to be bound by a seemingly insubstantial (yet magic) leash created at Odhinn's command. Fenrir was suspicious, but Tyr offered his hand as surety of the gods' innocent intentions, placing his hand in Fenrir's mouth. When the bonds proved unbreakable, Fenrir bit off Tyr's hand. In this tale Dumézil sees the two poles of sovereignty at work in dealing with external enemies. The sovereigns' two techniques, he says, are superior to those of the warrior, who, like *Thunraz-Thôrr 'wins wars without resorting to finesse, by fighting, by relying on his strength alone'. For rather than fighting, '*Wôdhnanaz-Odhinn* terrifies the enemy, petrifies him with the marvels of his magic, while *Tyr-*Tîwaz* circumvents and disarms him with the ruses of the law.'[31]

Dumézil draws a parallel between the one-eyed Odhinn/one-handed Tyr and the Roman heroes Horatius Cocles and Mucius Scaevola, two key figures in the Roman war against Lars Porsena, king of Clusium. Cocles, whose name means 'one-eyed', valiantly defended the Sublicius Bridge, the sole access to Rome, by facing the enemy at the front of the bridge while Roman soldiers destroyed it behind him. He fought with superhuman strength and escaped at the last minute by diving into the river and swimming to the other shore. Later, with Rome under siege by the Clusians, Scaevola (whose name means 'left-handed') snuck into the camp of Lars Porsena in an attempt to assassinate the king. Scaevola was captured, but when brought before the king, he declared that three hundred more Romans would be following him in the same mission, and as a demonstration of his bravery and scorn for his own safety, he plunged his hand into a sacrificial fire and held it there until it was consumed by the flames. Porsena was so impressed by this act that he ended the siege and made peace with Rome.

Dumézil links the one-eyed Odhinn and Cocles to the Irish warrior Cúchulainn and the Viking warrior Egill, both of whom 'practiced a heroic grimace' whenever 'gripped by warlike fury',[32] closing one eye and opening the other until it became unusually large. Via this association of the one-eyed Odhinn/Cocles and the one-eyed grimace Dumézil draws a third parallel to the Odhinn–Tyr and Cocles–Scaevola pair in the Irish gods Nuada and Lug, who led the Irish in the conquest of the demonic Formorians. In the first campaign, Nuada lost his arm, but later had it restored with a silver hand. In the second and decisive series of battles, Lug conquered the Formorians through the use of his paralysing grimace. The one-eyed/one-handed order is reversed in this tale, but the poles remain the same. Dumézil concludes from these narratives of Odhinn–Tyr, Cocles–Scaevola and Nuada–Lug that the Norse, the Celts and the Latins all inherited 'a philosophy of sovereignty . . . from their Indo-European ancestors', and that they preserved 'in an original fictional form, the double symbolism of the one-eyed sovereign and the one-handed sovereign'.[33]

Deleuze and Guattari make creative use of Dumézil's one-eyed and one-handed sovereigns, claiming that if 'war kills, and hideously mutilates', 'the State apparatus makes the mutilation, and even death come first'. The State 'needs them preaccomplished, for people to be born that way, crippled and zombielike . . . The State apparatus needs, at its summit as at its base, predisabled people, preexisting amputees, the still-born, the congenitally infirm, the one-eyed and one-armed' (TP 425–6). For Deleuze and Guattari, the one-eyed and one-armed are figures of the State apparatus, diametrically opposed to the warrior and the war machine. Similarly, Dumézil sees the one-eyed and one-handed as symbols of sovereignty, but the separation of sovereign and warrior is only partial in his account. Neither Cocles nor Scaevola is a sovereign – Cocles is an army officer, Scaevola a citizen-soldier. Cúchalainn and Egill are quintessential warriors, and though their heroic grimaces are like Odhinn's one-eyed 'army-bond' gaze, there is no indication that their grimaces are the gift of a sovereign figure (as is the case of the grimaces of the *berserkir*), nor that their warrior prowess is deployed in the defence of a sovereign power.

Deleuze and Guattari also cite Dumézil's studies of the 'three "sins" of the warrior' (TP 354) to emphasise the opposition of the warrior to the sovereign, summarising those sins as ones committed 'against the king, against the priest, against the laws originating in the State (for example, a sexual transgression that compromises the distribution of men and women, or even a betrayal of the laws of war as instituted by the State)' (TP 354). Dumézil does indeed see a motif in Indo-European cultures in which warriors commit three sins, but in his analysis the three sins are committed against the three functions, not the king, priest and their laws. Indra participates in *brahmanicide* (first function), abrogates a treaty through a cowardly use of force (second function) and commits adultery (third function). The Norse hero Starcatherus (or Starkadr) strangles a king after gaining his trust (first function), panics and succumbs to cowardice in battle (second function) and kills another king for money (third function, in that venality is related to the material realm of production and fecundity). And Heracles kills his children in defiance of an oracle commanding him to serve a king (first function), shows cowardice in hurling the weak, unarmed son of King Eurytos from a tower to his death (second function), and deserts his second wife (third function).[34]

For Deleuze and Guattari, the warrior's sins threaten the State apparatus, whereas for Dumézil they threaten all aspects of the trifunctional social system. Yet Dumézil's view of the warrior is fundamentally very close to that of Deleuze and Guattari. Warriors surrender to the intoxication of *furor*, and are thereby 'transfigured', but also 'made strangers in the society they protect'. They are 'dedicated to Force . . . which proves itself only by surpassing boundaries'.[35] The warrior seeks to be not simply strong 'but strong absolutely, the strongest of all – a dangerous superlative for a being who occupies the second rank'.[36] The warrior, hence, is an inherently dangerous force in a hierarchical society. But he also opens alternatives to the rigid justice of sovereign law, suspending 'the strict determinism of human relations' and introducing mercy. 'Throughout the world', says Dumézil, 'the "advent of the warrior"' represents a 'revolution' that 'constitutes one of the great openings of societies to progress'.[37]

Where Deleuze and Guattari differ most from Dumézil is in their understanding of the sovereign. Deleuze and Guattari draw a clear distinction between the sovereign and the warrior, whereas Dumézil views the sovereign as a fluid figure with connections to all three social functions. The warrior 'societies of men' belong to the second function (Indra's Marut), but they are also associated with the terrible sovereign (Varuna's Gandharva and Romulus' Luperci). For this reason, Dumézil can frame the opposition of the two sovereigns as one of *celeritas* (the trait of the Gandharva and Luperci, as well as the Marut) versus *gravitas* (whereas for Deleuze and Guattari, the *celeritas/gravitas* opposition is that of the war machine versus the State apparatus).[38] With the Indo-European king – 'Vedic *rāj-*, the Latin *rēg-* the Gaulic *rīg-*' – there is 'a certain floating in the representation or definition of the three functions', says Dumézil.[39] In one sense, the king is superior to the trifunctional structure as a whole, presiding over priests, warriors and herders/cultivators. In another, he is the partner of the priest, and as king-priest the most prominent representative of the first function. But 'yet again, the king presents a variable mixture of elements taken from the three functions, and notably from the second, that is, from the warrior function and indeed from the warrior class out of which he most often arises'.[40] In the war culture of the ancient Germans, the sovereign and warrior functions are especially confused. Here, 'one witnesses more than an osmosis: a veritable overflowing of war into the ideology of the first level, an inundation'.[41] And in the figure of Romulus Dumézil finds all three functions – Romulus the shepherd (third function), Romulus the warrior (second function) and Romulus the king (first function).[42]

For Deleuze and Guattari the State apparatus/war machine opposition is a *de jure* distinction, the two representing qualitatively distinct tendencies that manifest themselves in *de facto* mixtures. Dumézil's three functions, one might say, are something like *de jure* distinctions, in that 'the "tripartite ideology" does not necessarily entail a *real* tripartite division of that society' but may serve only as 'an ideal',[43] which then appears in various complicated *de facto* mixtures in diverse societies. But Dumézil's *de jure* three functions, he insists, are specific to Indo-European cultures. He agrees that all societies have governments, make war and cultivate the land, but he maintains that the trifunctional ideology is the basis of social organisation only in the Indo-European world. For Deleuze and Guattari, by contrast, the *de jure* opposition of the State apparatus and the war machine is universal. In Dumézil they find a vast body of mythological materials that point toward the *de facto* separation of the State apparatus from the war machine, and above all, suggest the possibility of an alternative politics in the ethos of the warrior. Dumézil glimpses something of the revolutionary potential of the warrior, but his main task is to conduct an empirical investigation of Indo-European trifunctionality and situate the warrior within that schema. He focuses on the tensions the warrior induces in Indo-European societies, the threats he poses to collective order as a whole, and the ways in which the war function is uneasily accommodated within those societies. It remains to Deleuze and Guattari to seize on the warrior ethos as articulated by Dumézil and explore its viability for the conception of a different mode of social existence outside the confines of the State apparatus.

Notes

1. Deleuze and Guattari cite the following works by Dumézil: *Mythes et dieux des Germains* (Paris: Ernest Leroux, 1939), *Horace et les Curiaces* (Paris: Gallimard, 1942), *Servius et la Fortune* (Paris: Gallimard, 1943), *Mitra-Varuna: Essai sur deux représentations indo-européennes de la souveraineté*, 2nd edn (Paris: Gallimard, 1948) [*Mitra-Varuna: An Essay on Two Indo-European Representations of Sovereignty*, trans. Derek Coleman (New York: Zone, 1988)], *Le Troisième Souverain* (Paris: Maisonneuve, 1949), *Heur et malheur du guerrier: Aspects mythiques de la fonction guerrière chez les Indo-Européens* (Paris: Presses universitaires de France, 1969) [*The Destiny of the Warrior*, trans. Alf Hiltebeitel (Chicago: University of Chicago Press, 1970)] and *Mythe et épopée II* (part one) (Paris: Gallimard, 1971) [*The Stakes of the Warrior*, trans. David Weeks (Berkeley: University of California Press, 1983)]. Of these, *Servius et la Fortune* and *Le Troisième Souverain* play only a minor role. Deleuze and Guattari cite *Servius* 'on the role of the ancient poet as a "functionary of sovereignty"' (TP 556) and claim that in this book 'Dumézil stresses the role played by the arithmetic element in the earliest forms of political sovereignty' (TP 559). Dumézil does focus on Servius as inventor of the census, but says very little about 'the arithmetic element' of the census, concentrating instead on the etymological associations of the census with the people's praise of the sovereign and the sovereign's evaluation and classification of the people (not their enumeration).
2. N. J. Allen, 'Debating Dumézil: Recent Studies in Comparative Mythology', *Journal of the Anthropological Society of Oxford* 24:2 (1993), p. 121. In Dumézil's *Entretiens avec Didier Éribon* (Paris: Gallimard, 1987), Éribon asks Dumézil how many books he has written, to which he responds, 'I don't know precisely. About sixty [*Une soixantaine*]' (p. 20). All unattributed translations are my own.
3. Deleuze concludes his remarks on Dumézil by citing Edmond Ortigues's *Le Discours et le symbole* (Paris: Aubier, 1962). It seems likely that Deleuze based his discussion of Dumézil on Ortigues's synoptic account of Dumézil's oeuvre (pp. 191–201).
4. In *Mythe et epopee III. Histoires romaines* (Paris: Gallimard, 1973),

p. 14, Dumézil says: 'In the course of the last several years the word "structure" has become ambiguous . . . Some have taken it upon themselves to rank my work . . . among the current manifestations or, given the dates involved, among the forerunners of structuralism . . . I should like to put an end to these pointless favors: I am not, I have never been, nor will I ever be a structuralist' (cited in C. Scott Littleton, *The New Comparative Mythology: An Anthropological Assessment of the Theories of Georges Dumézil*, 3rd edn [Berkeley: University of California Press, 1982], p. 275; trans. Littleton).

5. Dumézil, *Entretiens*, pp. 118–19. The Victor Goldschmidt in question is also the author of *Le Système stoïcien et l'idée de temps* (Paris: Vrin, 1953), upon which Deleuze relies heavily in his account of the Stoic concept of time in *The Logic of Sense* (see LS 144, 147, 340, 348).
6. Useful introductions to Dumézil in English are Littleton's *The New Comparative Mythology* and Bernard Sergent, 'Georges Dumézil', trans. Chet Wiener, https://greekromanworld.wordpress.com/2013/05/023/georges-dumezil.
7. Dumézil, *Entretiens*, p. 90. When asked how many of those languages he spoke perfectly, Dumézil responded, 'None'. He added that 'Turkish is the language that I speak the least badly' (p. 91).
8. 'These were my fairy tales', Dumézil tells Éribon. 'I liked Little Thumb [*le Petit Poucet*], I liked Donkey Skin [*Peau-d'Âne*], but I preferred Hercules and Jason. That was my first contact with mythology' (Eribon, *Entretiens*, p. 29).
9. Dumézil, *Entretiens*, p. 39.
10. Dumézil's role in the preservation of Ubykh is noteworthy. When Dumézil left Turkey in 1931 there were still a few speakers of the language alive, but in the years after the Second World War only one speaker survived, Tevfik Esenç. Dumézil learned of his existence and brought him to Paris four times during the 1960s and 1970s. Dumézil recorded several hundred hours of Esenç speaking Ubykh, and together they published an Ubykh–French dictionary (Dumézil, *Entretiens*, pp. 85–9).
11. Dumézil, *Entretiens*, p. 66.
12. *L'Idéologue tripartie des Indo-Européens*, Collection Latomus, vol. 31 (Brussels: Latomus, 1958), p. 91. Translation by C. Scott Littleton (Littleton, *The New Comparative Mythology*, p. 139).
13. This is hardly surprising, given Dumézil's temperament as a researcher. At one point in the *Entretiens*, Éribon asks Dumézil, 'So, the ideal for you would be to be able to rewrite each of your books after each discovery?', to which Dumézil responds, 'That's about right. It would require several secretaries and an army of temporary workers' (pp. 69–70). It is this practice of constantly modifying and correcting his positions that has maddened Dumézil's critics, who claim that his views

are at times inconsistent – a charge to which he readily admits, while suggesting that his critics consult his most recent works before finding fault with his analyses.

14. Unsurprisingly, Dumézil's critics have not been swayed by Éribon's defence. I find the charges of Dumézil's foes unconvincing and Éribon's refutation decisive. In my view, Dean A. Miller offers the most cogent and perceptive summation and evaluation of the controversy in the closing section of 'Georges Dumézil: Theories, Critiques and Theoretical Extensions' *Religion* 30 (2000), pp. 27–40.
15. Dumézil, *Mitra-Varuna*, p. 72.
16. Ibid., p. 51.
17. Ibid., p. 29.
18. Ibid., p. 44.
19. Ibid., p. 40.
20. Ibid., p. 45.
21. Ibid., p. 98.
22. On the *nexum* and *mutuum* and the account from Livy, see Dumézil, *Mitra-Varuna*, pp. 99–104, 109–11.
23. Dumézil, *Mitra-Varuna*, p. 208.
24. Ibid., p. 28.
25. Ibid., p. 107.
26. Dumézil, *Horace et les Curiaces* pp. 18–19. Dumézil elaborates further on the *Wut* of the *berserkir* in chapter 6 of *Mythes et dieux des Germains*, pp. 79–91. The warrior's becoming-animal is detailed in part III, chapter 3 of *The Destiny of the Warrior*, pp. 139–47.
27. Dumézil, *Mitra-Varuna*, p. 127.
28. Ibid., p. 127. Deleuze and Guattari echo Dumézil when they say, 'the two men of State are always getting mixed up in affairs of war'. The 'magic emperor sends to battle warriors who are not his own . . . "he binds without combat"', whereas 'the jurist-king is a great organizer of war . . . he gives it laws . . . subordinates it to political ends' (TP 425).
29. Dumézil, *Mitra-Varuna*, p. 127.
30. Ibid., p. 127. Dumézil describes the gifts of Odhinn in greater detail in *Mythes et dieux des Germains*, pp. 26–7. There he makes the point that Odhinn's paralysing power in battle is called the *her-fjöturr*, the 'army-bond [*lien*]', or 'army-shackle [*entrave*]'.
31. Dumézil, *Mitra-Varuna*, p. 143, translation modified.
32. Ibid., p. 146.
33. Ibid., p. 158.
34. Dumézil details the sins of Indra, Starcatherus and Heracles in *The Destiny of the Warrior*, pp. 65–104. In *The Stakes of the Warrior*, he elaborates further on Starcatherus and his sins and compares him to the Indian figure Śiśupāala, who also commits three sins.

35. Ibid., p. 106.
36. Ibid., p. 107.
37. Dumézil, *Mitra-Varuna*, pp. 108–9.
38. Deleuze and Guattari recognise that Dumézil 'has established the mythological importance' of the *celeritas/gravitas* opposition 'precisely in relation to the State apparatus and its natural "gravity"' (TP 371), but they argue that *celeritas* belongs properly to the war machine.
39. Dumézil, *L'Idéologie tripartie des Indo-Européens*, p. 32.
40. Ibid., p. 33.
41. Ibid., p. 57.
42. Georges Dumézil, *Archaic Roman Religion*, trans. Philip Krapp (Chicago: University of Chicago Press, 1970), pp. 255–6.
43. Georges Dumézil, *Mythe et épopée I: L'idéologie des trois fonctions dans les épopées des peuples indo-européens* (Paris: Gallimard, 1968), p. 15.

André Leroi-Gourhan

Daniel W. Smith

André Leroi-Gourhan (1911–86) was a French palaeontologist, archaeologist and ethnologist who held the chair of Prehistory at the Collège de France from 1968 until his retirement in 1982. During the 1960s and 1970s Leroi-Gourhan's impact on palaeontology was on a par with that of Claude Lévi-Strauss, his colleague at the Collège de France, in anthropology.[1] He was an extraordinary polymath, having received degrees in Russian (1931) and Chinese (1933). In 1936, while working at the Musée de l'Homme in Paris, he went on an ethnographic expedition to the Far East,[2] where he collected materials for his 1944 dissertation at the Sorbonne, which was entitled 'The Archaeology of the North Pacific' and directed by Marcel Mauss. His wide-ranging work focused primarily on prehistoric art, the history of technology, and human evolution. Among his many enduring legacies are the 'Techniques et Cultures' school of cultural anthropology,[3] the *chaîne opératoire* approach to technology, and the *decapage* method of excavation. He is well known to archaeologists for his pioneering studies of area excavations at Arcy-sur-Cure[4] and, especially, Pincevent.[5] Outside France, Leroi-Gourhan initially became known for his studies of Palaeolithic art,[6] for which he was often credited, somewhat simplistically, with having provided a 'structuralist' interpretation.[7] In the 1940s he achieved international recognition with the publication of *Evolution and Techniques* (in two volumes, *Man and Matter* [1943] and *Milieus and Techniques* [1945]), a massive ethological study of the evolution of technology that remains a touchstone in the field.[8]

But Leroi-Gourhan's *magnum opus* was his two-volume masterpiece *Gesture and Speech* (*Technique and Language* [1964] and *Memory and Rhythms* [1965]), a work of extraordinary scope that presents a synthetic account of the course of human evolution from a philosophically informed viewpoint.[9] The work had an immediate impact in France and was taken up by several philosophers: Jacques Derrida discusses the book in his 1967 *Of Grammatology* (primarily with regard to Leroi-Gourhan's analyses of the linearity of phonetic writing),[10] and Deleuze and Guattari appeal to it throughout their works. It would take more than thirty years for the book to be translated into English, in 1993, and its impact in the English-speaking world, especially in philosophy, has remained limited. It is true that in hindsight, more than fifty years after its publication, it is easy to identify aspects of the book that are outdated. Even in 1964, for example, Leroi-Gourhan was using an idiosyncratic terminology that was already becoming obsolete: he calls the biface makers 'Archanthropians', and their predecessors, 'Australanthropians'. Moreover, *Gesture and Speech* was written long before the discoveries of *Homo habilis* in Africa and the famous *Australopithecus afarensis* named 'Lucy', and its analyses necessarily must be reconsidered in light of subsequent fossil evidence. At times, the text even betrays a certain anthropocentrism that would be shared by few contemporary palaeontologists.[11]

Despite such caveats, the vision of human development presented in *Gesture and Speech* retains all its topicality and contemporaneity, for several reasons. The first is Leroi-Gourhan's morphological approach to human evolution. As Tim Ingold has noted, Leroi-Gourhan's work is derived as much from the tradition of Geoffroy Saint-Hilaire and Cuvier as it is from Buffon and Darwin.[12] For Leroi-Gourhan, *On the Origin of Species* did not so much inaugurate a new era in science as it brought an end the tradition of natural history started by Buffon, which firmly anchored humans in the natural world.[13] Cuvier's work, by contrast, had focused on the relations between the morphological components of the body, and Leroi-Gourhan's presupposition is that adaptations (variation and selection) can take place only within a fairly demarcated space of possible bodily transformations. Morphology is the *condition* for corporeal adaptations, and on this score animal species have two fundamental morphological patterns: *radial* symmetry (hydras, sea anemones, polyps) and *bilateral* symmetry (worms, molluscs, crustaceans). Humans belong to the second group, in which 'the entire organism is placed *behind* the aperture for ingesting food', or what Leroi-Gourhan calls the *anterior field* (27–8). Leroi-Gourhan's analysis of human evolution begins with the general morphology of bilateral symmetry, which polarises the front and rear, and locates the organs of prehension, ingestion and responsiveness in the anterior field in the front of the body.

Second, given this starting point, Leroi-Gourhan analyses the evolutionary transformations that took place within this bilateral morphology, which included changes in the mechanical organisation of the spinal column and limbs, the position of the skull, the size and layout of the teeth, the organisation of the forelimb (the hand) and the size of the brain. Leroi-Gourhan is highly critical of 'celebralist' theories (Rousseau, Teilhard de Chardin) which presume that human evolution was guided by intelligence (10, 19), arguing instead that it was the *foot*, and not the brain, that played the determinative role in human evolution, since the size of the human brain was dependent on the development of an erect posture (bipedality). In other words, *mobility*, and not intelligence, was 'the significant feature of evolution toward the human state' (26). The reason for this is strictly mechanical: a brain of human size and weight simply could not exist in quadrupeds with a horizontal backbone. For the human brain to develop, the vertebral column had to become vertical, and the skull had to be foreshortened in the front (including the face and dentition) and considerably extended over the convex 'roof' of the cranium – what Leroi-Gourhan calls the opening of the 'cortical fan'.[14] Leroi-Gourhan is in no way denying the important role that the brain played in the development of human societies – a factor Darwin famously emphasised.[15] His point is that, from an evolutionary perspective, cerebral development is a derivative phenomenon, an *effect* of bipedalism. Put differently, Leroi-Gourhan sketches the portrait, not of an embodied mind, but of an enminded body. The ongoing privilege accorded to intelligence and cognition has its roots in the longstanding bias that favours the mental rather than the corporeal, the mind rather than the body. In this sense, *Gesture and Speech*, although it never mentions his name, follows Nietzsche's advice to philosophers: 'Essential: to start from the body and employ it as a guide. It is a much richer phenomenon [than the mind], and admits of clearer observation.'[16]

Third, Leroi-Gourhan provides a detailed account of the evolutionary emergence of the bipedal body with erect posture, starting from a stable way of life in an aquatic medium, and proceeding through a series of what Leroi-Gourhan calls 'liberations': the initial liberation from the aquatic medium (amphibiomorphism), the freeing of the head (which distinguishes reptiles from fish), the acquisition of erect quadrupedal locomotion ('walkers'), the acquisition of seated posture ('graspers'), and, finally, the acquisition of erect posture (anthropomorphism), which entails the liberation of the hands and the mouth (36–60). Deleuze and Guattari will call these transitions 'deterritorialisations' rather than 'liberations' – in the upright position, the hand and mouth are literally de-territorialised and removed from the ground (*terre*) (DR 86–7). Our front paws gradually lost their faculty of locomotion, but in the process they became hands, which can do many more things than simply walking, such as the fabrication of tools. At the same time, the mouth lost its capacity for prehension, which was taken over by the hand, but in the process it gained the capacity for speech. In being deterritorialised, the forelimb and the mouth were *reterritorialised* on new actions, gestures and tool-making (for the hand) and speech (for the mouth). The is the source of the title of Leroi-Gourhan's book *Gesture and Speech*, and the most original aspect of the book is its analysis of these two morphological poles: the hand (gestures and tools) and the face/mouth (speech), and their complex interactions.

Indeed, the fundamental claim of *Gesture and Speech* is that 'tools, language, and rhythmic creation are three contiguous aspects of one and the same process' (336) – all of which are linked to the enlargement of the human brain, though not derived from it. The appearance of an erect bipedal body in humans *at one and the same time* freed the forelimb from the function of locomotion and created the hand; freed the mouth from the function of prehension and created language; and allowed the brain to expand by placing the cranium at the top of the now-erect spinal column, which led to the externalisation of visceral bodily rhythms in space and time. Though separable, these three changes in the human body were the result of the same morphological process, and can thus be considered as a single event. Since they are the result of one evolutionary process, Leroi-Gourhan will argue that there are inevitable parallels in the evolution of 'technics, language, and aesthetics' (275)

In what follows, we can do little more than provide a summary overview of each of these three poles, and the elements that Deleuze appropriated from Leroi-Gourhan, although it is no doubt the first pole (technics) that had the greatest impact on Deleuze.

First Pole: The Hand (Gestures and Tools)

Leroi-Gourhan belongs to a long tradition that interprets technical artefacts as *biological* phenomena. 'Leroi-Gourhan', Deleuze and Guattari write, 'has gone the farthest toward a technological vitalism taking biological evolution in general as the model for technical evolution', positing the existence of a 'university tendency' (which Deleuze and Guattari will term the 'machinic phylum') that traverses both the technical and internal milieus of organisms (TP 47). Perhaps the key term in Leroi-Gourhan's account of technology is the notion of *externalisation*. The evolution of the hand produced an entire series of manual gestures that went far beyond the locomotive of the paw: prehension, percussion, rotation, grasping, kneading, transmission and so on. The hand became a tool that could undertake numerous complex operations such as crushing, moulding, scraping, cutting, digging and so on. But these motor skills, in turn, were then externalised in technical artefacts, in relation to which the hand ceased to be a tool itself and became the motor force of these externalised tools. I can attempt to pound a stake into the ground with my fist, but I do a much better job at the task with a hammer, which externalises my forearm and fist in wood and metal. Similarly, a baby's bottle externalises the mother's breast; an oven externalises the stomach; writing externalises memory; and so on. Technical artefacts are biological phenomena because they are extensions or 'externalisations' of the motor skills and organs of the body. Ernst Kapp, a contemporary of Marx, seems to have been the first to make this argument in his *Prinicples of a Philosophy of Technology* (1877), which was taken up in France by Alfred Espinas in his 1897 book *The Origins of Technology*.[17] In the English-speaking world, the same tradition was revived in Marshall McLuhan's 1964 *Understanding Media*, which was published in the same year as Leroi-Gourhan's *Gesture and Speech*, and bore as its subtitle, precisely, *The Extensions of Man*.[18] Yet the characterisation of tools as 'externalisations', while a useful and perhaps necessary starting part, must be qualified in at least two ways.

On the one hand, long before any process of externalisation, one can find a 'proto-technicity' throughout the plant and animal kingdoms. Evolution, in other words, *produces its own technology*. Oviparous animals (birds), for instance, followed an evolutionary path that externalised the ovum through the action of laying eggs, objects that are half living (the embryo) and half technological objects (the calcium shell). In this sense, one could say that oviparous animals had already produced the 'objective', and that the egg could perhaps be considered one of the material origins of technology.[19] But birds were simply continuing an immense movement that had commenced with invertebrates such as arthropods (insects and molluscs), who secreted armours of chitin, or even scallops and shellfish, who produced an exoskeleton to protect themselves – just as masons build our houses, through another type of externalisation. From this viewpoint, one could push the advent of technology back half a billion years to the Cambrian explosion, the Palaeozoic era in which exoskeletons appeared – the exterior of an interior, a protective framework for soft and fragile parts. Later, in the vertebrates, feathers, hair, hooves, nails and teeth, the shells of the turtles and the scales of anteaters will continue this vital flux of proto-technicity. From the most ancient exoskeletons to the appearance of the most recent 'appendages' (*phanères*), we can follow a gigantic chain of 'natural' technologies. Even if they have not yet been detached from the body, they are nonetheless the precursors of subsequent externalisations. Indeed, are the ancient ruins of long-vanished civilisations or even modern junkyards filled with the carcasses of rusting automobiles all that different from the fossilised remains of the Cambrian period that are found in the Burgess Shale in the Canadian Rockies, about which Stephen Jay Gould wrote his superb book *Wonderful Life*?[20] They are *all* cemeteries of externalised techniques.

One could push this analysis even further. Bergson observed that a unicellular animal such as an amoeba can digest food, react to its surroundings, and even 'think', although it does not have a digestive tract, sensory organs or a brain.[21] To use Deleuze's terminology, taken from Artaud, an amoeba is a *body without organs*. Lacking organs, the amoeba is nonetheless capable of unified behaviour such as self-direction, conditioned reflexes, learning, adaptation, instinctive habits and so on. In so-called higher animals, these 'functions' become localised in specific organs such as the stomach and the brain, but clearly the functions do not require the specialised organs.[22] Raymond Ruyer drew the obvious conclusion: *bodily organs are themselves technical artefacts*, that is, they are specialised 'tools' that have been fabricated by the organism.[23] I do not necessarily need a hammer to drive a stake into the ground, but I can do it more quickly and efficiently if I have one. Similarly, organisms do not need a stomach to digest, or a nervous system to interact with the environment, but they perhaps digest and interact better if they have specialised organs devoted to these tasks. In other words, technologies may be externalisations of our organs, but our organs are themselves technologies that have been invented by the organism over the course of evolution. In his book *Climbing Mount Probable*, for instance, Richard Dawkins has a marvellous chapter, aptly titled 'The Forty-Fold Path to Enlightenment', that analyses the fact that eyes – which Dawkins calls 'a remote sensing technology' – have evolved no fewer than forty times in the animal kingdom in accordance with nine distinct principles.[24] Indeed, the greatness of Darwin, as Marx said in a famous text, was that he 'directed attention to the history of *natural technology*, that is, the formation of the organs of plants and animals'.[25] Variation and selection are the two mechanisms of this natural technology.

However one sketches this history of proto-technicity, it is clear that 'technology' is a product of evolution. Although we consider technological objects to be artificial, these artificial objects have a 'natural' origin. It was Plato and Aristotle who separated *tekhne* from *episteme*, and devalued the former in favour of the latter.[26] But this has had a pernicious effect in philosophy: far from being a mere application of science or 'theory', technology long preceded science and in certain respects conditions it.

On the other hand, even if one limits the idea of technical artefacts to objects outside the body, it is obvious that many species besides hominids fabricate external artefacts: beavers construct dams, birds create nests, spiders weave webs.[27] In these cases, however, technical activity is 'a faithful reflection of biological status' (137), that is, the technical artefacts fabricated by animals seems to be largely tied to their genetic makeup, as if they had been 'secreted' (91) or 'exuded' (239) by the organic body. Here, too, the artefact/organ distinction becomes blurred: a spider's web can be seen as one of the organs of the spider, even though it is external to its body. The artefacts fabricated by animals are what Richard Dawkins calls their 'extended phenotype', and he suggests that even the lake behind a beaver's dam 'may be regarded as a huge extended phenotype'.[28] It is well known that animals do not simply *adapt* to environments but actively *create* their environments (niche construction).[29] As Deleuze and Guattari write, 'an organic form is not a simple structure but a structuration, the constitution of an *associated milieu* . . . The spider web is no less "morphogenetic" than the form of the organism.'[30] Jacob von Uexküll pioneered the ethological analysis of such animal environments, and Deleuze frequently cites his analysis of the world of a tic, with its active, perceptive and energetic characteristics.[31]

What seems specific to the human species is that its externalised organs become *detachable*, removeable, separated from the body, which provides the advantage of mobility. A lion's fur, for instance, forces it to rather quickly halt a chase when it becomes overheated; but when fur is externalised in a coat, it can be put on and off at will, in accordance with quickly changing conditions. An important consequence follows from this detachability. Although 'tools and skeletons evolved synchronously' (97) for most of human existence, Leroi-Gourhan suggests that, at some point, these detached technical objects, or externalised organs, began to enter their own evolutionary history – a trajectory that Michel Serres has termed an 'exodarwinism'.[32] Evolution bifurcated: one might say that we have moved from creative evolution (Bergson) to being ourselves creative of evolution. Evolution produces organisms, with their own proto-technicity; but these organisms then produce technical artefacts that interconnect with each other to produce a new body with its own moving tissue. Each of us now lives in two bodies: the organic body created by the embryo, and the eternalised technological body created by our brains and our hands, a hyperbiological body that Kevin Kelly has aptly termed the *technium*.[33] The evolution of this second body not only moves at a *faster* pace than normal evolution, but it is moving at an increasingly *accelerated* pace: it is this *other* evolutionary time people are referring to when they talk about the fast pace of modern life.[34] Each of us thus participates in two evolutionary temporalities as well: the extremely slow-moving evolutionary process that sculpted our organic body, and fast-moving evolution of our technological body, which Serres calls a movement of 'hominisation'.[35] Put differently, our life takes place between two circuits: the internal circuit of our bodily organs, and the external circuit of our technological organs.

Interregnum: The Enigma of the Biface

But this raises the question of when and why technical artefacts became so detached from the human body that they could enter their own evolutionary sequence, and Leroi-Gourhan confronts this question by considering the enigma of the biface (or hand axe). The first tool created by hominids, dating back 2.7 million years, seems to have been the Oldowan 'chopper', which was created by a single movement of striking one stone against another to create a sharp edge – the same gesture that would serve 'to split a bone, crack a nut, or bludgeon an animal' (92). The concept of an 'operating sequence' (*chaîne opératoire*) was introduced by Leroi-Gourhan as a mean of analysing the process of production of technical artefacts, and particularly lithic artefacts, and the chopper can be identified as the earliest tool because it is the product of the most basic 'operating sequence': simple percussion. Around 1.7 million years ago, the chopper gave way to the biface, which has a pointed oval shape with two convex faces that meet at a sharp edge all around. The biface, which characterises the Acheulean period of artefact production, was the product of a far more complex production process, requiring 'at least six series of operations performed in strict sequence, each series being conditional upon the others and presupposing a rigorous plan' (100). Around 300,000 years ago, the biface gave way to Levalloisian points and microliths (136–8), which seems to have been the starting point of an exponential expansion of techniques – a literal explosion of technological development

What is remarkable about bifaces is that they have been found across Africa, Asia and Europe during a period that spans 'several hundreds of thousands of years' (144). Indeed, current research indicates they persisted for close to a million years, almost five times as long as the existence of *Homo sapiens*. Despite regional variations, the form of the biface, with its bilateral symmetry, remained consistent during this entire period, and even achieved increasing precision. The Acheulean was an industry of awesome stability: the biface was the first 'standardised' tool.

But why did the form of the biface remain constant for such a long period? In *Gesture and Speech*, Leroi-Gourhan oscillates between two responses to this question. One response is that the human biface was akin to the spider's web, the bird's nest or the beaver's dam, all of which are externalised artifacts derived from the species' genetic makeup, part of its extended phenotype. In this case, 'technical activity is a faithful reflection of biological status' (137). A second, and more persistent, response presumes that the explanation of the existence of the tool must be found, not in genetics, but rather in the growing capacities of the human mind, either in the form of a 'mental image' or a 'concept' or a 'representation'.[36] The form of the biface, Leroi-Gourhan writes, can be traced back to 'a shape that must be preexistent in the maker's mind' (97), implying that, in humans at least, technical artefacts bear witness to a conscious intentionality in the maker's mind.[37] On this score, Leroi-Gourhan suggests that what he calls the 'prefrontal event' was 'perhaps the most important technical revolution in human history' (136), since it was at this point that technical development ceased to be 'a faithful reflection of biological status' (137) and 'cell development' (139) and instead started 'to exteriorize itself completely – to lead, as it were, a life of its own' (139). Until this moment, increase in brain volume and industrial progress moved in parallel: *technicity was tied to biology*. After the prefrontal event, 'brain volume had apparently reached its peak, and the industry curve, on the contrary, was at the start of its vertical ascent' (141). In other words, at some point, technicity wound up *detached* from the body because of the expansion of the brain.

Yet Leroi-Gourhan himself nonetheless questions if it is possible to make such an easy distinction between the technical and the intellectual? 'One could ask whether techniques have a fundamentally intellectual nature, or whether the distinction often drawn between the intellectual and the technical actually reflects a paleontological reality' (106). What is at stake in these questions is what might be called 'archaeology of cognition'.[38] Deleuze, following Simondon, challenged the 'hylomorphic' (*hyle*, 'matter' + *morphē*, 'form') assumption that the production of material bifaces would have presupposed the concept of a pre-existing form for their production. In a later text, Leroi-Gourhan would note that 'the production of tools assumes the ability to preserve technological knowledge', but he argued that *this knowledge is stored in the tool itself*, and not in either the genome or the mind.[39] Recent scholars such as Gary Tomlinson, who is indebted to Leroi-Gourhan, have suggested that we should 'conceive of Acheulean workmanship without the aid of modern foresight or mental representation, without a teleological approach to a preconceived end – without, finally, a recognizably modern human agency at work'.[40] Rather, Tomlinson extends Leroi-Gourhan's concept of operating sequences to argue that the persistence of the biface form for so many millennia did not imply 'abstractable concepts' or even a 'symbolic communicative capacity', but was the result of externalised operating sequences that had become habituated patterns of movement, transmitted from generation to generation. The continuity of the biface-form was the result of the mutual interactions between the rhythmic gestures of the operating sequence and the material affordances of the stone and the environment – what Tim Ingold has termed a 'taskscape'.[41] Instead of seeing stone tools as proxies for the mind, we should see the mind as an outgrowth of the body–stone interface. Tomlinson's work at least suggests that Leroi-Gourhan's concept of the *chaîne opératoire* – the meeting of the body and the material world in a rhythmicised landscape – provides an explanation of the puzzle of the biface that is 'more in keeping with our picture of million-year-old hominins that models involving mental templates, multistep foresight, and top-down planning'.[42]

Second Pole: The Mouth (Speech and Language)

If we began with Leroi-Gourhan's analysis of technology, derived from the hand, it is in part because it becomes the model through which he approaches the externalisations of the mouth and bodily rhythms. If the deterritorialisation of the hand is linked to the genesis of tools and technology, the deterritorialisation of the mouth is linked to the genesis of speech and language, and more generally the status of semiotics or signal-sign systems – a theme Deleuze and Guattari take up in their analyses of 'regimes of signs'.[43] Karl Popper argued that an organism's most fundamental contact with external reality takes place with the ingestion of foodstuffs,[44] which led his disciple Donald T. Campbell to suggest that all types of knowing and perceiving are substitutes for *touching*.[45] Single-celled organisms such as amoebae gain most of their knowledge of the environment through direct physical contact – a mode of knowledge that is both accurate (what one touches certainly exists) and dangerous (if one encounters something hostile). From this viewpoint, one advantage of senses such as hearing, smell and vision is that they allow organisms to gain knowledge of their environment in a more distanced and indirect manner, although such modes of perception, while safer, are often less accurate and more susceptible to error. For Leroi-Gourhan, *detachment* ('thinking at a distance') is as much a theme in sensibility and thought as it is in technology, and these sensory modes of cognitive displacement are extended even further in modes of symbolic abstraction. This is why Ruyer can note that language is less a means of communication than a means of *interrupting* communication, in so far as both speech and writing interpose a sign between humans and the world.

> An immediate suspension of action and communication is the indispensable condition for symbolic behavior . . . The decisive step toward humanity was crossed when the stimulus-signal became the symbol-sign, that is, when it is no longer understood as announcing or indicating something nearby [in space] or the next object or a situation [in time], but as something capable of being used in itself in order to conceive an object even in the absence of this object.[46]

Here too, of course, we can identify a 'proto-symbolism' that exists within the organism itself, not only in its genetic structure, but in the complex chemical signalling that takes place between cells, a domain explored by the field of 'bio-semiotics'.[47] Such chemical signalling is often externalised in the extended phenotype of species such as ants, who communicate by secreting trail pheromones.[48] In humans, however, symbolisation is primarily linked to speech, that is, the production of sound and not chemical molecules. Although Leroi-Gourhan does not speculate on the origins of speech,[49] he makes two essential points about the *conditions* of its origin. First, as we have seen, the liberation of the mouth is directly linked to the liberation of the hand and the brain: 'manual liberation and the reduction of stresses exerted upon the cranial dome are two terms of the same mechanical equation' (60).[50] His analyses constantly focus on the reciprocally determined triangle of the hand, the mouth and the sensory-motor cortex. In other words, Leroi-Gourhan does not see the hand–mouth relationship 'as the commonplace one whereby the hand participates in speech through gesticulation, but as an *organic* one, manual expertise corresponding to the degree of freedom of operation of the facial organs thus made available for speech' (36). For this reason, second, 'there is a close synchronism between the evolution of techniques and that of language' (215), between the production of the technium and the production of the symbolic world, and the evolution of the former sheds light on the latter. 'The extraordinary acceleration of the development of material techniques following the emergence of *Homo sapiens*' implies that one can track a similar evolutionary development in language. Leroi-Gourhan argues that one can track a similar evolutionary development in language (215).

Of the many riches in his analyses of human symbolisation, we will simply highlight the fact that, for Leroi-Gourhan, like many others (Havelock, Ong, Goody), the singular moment in the long history of language was the advent of *writing*.[51] Phonetic writing – a subset of the more general phenomenon of 'graphism' – constituted an externalisation of human memory, which made the archiving of knowledge possible. The implications of writing and literacy are immense, and have been the object of numerous studies, and the three remarkable chapters Leroi-Gourhan devotes to the topic (219–66) are among his most prescient. But, from Leroi-Gourhan's morphological viewpoint, what is most significant about the invention of graphic symbolism is that it signified a 'subordination' of the hand to the mouth, and thus an entirely *new* relation among the three poles of his analyses. In oral societies, the graphic system is *independent* of the voice (drawing, art), and it was the alignment and subordination of the hand to the voice that ultimately allowed writing to *supplant* the voice In *Anti-Oedipus*, Deleuze and Guattari examine Leroi-Gourhan's analyses of this new hand–voice–graphism relation in some detail, coupling it with Nietzsche's analyses in the *Genealogy of Morality*, in order to produce their concept of the 'magic triangle' (voice–audition, graphism–body and eye–pain) that characterises ancient despotic states.[52]

Third Pole: Rhythm (space and time)

Leroi-Gourhan does not turn to the third pole of his analyses until the last part of *Gesture and Speech*, which includes a phenomenologically oriented chapter entitled 'The Body as the Source of Values and Rhythms' (281–97). For most of the living world, he notes, time and space have no other reference than the body's visceral rhythms: waking and sleeping, digestion and appetite, heartbeat and breathing; the movement of bowels and the muscles, the organs of balance (the labyrinth of the ear), and so on. '*Hunger*, *balance*, and *motion* are the tripod upon which rest the higher reference senses of touch, smell, hearing, and sight' (289). But, as with the motor functions of the hand and mouth, these bodily rhythms are likewise externalised in 'a checkerwork of scales and measures', which ensconce human behaviour in 'a time and a space proper to humankind' (283). 'For thousands of years our favorite game has been to organize time and space in rhythms, in the calendar, in architecture' (288).[53] Leroi-Gourhan is quick to point out the complexities of this externalised, artificial rhythmicity. On the one hand, it tends to produce a 'rhythmic uniformization' or normalisation, 'the reduction of individuals to a conditioned crowd' (287). On the other hand, and more interestingly, the various 'techniques of the self', as Foucault termed them, found in domains such as religion and philosophy, are largely directed towards taking human beings *outside* their daily rhythmic cycles (284). 'Acrobatics, balancing exercises, the dance, are to a large extant the material expression of the attempt to break away from normal operating sequences' (286), and philosophy has always fed on the conquest of eternity as a suspension of these rhythms.

Deleuze appropriates two important themes from Leroi-Gourhan's analysis of rhythm. The first is the concept of the 'abstract line'. Deleuze and Guattari cite with approval Leroi-Gourhan's observation that 'rhythmic markings precede explicit figures'.[54] Primitive art, in other words, begins with these abstract and prefigurative lines that are derived from the rhythms of the body and the cosmos, and the origins of art could not have been otherwise (188–90). 'Prehistoric art is fully art because it manipulates the abstract, though nonrectilinear, line' (TP 497). The second is the concept of rhythm itself, which comes to the fore in Deleuze's 1981 book, *Francis Bacon: The Logic of Sensation*. It is not simply that rhythm lies at the origin of prehistoric painting; Deleuze argues that rhythm is the essence of *all* painting. In Bacon's paintings, in particular, it is rhythm itself that becomes the characters, the objects and the Figures. Following Messiaen, Deleuze argues that, as in music, one can find three different types of rhythm in Bacon: a steady or 'attendant' rhythm, and then two other rhythms, a rhythm of crescendo or simplification (climbing, expanding, diastolic, adding value), and a rhythm of diminuendo or simplification (descending, contracting, systolic, removing value).[55]

Conclusion

We have simply presented here the broad outlines of the vision of human evolution developed by Leroi-Gourhan in *Gesture and Speech*. If there is one aspect of Leroi-Gourhan's analyses that Deleuze and Guatarri put in question, however, it is the notion of externalisation. There is a 'classic schema', they write, that sees 'the tool as the extension and projection of the living being', but they suggest that this schema has several drawbacks.[56] It presumes that technical artefacts have their origin in the body and are coupled with it, even though the body *itself* is constituted by a proto-technicity. In other words, the concept of externalisation neglects the determinative role that assemblages (*agencements*) in evolution, technological or otherwise. 'Functioning as a component part in conjunction with other parts [in an assemblage]', they write, "is very different from being an extension or a projection.'[57] In a sense, one could argue that Deleuze and Guattari created the concept of an assemblage as a corrective to Leroi-Gourhan's analyses, and it is sometimes presented as such by them.[58] The hand–tool pole is generalised into the concept of a *machinic assemblage of bodies*, or form of content, and the mouth–language pole is generalised into the concept of a *collective assemblage of enunciation* (regime of signs), or form of expression (ATP 88), with each of these poles characterised by vectors of de- and re-territorialisations. Evolution is itself a series of such de- and re-territorialisations, and as Deleuze and Guattari write, 'maps should be made of these things, organic, ecological, and technological maps [that] one can lay out on the plane of immanence' (ATP 61).

If *Gesture and Speech* can and should be read as a work of philosophy, and not simply palaeontology, it is because one of its achievements is to have vastly extended the scope of the philosophical enterprise. One of the great successes of the contemporary sciences is their development of techniques of *dating*, which have now provided us with what Serres calls the 'Grand Narrative' of the universe: the 'big bang' (if it occurred) took place 13.79 billion years ago; the Earth was formed 4.54 billion years ago; life (the first prokaryotes) began 3.5 billion years ago; the first hominids appeared 2 million years ago; and *Homo sapiens* made its appearance 200,000 years ago.[59] Though these dates will inevitably be modified, the development of this Grand Narrative means that the history of thought itself must be extended far beyond the origins of philosophy in Greece in the sixth century BCE. Among its many ambitions, *Gesture and Speech* was an early effort to attempt such a project, analysing the nature of thought and cognition in a context that must now span thousands and indeed millions of years.

Notes

1. See the article by Françoise Audouze, one of Leroi-Gourhan's students, 'Leroi-Gourhan, a Philosopher of Technique and Evolution', *Journal of Archaeological Research* 70:4 (Dec. 2002), pp. 277–306, which not only presents an overview of Leroi Gourhan's career and contributions, but also analyses the difficulties that hindered the more general reception of Leroi-Gourhan's work outside his technical areas of specialisation.
2. Leroi-Gourhan's writings from this period have only recently been published as *Pages oubliées sur le Japon* (Grenoble: Jérôme Millon, 2004).
3. See Pierre Lemmonier, 'Leroi-Gourhan: ethnologue des techniques', in *Nouvelles de l'archéologie* 48/49 (1992), pp. 13–17.
4. André Leroi-Gourhan, 'Les fouilles d'Arcy-sure-Cure (Yonne)', *Gallia préhistoire* 4 (1961), pp. 1–16; André Lerois-Gourhan and Arlette Leroi-Gourhan, 'Chronologie des grottes d'Arcy-sur-Cure (Yonne)', *Gallia préhistoire* 7:1 (1964), pp. 1–64.
5. André Leroi-Gourhan and Michel Brézillon, *Fouilles de Pincevent: Essai d'analyse ethnographique d'un habitat magdalénien*, 2 vols (Paris: Éditions du CNRS, 1983); André Leroi-Gourhan, *Pincevent: Campement magdalénien de chasseurs de Rennes* (Paris: Ministère de

la Culture, 1984); and André Leroi-Gourhan and Michel Brézillon, 'L'habitation magdalenienne no. 1 de Pincevent près Montereau (Seine-et-Marne)', *Gallia préhistoire* 9:2 (1966), pp. 263–363.

6. See André Leroi-Gourhan, *Treasures of Prehistoric Art*, trans. Norbert Guterman (New York: Harry N. Abrams, 1967), a translation of *Préhistoire de l'art occidental: L'art et les grandes civilisations* (Paris: Lucien Mazenod, 1965); and André Leroi-Gourhan, *The Dawn of European Art: An Introduction to Palaeolithic Cave Painting*, trans. Sara Champion (Cambridge: Cambridge University Press, 1982), a translation of *I piu' antichi artisti d'Europe* (Milan: Jaca Book, 1980).
7. For a more nuanced assessment, see Oscar Moro Abadía and Eduardo Palacio-Pérez, 'Rethinking the Structural Analysis of Palaeolithic Art: New Perspectives on Leroi-Gourhan's Structuralism', *Cambridge Archaeological Journal* 25:3 (August 2015), pp. 657–72. Paul Graves discusses Leroi-Gourhan's reception in the English-speaking world in his interesting piece 'My Strange Quest for Leroi-Gourhan: Structuralism's Unwitting Hero', *Antiquity* 68: 259 (1994), pp. 438–41.
8. André Leroi-Gourhan, *Evolution et techniques*, vol. 1, *L'Homme et la matière* (Paris: Albin Michel, 1943), and vol. 2, *Milieu et techniques* (Paris: Albin Michel, 1945). The two volumes were reprinted in 1971 and 1973, with minor additions and modifications.
9. André-Leroi Gourhan, *Gesture and Speech*, trans. Anna Bostock Berger (Cambridge, MA: MIT Press, 1993). Page numbers for references to *Gesture and Speech* are included in the text in parentheses.
10. Jacques Derrida, *Of Grammatology* [1967], trans. Gayatri Chakravorty Spivak (Baltimore: Johns Hopkins University Press, 1977), pp. 83–6.
11. See, for instance, Leroi-Gourhan, *Gesture and Speech*, p. 58: 'All evolutionists agree that the stream upon which we are borne forward is *the* stream of evolution. Like the giant dinosaur, lichen, jellyfish, oysters and giant turtles are no more than spray from the central jet that gushes human-ward.'
12. Tim Ingold, '"Tools for the Hand, Language for the Face": An Appreciation of Leroi-Gourhan's *Gesture and Speech*,', *Studies in History and Philosophy of Biological and Biomedical Sciences* 30:4 (1999), pp. 411–53 (p. 416).
13. See Leroi-Gourhan, *Gesture and Speech*, p. 8: 'When Darwin's Origin of Species was published in 1859, it bore little relation to the barely nascent science of prehistory. Rather it marked the conclusion of the movement begun by Buffon. Like the eighteenth-century naturalists, Darwin – himself a naturalist, not a prehistorian or an anthropologist – grew from the subsoil of stratigraphic zoology, paleontology and contemporary zoology, for in the last analysis . . . humans can only be understood as part of a terrestrial totality. With Darwin, the encyclopedists' thirst was satisfied once and for all.'

14. See Leroi-Gourhan, *Gesture and Speech*, pp. 64–89. Leroi-Gourhan devoted a separate book to a detailed analysis of the development of the human skull: *Méchanique vivante: Le crâne des vertébrés du poisson à l'homme* [Living Mechanics: The Skull in Vertebrates from the Fish to Humans] (Paris: Fayard, 1983).
15. See Charles Darwin, *The Descent of Man*, 2nd edn [1879] (London and New York: Penguin Classics, 2004), chapter 5, 'On the Development of the Intellectual and Moral Faculties, during Primeval and Civilized Times', p. 153: 'In the rudest state of society, the individuals who were the most sagacious, who invented and used the best weapons or traps, and who were best able to defend themselves, would rear the greatest number of offspring.'
16. Friedrich Nietzsche, *Will to Power*, trans. Walter Kaufmann and R. J. Hollingdale (New York: Random House, 1967), §532, 289; cf. §489, 270.
17. See Ernst Kapp, *Grundlinien einer Philosophie der Technik: Zur Entstehungsgeschichte der Kultur aus neuen Geschichtspunkten*) [Principles of a Philosophy of Technology: Towards a History of Culture from New Viewpoints] (Braunschweig: George Westermann, 1877). French translation: Ernst Kapp, *Principes d'une philosophie de la technique*, trans. Grégoire Chamayou (Paris: Vrin, 2007). For Kapp, the necessity for technics derives from man's organ deficiencies, and he distinguished between the principles of organic relief (*Organentlastung*), organic substitution or replacement (*Organersatzes*) and organic strengthening or improvement (*Organüberbeitung*). Kapp's work seems to have entered France through Alfred Espinas's *Étude sociologique: les origines de la technologie* (Paris: Félix Alcan, 1897). Neither Leroi-Gourhan nor Deleuze cite Kapp or Espinas. Konrad Lorenz similarly suggested that 'a behavior pattern can be treated as an anatomical organ' (cited in Richard Dawkins, *The Extended Phenotype* [Oxford: Oxford University Press, 1982], p. 2).
18. Marshall McLuhan, *Understanding Media: The Extensions of Man* [1964], critical edition edited by W. Terrence Gordon (Berkeley: Ginko Press, 2013). For an overview of the idea that technology is an 'order of extension', see David Rothenberg, *Hand's End: Technology and the Limits of Nature* (Berkeley: University of California Press, 1995), chapter 3, 'Extension's Order', pp. 28–53.
19. See Michel Serres, *Rameaux* (Paris: Pommier, 2004), pp. 179–80. In viviparous animals, such as mammals, by contrast, the embryo is reintegrated into the maternal body, and the fixed stock of nourishment in the egg is changed into a secretion from the breast, which varies according to demand.
20. Stephen J. Gould, *Wonderful Life: The Burgess Shale and the Nature of History* (New York: W. W. Norton, 1990).

21. Henri Bergson, 'Life and Consciousness', in *Mind-Energy*, trans. H. Wildon Carr (London: Macmillan, 1920), pp. 1–28 (p. 7).
22. This argument applies equally to plant life. See Stefano Mancuso and Allessandra Viola, *Brilliant Green: The Surprising History and Science of Plant Intelligence*, trans. Joan Benham, foreword by Michael Pollan (Washington, DC: Island Press, 2015). Plants are not 'individuals' (*in*, 'not' + *dividuus*, 'divisible'), since even if a plant is cut in half, the two parts can still live independently (p. 36), in part because plants have not localized their life functions in organs ('they can see without eyes, taste without taste buds, smell without a nose, and even digest without a stomach' [p. 73])
23. Renaud Barabas, 'Vie et extériorité: le problème de la perception chez Ruyer', *Les Études philosophiques* 80:1 (2007), pp. 5–37 (25), citing Raymond Ruyer, *Éléments de psychobiologie* (Paris: Presses universitaires de France, 1946), p. 22. See also Raymond Ruyer, 'Le paradoxe de l'amibe et la psychologie', *Journal de psychologie normale et pathologique*, July–Dec. 1938, pp. 472–92; and 'Du vital au psychique', in *Valeur philosophique de la psychologie*, Treizième semaine de synthèse (Paris, Presses universitaires de France, 1951).
24. Richard Dawkins, *Climbing Mount Probable* (New York and London: W. W. Norton, 1996), pp. 138–9.
25. Karl Marx, *Capital: A Critique of Political Economy*, vol. 1, trans. Ban Fawkes (London: Penguin, 1990), chapter 15, 493n., as cited in Bernard Steigler, *Technics and Time 1: The Fault of Epimetheus* [1994], trans. Richard Beardsworth and George Collins (Stanford: Stanford University Press, 1998), p. 26.
26. See Steigler, *Technics and Time 1*, p. 1.
27. James L. Gould and Carol Grant Gould, *Animal Architects: Building and the Evolution of Intelligence* (New York: Basic Books, 2012).
28. Dawkins, *The Extended Phenotype*, p. 200. Dawkins notes that these externalised organs sometimes assume persistent genetic idiosyncrasies: 'One female *Zygiella-x-notata* was seen to build more than 100 webs, all lacking a particular concentric ring' (pp. 198–9).
29. See, for instance, Richard Lewontin, 'Organism and Environment', in *The Triple Helix: Gene, Organism and Environment* [1998] (Cambridge, MA: Harvard University Press, 2000), pp. 41–68.
30. TP 51. Deleuze and Guattari have proposed a complex concept of the 'milieu': 'the living thing has an *exterior* milieu of materials, an *interior* milieu of composing elements and composed substances, an *intermediary* milieu of membranes and limits, and an *annexed* [or *associated*] milieu of energy sources and actions-perceptions' (TP 313).
31. Jacob von Uexküll, *A Foray into the Worlds of Animals and Humans* [1934], trans. Joseph D. O'Neill (Minneapolis: University of Minnesota Press, 2010), pp. 44–5. See TP 51.

32. Serres, *Rameaux*, pp. 175–6.
33. Kevin Kelly, *What Technology Wants* (New York: Penguin, 2010), pp. 11–12.
34. See, for instance, the title of James Gleick's book, *Faster: The Acceleration of Just about Everything* (New York: Vintage, 2000).
35. Michel Serres, *L'Hominescence* (Paris: Éditions Le Pommier, 2001).
36. For three instances of this claim, see Ralph Holloway, 'Culture, a Human Domain', *Current Anthropology* 10 (1969), pp. 395–412; Jacques Pelegrin, 'A Framework for Analyzing Prehistoric Stone Tool Manufacture and a Tentative Application to Some Early Stone Industries', in A Berthelet and J. Chavaillon (eds), *The Use of Tools by Humans and Non-Human Primates* (Oxford: Clarendon Press, 1993), pp. 302–14; and Thomas Wynn, *The Evolution of Spatial Competence* (Urbana: University of Illinois Press, 1989).
37. Gary Tomlinson, *A Million Years of Music: The Emergence of Human Modernity* (New York: Zone Books, 2016), pp. 57, 60.
38. Tomlinson, *A Million Year of Music*, p. 52. On the 'archaeology of mind', see Lambros Malafouris, *How Things Shape the Mind: A Theory of Material Engagement* (Cambridge, MA: MIT Press, 2013).
39. André Leroi-Gourhan, *The Hunters of Prehistory* [1983], trans. Claire Jacobson (New York: Atheneum, 1989), p. 48. See pp. 59–60: 'The tool itself sums up and keeps alive for us the thoughts of all preceding generations.'
40. Tomlinson, *A Million Years of Music*, p. 61.
41. Tim Ingold, 'The Temporality of the Landscape', in *The Perception of the Environment: Essays on Livelihood, Dwelling, and Skill* (London: Routledge, 2000), pp. 189–208
42. Tomlinson, *A Million Years of Music*, p. 69.
43. See *A Thousand Plateaus*, chapter 5 ('On Several Regimes of Signs') (TP 111–48).
44. Karl Popper, *Objective Knowledge: An Evolutionary Approach*, rev. edn (Oxford: Oxford University Press, 1972), p. 37.
45. Donald T. Campbell, 'Evolutionary Epistemology', in *The Philosophy of Karl Popper*, ed. Philip Schilpp (LaSalle: Open Court, 1974), pp. 412–63.
46. Raymond Ruyer, *L'Animal, l'homme, la function symbolique* (Paris: Gallimard, 1964), p. 97.
47. See Jesper Hoffmeyer, *Biosemiotics: An Examination into the Signs of Life and the Life of Signs*, ed. Donald Favareau (Scranton, PA: University of Scranton Press, 2009), and Steven Rose, *The Chemistry of Life*, 4th edn (London: Penguin Books, 1999).
48. E. O. Wilson was one of the pioneers in the study of ants and their chemical semiotics. Among his many works, see *The Insect Societies* (Cambridge, MA: Harvard University Press, 1971) and *The Ants*,

with Bert Holldobler (Cambridge, MA: Harvard University Press, 1990).

49. In this, Leroi-Gourhan is perhaps following the lead of the Société de linguistique de Paris, which, in 1865, famously informed its members that it would no longer accept 'any submissions concerning the origin of language' in order to avoid sterile quarrels and eccentric theses.
50. See also pp. 88–9: 'Bipdeal posture and a free hand automatically imply a brain equipped for speech.'
51. See Eric A. Havelock, *Preface to Plato* (Cambridge, MA: Harvard University Press, 1963), especially chapter 9, pp. 145–64; Walter J. Ong, *Orality and Literacy: The Technologizing of the Word* (London and New York: Routledge, 1982); and Jack Goody, *The Interface between the Written and the Oral* (Cambridge: Cambridge University Press, 1987).
52. See AO 202–4.
53. For an accessible analysis of externalised systems of measurement, see Robert P. Crease, *World in the Balance: The Historic Quest for an Absolute System of Measurement* (New York: Norton, 2011).
54. Leroi-Gourhan, *Gesture and Speech*, p. 372, cited TP 574 n. 33.
55. See FB chapter 9.
56. Gilles Deleuze and Félix Guattari, 'Balance-sheet for "Desiring-Machines"', in Félix Guattari, *Chaosophy: Texts and Interviews, 1972–1977*, ed. Sylvère Lotringer and trans. David L. Sweet, Jarred Becker and Taylor Adkins (New York: Semiotet(e), 1992), p. 92.
57. Ibid.
58. See TP 60: 'Leroi-Gourhan's analyses give us an understanding of how contents came to be linked with the hand-tool couple and expressions with the face-language couple.' (See also TP 64, 302.)
59. Michel Serres, *L'Incandescent* (Paris: Pommier, 2003), pp. 9–62.

Henri Maldiney

Ronald Bogue

In his writings on painting, Deleuze makes use of a number of commentators on art, including Hubert Damisch, Mikel Dufrenne, Elie Faure, Henri Focillon, Michael Fried, Clement Greenberg, Maurice Merleau-Ponty, Aloïs Riegl, Heinrich Wölfflin and Wilhelm Worringer. But perhaps the most important influence on his approach to painting is Henri Maldiney. Such a claim might seem exaggerated, were one to judge Maldiney's impact by the number of times Deleuze cites his work, or by the proximity of Maldiney's thought to Deleuze's. Only upon consultation of *Regard Parole Espace* (Gaze Speech Space), the sole publication of Maldiney's cited by Deleuze, does the significance of Maldiney become evident. Here one finds not only a profound meditation on art but also a source book of commentators and citations upon which Deleuze draws, as well as a history of painting whose broad outlines Deleuze makes use of in his own works.

Born 4 August 1912 in Meursault (in the Côte d'Or region), Maldiney began his studies in philosophy at the Lycée du Parc in Lyon. In 1933 he was admitted to the École normale supérieure in the rue d'Ulm in Paris, where he wrote a thesis on Fichte under the direction of Léon Brunschvicq. After completing his *agrégation* in philosophy in 1937, he taught briefly at the Briançon *lycée* before being inducted into the army in 1939. He was captured by the Germans in 1940 and spent the remainder of the war in a prison camp. There, he was able to study key texts of Husserl and Heidegger, most notably Heidegger's *Sein und Zeit*. After the war, he secured a position in the École des hautes études at the University of Ghent in Belgium, where his primary duties were teaching literature. In 1947 he met the painter Elsa Vervaene, who soon became his wife, and Jacques Schotte, one of his students, who introduced Maldiney to Ludwig Binswanger and Roland Kuhn, proponents of Dasein analysis. This encounter initiated Maldiney's lifelong interest in psychoanalysis and psychiatry and his interaction with such notable figures as Eugène

Minkowski, Jacques Lacan, Gisela Pankow, Léopold Szondi and Jean Oury (founder of the La Borde clinic, where Guattari worked for several years).

In 1953 Maldiney accepted a position at the University of Lyon, where he remained until his retirement in 1977. He taught a wide range of courses in philosophy, phenomenological anthropology, psychology and aesthetics, yet despite his international reputation as an important and original exponent of phenomenology, he remained marginalised as an adjunct professor during much of his tenure at Lyon. Such was his status when Deleuze joined the Lyon philosophy faculty in 1964. Upon Deleuze's arrival, the two soon became friends, and throughout his five years in Lyon Deleuze remained Maldiney's advocate.[1]

No doubt one difficulty Maldiney faced in seeking a more secure position was that he did not have a book to his name, only a series of extremely dense articles in diverse venues. That situation changed in 1973, when, at the age of sixty-one, he published his first book, *Regard Parole Espace*, a selection of seven previously published studies and five new essays. The following year, he brought out a second book, dedicated to the poetry of his close friend Francis Ponge, *Le Leg des choses dans l'oeuvre de Francis Ponge* (The Legacy of Things in the Work of Francis Ponge). With the assistance of Paul Ricœur, in 1974 he was able to defend his *thèse de Doctorat d'État* at Nanterre before a jury consisting of Ricœur, Emmanuel Levinas, Clémence Ramnoux and Marc Le Bot, and at long last attain the rank of professor. That *thése* appeared in 1975 under the title *Aîtres de la langue et demeures de la pensée* (Enclosures of Language and Dwellings of Thought). After his retirement in 1977, Maldiney continued to publish regularly, with several books to his credit when his students and colleagues gathered to celebrate his hundredth birthday in 2012. That year the Éditions du Cerf launched the publication of the complete philosophical works of Maldiney, of which to date five volumes have appeared. Maldiney died on 7 December 2013 at the age of 101.[2]

Maldiney's philosophy is squarely within the phenomenological tradition, but he departs from Husserl in arguing against the primacy of intentionality in consciousness. In Binswanger's Dasein analysis Maldiney finds the concept of a pre-intentional 'thymic space' (*gestimmter Raum*, rendered in French as an *espace thymique*), which is neither objective nor subjective, but an atmospheric affective space with no delineation of inside or outside, subject or object. In such a thymic space there is no Husserlian intentionality, since there is no subject to bear that intention. Binswanger's concept of the thymic Maldiney equates with Erwin Straus's notion of the *pathic*, which Straus identifies as the domain of sensation. If Binswanger is Maldiney's guide in his psychoanalytic writings, it is Straus who provides the inspiration for the development of Maldiney's aesthetics.

In his 1935 *Vom Sinn der Sinne* (translated as *The Primary World of Senses: A Vindication of Sensory Experience*), Straus undertakes a critique of Pavlov and behavioural psychology, arguing that Pavlov and his followers go astray by concentrating their analyses solely on perception while ignoring the existence of sensation, a dimension of experience that serves as the precondition of all their studies. Straus sees perception as a secondary organisation of primary sensation, perception being a rational configuration of time, space, self and other, and sensation a non-rational, alinguistic being-with the world, in which near and far form a single Here in a perpetual Now. The primary world of sensation is one we share with animals, one in which subject and object are merely emergent tendencies within a space of movement and affect.

> The being present of sensory experience – and thus sensory experience in general – is the experiencing of a being-with (*Mit-Sein*) which unfolds into a subject and an object. The sensing subject does not have sensations but, rather, in his sensing he has first himself. In sensory experience, there unfolds both the becoming of the subject and the happenings of the world. I become only insofar as something happens, and something happens (for me) only insofar as I become. The Now of sensing belongs neither to objectivity nor to subjectivity alone, but necessarily to both together. In sensing, both self and world unfold simultaneously for the sensing subject; the sensing being experiences himself and the world, himself in the world, himself with the world.[3]

In perception, space is organised according to a uniform system of coordinates, independent of any given perspective, and time is measured in an abstract succession of discrete moments. In sensation, by contrast, space is perspectival, a surrounding environment delineated by a shifting horizon that perpetually moves with the moving inhabitant, and time is inseparable from the Now of the moving inhabitant's *Mit-Welt*. Sensation always unfolds toward the poles of subject and object, but the two never become fully detached from one another; instead, a continual process of simultaneous separation and union establishes a communication between world and self through their mutual movement and interaction. Sensation is neither 'within' nor 'without', and 'the body is the mediator between the self and the world. It belongs fully neither to the "inner" nor to the "outer"'.[4]

Straus develops the opposition of perception and sensation by differentiating *geography* from *landscape*. The world of geography, he says, 'is a world of things with fixed and inalterable properties in universal objective space and universal objective time'.[5] The landscape, by contrast, is the world of a perspectival, sensory moving space-time. Despite the primacy of the landscape of sensation, we have difficulty discerning it, since our practical negotiation of the world relies so heavily on our rational organisation of space and time. But in great landscape painting, says Straus, we are brought into the world of sensation.

> Landscape painting does not depict what we see, i.e., what we notice when looking at a place, but – the paradox is unavoidable – it makes visible the invisible, although it be as something far removed. Great landscapes all have a visionary character. Such vision is of the invisible becoming visible.[6]

In such a landscape, we enter the *Mit-Welt* of an emerging self-world: 'the more we absorb it, the more we lose ourselves in it'.

Straus's statement that the landscape 'makes visible the invisible', Maldiney notes, is remarkably similar to Paul Klee's dictum that 'art does not render the visible but renders visible'.[7] Maldiney argues that all genuine art is like Straus's landscape, a means of making visible the invisible realm of sensation, the 'Real', which 'one never expects – and yet which is always already there'.[8] In Straus's identification of primary sensation with the landscape Maldiney sees the possibility of bringing together the two senses of the aesthetic in Kant – that of sense experience in *The Critique of Pure Reason*, and that of art in *The Critique of Judgement*. Art's function, then, is not to represent objects or express concepts, but to render visible sensations, such that the primary world of the senses, veiled by the habits of rational perception, 'appears'. A painting is not 'an image: it is an apparition. Every painting is an event: and it is so to the extent that it offers us a surprise' (RPE 6/37). The apparitional event of the painting is an 'encounter' (RPE 248/316) that offers us 'the astonishment of the "there is" [*il y a*], the surprise of *being* and *being-there*' (RPE 152/207) .

In both sense experience and art, the aesthetic 'concerns not a *what* but a *how*' (137/190), an interplay of form and rhythm that together constitute the 'how' of style. A form is not a sign, for which reason art is not a discourse or language. Citing Henri Focillon, Maldiney asserts, 'The sign signifies, the form signifies *itself* [*Le signe signifie, la forme se signifie*]' (RPE 131/183). Nor is a form static or determined by fixed relations. Indeed, as the 'how' of sensation, it cannot be, for the world of sensation is one of movement and becoming. A form is a 'forming', not a *Gestalt*, but a *Gestaltung* (as Klee puts it). The painting's apparition is the spontaneous emergence of its self-forming, a 'sudden arising [*surgissement*] of itself to itself' (RPE 132/184). And the unfolding patterning of the self-shaping activity of form is rhythm. 'This sense of form in formation, in perpetual transformaon in the return of the same, is properly the sense of rhythm' (157/213). Maldiney does not ignore the representational aspect of much art, but he argues that a representational work 'has two dimensions: an "intentional-representative" one according to which it is an image, and a "genetic-rhythmic" one, which makes it a form. The rhythm of the form commands and assumes the motricity of the image, and it determines the affective tonality by way of which – before any objective sensible representation – we haunt the world' by passing 'through the image' (RPE 155–6/211).

Maldiney delineates three moments in the artistic creation of forms: a disorienting surging-forth of a chaotic world of sensation; a systolic coming-together of elements in emergent shapes; and a diastolic expansion of forces that transforms the shapes into components of a pathic inter-communicative whole. Straus observes that often the manifestation of sensation comes in an abrupt break in common-sense perception, and in that break we feel confused, dazed and 'lost (*verloren* – forlorn)'.[9] Maldiney asserts that this vertiginous emergence of sensation is what Cézanne described so aptly when he told Gasquet,

> At this moment I am one with my canvas [not the painted canvas, in Maldiney's reading, but the world to be painted]. We are an iridescent chaos. I dream in front of my motif, I lose myself there . . . The sun dully penetrates me like a distant friend, warming my laziness, fecundating it. We germinate. (Cited in RPE 150/204)

Maldiney also finds this moment elaborated in Klee's notion of the grey point, neither black nor white, cold nor warm, high nor low, 'a non-dimensional point, a point between dimensions'.[10] This is the point of chaos, a 'nonconcept', a 'nowhere-existent something' or 'somewhere-existent nothing'.[11]

Klee's chaotic grey point does not remain inert and undetermined, however. Miraculously, the point gives rise to 'the cosmogenetic moment': 'A point in chaos: Once established the grey point leaps into the realm of order.'[12] This spontaneous originary leap, this *Ur-sprung* as Maldiney calls it (RPE 132/184), inaugurates the second moment of systolic condensation. In characterising this moment, Cézanne interlocks his hands and squeezes them together. '"Slowly the geological strata appear before me . . . Everything falls straight down . . . I begin to separate myself from the landscape, to see it"' (cited in RPE 150/204–5). As distinct compositional elements emerge, says Cézanne, the '"stubborn geometry"' and the '"measure of the earth"' (cited in RPE 150/204) begin to exert their presence. At this juncture, the amorphous potentialities of chaos take on a specific configuration, a rhythmic articulation of space and time that is 'the most unpredictably necessary. Such, among a thousand possible, is the right line [*ligne juste*], whose reality annuls the possibility of all the others' (RPE 166/223).

Yet this systolic moment is succeeded by a third, diastolic moment, in which the condensation of elements gives way to 'the expansive eruption of color, in the diastole of the painting and of the world, in the diastole of ex-istence' (RPE 185/244). A pathic communication unites the surrounding world. At this moment, says Cézanne, he '"breathes the virginity of the world"' (cited in RPE 150/204), and man is '"absent from but entirely within the landscape"' (cited in RPE 185/245). Cézanne speaks of '"the radiation of the soul, the look, the mystery of light . . . the colors! An aerial, colored logic suddenly replaces the stubborn geometry. The geological strata, the preparatory labor, the moment of design collapse, crumble as in a catastrophe"' (cited in RPE 185/244). It is this aerial colored logic, says Maldiney, that inspires Cézanne's exclamation to his coachman, '"Look! The blues! The blues down there under the pines"' (cited in REP 138/191). Similarly, Maldiney asserts, when Van Gogh writes to his brother of his efforts to '"attain the high yellow note of this summer"', he uses a musical metaphor 'because in this yellow the world sounds; and it sounds to the extent that Van Gogh, in this yellow, inhabits a world that has not yet crystallized into objects, and with which he communicates in the rhythm of an ascending vertigo' (RPE 137/191).

In chapter 6 of *Francis Bacon: The Logic of Sensation*, Deleuze presents the book's central concept of sensation, and throughout the exposition one finds echoes of Maldiney. Deleuze opens the chapter by considering Bacon's rejection of the extremes of conventional representation and abstraction in favour of the Figure, arguing that Bacon's treatment of the Figure should be understood in terms of what Cézanne called sensation. Clearly, what Deleuze refers to as the Figure Maldiney would include within the concept of form: 'The Figure is the sensible form related to a sensation; it acts immediately upon the nervous system, which is of the flesh, whereas abstract form is addressed to the head and acts through the intermediary of the brain, which is closer to the bone' (FB 31). Deleuze alludes here to Bacon's observation that 'some paint comes across directly onto the nervous system and other paint tells you the story in a long diatribe through the brain',[13] but also to Cézanne's opposition of the 'logic of the senses' and the 'logic of the brain', an opposition to which Maldiney calls attention in his differentiation of sensation from cognitive-mediated perception (RPE 138/191, 275/346). Deleuze continues that sensation has one face turned towards the subject and a second towards the object, 'Or rather, it has no faces at all, it is both things indissolubly, it is Being-in-the-World, as the phenomenologists say: at one and the same time I *become* in the sensation and something *happens* through the sensation, one through the other, one in the other' (FB 31). Deleuze cites Maldiney as the source of this observation,[14] but of course it is Straus who is being paraphrased here: 'In sensory experience, there unfolds both the becoming of the subject and the happenings of the world.[15] Deleuze then elaborates, 'And at the limit, it is the same body that, being both subject and object, gives and receives the sensation. As a spectator, I experience the sensations only by entering the painting, by reaching the unity of the sensing and the sensed' (FB 31). Here, we discern echoes of Straus's assertion that 'the body is the mediator between the self and the world',[16] but, more importantly, we find in these words an apt summary of Maldiney's understanding of the function of art. As Maldiney repeatedly asserts, art renders visible the world of sensation, a world with no differentiation of subject and object, and when we view a painting, we enter that world through the painting and experience it within the painting.

After presenting the basic concept of sensation, Deleuze explores the significance of Bacon's frequent references to 'orders of sensation', 'levels of feeling', 'areas of sensation' and 'shifting sequences' (FB 33), concluding that for Bacon sensation has an 'irreducibly synthetic character' (FB 33). How should we understand sensation's synthetic nature? Deleuze asks. Not in terms of the represented objects, of course; not through 'an ambivalence of feelings' (FB 35), since sensation is a matter of affect rather than emotion; and not as a function of movement, since it is sensation that generates movement, not the reverse. More promising, Deleuze says, is a phenomenological approach, in which the synthesis would be 'an existential communication' among the body's five senses in a '"pathic" (non-representative) moment' (FB 37). According to this interpretation, 'The painter would thus *make visible* a kind of original unity of the senses' (FB 37). But this account limits sensation to the domains of the lived human body, and sensation is 'a vital power that exceeds every domain and traverses them all' (FB 37). This power 'is Rhythm, which is more profound than vision, hearing, etc.' Rhythm discloses

> a 'logic of the senses', as Cézanne said, neither rational nor cerebral. What is ultimate is thus the relation between sensation and rhythm, which places in each sensation the levels and domains through which it passes . . . It is diastole–systole: the world that seizes me by closing in around me, the self that opens to the world and opens the world itself. (FB 37)

As Deleuze duly notes (FB 157), it is Maldiney who points the way beyond phenomenology through this analysis of sensation in terms of the systolic and diastolic rhythm of forms. Deleuze speaks little of forms, in Maldiney's sense of the word, and utilises the terms 'systole' and 'diastole' only in his discussion of the Figure's relationship to its surrounding structure (FB 29–30), but rhythm serves as the master concept in his formal analyses of Bacon's paintings (see especially FB 37–8, 60, 63–9, 83, 86–7). Where Deleuze departs from Maldiney is in tying rhythm to forces and sensation to the body without organs. Maldiney does occasionally speak of forces and energy in his analyses of forms and rhythms,[17] but primarily as a means of characterising the dynamism of sensation – its multiple, interacting movements of contraction and dilation, condensation and expansion, surging-forth and fading-away. These movements are manifest in the *aesthēsis* of sense experience and the *aesthēsis* of the work of art, but they are conceived of only as movements within a human world, albeit one in which subject and object are indiscernible. When Maldiney cites Klee's dictum that art 'renders visible', he means that art renders visible the experiential world of sensation. Deleuze, by contrast, uses the phrase to insist that art renders visible invisible forces, just as music renders audible inaudible forces, and those forces permeate the human and the non-human. They are forces of 'nonorganic life' (FB 40), which reveal, beyond the lived body, the body without organs, 'an intense and intensive body . . . traversed by a wave that traces levels or thresholds' (FB 39). Here the distance between Deleuze and Maldiney is quite evident, but in Maldiney's phenomenological analyses of individual paintings the distance is less pronounced, for in those analyses Maldiney virtually ignores the lived body and focuses instead on the autonomous movements of form and rhythm that play through the cosmos made manifest in the canvas. It is this aspect of Maldiney's work especially that opens the way beyond phenomenology towards Deleuze's account of painting as the capture of forces and the creation of a body without organs.

Maldiney also plays an important role in Deleuze's remarks on the history of painting in *Francis Bacon*. In chapter 14, Deleuze entertains the hypothesis that all painters recapitulate the history of painting in their own ways, arguing that in Bacon one finds echoes of Egyptian, classical Greek, Christian, Byzantine and Gothic art, as well as the colouristic practices of Cézanne and Van Gogh. Deleuze organises this history in terms of the haptic and the optic, an opposition he draws from Aloïs Riegl. In his *Late Roman Art Industry* (1901), Riegl asserts that there are two kinds of vision, one that is *nahsichtig* ('near seeing'), tactile or haptic (from the Greek *hapto*, to touch); and one that is *fernsichtig* ('far-seeing') or optic. Haptic vision stresses the individuality and impenetrability of objects while suppressing the sense of depth as an infinite space. Optic vision, by contrast, situates objects within an infinite space and subordinates them to the variegations of light within that space. Riegl argues that Egyptian art is primarily haptic, classical Greek art haptic-optic (neither *nahsichtig* nor *fernsichtig* but *normalsichtig*, or 'normal-seeing') and late Roman art predominantly (but not fully) optic.

Maldiney provides his own treatment of Riegl in chapter 9 of *Regard Parole Espace*, 'L'Art et le pouvoir du fond' (Art and the Power of the Ground), and there is evidence that Deleuze's reading of Riegl is filtered through Maldiney. Maldiney sees in Riegl's haptic/optic analysis of ancient art a means of understanding the relation between motif and ground (*fond*) in all art. This artistic relation, says Maldiney, 'is the aesthetic expression of the ontological relation of existence to ground' (RPE 173/232). We stand in the world surrounded by space, our feet on the ground and our eyes on the horizon. Our most active senses, touch and sight, engage the ground and horizon by grasping the world through touch and extending ourselves into the world through sight. This opposition of touch and sight gives rise to two different spaces and two different ways of seeing, one haptic, the other optic. In haptic space, the individual object, or motif, is something one grasps, seizing it with the eyes as an individual entity emergent from an immobile ground. In optic space, by contrast, the motif 'is given starting from free space and, as a result, the motif is moving and tends to make the ground move'.[18] In haptic space, viewers face the motif and project themselves into the world and possess objects, whereas in optic space viewers are possessed by the luminous space of the motif and its shifting ground, entering into pathic communication with the world of ground and object. Maldiney identifies haptic space with the systolic moment of condensation, in which individuated entities begin to take shape, and optic space with the diastolic moment of expansion, in which all becomes colour and light. In the interplay of systole and diastole, of haptic and optic space, one finds 'the ontological relation of existence to ground', which is rendered in art as the aesthetic relation of motif to ground. In a limited sense, the artistic ground, or *fond*, is the background against which the motif appears, but in a larger sense that *fond* is the systolic ground of sensation that emerges from an originary chaos and partakes of a rhythmic process of systolic–diastolic grounding (*fondement*), whereby the motif becomes the grounding of the ground from which it surges forth.

On the basis of this broad interpretation of the haptic and the optic, Maldiney reviews Riegl's history of Egyptian, classical Greek and late Roman art. He concurs with Riegl that Egyptian art aptly exemplifies the haptic relation between motif and ground, and he follows Riegl in his description of Egyptian art's basic characteristics. The space of the Egyptian artwork is structured according to the close view, as if the eye were touching its surfaces. The goal of Egyptian art is to protect the object from change, the corruption of time and the uncertainties of spatial variations of light and shadow. The motif's contour separates it from the ground, but any sense of depth is suppressed, since depth exposes the object to the world of becoming. Compositions are planar, and forms are symmetrical, regular and stable. Between motif and ground there is no dialogic space, which might expose the motif to the forces of change. The ground is suppressed, and the motif itself becomes a ground, a static instance of the eternal afterlife that transcends our earthly existence.

Maldiney also seconds Riegl's assessment of classical Greek art as haptic-optic, but his characterisation of Riegl's analysis conflates Riegl's treatment of classical Greek and late Roman art. In Riegl's view, classical Greek art's modelling of the figure implies projections from the compositional plane within a three-dimensional space, the figure rising from the ground in three-quarter view, its movements more lively than those of Egyptian art. Yet the artworks remain essentially planar, the ground serving a calming, haptic function, the figure's movements partaking of another plane that is partially but not completely separated from the background plane. Only in late Roman art, Riegl argues, does the figure take on a truly spatial, optic configuration. The figure is sharply delineated from the ground, the figure's modelling employs deep shadows to sever the figure from the ground, and a rhythmic handling of light and dark organise the composition. Nonetheless, the figure is not open to an unlimited optic space. Rather, it exists in an enclosed cubic space, the cube superimposed against a planar background. Hence, late Roman art is not purely optic, only relatively so in its invention of a cubic space for the figure.

In his summary of Riegl, Maldiney attributes to classical Greek art not only the three-quarter view and animated movement of the figure but also the figure's placement within a cubic space affixed to a planar background, thereby collapsing Riegl's clear demarcation of classical Greek and late Roman art. Instead, Maldiney presents Riegl's late Roman art merely as a transitional phase in which classical Greek haptic elements slowly dissolve and make way for the emergence of the purely optic space of Byzantine art. Maldiney claims Riegl as his predecessor in viewing Byzantine art as purely optic, and there is some evidence to support this claim, but Maldiney's detailed analysis of Byzantine art is entirely his own.[19] In the mosaics and murals of such structures as Ravenna's basilica of Sant'Apollinare Nuovo and the cathedral at Cefalù, Sicily, Maldiney discerns a new relation between motif and ground, in which the ground is an infinite field of light and the figure an emergent expression of that field. What Byzantine art discovers, according to Maldiney, is 'the spatializing energy of color', the 'movement of space spacing itself in the irradiation of its ubiquity' (RPE 202–3/263, 265). Byzantine figures inhabit the space in front of them that extends to include the viewer. Here, 'Color generates space before serving the elucidation of form. Space is the auto-moving con-sistence of heterogeneous moments whose isolation or tension is resolved in the diffusive unity of a radiant matter' (RPE 204/266).

Deleuze begins his history of painting with a recapitulation of Riegl's analysis of the haptic characteristics of Egyptian art. His summary is an amalgam of points made by Riegl and Maldiney, with his own added stress on Egyptian art's static forms as essences, the 'very mystery' of this art being 'the mystery of essence' (FB 100). This focus on essence allows Deleuze to invoke the traditional essence–accident opposition and comment on Christian art as an exploration of the accidental within the divine, the incarnation exposing the eternal to the vicissitudes of the world and thereby providing 'a germ of tranquil atheism', which eventually collapses with the advent of modern painting, 'when man no longer experiences himself as an essence, but as an accident' (FB 100–1). After this aside, Deleuze returns to his primary theme of the haptic and optic with his description of classical Greek art. Here, his analysis is fully aligned with Maldiney's, most tellingly in his association of the figure's cubic space with Greek art (FB 101), and it is Maldiney Deleuze cites when he identifies Greek art's space as 'a *tactile-optical space*' (FB 102). Deleuze then discusses Byzantine art in terms of a purely optic space, again drawing on Maldiney for most of the details of his analysis.

Where Deleuze parts from Maldiney is in his treatment of the haptic outside Byzantine art. In Gothic art, to which Maldiney makes no reference in *Regard Parole Espace*, Deleuze sees a new haptic sensibility, expressed primarily in the Gothic line, described by Wilhelm Worringer in *Form in Gothic* (1912), a line animated by 'an intense kind of life, a *nonorganic* vitality' (FB 104). Deleuze also discovers a haptic dimension in the colourism of Cézanne and Van Gogh, which is evident in Cézanne and Van Gogh's use of 'broken tones' (created through a mixture of paints of complementary colours). For Maldiney, Cézanne and Van Gogh create a purely optic space of light and colour that is similar to the optic space of Byzantine art. For Deleuze, by contrast, Cézanne and Van Gogh are simultaneously optic and haptic colourists. Deleuze identifies two types of colour relations: relations of value, which involve relations of light and 'a purely optic function of distant vision'; and relations of tonality, which involve relations of hue, 'near vision' and 'a properly *haptic* function' (FB 85). Whereas Maldiney makes no distinction between light and colour, Deleuze differentiates light from hue, thereby granting colour a dual role as a force of optic light and haptic hue.

Maldiney's presence in Deleuze's thought is most evident in *Francis Bacon*, but it may be discerned as well in *Cinema 1: The Movement-Image* and *What is Philosophy?*. Deleuze uses Maldiney briefly in *Cinema 1* when he prefaces his discussion of the films of Kurosawa and Mizoguchi by identifying two central principles in Chinese painting, as summarised by Maldiney in his 1967 essay 'L'esthétique des rythmes' (The Aesthetic of Rhythms). Maldiney finds in the sixth-century theorist Xie He an articulation of the same principles of diastole and systole that inform Cézanne's aesthetic. Xie advises the painter first 'to reflect the vital breath', and then 'to seek the skeleton' (*ossature* in Maldiney's French translation, *ossature* meaning 'the disposition of the skeleton's bones' as well as 'any framework of elements structuring a whole), achieving the first by creating movement and the second by knowing how to use the brush (cited in RPE 167/224). In Maldiney's reading, to reflect the vital breath is to capture 'the cosmic respiration' of diastole and systole, and to seek the skeleton is to create a systolic 'living line of the universe' (RPE 167/224), the line of the universe being the counterpart of Cézanne's 'stubborn geometry', a line that only becomes a living line when it enters into the process of cosmic respiration. Deleuze takes this opposition of vital breath and skeleton and proposes that the large form of the cinematic action image discloses a '*respiration-space*' (*espace-respiration*) and the small form a '*skeleton-space*' (*espace-ossature*) (MI 168). He then presents Kurosawa as an exemplary creator of an all-inclusive respiration space and Mizoguchi as a master of the line of the universe that passes through a skeleton-space.[20]

In *What is Philosophy?* Deleuze and Guattari mention Maldiney only twice, once when they remark, 'Phenomenology needs art as logic needs science; Erwin Straus, Merleau-Ponty or Maldiney need Cézanne or Chinese Painting' (WP 149), and again when they cite him in a note on chaos, Cézanne and Klee (WP 233). Despite such scant reference to Maldiney, however, he must be seen as one of the more important inspirations for Deleuze and Guattari's philosophy of art, given their definition of the work of art as 'a being of sensation and nothing else' (WP 164). Maldiney may also have contributed to Deleuze and Guattari's notion that the work of art 'exists in itself' and, when successful, constitutes 'a monument' (WP 164). In the opening paragraphs of *What is Philosophy?*, Deleuze and Guattari argue that the work of art preserves sensation, in that the sensation captured by the work is autonomous, separate from its creator, any specific audience, or its referential content:

> The young man will smile on the canvas for as long as the canvas lasts . . . In a novel or a film, the young man will stop smiling, but he will start to smile again when we turn to the page or that moment . . . The young girl maintains the pose that she has had for five thousand

> years, a gesture that no longer depends on whoever made it. (WP 163)

The artist must utilise materials to create the work, but the artwork's captured sensations are separate from the material: 'Even if the material lasts for only a few seconds it will give sensation the power to exist and be preserved in itself *in the eternity that coexists with this short duration*' (WP 166). Maldiney makes a similar point when he characterises the time of the work of art. In the cave paintings of Lascaux, says Maldiney, we do not confront a dead record of a prehistoric era, but 'the instant of truth' which 'was for this race of hunters the apparitional moment, in which the surging-forth of the animal was one with the startled leap [*sursaut*] of the entire space of the Umwelt', a world 'suddenly haunted . . . by the event-advent [*événement-avènement*] of a disruptive presence [*une presence bouleversante*]' (RPE 139/192). When we view the Lascaux paintings, we enter that apparitional moment. 'The work of art is contemporary with the spectator and the auditor because it renders them contemporary with its instant' (RPE 139/192). That instant is in a perpetual present, but not the present of ordinary time. Maldiney likens the artwork's present to what the linguist Gustave Guillaume calls an 'implicated time', one that is opposed to the explicated time of actions 'divisible into epochs, past, present, future' (RPE 160/216).[21] The artwork's present, says Maldiney, is what Boulez calls amorphous or smooth time, as opposed to pulsed and striated time (RPE 159/214–15).[22] The artist renders visible the rhythms of this implicated, smooth time, allowing forms to surge forth in their self-formation, and spectators enter that same pathic time of sensation whenever they engage the artwork as an encounter.

Deleuze and Guattari state that in order for an artwork to preserve sensation, it must '*stand up on its own*' (WP 164), and that when it does so, it is 'a monument, but one that may be contained in a few marks or a few lines [*en quelques traits ou quelques lignes*]' (WP 164–5). The work must conserve a compound of sensations that cohere, a compound, in Cézanne's words, sufficiently '"solid and lasting like the art of the museums"' (cited in WP 165). In 'Art and the Power of the Ground', Maldiney also explores the concept of the artwork as monument, approaching the concept via the German word for monument, *Denkmal*:

> Denkmal is at once the body and the sign (*sōma sēma*) of a thought whose expression is one with its formation. *Mal* is the ground [*fond*]

> through which the thought *is*; and *Denken* (thought) the grounding [*fondement*] through which the ground [*fond*] *ex-ists*. But the ground and the grounding here are one. (RPE 174–5/233–4)

The body-sign thought of the artistic *Denkmal* is not a concept, however, but sensation, and the artwork as monument is the surging forth of its self-formation. The artwork's origin is the *Mal*, which Maldiney translates as *tache* (spot, stain, mark), through which the quotidian 'abruptly goes beyond itself toward a new depth and dimension of presence' (RPE 175/234). The *Mal*, 'be it block, spot, mark or point [*bloc, tache, trait ou point*]', is 'the fixation of a point in chaos [that] constitutes the cosmogenetic moment, as Paul Klee puts it' (RPE 181/240). When the systolic–diastolic rhythm initiated by the *Mal* reaches its full artistic expression, the work attains the solidity of 'stubborn geometry' but also the resonance of expanding light and colour. For this reason, says Maldiney, Cézanne wants to create '"something solid and lasting like the art of the museums"' (RPE 189/250), but also something that discloses '"the virginity of the world"' (cited in RPE 150/204) in which man is '"absent from but entirely within the landscape"' (cited in RPE 253/322). It is in this sense that Cézanne aspires to create a *Denkmal*, a monument.

Maldiney's treatment of the monument differs sufficiently from Deleuze and Guattari's that one might judge the similarity coincidental, but the identical citation from Cézanne and the echo of Maldiney's 'bloc, tache, trait ou point' in Deleuze and Guattari's 'quelques traits ou quelques lignes' suggest at least the plausibility of Maldiney's being an instigating source for Deleuze and Guattari's reflections on the artwork as monument. And as an instigating source, Maldiney's concept of the monument may serve as a paradigm of Deleuze's relationship to Maldiney in general. In all his engagements with other philosophers, Deleuze offers astute readings of their thought, extracts key concepts, and then uses them in the pursuit of his own philosophical project. In Maldiney's case, the concept of sensation that Maldiney derives from Straus allows Deleuze to move beyond phenomenology and develop a philosophy of painting that centres on sensation as the capture of forces and creation of a body without organs (*Francis Bacon*) and a philosophy of the arts in general as the preservation of the being of sensation (*What is Philosophy?*). Maldiney's history of the haptic and optic from Egyptian, classical Greek and Byzantine art to Cézanne provides Deleuze with a schema for analysing Bacon's recapitulation of the history of painting, a schema he ingeniously modifies by disclosing a haptic as well as an optic colourism in Cézanne and Van Gogh. Some elements of Maldiney's work serve more modest ends for Deleuze, such as Maldiney's analysis of Chinese painting's 'cosmic respiration' and 'the line of the universe' and the notion of the artwork as monument. And then there are the citations Deleuze draws from Maldiney and weaves into his own work, such as Cézanne's 'man absent from but entirely within the landscape' and Klee's 'art does not render the visible but renders visible', as well as Maldiney's allusions to concepts that Deleuze develops in his own way, such as Klee's grey point (in the Refrain Plateau of *A Thousand Plateaus*) or Boulez's smooth and striated time (in the Smooth and Striated Plateau).

A theory is a tool box, Deleuze asserts (DI 208), and one might say the same of certain books. Maldiney's *Regard Parole Espace* is a box full of tools, both major and minor, which Deleuze uses to construct significant portions of his philosophical edifice. Clearly, among Deleuze's many encounters with other philosophers, his encounter with Maldiney is an important one that has gone largely unrecognised and needs to be given fuller consideration.

Notes

1. See Francois Dosse, *Gilles Deleuze and Félix Guattari: Intersecting Lives*, trans. Deborah Glassman (New York: Columbia University Press, 2010), pp. 135–7, 170, 185–7 for details about Deleuze's tenure at Lyon. See, especially, Dosse's amusing account of Lacan's visit to Lyon in 1967 (pp. 185–6), which ended in an impromptu gathering at Deleuze's house (per Lacan's request), with Maldiney vainly searching Lyon at 11:00 pm for cigars demanded by the diva.
2. None of Maldiney's writings has been translated into English, nor have any studies devoted solely to Maldiney appeared in English. For works on Deleuze and Maldiney in English, see Tomas Geyskens, 'Painting as Hysteria: Deleuze on Bacon', *Deleuze Studies* 2:2 (2008), pp. 140–54, and Ronald Bogue, *Deleuze on Music, Painting, and the Arts* (New York: Routledge, 2003), especially pp. 116–21 and 139–46. Students of Maldiney have established a Maldiney website, http://www.henri-maldiney.org, which includes a full bibliography of Maldiney's works and of studies dedicated to his philosophy. A useful introduction to Maldiney's thought is Jean-François Rey's *À dessein de soi. Introduction à la philosophie d'Henri Maldiney* (Argenteuil: Le Cercle herméneutique, 2014). For an intriguing analysis of Maldiney's influence on Deleuze, see Jean-Christophe Goddard's 'Henri Maldiney

et Gilles Deleuze. La station rythmique de l'œuvre d'art', *Revista Filosófica de Coimbra* 33 (2008), pp. 109–24. Goddard also makes use of Maldiney and Deleuze in developing his own theory of subjectivity in *Violence et subjectivité: Derrida, Deleuze, Maldiney* (Paris, Vrin, 2008).

3. Erwin Straus, *The Primary World of Senses: A Vindication of Sensory Experience*, trans. Jacob Needleman (London: Free Press, 1963), p. 351.
4. Ibid., p. 245.
5. Ibid., p. 117.
6. Ibid., p. 322.
7. Paul Klee, *Notebooks*, vol. 1, trans. Ralph Mannheim (New York: Wittenborn Art Books, 1961), p. 76, translation modified.
8. Henri Maldiney, *Regard Parole Espace* (Lausanne: L'Âge d'Homme, 1973), p. 152. *Regard Parole Espace* is now available as a volume of the *Œuvres philosophiques* (Paris: Éditions du Cerf, 2012). Henceforth, *Regard Parole Espace* will be cited as RPE followed by page references first to the 1973 edition and then to the 2013. (For example, this reference would be RPE 152/207.)
9. Straus, *The Primary World of Senses*, p. 319.
10. Klee, *Notebooks*, p. 3.
11. Ibid., p. 3.
12. Ibid., p. 4.
13. David Sylvester, *The Brutality of Fact: Interviews with Francis Bacon*, 3rd edn expanded (New York: Thames & Hudson, 1963), p. 18.
14. In his note citing Maldiney, Deleuze also cites as a source Merleau-Ponty's chapter on sense experience in *Phenomenology of Perception*, trans. Colin Smith (London: Routledge, 1962), pp. 207–42. There is no doubt that Merleau-Ponty's and Maldiney's views are largely concordant, but it is clear that Deleuze is drawing primarily on Maldiney in his characterisation of the phenomenological approach to sensation. Deleuze says in the note, for example, that Merleau-Ponty and Maldiney discern in sensation 'the "pathic moment"', and that 'Hegel's phenomenology short-circuits this aspect of sensation, which nonetheless forms the basis for every possible aesthetic' (FB 156). In the chapter of *Phenomenology of Perception* cited by Deleuze, Merleau-Ponty makes no reference to the 'pathic moment' or to Hegel. Maldiney alone speaks of the Strausian 'pathic moment', and he alone critiques Hegel's phenomenology as one in which sensation is 'short-circuited' (RPE 114/162; 126/177; 152/207; 202/264, 261/331). For Maldiney's critique of Hegel, see RPE 127–33/176–85; 254–321/323–99.
15. Straus, *The Primary World of Senses*, p. 351.
16. Ibid., p. 245.

17. Maldiney's uses of the word 'force': RPE 8/39; 11/43; 17/48; 65/105; 155/211; 252/321; 'energy': RPE 166/223; 191/251; 202/263.
18. RPE 195/255.
19. On Riegl's understanding of Byzantine art, see Bogue, *Deleuze on Music, Painting and the Arts*, p. 204; see also pp. 143–7 for a detailed summary of Maldiney's approach to Byzantine art.
20. On Kurosawa and Mizoguchi, see MI pp. 186–96, and Ronald Bogue, *Deleuze on Cinema* (New York: Routledge, 2003), pp. 89–99.
21. For more on Guillaume, see Bogue, *Deleuze on Music, Painting, and the Arts*, p. 201. Deleuze also makes use of Guillaume's linguistics at several points: DR 205; LS 351, 355; TI 241, 262; TP 349, 541; ECC 108–9. Deleuze may have come upon Guillaume through Maldiney, but it is also possible that he became aware of Guillaume through Edmond Ortigues's *Le Discours et le symbole* (Paris: Aubier Montaigne, 1962), which he cites as a secondary source on Guillaume (DR 327; LS 351; TI 330), in which case Maldiney and Deleuze merely shared a common interest in the linguist.
22. Deleuze does not mention Boulez before *Dialogues* (1977; D 94), and he makes no reference to the smooth and striated before *A Thousand Plateaus* (1980), which leads me to believe that Deleuze's interest in the smooth and striated was initially piqued by Maldiney's remarks on Boulez.

Michel Foucault

Paul Patton

After Félix Guattari, Michel Foucault was Deleuze's most significant contemporary intellectual and political relationship. He regarded Foucault as the greatest thinker of his time, and the author of one of 'the greatest of modern philosophies' (N 94). His *Foucault* (1986) was the only book he wrote on a contemporary philosopher. They were also close friends, at least for a period from the 1960s to the 1970s. In *Dialogues*, Foucault is mentioned among the small group of Deleuze's closest associates, which included his lifelong friend Jean-Pierre Bamberger, his wife Fanny, his friend and publisher Jérôme Lindon, and Guattari (D 17–18). After 1976, for a variety of reasons, they drifted apart and rarely spoke in the years before Foucault's untimely death in 1984. Some years later Deleuze reflected on this period in their relationship:

> We worked separately, on our own. I am sure he read what I wrote. I read what he wrote with a passion. But we did not talk very often. I had the feeling, with no sadness, that in the end I needed him and he did not need me. Foucault was a very, very mysterious man. (TRM 286)

Deleuze and Foucault are widely considered to be intellectual as well as political fellow travellers, especially during their intense period of activism between 1969 and 1976. François Dosse denies that one can speak of a 'Foucault–Deleuzianism' that would eliminate the singularity of each thinker and overlook their real disgreements, but suggests that they formed a 'disjunctive synthesis' similar to the relationship between Deleuze and Guattari.[1] In fact, there were significant differences in their approaches to philosophy and politics. After sketching the history of their relationship, I will focus on their supposed convergence in relation to the idea of 'control society'. Closer examination of Deleuze's efforts to give this concept a Foucaultian provenance only highlight their philosophical differences.

Brief History of Their Relationship

The early careers of Deleuze and Foucault took different paths. Deleuze was born in 1925 in Paris where he completed his secondary schooling. After failing the entrance exam for the École normale supérieure he was awarded a *bourse d'agrégation* at Strasbourg, where he attended classes by Canguilhem. He also enrolled at the Sorbonne where he took courses by Alquié, Bachelard and Wahl, among others. He passed the *agrégation* in 1948 and subsequently taught at a number of *lycées* before returning to the Sorbonne in 1957. In 1953 he published his thesis for the *diplôme d'études supérieures* on David Hume, *Empirisme et subjectivité*.

Foucault was a year younger than Deleuze and grew up in the provincial city of Poitiers. He moved to Paris in 1945 to prepare for the École normale supérieure entrance exam. Admitted in 1946, he graduated with a *diplôme d'études supérieures* in 1949 and passed the *agrégation* in 1951. In 1960 he completed his *doctorat d'état* and obtained his first tenured position in philosophy at the University of Clermont-Ferrand. His doctoral thesis was published the following year as *Folie et déraison: Histoire de la folie à l'âge classique*. Following the departure of Jules Vuillemin for the Collège de France in 1962, he tried and failed to have Deleuze appointed at Clermont-Ferrand. It was around this time that they became friends, although they had first met a decade earlier after Deleuze and Bamberger attended a lecture by Foucault.[2] Deleuze had just published *Nietzsche and Philosophy* (1962), which left a lasting impression on Foucault.[3] In a 1983 interview with Gérard Raulet, Foucault commented on the role of Deleuze's 'superb' book in the French rediscovery of Nietzsche during the 1960s.[4] In 1962 Foucault was finishing *The Birth of the Clinic*, along with *Raymond Roussel* which Deleuze reviewed in 1963.[5] He also reviewed *Les Mots et les choses* shortly after its publication at the peak of French structuralism in 1966, describing it as 'a great book, brimming with new thoughts'.[6]

Their shared interest in Nietzsche led to their first intellectual collaboration in 1966 when they became co-editors of the French edition of Colli-Montinari's *Complete Works of F. Nietzsche*. Their co-authored 'General Introduction' published in 1967 expressed the hope that this edition would bring about a 'return to Nietzsche'.[7] In 1969 Foucault published a short review of *Difference and Repetition*, describing this book as 'the theatre, the stage, the rehearsal of a new philosophy.'[8] This was followed by a much longer article in 1970,

'Theatrum Philosophicum', which discussed both *Difference and Repetition* and *Logic of Sense*.[9] It began with the much quoted remark that 'perhaps one day, this century will be known as Deleuzian'. Less frequently noted is the first part of this sentence in which Foucault places Deleuze's work in 'enigmatic resonance' with that of Pierre Klossowki, another interest that they shared during the 1960s.[10] Deleuze's 'Klossowski or Bodies-Language' appeared in *Critique* (1965) before reappearing in modified form as an appendix to *Logic of sense* in 1969.[11] 'The Prose of Actaeon', published in *La Nouvelle Revue française* (1964), is one of three works by Foucault listed in the bibliography to *Difference and Repetition*, alongside *Raymond Roussel* and *Les Mots et les choses*.[12]

Foucault's reading of Deleuze in 'Theatrum Philosophicum' invoked several themes shared with Klossowski such as the overturning of Platonism and the revaluation of simulacra. At the same time, he pointed to the overriding concern of both books with the nature of thought. He noted that Deleuze's search for a new image and a new practice of thought required abandoning the subordination of both difference and repetition to figures of the same in favour of a thought without contradiction, without dialectics and without negation. This would be a form of thought that embraced divergence and multiplicity, in particular 'the nomadic and dispersed multiplicity that is not limited or confined by the constraints of the same'.[13] It would be an acategorical thought involving a univocal conception of being that revolved around the different rather than the same, following Deleuze's interpretation of Nietzsche's eternal recurrence as the recurrence of difference. Foucault suggested that Deleuze's texts express such a thought and that, as a consequence, 'new thought is possible; thought is again possible'.[14] Deleuze reaffirmed their shared commitment to a new image and practice of thought at Foucault's funeral in June 1984, where he read a passage from the preface to *The Use of Pleasure* in which Foucault asked the rhetorical question what does philosophy consist in 'if not the endeavor to know how and to what extent it might be possible to think differently?' In his seminar in May 1986, shortly before the publication of his *Foucault*, he suggested that 'Only one thing has ever interested Foucault: what does it mean to think?'[15]

Political Activism

Neither Deleuze nor Foucault was directly involved in the events of May 1968, although both were deeply affected by them. In 1969 Foucault was responsible for Deleuze's appointment to the Philosophy Department at the newly established University of Paris VIII at Vincennes. Throughout the early 1970s they collaborated on a number of political activities such as the Prisoner's Information Group established by Foucault, Defert and others at the beginning of 1971, and the anti-racism movement inspired by the shooting of a young Algerian in the Paris neighbourhood known as the Goutte d'Or.[16] Deleuze participated in Foucault's seminar at the Collège de France in 1971–2 devoted to the case of Pierre Rivière and which led to the collaborative publication *I, Pierre Rivière, Having Slaughtered My Mother, My Sister and My Brother* (1973). Both contributed to several issues of the journal *Recherches*, published by Guattari's Centre d'études, de recherches et de formation institutionelles (CERFI), including the infamous issue on homosexuality entitled 'Trois milliards de pervers'.[17]

A high point of their mutual political and theoretical engagement was undoubtedly the 'Intellectuals and Power' interview, conducted in March 1972 and published later that year in the issue of *L'Arc* devoted to Deleuze.[18] Both rejected the Marxist idea that there is a single 'totalising' relation between theory and practice in favour of a plurality of such relations. On their view, theory is neither the expression nor the translation of a practice while practice is neither the application of theory nor the inspiration of a theory to come. Theory is itself a local practice that operates as a relay from one practice to another, while non-theoretical practices form relays from one theoretical moment to the next. Foucault suggested that it was one of the lessons of the upsurge of political action in France at the end of the 1960s that the masses have no need of enlightened consciousness produced by intellectuals in order to understand their situation. The problem is rather that their own forms of knowledge are blocked or invalidated. The role of the intellectual therefore consists of working within and against the order of discourse within which forms of knowledge appear or fail to appear. More generally, it consists of struggling against the forms of power of which the intellectual is both the object and the instrument.

Foucault considered existing theories of the state and state apparatuses, along with the theory of class power, associated with Marxism to be inadequate for understanding the nature of power and the forms of its exercise. He credited Deleuze's *Nietzsche and Philosophy* as well as his work with Guattari with advancing the manner in which this problem is posed. He implicitly referred to his earlier comments about working within the order of discourse and knowledge in suggesting that identifying and speaking publicly about the centres of power within society is already a first step in turning power back on itself: 'If the discourse of inmates or prison doctors constitutes a form of struggle, it is because they confiscate at least temporarily the power to speak on prison conditions – at present, the exclusive property of prison administrators and their cronies in reform groups' (DI 211; translation modified). Much of Foucault's work during the 1970s sought to develop new conceptual tools for understanding power and its relation to knowledge. The opening lectures of his 1976 course at the Collège de France, *'Society Must Be Defended'*, take up the question implicitly posed by his 1972 remarks about the relative lack of understanding of the nature of power on the Left. He set out a series of heuristic principles designed to reorient the study of power away from the juridical, political and ideological apparatuses of the state and towards the material operations of domination and subjectification throughout society.[19]

Many of the points made in Deleuze and Foucault's 1972 interview reverberated throughout their publications in the years that followed. For example, Foucault's 1982 essay 'The Subject and Power' offers much the same analysis of the totalisation of micro-powers by a dominant or ruling power that he gave in the interview with Deleuze a decade earlier.[20] However 'Intellectuals and Power' also showed signs of their future divergence. At one point, Deleuze endorsed and attributed to Foucault the idea that theory is 'by nature opposed to power', even though Foucault had just suggested that theory always takes place within an order of discourse and knowledge that is governed by forms of power (DI 208). Deleuze appears to have understood the vocation of 'theory' and its relation to power along similar lines to the conception of philosophy that he later defined as the creation of concepts that 'in itself' called for 'a new earth and a people that do not yet exist' (WP 108). In addition, when he referred to the radical fragility of the system of power and its 'global force of repression' he appears to have relied on the repressive conception of power that Foucault soon came to challenge (DI 2008; translation modified).

The publication in 1976 of Foucault's *History of Sexuality Volume*

1, which strongly criticised the repressive conception of power, marked the beginning of an increasing distance between them. A letter that Deleuze wrote to him in 1977, published after Foucault's death in 1994 as 'Desire and Pleasure', set out a series of questions that reflected some of the differences between their respective concepts of apparatuses (*dispositifs*) and assemblages (*agencements*) of power and desire (TRM 122–34).[21] Deleuze insisted on the priority of desire and the derivative status of dispositifs of power in relation to the deterritorialising movement of desire. He reaffirmed his reluctance to abandon the repressive effects of power and reiterated his reservations about the concepts of truth and pleasure that Foucault employed in *History of Sexuality Volume 1*.[22]

In response to questions from James Miller some years later, Deleuze insisted that there was no single cause of their drifting apart, but a number of contributing factors: 'The only important thing is that for a long time I had followed [Foucault] politically; and at a certain moment, I no longer totally shared his evaluation of many issues.'[23] First, unlike Foucault, Deleuze actively supported the Palestinian cause, collaborating in interviews with Elias Sanbar and assisted him in establishing the *Revue d'études palestiniennes*. Second, he took a different view of the 'new philosophers'. In 1977 Foucault published a three-page review of André Glucksmann's *Les Maîtres penseurs* that praised the book for tracing the origins of the Soviet Gulag to the manner in which nineteenth-century German philosophy linked the state and the revolution.[24] One month later, Deleuze published a denunciation of the new philosophers in which he expressed his disgust at their martyrology of the victims of the Gulag and accused them of trafficking in large empty concepts such as The Law, The Power, The Master and so on (TRM 139–47). Third, there is a suggestion that Deleuze and Foucault disagreed in their analyses of West Germany. Both joined a Committee established in 1977 to oppose the extradition and agitate for the release from prison of Klaus Croissant, one of the defence lawyers for the Red Army Faction. While Foucault published several pieces against the extradition of Croissant, he refused to sign a petition circulated by Guattari and signed by Deleuze, among others. The reason for his refusal is unclear: Macey claims that he objected to the characterisation of the West German state as 'fascist' while Eribon suggests that it was rather the characterisation of West Germany as drifting towards 'police dictatorship'.[25] Whatever may have been the text of the petition, Deleuze and Guattari's opinion piece in *Le Monde* on 2

November contains no characterisation of the West German state as fascist nor any suggestion that it was becoming a police dictatorship, although it does reflect a more critical stance towards 'the German governmental and judicial model' which they describe as in 'a state of exception' (TRM 149). From this point on, Foucault and Deleuze rarely saw one another.

Deleuze on Foucault: Actuality and Control

A little more than a year after Foucault's death in June 1984, Deleuze devoted his 1985–6 course to the study of Foucault's philosophy. These lectures provided a workshop for his *Foucault*, published in 1986, which also included revised versions of the reviews that he had previously published of *The Archaeology of Knowledge* and *Discipline and Punish*.[26] This book, was not a detailed academic account of Foucault's work but rather a 'portrait' of Foucault's philosophy that sought to discern the inner logic that propelled its movement from the history of systems of thought to apparatuses of power and then to processes of subjectification (N 84, 94, 102). A helpful summary of the main themes is provided in Deleuze's contribution to the international conference *Michel Foucault Philosopher* held in Paris in January 1988. He presents Foucault's philosophy by way of an analysis of the concept of apparatus (*dispositif*) that was a constant feature of his genealogies of modern punishment and sexuality during the 1970s. Deleuze generalises this concept and the different kinds of line that make up *dispositifs* to encompass the different axes of Foucault's entire oeuvre: knowledge, power and subjectivity. In relation to knowledge, it is in the first instance a question of regimes of visibility and sayability; in relation to power, a question of regimes of force; and in relation to subjectivity, a question of regimes or lines of subjectivation:

> Apparatuses are therefore composed of lines of visibility, utterance, lines of force, lines of subjectivation, lines of cracking, breaking and ruptures that all intertwine and mix together and where some augment the others or elicit others through variations and even mutations of assemblage. (TRM 347, translation modified)

The subtle shift of terminology from apparatus (*dispositif*) to assemblage (*agencement*) in the last line only confirms what is already apparent in Deleuze's analysis of Foucault's apparatuses, namely that these are described in the terms of his own concept of assemblages.

It is true that these resemble one another in several respects, but they also differ in significant ways.[27] Deleuze suggests that two important consequences follow from Foucault's *dispositif* philosophy, both of which accord with key principles of his own thought. The first is the repudiation of universals in whatever form, whether universal forms of the subject, the object, truth or reason. As Deleuze comments here and in many places in his own work: 'The universal explains nothing, it is rather it that needs to be explained' (TRM 347).

The second is a shift of orientation away from the universal towards the new, by which he means the orientation that emerged in twentieth-century philosophy towards the question 'How is it possible that something new is produced in the world?' (TRM 349). In 'Breaking Things Open, Breaking Words Open' Deleuze suggests that this concern with the emergence of the new, rather than the timeless, was one of the things that he shared with Foucault (N 86). This concern with the question of the new lies behind his own increasing insistence on the distinction between history and becoming (N 170). In the terms of this distinction, History is incapable of engaging with the conditions of possibility of newness because it only deals with the event as actualised in states of affairs or lived experience. Philosophy, by contrast, is the discipline that creates concepts capable of expressing events as pure becomings that are the condition of novelty or change in the world: 'the event in its becoming, in its specific consistency, in its self-positing as concept, escapes History' (WP 110). On this basis, Deleuze argues that Foucault is not a historian in the traditional sense of the term, but a genealogist who studies the *dispositifs* in terms of which we think, speak and act. In particular, he insists, Foucault's concern is less with the past than the future:

> Some have thought that Foucault was painting the portrait of modern societies as disciplinary apparatuses (*dispositifs*) in opposition to the old apparatuses of sovereignty. This is not the case: the disciplines Foucault described are the history of what we are little by little ceasing to be, while our actuality is sketched out in the arrangements (*dispositions*) of open and continuous *control* that are very different from the recent closed disciplines. (TRM 350)

This characterisation raises a number of questions about Deleuze's account of Foucault's philosophy and its relation to his own. In the remainder of this chapter, I will focus on two: first, whether it is plausible to present Foucault as a philosopher concerned with the question of the new in the manner that he does, namely as one who writes from the perspective of the actual in a sense close to Deleuze's concept of becoming. As he explains in *What is Philosophy?* 'actual' here is not to be understood in the everyday French sense of the term (*actuel*), which refers to what is current, but in a sense closer to Nietzsche's concept of the untimely. It is not a question of what already exists or is present in a given historical moment but of what is coming about or what is in the process of becoming.[28] Second, I will focus on the concept of control in order to ask whether there is any justification for attributing to Foucault the diagnosis that disciplinary societies are giving way to control societies in the sense that Deleuze elaborates in his 'Postscript on Control society'. Both questions I suggest should be answered in the negative.

Foucault, Philosopher of 'Actuality'

Deleuze defends his assimilation of Foucault's 'actuel' to Nietzsche's 'untimely' and to his and Guattari's 'becoming' by reference to a passage in *The Archaeology of Knowledge*, in which Foucault draws a distinction between the present and 'the border of time that surrounds our present, which overhangs it and which indicates it in its otherness'.[29] Foucault's remark occurs in the context of a discussion of the overall system of the different discursive practices present in a given society at a given time that Foucault calls the archive. This archive is 'the law of what can be said, the system that governs the appearance of statements as unique events'.[30] Given that all statements, including those of the archaeologist of discourse, are subject to rules governing what can be said, Foucault's problem is to explain how and when it becomes possible to describe such an archive. It is clearly not possible to describe the archive within which we speak and write. However, it is possible to describe the archive of those discourses which are no longer our own. In this sense, a condition of possibility of the archaeology of discourse undertaken by Foucault is 'the discontinuity that separates us from what we can no longer say and from that which falls outside our discursive practice'.[31] It is of this discontinuity, this difference, that Foucault speaks in referring to the 'border of time that surrounds our present' and that must therefore be understood as different from our present (*actualité*).

Deleuze is simply wrong to suggest that this border that surrounds the present is what Foucault calls the actual. Foucault explicitly contrasts this border region with 'our actuality':

> The analysis of the archive, then, involves a privileged region: at once close to us and different from our actuality, it is the border of time that surrounds our present (*notre actualité*), which overhangs it, and which indicates it in its otherness; it is that which, outside ourselves, delimits us.[32]

In the extended commentary on this passage in 'What is a *Dispositif*?' Deleuze goes further than the mere transposition of the term 'actuality' so that it becomes identified with the border of time that surrounds our present. He suggests that this border that surrounds the discursive present in which we speak and write is not simply a backward-looking difference that allows us to identify and describe the archive of discursive practices that are no longer our own, but a forward-looking difference that acquires the positive meaning of a becoming, in the sense of what we will become in the future. In Foucault's text, the border of time that separates us from what we can no longer say is a becoming only in the most negative and minimal sense of the term. In Deleuze's commentary, it is turned into the actual in the sense of what we are becoming or what we will become:

> The actual is not what we are but rather what we are becoming, what we are in the process of becoming, that is to say the Other, our becoming-other. In every *dispositif* we must distinguish what we are (what we are already no longer) and what we are becoming: *the part of history and the part of the actual*. History is the archive, the design of what we are and cease being while the actual is the sketch of what we will become. (TRM 350, translation modified)[33]

Deleuze's interpretation of Foucault as a philosopher of what we are becoming is not only not justified by the textual support he offers, but also difficult to reconcile with Foucault's published work. In the terms of Deleuze's hypothesis, *Discipline and Punish* should have analysed what prisons are in the process of becoming rather than confining itself to the analysis of the disciplinary techniques of power that they embodied, at least in principle, since the early nineteenth century. Yet we search in vain for analyses of what is coming about or what prisons are becoming. Moreover, Foucault's own retrospective accounts of his genealogical method present it in a rather different light, namely as attempting to draw attention to and exacerbate those hitherto imperceptible borders that separate the recent past from our present.[34] In this more limited sense, his genealogies seek to assist the emergence of new ways of thinking, speaking and acting.

Deleuze's response to this problem is to suggest that we need to enlarge our understanding of Foucault's oeuvre to include not only his books but also his interviews. The books that address a particular archive, whether in relation to madness, the clinic, disciplinary power or sexuality, are only half the story: the other half is made explicit in the interviews that Foucault gave alongside the publication of his major works, in which he comments on the bearing of his historical studies on current problems:

> Foucault attached so much importance to his interviews in France and even more so abroad, not because he liked interviews but because in them he traced lines of actualization that required another mode of expression than the assimilable lines in his major books. The interviews are diagnoses. (TRM 352)[35]

There is some truth to Deleuze's claim about the role of interviews in Foucault's oeuvre, although the publication of Foucault's Collège de France lectures further complicates this two-series partition of Foucault's oeuvre.[36] However, Foucault rarely goes so far as to prognosticate on what is coming to be in the manner suggested by Deleuze's account of his relation to the diagnosis of an emerging control society.

Control, Discipline and Mechanisms of Security

Deleuze's conception of Foucault as a thinker of actuality is clearly at work in his 'Postscript on Control Societies', where he places him among those who saw that disciplinary societies were giving way to control societies are taking over from. Foucault's interviews do support his claim in Deleuze's 'Control and Becoming' interview with Negri that Foucault 'was actually one of the first to say that we're moving away from disciplinary societies' (N 174).[37] However, there is no support in interviews or anywhere else for the stronger claim that he thought disciplinary societies were giving way to societies of control. Despite the lack of direct textual support, Deleuze in 'Postscript' aligns the work of Foucault with the diagnosis of the present as one in which '*Control societies* are taking over from disciplinary societies' (N 178). First, he reiterates the thesis of *Discipline and Punish* that disciplinary societies succeeded sovereign societies and then suggests that, after the Second World War, the government of lives by means of disciplinary techniques deployed in closed institutions such as the family, school, barracks, factory, hospital and, for some, prison, began to break down: 'we were no longer in disciplinary societies, we were leaving them behind' (N 178). Second, he argues that, in the latter half of the twentieth century, disciplinary power was being replaced by control society and that Foucault, like William Burroughs and Paul Virilio, saw that this new model was 'fast approaching' (N 178).

Prima facie it seems that control can be differentiated from discipline in terms of the Aristotelian schema that Foucault often uses to identify distinct practices: material, formal, efficient and final causes. This schema is applied to ethical practice in the Introduction to *The Use of Pleasure*, where it allows a characterisation of distinct forms of relation to the self in terms of their object, mode of subjectification, ethical work and desired goal, or *telos*.[38] Applied to practices of punishment, it allows him to distinguish the different technologies of power proposed to deal with criminals at the end of the eighteenth century.[39] He follows a similar procedure in contrasting biopower with disciplinary power in the last chapter of *History of Sexuality Volume 1*: they do not have the same objects (populations as opposed to bodies and their forces), the same mechanisms (mechanisms of security as opposed to techniques of training), modes of operation (regulation of collective phenomena as opposed to control of individuals and groups) or the same goals (statistical norms as opposed to docile bodies).

In these terms, it is clear that control mechanisms are different from those of discipline. Control does not have the same object, techniques, modes of regulation of individual and group behaviour, nor the same objective, as disciplinary power. Control does not operate on the physiological, affective and intellectual capacities of human bodies to produce individuals, as Foucault famously argued disciplinary power does. Unlike disciplinary societies, control societies do not 'mould' individuals to produce docile and obedient subjects. Rather, they 'modulate' certain 'dividuals', where these are not whole persons but partial persons defined by particular functional aspects identified in relation to particular ends. The same biological person might correspond to a financial capacity to repay a bank loan, as defined by their age, income, lifestyle and existing level of debt; to an intellectual capacity to undertake a given programme of study, as defined by their prior education and levels of achievement; and to a physiological capacity to qualify for a certain insurance product based on their medical history, genetic makeup and lifestyle. Each of these financial, intellectual and physiological dividuals can be tabulated and recorded along with others of the same kind to form a data or population sample that can be analysed and exploited for commercial, governmental or other ends.

Control establishes series of thresholds through which individuals can only pass with the right password. As individual members of control societies, we carry with us an increasingly long and potentially endless chain of passwords. However, Deleuze means more than this everyday sense of 'password'. He points to the ways in which we are coded to indicate that we meet the criteria for access to particular services and contrasts these codes or passwords with the 'order-words' that, in disciplinary societies, accomplished the transition from one phase or state of life to the next: childhood to adulthood, failure to success, good health to ill-health, and so on.

In contrast to discipline, control does not establish institutional spaces of confinement where the actions of individuals can be strictly ordered in space and time. Control operates in the open rather than in confined spaces, by means of various digital and electronic technologies. To take an example that has emerged since Deleuze wrote his 'Postscript', consider the manner in which GPS location has become utilised in a whole series of devices, from mobile phones to electronic watches and other tracking devices. Olivier Razac comments that

> GPS represents the final stage of this evolution [from discipline to control]. Even the electronic bracelet remains essentially disciplinary, transforming the home into a prison and trapping the condemned as though in his apartment burrow. By contrast, mobile technologies of surveillance in real time liberate the individual. They liberate his energy and his desire so that he can work at his own always ephemeral and perfectible integration.[40]

At the level of the modality of action, control mechanisms do not impose particular moulds according to the nature of the institution in which they are employed, producing a certain kind of subject, body or relationships. Rather, they involve the continuous modulation of behaviours or performances in and by means of their relations to one another. Deleuze writes that 'enclosures are moulds, distinct mouldings, but controls are modulations, like an auto-deforming [self-transmuting] mould that would continuously change from one moment to the next' (N 178–9). Modulation is a concept that he takes from Simondon and uses in a variety of contexts to outline an alternative metaphysics, for example in his elaboration of a transcendental empiricism in *Difference and Repetition*.

Deleuze associates the emergence of control with a mutation in the nature of capitalism that he describes in terms that partly recall the transition from Fordist to post-Fordist techniques of production, but also the transition from economies of production to economies of services and to the marketing of products produced elsewhere. Capitalism in its present form, he argues, relies on metaproduction rather than production:

> It no longer buys raw materials and no longer sells finished products: it buys finished products or assembles them from parts. What it seeks to sell is services, and what it seeks to buy are activities. It's a capitalism no longer directed towards production but toward products, that is, toward sales or markets. (N 181)

Whereas discipline was a long-term, infinite and discontinuous process, control is 'short-term and rapidly shifting, but at the same time continuous and unbounded' (N 181). This is consistent with the replacement of apparent acquittal by unlimited deferral of judgement in the judicial sphere, the replacement of examinations by continuous assessment in the educational sphere, the replacement of manufacture by the sale of services or immaterial products in the economic sphere, and so on.

Not everybody is convinced by Deleuze's attempt to differentiate discipline and control. Mark Kelly notes that Foucault uses the word 'control' in relation to the operation of disciplinary power and argues that Deleuze's essay advances a thesis that is 'partly redundant, inasmuch as he is talking about things already covered by Foucault's notion of discipline, and partly simply false, describing as changes things which are either not new or are not happening at all'.[41] He argues that disciplinary techniques have not been superseded by mechanisms of control and that the phenomena mentioned by Deleuze as examples of control do not amount to a new form of power. Many of the details among the 'dense catalogue of phenomena which Deleuze presents as indicative of the new control society' do not amount to changes in the technology of power, either because they are not taking place or, if they are, then they are little more than intensifications of the logic of disciplinary power.[42]

Others see continuity between Deleuze's concept of control and Foucault's discovery of biopower. Dosse suggests that Deleuze's analysis of control society 'follows from Foucault's work' and that the concept of control encompasses the range of technologies of power that Foucault discussed under the heading of 'biopower'.[43] A similar view is expressed in the entry on 'Control' in Jeffrey Nealon's *Cambridge Foucault Lexicon* (2014), where the concept is implicitly treated as Foucault's and taken to cover all of the 'lighter, more effective, and more diffuse methods of subject production' discussed in Foucault's work after *Discipline and Punish*.[44] Thomas Nail also defends the continuity thesis, drawing on Deleuze's lectures on Foucault in 1986 to suggest that he establishes 'a clear equivalence between biopower and control in both content and form'.[45] Biopower and control both take as their object the life of populations and both work through the management of probabilities. The reference to probabilities recalls Foucault's analysis of mechanisms of security in his 1977–8 lectures, *Security, Territory, Population*.[46] Foucault's aim in these lectures was to describe a particular kind of power, operating at the level of whole societies or populations and involving a different substance, mechanism, mode of operation and objective to those associated with discipline. At the end of his previous course in 1975–6 and in the final chapter of *History of Sexuality Volume 1* he called this 'biopower'. In the further development of his thought in 1978 and 1979 it became associated with liberal governmentality.

In the opening lectures of *Security, Territory, Population*, Foucault outlined the distinguishing features of mechanisms of security, which he contrasted both to juridical and to disciplinary mechanisms of power. He argued that security mechanisms involve forms of action on a population, where this is supposed to be a natural phenomenon subject to various kinds of regular behaviour: economic, demographic, epidemiological and so on. As such, this kind of power required knowledge of the relevant dimensions of the behaviour of populations. The new sciences of statistics and political economy no longer considered a population as a collection of subjects of right but as 'a set of processes to be managed at the level and on the basis of what is natural in these processes'.[47] Security mechanisms deal with probable rather than actual events and seek to respond to these on the basis of calculations of cost and in terms of a norm of acceptable outcomes rather than a binary division between the permitted and prohibited. The editors of the issue of *New Formations* devoted to 'Control Societies', Jeremy Gilbert and Andrew Goffey, suggest the modality of power described in Foucault's analysis of security mechanisms 'can usefully be equated with' Deleuze's 'control'.[48]

One obvious problem with the proposed equivalence between control, biopower and mechanisms of security involves historical periodisation. Deleuze situates the transition to control societies in the latter half of the twentieth century whereas Foucault locates the emergence of techniques of security in the latter half of the eighteenth century. More generally, Foucault's lectures show that, while he analyses different forms of 'government' of individual and collective behaviour, he did not support the kind of historicism that supposed a succession of monolithic regimes or 'diagrams' of power. So, for example, he acknowledged the differences between juridical, disciplinary and security mechanisms of power, but denied that they succeeded one another in the history of modern government. All three have been present in differing degrees throughout the early modern period and what changes there are involve the 'system of correlation between juridico-legal mechanisms, disciplinary mechanisms, and mechanisms of security'.[49]

Apart from these historical difficulties, there are significant conceptual differences. The shift of focus in Foucault's work from the direct control of the activity of individuals and groups to the indirect control of populations behaviour related to a series of questions about the nature of power and the terms of his analysis that he raised at the beginning of his 1975–6 lectures *'Society Must Be Defended'*. He raised doubts about what he called the 'war model' of power as conflict of forces, a model that he had relied on in his analysis of discipline. The analysis of mechanisms of security and forms of governmentality eventually led to his formulation of a quite different conception of power from the one that he relied upon in *Discipline and Punish* and that he elaborated in a 'The Subject and Power'. According to this conception, the exercise of power involves a certain kind of action upon the action, or the field of possible actions, of others:

> In effect, what defines a relationship of power is that it is a mode of action that does not act directly and immediately on others. Instead, it acts upon their actions: an action upon an action, on possible or actual future or present actions.[50]

Henceforth, Foucault understands the exercise of power in terms of relations of government rather than war. This implies a conception of power as action on the actions of others, where this takes the material on which power is exercised to be free agents. By contrast, Deleuze's control essay tends to treat the material on which power is exercised differently, as dividuals rather than individual agents, regulated by codes or passwords rather than formed as docile or obedient subjects. Foucault's conception of power as action upon the actions of others implies that power is exercised over individual and collective agents, subjects of power and freedom, rather than dividuals, masses or legal, medical or other 'cases'. Unlike the spatial and temporal ordering of bodies and gestures that is at the heart of discipline, liberal government involves the kind of indirect regulation of behaviour exemplified in market mechanisms. Deleuze's conception of control tends to focus on systems that regulate behaviour in ways that bypass individual agency: dividuals are not agents. In effect, control is closer to what Deleuze and Guattari call in *A Thousand Plateaus* 'machinic subjection' than it is to what Foucault came to call 'government'.[51]

Close examination of Deleuze's efforts to enlist Foucault as a philosopher of assemblages of power and desire, of actuality, or as a diagnostician of control society shows these to be unconvincing. More generally, it suggests that their philosophical approach and concepts were not as close as Deleuze and many others took them to be.

Notes

1. François Dosse, *Gilles Deleuze and Félix Guattari: Intersecting Lives* (New York: Columbia University Press, 2011), p. 328. Chapter 17 of this book, 'Deleuze and Foucault: A Philosophical Friendship', is reprinted in Nicolae Morar, Thomas Nail and Daniel W. Smith (eds), *Between Deleuze and Foucault* (Edinburgh: Edinburgh University Press, 2016), pp. 11–37.
2. Dosse, *Gilles Deleuze and Félix Guattari*, p. 307. See also David Macey, *The Lives of Michel Foucault* (New York: Pantheon, 1994), p. 109.
3. Dosse, *Gilles Deleuze and Félix Guattari*, p. 307.
4. Michel Foucault, *Essential Works of Foucault, 1954–1984, Volume 2: Aesthetics, Method and Epistemology*, trans. Robert Hurley et al. and ed. James D. Faubion (New York: New Press, 1998), pp. 438, 445.
5. 'Raymond Roussel ou L'Horreur du vide', *Arts* 933 (23–9 Oct. 1963), p. 4. Translated (without notes) as 'Raymond Roussel or the Abhorrent Vacuum' [*sic*] in DI 72–3.
6. 'L'homme, une existence douteuse', *Le Nouvel Observateur* 81 (1–7 June 1966), pp. 32–4. Translated as 'Humans: A Dubious Existence' in DI 90–3.
7. This co-authored 'General Introduction' was not included in Deleuze's *Desert Islands and Other Texts, 1953–1974*, but does appear as 'Introduction' in *Œuvres philosophiques complètes de F. Nietzsche* (Paris: Gallimard, 1977), vol. 5, pp. i–iv, and in Michel Foucault, *Dits et écrits* (Paris: Gallimard, 1994), vol. I, pp. 561–4.

8. 'Ariane s'est pendu,' *Le Nouvel Observateur* 229 (31 Mar. – 6 Apr. 1969), pp. 36–7. Reprinted in Foucault, *Dits et écrits*, vol. I, pp. 767–71.
9. 'Theatrum Philosophicum', *Critique* 282 (1970), pp. 885–908. Translated in Foucault, *Essential Works, Volume 2*, pp. 343–68.
10. Ibid., p. 343.
11. 'Pierre Klossowski ou les corps-langage', *Critique* 214 (Mar. 1965), pp. 199–219. Translated as 'Klossowski or Bodies-Language' in LS 280–301.
12. *La Nouvelle Revue française* 135 (Mar. 1964), pp. 444–59. Translated as 'The Prose of Actaeon', in Foucault, *Essential Works, Volume 2*, pp. 123–35.
13. Foucault, *Essential Works, Volume 2*, p. 358.
14. Ibid., p. 367.
15. Dosse, *Gilles Deleuze and Félix Guattari*, p. 309.
16. Dosse, *Gilles Deleuze and Félix Guattari*, pp. 309–13. On the Prisoner's Information Group and Deleuze's role in it, see Defert and Donzelot, 'La charnière des prisons', *Le Magazine littéraire* 112–13 (May 1976), pp. 33–5, and Alberto Toscano, 'The Intolerable Inquiry: The Documents of the Groupe d'information sur les prisons', *Viewpoint Magazine*, Issue 3: Worker's Inquiry, 2013. https://viewpointmag.com/2013/09/30/issue-3-workers-inquiry/
17. Félix Guattari (ed.), *Trois milliards de pervers. Grande encyclopédie des homosexualités* (Paris: Recherches, 1973).
18. Gilles Deleuze, 'Les intellectuels et le pouvoir: Entretien avec Michel Foucault du 4 mars 1972', *L'Arc* 49 (1972), pp. 3–10. Translated as 'Intellectuals and Power', DI 206–13.
19. Michel Foucault, *"Society Must Be Defended': Lectures at the Collège de France, 1975–1976*, ed. Mauro Bertani and Alessandro Fontana, trans. David Macey (New York: Picador, 2003), pp. 27–34.
20. Michel Foucault, *Essential Works of Foucault 1954–1984, Volume 3: Power*, ed. James D. Faubion, trans. Robert Hurley et al. (New York: New Press, 2000), pp. 326–48.
21. 'Désir et plaisir' appeared in the *Magazine littéraire* 325 (October 1994), pp. 57–65. An English translation by Daniel W. Smith was published in Arnold I. Davidson (ed.), *Foucault and His Interlocutors* (Chicago: University of Chicago Press, 1997), pp. 183–92 and is reproduced in Morar et al. (eds), *Between Deleuze and Foucault*, pp. 223–31. See also TRM 122–34.
22. Wendy Grace provides a detailed account of the differences between Deleuze's approach to sexuality and psychoanalysis and that of Foucault in '*Faux Amis*: Foucault and Deleuze on Sexuality and Desire', *Critical Inquiry* 36 (Autumn 2009), pp. 52–75. Nicolae Morar and Marjorie Gracieuse argue for the compatibility of their different approaches in chapter 14, 'Against the Incompatibility Thesis: A Rather Different

Reading of the Desire-Pleasure Problem', in Morar et al. (eds), *Between Deleuze and Foucault*, pp. 232–46.

23. James Miller, *The Passion of Michel Foucault* (New York: Doubleday, 1993), p. 298.
24. Michel Foucault, 'La grande colère des faits', *Le Nouvel Observateur* 652 (9–15 May 1977), pp. 84–6. Reprinted in Foucault *Dits et écrits*, vol. 3, pp. 277–81. André Glucksmann, *Les Maîtres penseurs* (Paris: Grasset, 1977) is translated by Brian Pearce as *The Master Thinkers* (New York: Harper & Row, 1980).
25. Macey, *The Lives of Michel Foucault*, p. 394; Didier Eribon, *Michel Foucault*, trans. Betsy Wing (Cambridge, MA: Harvard University Press, 1991), p. 260.
26. Gilles Deleuze, 'Un nouvel archiviste', *Critique* 274 (Mar. 1970), pp. 195–209; 'Ecrivain non: un nouveau cartographe', *Critique* 343 (Dec. 1975), pp. 1207–27.
27. Differences include the relation of desire to power and the primacy of movements of deterritorialisation or lines of flight in any given assemblage. These were set out in 'Desire and Pleasure' (see note 21) and restated several years later in a footnote in *A Thousand Plateaus* (TP 530–1).
28. Dosse registers both the specific sense of actual in Deleuze's text and his assimilation of Foucault to his own way of thinking about events in commenting that this was an understanding that was 'fundamentally untimely and inactual according to the Nietzschean conception that Foucault shared' (Dosse, *Gilles Deleuze and Félix Guattari*, p. 323).
29. Michel Foucault, The *Archaeology of Knowledge*, trans. A. M. Sheridan (London: Tavistock, 1972), p. 130, translation modified.
30. Ibid., p. 129.
31. Ibid., p. 130.
32. The original reads: 'L'analyse de l'archive comporte donc une région privilegiée: à la fois proche de nous, mais différente de notre actualité, c'est la bordure de temps qui entoure notre présent, qui le surplombe et qui l'indique dans son alterité; c'est ce qui, hors de nous, nous délimite' (Foucault, *L'Archéologie du savoir* [Paris: Gallimard, 1969], p. 172).
33. Similarly, In *What is Philosophy?*, Deleuze suggests that 'for Foucault, what matters is the difference between the present and the actual. The actual is not what we are but, rather, what we become, what we are in the process of becoming – that is to say, the Other, our becoming-other' (WP 112).
34. See, for example, 'What is Enlightenment?', in *Essential Works of Foucault, 1954–1984, Volume 1, Ethics*, ed. Paul Rabinow, trans. Robert Hurley et al. (New York: The New Press, 1997), pp. 303–19.
35. Similar claims about the role of interviews as an integral part of

Foucault's oeuvre are presented in Foucault (F 115) and in 'A Portrait of Foucault' (N 106).

36. See Patton, 'From Resistance to Government: Foucault's Lectures 1976–1979', in C. Falzon, T. O'Leary and J. Sawicki (eds), *A Companion to Foucault* (Oxford: Blackwell 2013), pp. 172–88.
37. In a 1977 discussion of Bentham's Panopticon with historians, Foucault commented that 'the procedures of power at work in modern societies are much more numerous, diverse and rich' than the principles of permanent visibility so important to Bentham and that it 'would be wrong to say that the principle of visibility governs all technologies of power used since the nineteenth century (*Michel Foucault: Power/Knowledge: Selected Interviews and Other Writings, 1972–1977*, ed. Colin Gordon [Hemel Hempstead: Harvester Wheatsheaf, 1980], p. 148). He noted that 'disciplinary power was in fact already in Bentham's day being transcended by other and much more subtle mechanisms for the regulation of phenomena of population, controlling their fluctuations and compensating their irregularities' (*Michel Foucault: Power/Knowledge*, p. 160). In a 1978 interview in Japan, Foucault commented in terms close to those employed by Deleuze that 'Discipline, which was so effective in sustaining power, has lost some of its efficacy. In industrialised countries, the disciplines are in crisis' ('La société disciplinaire en crise', in *Dits et écrits*, vol. III, pp. 532–5). See also the 'Body/Power' interview from 1975, in which Foucault suggests that 'From the eighteenth to the early twentieth century I think it was believed that the investment of the body by power had to be heavy, ponderous, meticulous and constant. Hence those formidable disciplinary regimes in the schools, hospitals, barracks, factories, cities, lodgings, families. And then, starting in the 1960s, it began to be realised that such a cumbersome form of power was no longer as indispensable as had been thought and that industrial societies could content themselves with a much looser form of power over the body' (*Michel Foucault: Power/ Knowledge*, p. 58)
38. Michel Foucault, *The Use of Pleasure: The History of Sexuality Volume Two* (New York: Pantheon, 1985), pp. 26–8.
39. Mitchell Dean draws attention to the parallels between Foucault's conceptualisation of ethical practices and his characterisation of practices of punishment in *Discipline and Punish*: see his *Critical and Effective Histories: Foucault's Methods and Historical Sociology* (London and New York: Routledge, 1994), pp. 160–1, 196f.
40. Olivier Razac, *Avec Foucault, Après Foucault: Disséquer la société de contrôle* (Paris: L'Harmattan, 2008), p. 61.
41. Mark Kelly, 'Discipline is Control: Foucault contra Deleuz,e' *New Formations* 84–5, (2015), p. 151.
42. Kelly, 'Discipline is Control', p. 157.
43. Dosse, *Gilles Deleuze and Félix Guattari: Intersecting Lives*, p. 329.

44. Jeffrey Nealon, 'Control', in Leonard Lawlor and John Nale (eds), *The Cambridge Foucault Lexicon* (Cambridge: Cambridge University Press, 2014), p. 84.
45. Thomas Nail, 'Biopower and Control', in Morar et al. (eds), *Between Deleuze and Foucault*, pp. 247–63, 257.
46. Michel Foucault, *Security, Territory, Population: Lectures at the Collège de France, 1977–1978*, ed. Michel Senellart, trans. Graham Burchell (Basingstoke and New York: Palgrave Macmillan, 2007).
47. Foucault. *Security, Territory, Population*, p. 70.
48. Jeremy Gilbert and Andrew Goffey, 'Control Societies: Notes for an Introduction', *New Formations* 84–5 (2015), p. 9. Razac also notes the way that both security mechanisms and control techniques describe the mode of regulation of a given material in terms of 'continuous modulation and the treatment of the object of power adapted in real time to what actually occurs' (Razac, *Avec Foucault, Après Foucault*, p. 40).
49. Foucault, *Security, Territory, Population*, pp. 8, 107.
50. Michel Foucault, *Society Must Be Defended: Lectures at the Collège de France, 1975–1976*, ed. Mauro Bertani and Alessandro Fontana, trans. David Macey (Basingstoke and New York: Palgrave Macmillan, 2003), p. 340.
51. The 'Postscript' is not entirely consistent on this point: Deleuze does talk about marketing as an instrument of social control (N 181), which does seem to imply agents who are *subjects* of desire and freedom, but this calls for further analysis not undertaken in this short essay.

Pierre Clastres

Jon Roffe

On the evening of 29 July 1977 a car carrying Pierre Clastres (1934–1977) and his wife Hélène crashed while crossing a narrow bridge in the Gabriac region in the South of France. The accident ended the life and already remarkable career of the forty-three-year-old anthropologist.[1] At the time of his death, aside from a pair of anthologies cataloguing the myths and sacred texts of certain tribes that continue up until the present to live in modern-day Paraguay, Clastres's output was contained in a handful of articles, a scintillating ethnography and a modest collection of essays entitled *Society against the State*.[2]

The essential thesis of these works can be put with equal brevity: there exist societies that are organised so as to counter the rise of a separate organ of power, that is, the formation of a State. This is a decisive thesis for the work of Gilles Deleuze. While he only engages with Clastres in the works published in the 1970s with Félix Guattari and Claire Parnet, it constitutes an essential point of reference in the account of society that these works advance. Indeed, it would be fair to say that without Clastres's account of counter-State societies, Deleuze and Guattari's entire social theory would be inconceivable in its current form – up to and including the broader framework of a 'universal history of contingency' (AO 140) within which this theory unfolds.

The case of Clastres also sadly provides us with a rather unique aperture on the way in which Deleuze and Guattari make use of other theoretical resources. They cite his first published article 'Exchange and Power' (1962) in *Anti-Oedipus* (AO 148); their most significant treatment of his thought appears in *A Thousand Plateaus* under the parenthetical heading 'a tribute to the memory of Pierre Clastres'.[3]

Clastres's Intellectual Heritage

The first significant contextual element and intellectual resource that plays into Clastres's work is the structural anthropology of Claude Lévi-Strauss.[4]

Structuralism

Clastres's assessment of the then-dominant strain of ethnographic thinking was a complex one. Lévi-Strauss's work was avowedly the influence that opened Clastres on to his own intellectual trajectory, and was, moreover, the central influence on a group of thinkers with whom he worked closely from the early 1950s until his death – one of whom (Alfred Adler) recalled that Clastres read Lévi-Strauss's *Tristes tropiques* 'four or five times'[5] over the course of 1956 alone.

Of these thinkers, it was perhaps his fellow anthropologist Louis Sebag who had the most influence on Clastres in the 1950s and early 1960s – arguably up to Sebag's suicide in 1965.[6] In addition to his *Marxism and Structuralism* (1963), Sebag was most interested in a problematic with respect to which structuralism had very clearly made groundbreaking progress on: the study of myth.

It is unsurprising, therefore, to read Clastres assert in a 1974 interview that the structuralist approach to the analysis of dreams and myth appeared to be the only viable option: 'it is likely that, if I was to take up a mythological corpus, I would do so in a strongly structuralist way. I don't see any other particularly strong way to analyse such a corpus in an extra-structuralist fashion.'[7] By the time of his death, however, Clastres was not even willing to grant the structuralist perspective this capacity, writing that 'The classic or structuralist analysis of myths obscures the political dimension of Savage thought.'[8]

In a passage from the same piece, one particularly reminiscent of the third chapter of *Anti-Oedipus*, Clastres writes that

> structuralist thought abolishes, in a particularly clear manner, the rapport with the social: it is the relation *between* the myths themselves that is privileged at the outset, thereby eliding the place of the production and invention *of* the myth: the society . . . Structuralism is only operative on the condition of cutting the myths from society, of seizing them, ethereal, floating at a distance from their place of origin.[9]

Despite this shifting boundary, Clastres was from the first to the last convinced that the Lévi-Straussian perspective – and, 'outside of a few rather clever disciples, capable at best of doing sub-Lévi-Strauss, who are the structuralists?'[10] – did not provide the means to understand, where it did not actively obscure it, the specifically political dimension of non-State societies.

Contra Marxism

There are two more important decisive intellectual posits attested to in Clastres's work, and the first is his hostility towards Marxism. Indeed, Clastres's serious engagement with Lévi-Straussian anthropology dates from 1956, the same year that he left the French Communist Party. On one side, this hostility reflected Clastres's sense that the teleological vision of history ensconced in party-line French Marxism was incapable of grasping so-called primitive societies on their own terms – hence the rhetorical questions posed in 'Copernicus and the Savages': 'what resources does Marxism really provide to understand primitive communism? And, further, is Marxism able to account for this transition from non-history to historicity and from non-coercion to violence?'[11]

Clastres's expression of these concerns with Marxism does not maintain the relatively indirect form of the rhetorical question for long. His final posthumous publication, 'Marxists and Their Anthropology', a biting and sarcastic attack on both its stated objects and structuralist anthropology, begins on a mischievous note: 'Though it will not be particularly entertaining to do so, we must reflect a little on Marxist anthropology, on its causes, its advantages and inconveniences.' But this is immediately followed with an explicit rejection: 'For if ethnomarxism, on the one hand, is still a powerful current in the human sciences, the ethnology of Marxists possesses, on the other, an absolute, or rather radical, nullity; it is null at its root.'[12]

Clastres objects to the 'militant obscurantism' of Marxist ethnologists – their tendency to assert that 'those who do not agree with Marxist anthropology are partisans of Pinochet. Cekomça'[13] – and for a general lack of theoretical sophistication, but of primary importance is their incapacity to account for the full range of social formations:

> For the Marxists, primitive societies are only, they proclaim eruditely, pre-capitalist societies . . . For them, primitive society only exists insofar as it can be reduced to the figure of society that appeared at the end of the 18th century, capitalism. Before that, nothing counts: everything is pre-capitalist. They do not complicate their lives, these guys. It must be relaxing to be a Marxist.[14]

Despite this – or rather, this is the motive for the critique itself – it is important to note the quintessentially political character of Clastres's work.[15] The subtitle of *Society against the State*, 'Essays in Political

Anthropology', is close to identical to the original French title of *The Archeology of Violence*, *Recherches d'anthropologie politique*. The essential problem with Marxism for Clastres, as for many other thinkers, is the way that it doubles down on the problems already present in Hegel: the latter correlates state, society and history; the former inflexibly insists that politics and economics also belong to this list.

Nietzsche

The second correlate of Clastres's critical debt to structuralism is his debt to the thought of Friedrich Nietzsche, or rather to the revival of Nietzche in that moment of French thought. Indeed, in Clastres's view, it is in Nietzsche rather than Marx that the resources for political thought can be found. Not only does Clastres's definition of power demonstrate a very explicit Nietzschean provenance – 'power only exists when exercised: a power that is not exercised is, in effect, nothing'[16] – *Society against the State* invokes *Beyond Good and Evil* in order to establish Nietzsche as the first real thinker of the political.

But the most prominent element Clastres draws on and extends is Nietzsche's account of the primacy of debt in social life of *On the Genealogy of Morals*. He also shows, however, that debt does not take a single form, and that the role it plays in counter-State and State societies in particular are symmetrically opposed. In the former case, it is precisely the chief who is in debt. 'The leader is in debt to society precisely because he is the leader. And he can never get rid of this debt, at least not as long as he wants to continue being the leader.' And it is 'In trapping the chief in his desire, [that] the tribe insures itself against the mortal risk of seeing political power become separate from it and turn against it.'[17] The status of debt in State society is reversed: it is the social body, the individuals who are not in power who bear this unpayable debt. In turn, 'To hold power, to impose tribute, is one and the same, and the despot's first act is to proclaim the obligation of payment.'[18]

To these we can add a third site of influence: Clastres's account of the link between torture and writing, 'torture and memory'.[19] As the powerful essay 'Of Torture in Primitive Societies' puts it, '*the law written on the body is an unforgettable memory*.'[20] It should come as no surprise, then, that Deleuze and Guattari's discussion of the ritual cutting of the liminal body in Clastres's ethnographic work is immediately followed by the assertion that 'The great book of modern ethnology is not so much Mauss's *The Gift* as Nietzsche's *On the Genealogy of Morals*' (AO 180).[21] We will return to all of these points in what follows.

Clastres's ethnographic work

As important as these intellectual influences were for Clastres, he remained convinced that it was the ethnographic research itself that was the final authority in thinking about the political character of social existence.

Clastres's ethnographic fieldwork took place over three visits to South America in the 1960s and early 1970s. The latter two were relatively restricted in length and considered in pieces included in *The Archeology of Violence*, notably its remarkable opening chapter on the Yanomami Indians of Venezuela. The most sizeable and, arguably, significant period was the year Clastres spent with the Guayaki Indians in the south-eastern part of Paraguay, a visit recorded in Clastres's first book, *The Chronicle of the Guayaki Indians*. Other analyses drawn directly from this same material can be found in *Society against the State*, including 'The Bow and the Basket', the first of Clastres's pieces cited by Deleuze and Guattari.

Without having space here to consider this work in detail, the following discussion will make reference to five topoi that are key touchpoints of this fieldwork, and which are in turn the points on which Deleuze and Guattari make reference to Clastres's writing.[22]

First Topos: Savage Society and the State

Deleuze and Guattari's engagement with, and perhaps interest in, Clastres turns around or is oriented by a single point: 'The prime interest in Pierre Clastres' theories is that they break with this evolutionist postulate' (TP 357). The theories in question assert that societies without a State are more primitive organisations than State societies, not having evolved political or economic structures bearing the necessary complexity in order for the State to arise, with the implication that 'primitive people "don't understand" so complex an apparatus' (TP 357).

Following Clastres, Deleuze and Guattari assert the opposite thesis: a fully fledged type of social formation existed and exists that does not incline towards the State as if to the realisation of its implicit tendencies, but presses in the opposite direction, 'Warding off the formation the formation of a State apparatus' (TP 357): whether we call it primitive, savage or counter-State, what is essential is that 'primitive society is a society against the State'.[23]

As I indicated at the beginning of this chapter, this is Clastres's own central claim and the guiding concern of his work. And for Clastres, the most significant evidence for this view was found in the field. The *Chronicle of the Guayaki Indians* introduces us to Jyvukugi, whose photograph bears a caption that already conveys the main point: 'Jyvukugi, "chief" of the Aché Gatu'.[24] He is clearly identified as the chief by the Aché, but as Clastres points out, this position does not convey on him any power to *do* anything. No sovereign agent, the chief functions only to recount the desires of the tribe. His agency is therefore enunciative rather than political: 'The obligation to use the instrument of non-coercion – language – *every time it is necessary* gives the group permanent control over the chief because every word he speaks is an assurance that his power will not menace the society.'[25]

Conversely, the chief desires the position of chief in order to affirm his personal prestige, but it is an affirmation whose burden is absolute: 'The "power" incarnated by the chief is not authoritarian . . . Permanently under the control of the group, the leaders cannot transgress the norms on which the whole life of the society is based.'[26] Indeed, the use of power in the instrumental sense is itself nothing other than the abuse of power in the sense of representing the desires of the group: 'Should the tribe locate the slightest abuse of power (that is, the use of power), the chief's prestige ends.'[27]

This form of political organisation – as Deleuze and Guattari note (AO 148) – also manifests itself in the sphere of hunting and eating:

> A man never eats his own game: this is the law that provides for the distribution of food among the Aché. A hunter kills an animal and his wife cuts it up, since he is forbidden to do it himself. She keeps a few pieces for herself and the children and the rest is given out, to relatives first, brother and brothers-in-law, and then to the others. No one is forgotten, and if there is not much meat, then the shares are small, but each person gets something.[28]

The consequence of not abiding by this distribution is to be stricken with *pane* – an inability to successfully hunt (to not find animals, to continually miss them with the bow). This result leads, by the logic of distribution itself, to an exclusion from both nature and society: 'When you do not mediate your relationship with food through your relationship with other people, you risk being completely cut off from the natural world and place outside it, just as you are pushed out of the social universe by refusing to share your goods.'[29]

Deleuze and Guattari reflect on two features of Clastres's central thesis in particular. The first is the position of the chief itself and, to be more precise, the status of political power. 'To be sure,' they write, 'primitive societies have *chiefs*. But the State is not defined by the existence of chiefs; it is defined by the perpetuation or conservation of organs of power' (TP 357). With Clastres, they will not hesitate to call the social formation in which a separation of the social body and the locus of power are distinct a State society, whose centre of power constitutes a 'higher unity' (AO 193), a locus from which it is 'possible to judge life and survey the earth from above' (AO 194).

The second feature they dwell on at considerably more length are the social functions by which counter-State societies rule out the advent of the State. The ensemble of these function is what Deleuze and Guattari will call 'warding' (*conjurer*). In a roundtable on the occasion of the publication of *Anti-Oedipus*, Clastres himself provides a succinct sense of what this operation entails:

> A primitive society directs all its efforts toward preventing its chief from becoming a chief (and that can go as far as murder). If history is the history of class struggle (I mean, in societies that have classes), then the history of classless societies is the history of their struggle against the latent State. Their history is the effort to encode the flows of power. (DI 227)

The correlate of this warding operation is a necessary anticipation of that which is to be kept at bay. This is why Deleuze and Guattari ultimately come to describe them as 'anticipation-prevention mechanisms' (e.g. TP 437); it is also why Clastres affirms a key thesis of *Anti-Oedipus* in the same roundtable discussion:

> the '*Urstaat*,' the cold monster, the nightmare, the State, which is the same everywhere and which 'has always existed.' Yes, the State exists in the most primitive societies, even in the smallest band of nomadic hunters. It exists, but it is ceaselessly warded off. It is ceaselessly prevented from becoming a reality. (DI 227)

But, Deleuze and Guattari want to know, what characterises the function of warding itself? It is true that Clastres's work implicitly presents the answer to this question in a variety of different contexts, but in their view a precise and explicit formulation is possible.[30] This formulation concerns the notion of the *threshold*. Here are Deleuze and Guattari: 'There exist collective mechanisms that simultaneously ward off and anticipate the formation of a central power. The appearance of a central power is thus a function of *a threshold or degree* beyond which what is anticipated takes on consistency or fails to' (TP 432).[31]

The State thus comes into being or attains consistency when this threshold is reached. This attainment is characterised by Deleuze and Guattari in terms of the economic theory of marginalism, despite the fact that something extra-economic is at stake.[32] Like the last word in an argument, the last axe made or the last bushel of seeds collected marks the point beyond which the social group would have to become something new. The last, that is to say, is always the 'next to last', what Deleuze and Guattari call the *limit*; the threshold is at once the real last and a first for a new assemblage. When a stockpile is created, it puts an organisational demand on a social group that can only be met by the group's very structure changing – just as the real last drink of the alcoholic necessitates a real change in their composition: sobriety or death. What appears as exchange is therefore a means of divesting the group of the avatar of stock, not the need to procure necessary items.

To anticipate-prevent is to structure all social activities with an eye to the performance of these activities that will necessitate a transformation of the social order. Every act is evaluated in terms of the limit that must not be crossed – indeed, as Deleuze and Guattari insist, it is this 'last' that constitutes the real source of all social values in their respective domains: 'The last as the object of a collective evaluation determines the value of the entire series' (TP 438).

So we can now see the rationale for summarising the position in the following terms:

> We previously defined primitive societies by the existence of *anticipation-prevention* mechanisms. Now we can see more clearly how these mechanisms are constituted and distributed: it is the evaluation of the last as limit that constitutes an anticipation and simultaneously wards off the last as threshold or ultimate (a new assemblage). (TP 439)

Second Topos: Bodily Inscription and the Law

According to Clastres, the constitutive counter-State rejection of any distinct organ of political power also provides the means to understand the phenomenon of torture in primitive society. At issue in particular is the ritual marking of the body. It is true, he notes, that inscriptions on the body function to identify their bearer as a member of a particular tribe, and that the ceremonies also involve 'measuring personal endurance'[33] against the yardstick of the ideals of the group. But for Clastres these two functions are not sufficient to explain the place and significance of ritual torture in primitive society.

The essential purpose of torture is rather to force its subject to remember: 'the body itself bears the memory traces imprinted on it; *the body is a memory*.'[34] And what it is made to remember is the central truth of the group:

> You are one of us. Each one of you is like us; each one of you is like the others . . . None of you is less than us; none of you is more than us. *And you will never be able to forget it.* You will not cease to remember the same marks that we have left on your bodies.[35]

As Clastres later puts it later in a text on La Boétie:

> To its children, the tribe proclaims: you are all equal, no one among you is worth more than another, no one worth less than another, inequality is forbidden, for it is false, it is wrong. And so that the memory of the primitive law is not lost, it is inscribed painfully – branded – on the bodies of the young people initiated into the knowledge of this law. In the initiatory act, the individual body, as surface of inscription of the Law, is the object of a collective investment which the entire society wishes for in order to prevent individual desire from transgressing the statement of the Law and infiltrating the social arena.[36]

Given this, the meaning of the pain's endurance also shifts: 'the initiates must remain silent under the torture. Silence gives consent. To what do the young people consent? They consent to accept themelves for what they are from that time forward: full members of the community.'[37]

And not only does the sense of these inscriptions militate against any one person asserting themselves as outside and therefore above the group. The fact that they are written on the body itself is key, in so far as it gives to the law an exclusively immanent location, foreclosing in turn the advent of a transcendent position from which it could be emitted. It is essential to note, for Clastres, that the law is on the body and only on the body; it is not knowledge about society, 'a knowledge exterior to it. It is, necessarily, the knowledge of society itself, a knowledge that is immanent to it, and that constitutes the very substance of society, its substantial self, what it is in itself.'[38]

Deleuze and Guattari also insist, following what 'Clastres says in an admirable text' (they are referring to the *Chronicle*), that the role of bodily inscription in counter-State societies is to affirm the immanence of every person to the social order and to the earth as its presupposed milieu: 'Furrowed skin, scarified earth, one and the same mark.'[39] But that the law thus written on the body is immanent to it means in turn that this writing must be conceived of as connotational rather than representational. It does not refer to something else (another sign, a signifier or a referent) as if to its meaning, but rather continually affects meaningful language use. Consequently, in the primitive use of the sign, 'everything is a matter of use and function' (AO 204), working to embed the descriptive function of spoken language in, or intertwine it with, the written law of the social order, according to which everyone is 'called by the same name'.[40]

Third Topos: State and Counter-State Societies in Economic Terms

A central feature of 'classical' ethnology is the notion that primitive society, unfolding at the greatest proximity to 'nature', is pitiless and grim. The prevalence of this view is remarkable, Clastres notes, for being unable to take in the massive evidence, concerning societies throughout the world, to the contrary: that far from being 'subsistence' societies, where survival characterises the whole of existence, they easily obtain what is required to survive, and spend a great deal of time in leisure.

This ethnology shares its economic pretentions – as he argues in a preface to Marshall Sahlins's decisive *Stone Age Economics* – with orthodox economics and Marxist anthropology. By endorsing a theoretical framework before looking at what is actually the case, they only manage to reproduce this framework in their results: 'Their pathetic undertakings are born in the same place and produce the same results. An ethnology of poverty. Sahlins has helped demonstrate the poverty of their ethnology.'[41] Clastres's own work demonstrates the same conclusion: primitive society is a self-sustaining autarky in which little work is required to provide everything the group needs: 'among the Yanomami,' for instance, 'all the needs of society are covered by an average of three hours of work per person, per day (for adults)'.[42]

But the inverse of this possible leisure is a necessary foreclosure of stockpiling, of the very notion of stock itself. 'Primitive society strictly limits its production lest the economic escape the social and turn against society by opening a gap between rich and poor.'[43] The advent of a stock is thus subject, in Vivieros de Castros's words, to an 'inhibition . . . by forced redistribution or ritual dilapidation.'[44] Contrary to the myriad blatantly ethnocentric characterisations of counter-State society, it is not that the poor primitives did not know how to produce well enough to constitute a stock, it is that they choose not to: 'if the primitive machine of production . . . could, if it wanted to, function longer and more quickly, produce surplus, form a stockpile. Consequently, if primitive society, though able, does nothing about it, it is because it does not want to.'[45]

We see here again the counter-State character of this society; and, indeed, for Clastres, various 'economic' features of these societies thus come to the same thing:

> the refusal of primitive societies to allow work and production to engulf them; by the decision to restrict supplies to socio-political needs; by the intrinsic impossibility of competition (in a primitive society what would be the use of being a rich man in the midst of poor men?); in short, by the prohibition – unstated but said nonetheless – of inequality.[46]

This all means in turn that there can be no question of conceiving exogenous group relations in economic terms, that is, as 'exchange'. There is no stock to exchange, and the very idea of an exchange that would presuppose that different groups were willing to adopt an even footing is undermined from the start: 'The constant problem of the primitive community is not: whom will we trade with? but: how can we maintain our independence?'[47] Or, as Clastres laconically puts it elsewhere, 'Commerce between tribes is not import–export.'[48]

Above all, these social processes must be understood as a part of the effort to ward off the advent of the State. It is not simply that 'The Savages produce to live, they do not live to produce';[49] the issue is rather to block the advent of a form of society in which one *must* produce, one in which 'living in order to produce' is the rule. We find here then a synonym for the 'society against the State': It is a 'society without economy, certainly, but, better yet, a society against economy'.[50]

This brings us to the category of *debt*, one whose value Clastres believes cannot be overstated:

> as a political category debt offers the surest criterion on which to evaluate the being of societies. The nature of society changes with

> the direction of the debt. If debt goes from the chieftainship toward society, society remains undivided, power remains located in the homogeneous social body. If, on the contrary, debt goes from society toward the chieftainship, power has been separated from society and is concentrated in the hands of the chief, the resulting heterogeneous society is divided into the dominating and the dominated.[51]

We have already seen Clastres's account of the way that debt holds symmetrically inverted positions in counter-State and State society. There is. however, the appearance of a contradiction in this account: on the one hand, counter-State societies are militantly egalitarian; on the other, they always put the chief in a position of subservience with respect to the group. The difficulty can be resolved by seeing that we are not merely dealing with an inversion of the direction of the debt, but two debts that differ in kind. The debt owed by the chief is a *finite* debt that ends at the moment that the chieftanship is ceded, a debt that is owed for the prestige that the chief garners while the chief. But the debt that is owed by the society to the ruler in State societies is *infinite* and unpayable. This debt is, moreover, for the very life of the members of the subjugated group; both its renunciation and its restitution are strictly and exclusively identical with death.

In sum, then, Clastres emphasises three features of primitive society with respect to the 'economy':

> 1. that the labour needed to produce enough to live is minimal, and that a great deal of primitive life is lived in leisure
> 2. that there is no interest in, and indeed resistance towards, any effort of stockpiling
> 3. that the chieftanship is a position which puts its occupant in a position of irredeemable debt to the society.

Deleuze and Guattari take up the latter two points in particular, devoting key pages of their social analysis in *Anti-Oedipus* to the second, and a decisive moment in *A Thousand Plateaus* to the third.

Anti-Oedipus on the role of debt in social formation

Deleuze and Guattari join with Clastres in identifying the structure of the debt relation in State society with the unilateral and inexhaustible debt of existence owed to the sovereign: 'The stocks form the object of an accumulation, the blocks of debt become an infinite relation in the form of the tribute' (AO 194). They considerably complicate his analysis of debt in counter-State societies, however. For Clastres, debt is located in the single relationship between the chief and the social body. For Deleuze and Guattari, it is ubiquitous in society, taking the form of the always dynamic, unequal relations of alliance.[52]

In a word, like the attempt to evict an air bubble from beneath a large sticker, every act of organisation that shifts the tapestry of social relations of (extra-filiative) alliance involves the displacement of finite debts. Debt is therefore 'a kinetic energy that is determined by the respective paths of the gifts and countergifts on the surface' (AO 149). Debt is the disequilibrium that never allows for it to remain as it is – and thus the very counter to the role of debt as permanent fixant in the State form, and the inversion of Lévi-Strauss's famous assertion of the primacy of exchange over debt. Conversely, Deleuze and Guattari closely follow the anthropological literature in taking the exchange of women for marriage as the principal case of the peristalsis of debt-alliance, including of course Clastres himself.[53]

Stock and code, stock and exchange

Summarising their conception of primitive exchange in *Anti-Oedipus*, Deleuze and Guattari affirm that 'exchange is known, well known in the primitive socius – but as that which must be exorcised, encasted, severely restricted, so that no corresponding value can develop as an exchange value that would introduce the nightmare of a commodity economy' (AO 186). This sentiment closely anticipates the more detailed analyses of *A Thousand Plateaus*, found at the heart of the 'Apparatus of Capture' plateau.

Before examining it, however, it is important to emphasise the less than categorical status given to the stockpile in *Anti-Oedipus*. Indeed, it would not be possible to speak of social reality at all in the terms of *Anti-Oedipus* if there was no stock, since the stock is ultimately nothing but the stability that belongs to the socially produced reality, that is, coded flows. Uncoded flows fall beneath the threshold of conscious experience. Consequently, as Deleuze and Guattari say, society has only one ultimate function: to code the flows (AO 139).[54] Invoking Clastres's *Chronicle*, they therefore write that 'there is always and already an encampment where it is a matter of stocking – however little – and where it is a matter of inscribing and allocating, of marrying, and of feeding oneself' (AO 148).

In *A Thousand Plateaus*, the correlative discussion turns around what Deleuze and Guattari term the *appearance of exchange*; we have already seen their analysis with respect to the notion of stock and the threshold/limit distinction. What must be emphasised once again and above all is that, at root, the sole aim of 'exchange' in counter-State societies is to ward off the advent of a transcendent locus of power; from this perspective, as a result, the notions of exchange and stock altogether change meaning.

On the one hand, exogenous exchange is only apparent for Deleuze and Guattari because it does not fulfil any of the goals of exchange as they are commonly: it is not entered into in order to address a lack (the fiction of barter), and it does not take place in the context of a neutral measure of value (as Deleuze and Guattari argue, both groups have their own measure of value, which is determined by the horizon of the 'last'). On the other hand, stock appears as the very emblem of State society.

Somewhat perversely, first of all, stockpiling begins at the precise moment when exchange has lost its interest (TP 440). Since, that is, exchange is an exercise in dispossession, the drive to constitute stock runs directly counter to the correlative primitive drive. Stock also necessarily summons or requires an owner, a manager, a 'sole and transcendent public-property owner, the master of the surplus or the stock' (TP 428), that is, induces a separate organ of power.

Fourth Topos: Warfare

At what was to be the very end of his life, Clastres turned to directly consider a problematic that is nevertheless ubiquitous in his work: war.[55] This is reflected in the title that Deleuze and Guattari give to their most detailed discussion of his work in *A Thousand Plateaus*: '*The exteriority of the war machine is also attested to by ethnology (a tribute to the memory of Pierre Clastres)*' (TP 357).

The elementary form of inter-group life, Clastres contends, is warfare. As he already asserts in the *Chronicle*, 'For a Guayaki tribe, relations with Others can only be hostile . . . There is only one language that can be spoken with them, and that is the language of violence.'[56] Indeed, Deleuze and Guattari, with reference to Clastres, position war as 'the surest mechanism directed against the formation of the State' (TP 357). It is war that establishes what Vivieros de Castros glosses as a 'meta-stable state of latent hostility'[57] between primitive social groups that are thereby unable to form a single group, and it is war that 'limits exchanges' (TP 357). Correlatively, the emphasis on exchange in accounts of primitive society has a disastrous analytic consequence for Clastres: it obscures the significance of warfare in the maintenance of societies resisting the formation of the State. In a key passage, he writes that

> The exchangist discourse on primitive society, in reducing this society wholly to exchange, is mistaken on two distinct but logically connected points. It is first of all unaware – or refuses to acknowledge – that primitive societies, far from always seeking to extend their field of exchange, tend on the contrary to reduce its significance constantly. This discourse consequently underestimates the real importance of violence, for the priority and exclusivity accorded to exchange leads in fact to abolishing war.[58]

In short, 'to be mistaken about war is to be mistaken about society'.[59] Once again, Deleuze and Guattari will affirm Clastres's analysis and extend it with the resources of their machinic social analysis, and, here in particular, by thinking the place of war in nomadic and primitive societies respectively.

If a single feature of Deleuze and Guattari's concept of the war machine is familiar, it is their *prima facie* paradoxical claim that 'the war machine does not necessarily have war as its object' (TP 417). This characterisation is underpinned by the idea that war itself does not have a single function, and varies in sense and object depending on the social formation in which it is put into play. Or, conversely: '*the war machine has an extremely variable relation to war itself*' (TP 422; see too 417). The war machine, consequently, is an agent that creates dynamisms that do not refer back to any underlying ordering of any kind, for instance the metric organisation of space brought about by the State, rather than being in any sense 'military'.

In keeping with the two senses of the figure of the nomad in *A Thousand Plateaus* – as a *de facto* social reality and *de jure* social type – there are two ways in which this relationship between the primitive and the nomadic can be thought through. On the one hand, we are dealing with an opposition between two concrete forms of social reality, a position that seems the dominant one in *A Thousand Plateaus*, for instance when they assert that 'primitive societies are defined by mechanisms of prevention-anticipation; . . . nomadic societies, by war machines' (TP 435). From this point of view, the war machine is the *de jure* element of interest, which finds its fullest expression in the nomadic formation: 'No doubt the war machine is realized more completely in the "barbaric" assemblages of nomadic warriors than in the "savage" assemblages of primitive societies' (TP 359; cf. D 141). In an important note, they are more precise again:

> We have seen that, according to Clastres, primitive war is one of the principal mechanisms warding off the State in that it maintains the opposition and dispersion of small segmentary groups. But also, from this viewpoint, primitive war remains subordinated to these preventive mechanisms and does not become autonomous as a machine, even when it comprises a specialized body. (TP 565 n. 12)

In other words, the war machine is at the centre of the putative nomadic social formation where it takes the form of creative social praxis, while in the primitive formation it is subordinated to the warding-off of the State in the direct form of generalised warfare or multilateral hostility. Deleuze and Guattari's account thus seems to imply that the State is already present in counter-State society in not one but two senses: as that threshold of consistency which is anticipated-prevented, and as the first instrumentalisation of the war machine that the State and then capitalism will generalise.

On the other hand, we can read the nomadic social form – identified by Clastres throughout with counter-State society – as the *de jure* element of interest, and it is ultimately something like this that Clastres argues for. Warfare must in turn be considered to be a particular expression of primitive society, but nothing in itself. To put the point more directly, for Clastres there is no nomadic society *de jure* or *de facto*. There are only the nomadic tendencies within a group, and the tendency, resisted in multifarious ways, towards the State. While this sounds in its own way very close to Deleuze and Guattari's analysis, its immediate consequence is not: for Clastres, there is no war machine.

Fifth Topos: 'The Meaning of Cannibalism'

A final *topos* can be added, even though it – like war, the economic and torture – is in truth a feature and consequence of the social organisation of counter-State societies: anthropophagy, and, to be more precise, endo-cannibalism, the eating of the bodies of one's own dead.

In a preliminary sense, the act of eating the dead is a straightforward analogue of burial. As the *Chronicle* puts it, 'The Guayaki were endo-cannibals in that they used their stomachs as the final resting place of their companions.'[60] And later: 'in some sense, they are walking cemeteries.'[61]

There is, however, a more serious, preventative function also in play: for the Aché, the dead are no longer people, but predators on the living: 'The dead want only Death to reign.'[62] The Guayaki rituals that follow upon death aim to fend off the return of the *Ove*, the spirit that occupied the now-dead person which seeks another to occupy. It is this threat to which Guayaki cannibalism responds:

> The Atchei eat the bodies of their dead, and this prevents the souls from penetrating the bodies of the living. The barrier against *Ove* is the very body it inhabited while it was alive, the body that is now exactly where it wants to go – within the bodies of the living people, who have ingested it . . . The joining through cannibalism of living and dead bodies is the disjoining of living beings and 'dead souls'; by doing away with the body in the form of food, *Ove* is forced to recognise once and for all what it is: a ghost without substance that no longer has anything to do with the living.[63]

In the 'Several Regimes of Signs' chapter of *A Thousand Plateaus*, Deleuze and Guattari's account of social machines is played out in terms of a complex analysis of the sign. Their essential claim is that the nature of the sign and its modes of operation radically differ depending on the socio-political conditions in which it is engendered and deployed. Once more, the distinction between the State and the counter-State forms appears, and, like the analysis of debt and inscription, it appears on the terrain of the sign. But whereas the opposition between the mark and writing discussed above is a counterposed description of two regimes of signs, the discussion of anthropophagy isolates a semiotic form of the warding operation itself.

As we have seen, counter-State formations deploy signs in a way that does not rupture the immanence of the social order. In the terms of *Anti-Oedipus*, the sign in primitive society is intertwined with bodily inscription and the shifting nature of social debt; in the terms of *A Thousand Plateaus*, the sign possesses a low degree of deterritorialisation: it is therefore pre-signifying. In both books, the passage to State society is the passage to the signifying regime in which the necessary (and unbroachable) space between mark and meaning is established. Signs refer to other signs, invoke a master signifier, and instantiate a neurotic-paranoid form of subjectivity. The historically specific truth of structuralist linguistics.

It is within this framework that Deleuze and Guattari take up Clastres's analysis. As I said, cannibalism functions to ward off the advent of the State in this semiotic register. As they memorably write, 'The meaning of cannibalism in a presignifying regime is precisely this: eating the name . . . Every time they eat a dead man, they can say:

one more the State won't get' (TP 118). By not allowing the name to be separated from the bodies of the dead, they cannot be the ground for the necrotic advance of the signifying regime. This account clearly goes further than the letter of Clastres's work – where the role of cannibalism, as we have seen, is to keep balance between the living and malicious spirits of the dead. But it is in keeping with the central claim of his thought, and this is because cannibalism in counter-State societies, on this reading, has the essential function of *warding*. In this case, what is to be warded off is precisely the arrival of an agent, transcendent in both origin and orientation, hostile to the immanent social order.

Deleuze and Guattari's Critique of Clastres

Whatever the virtues they assess it to have, Deleuze and Guattari frame their major discussion of Clastres's work in *A Thousand Plateaus* as a critique. Having lauded his rejection of the evolutionary–teleological vision of history embedded in the standard Hegelian-Marxist vision of the State, they add:

> However, one does not depart from evolutionism by establishing a clean break. In the final state of his work, Clastres maintained the preexistence and autarky of counter-State societies, and attributed their workings to an over-mysterious presentiment of what they warded off and did not yet exist. (TP 430)

This line of argument is not unique to Deleuze and Guattari. Claude Lefort perhaps gives its canonical formulation when he writes that 'The author of *Society against the State* has placed us in the presence of a system so closed that no event seems capable of unsettling it.'[64] But this critique misses its target. It is the case, first of all, that Clastres himself was quite aware of the problem. In his essay on La Boétie, for instance, he poses the question of the origin of the State and the concomitant origins of a desire for servitude:

> How does it begin? La Boétie has no idea. How does it continue? It is because men desire it to be this way, answers La Boétie. We have hardly advanced; objecting to this is easy. For the stakes, subtly but clearly fixed by La Boétie, are anthropological. Human nature itself poses the question: is the desire for submission innate or acquired? Did this desire pre-exist the misfortune which would then have allowed it to come into being? Or is its emergence due instead, *ex nihilo*, to the occasion of the misfortune, like a lethal mutation that

> defies all explanation? These questions are less academic than they seem, as the example of primitive society suggests.[65]

More than this, Clastres was also aware – contrary to what Vivieros de Castros implies[66] – of the solution to the problem that Deleuze and Guattari themselves pose. In contradistinction to the alleged sterility of Clastres's position, Deleuze and Guattari write that 'We are compelled to say that there has always been a State, quite perfect, quite complete. The more discoveries archaeologists make, the more empires they uncover. The hypothesis of the *Urstaat* seems to be verified' (TP 360). But Clastres himself asserts and agrees with this very claim, in Deleuze and Guattari's presence no less:

> the State, which is the same everywhere . . . 'has always existed.' Yes, the State exists in the most primitive societies, even in the smallest band of nomadic hunters. It exists, but it is ceaselessly warded off. It is ceaselessly prevented from becoming a reality. (DI 227)

Why then do his last essays on warfare in particular strengthen the impression, at least for Deleuze and Guattari, that no analytic passage from counter-State to State exists?

Another question without an easy answer. But we will leave the last word to Clastres himself, and to this passage from his scintillating take-down of Pierre Birbaum's misreading of his project:[67]

> up until now, I have never said anything regarding the origin of the State, that is, regarding the origin of social division, the origin of domination. Why? Because this is a matter of a (fundamental) question of sociology, and not of theology or philosophy of history. In other words, to pose the question of origin depends on an analysis of the social: under what conditions can social division surge forth from the undivided society? What is the nature of the social forces that would lead Savages to accept the division into Masters and Subjects? Under what conditions does primitive society as undivided society die? A genealogy of misfortune, a search for the social clinamen that can only be developed, of course, by questioning the primitive social being: the problem of origin is strictly sociological, and neither Condorcet nor Hegel, neither Comte nor Engels, neither Durkheim nor Birnbaum are of any help in this. In order to understand social division, we must begin with the society that existed to prevent it. As for knowing whether I can or cannot articulate an answer to the question of the origin of the State, I still do not know, and Birnbaum knows even less. Let us wait, let us work, there is no hurry.[68]

This is the response of an ethnographer: there remains work to be done. But the death of Clastres cut this work off, as if mid-sentence.

Alas, there was a hurry; five months after this piece was published, Clastres was dead. But this hurry owes itself not to research projects or the critical overreach practiced by impatient detractors, but to the indiscernible register of time – which is to say, to Death, who, as Clastres writes, 'mockingly asks his question'.[69]

Notes

1. Paul Auster, the translator of Clastres's first book, *Chronicle of the Guayaki Indians*, presents an account of the circumstances of Clastres's death in an online interview (also given in abbreviated form at the start of Clastres's *Chronicle*, pp. ix–x): 'I heard the terrifying story of Clastres's death from someone who had known him. It's an awful story. Apparently, there were a bunch of young anthropologists in France at the time, and they had all bought little houses in the country, not far from one another. Clastres's house was down in a valley, and they had friends who lived up in the mountains. One night, the friends invited Clastres and his wife to dinner. In order to get to the house, they had to go over a very narrow bridge. It seems that they all drank too much, and driving home, after the party, Clastres's car went off the bridge and crashed; he was killed, his wife survived.

   Two years later, when she was finally well enough to invite some people over, she invited these same friends, and they came down from the mountain over the little bridge, and down to her house for dinner. After dinner, driving home that night, their car went off the bridge and they were both killed. It's a frightening story' (Jill Owens, 'The Book of Paul Auster', *Powell's City of Books*, 24 Jan. 2007, http://www.powells.com/post/interviews/the book-of-paul-auster [last accessed 19/12/2016]).
2. The works of Clastres I will cite here are *Chronicle of the Guayaki Indians* [1972], trans. Paul Auster (New York: Zone Books, 1998); *Entretien avec* L'Anti-Mythe (Paris: sens&tonka, 2012); *Society against the State* [1974], trans. Robert Hurley and Abe Stein (New York: Zone Books, 1998); and *The Archeology of Violence* [1980], trans. Jeanine Herman (New York: semiotext(e), 2010).
3. It is also clearly the case that Clastres himself was clearly influenced by Deleuze and Guattari's work, and indeed attended some of Deleuze's seminars during the 1970s when aspects of *A Thousand Plateaus* were being worked out. Take, for example, the appearance of the concepts of deteritorialisation and anti-production in the pieces, collected in *The Archeology of Violence*, that were published after 1972. Unfortunately, considerations of space rule out a consideration of this other trajectory of influence. Eduardo Vivieros de Castros considers certain elements of this influence in both his introduction to *The Archeology*

of Violence ('The Untimely Again') and in his *Cannibal Metaphysics: For a Post-Structural Anthropology*, trans. Peter Skafish (Minneapolis: Univocal Press, 2014). Viveros de Castros's work on Deleuze and Guattari constitutes an important rejection of the less than rigorous critical readings of their work on and around anthropology. See, for instance, Christopher Miller, 'The Postidentitarian Predicament in the Footnotes of *A Thousand Plateaus*: Nomadology, Anthropology, and Authority', *Diacritics* 23:3 (1993), pp. 6–35, and Riccardo Ciavolella, 'Alterpolitics or Altertopies: A Critique of Nomadology with Reference to West African Fulbe', *Focaal* (Summer 2015), pp. 23–36. The latter of these pieces also includes a quite misleading presentation of Clastres's work. For another very helpful corrective, see Ron Bogue, 'Apology for Nomadology', *interventions* 6:2 (2004), pp. 169–79, which treats the role of Clastres for Deleuze and Guattari in a much more salutary fashion.

4. Cf. François Dosse, *History of Structuralism*, vol. 2, *The Sign Sets, 1967–Present*, trans. Deborah Glassman (Minneapolis: Minnesota University Press, 1997), p. 88.
5. Adler cited in François Dosse, *History of Structuralism*, vol. 1, *The Rising Sign, 1945– 1966*, trans. Deborah Glassman (Minneapolis: Minnesota University Press, 1997), p. 162. The chapter titles in Clastres's own ethnography closely resemble – in both their tone and narrative character – Lévi-Strauss's section headings in *Tristes tropiques*.
6. See Dosse, *The Sign Sets*, pp. 88–90; Vivieros de Castros, 'The Untimely Again', pp. 10–12.
7. Clastres, *Entretien*, p. 13.
8. Clastres, *Archeology*, p. 323.
9. Ibid., p. 224, translation modified, emphases added.
10. Ibid., p. 222.
11. Clastres, *Society against the State*, p. 25. See, too, his transformation of the infrastructure/superstructure pair in the same book (pp. 202–3)
12. Clastres, *Archeology*, p. 221, translation modified.
13. Ibid., p. 226.
14. Ibid., p. 235.
15. For this reason, Emmanuel Terray's assertion that, in his 'mature' work, Clastres supposes that 'primitive society is of its essence a society without a State and *without* power' is a completely incorrect one (Terray, 'Une nouvelle anthropologie politique?' *L'Homme* 110 (Apr.–June 1989), pp. 5–29 (p. 7)). As Clastres himself notes, this kind of claim forces us to buy into the idea that power is always coercive. But – anticipating, rather than rejecting in advance, in many regards the account that would appear three years later in *Discipline and Punish* – 'It is not evident to me that coercion and subordination constitute the essence of political power *at all times and in all places*' (Clastres,

Society against the State, p. 13). Or, as he puts it a little later, 'societies cannot be divided into two groups: societies with power and societies without power. On the contrary, it is our view (in complete conformity with ethnographic data) that political power is *universal*, [and] immanent to social reality' (Clastres, *Society against the State*, p. 22).

16. Clastres, *Archeology*, p. 208. This is despite the fact that he earlier – and incorrectly, at least from the point of view of more sophisticated readings of Nietzsche including Deleuze's – claims that for Nietzsche the exercise of power can be strictly identified with the exercise of violence (Clastres, *Society against the State*, p. 11).
17. Clastres, *Archeology*, pp. 203, 204.
18. Ibid., p. 204.
19. Clastres, *Society against the State*, p. 183.
20. Ibid., p. 188.
21. It should be equally unsurprising that in this same essay Clastres will write that 'As the authors of *L'Anti-Oedipe* have so forcefully argued, primitive societies are first of all societies that *mark*' (*Society against the State*, pp. 187–8). See also note 3 above.
22. Claude Lefort enumerates the first four of these points in *Writing: The Political Test*, trans. and ed. David Ames Curtis (Durham, NC: Duke University Press, 2000), p. 214.
23. Clastres, *Archeology*, p. 204. There is a clear sense in which Clastres's work on forms of societies that turn around a hostility towards the State constitute, for Deleuze and Guattari, a complement with the historical and linguistic work of Georges Dumézil that emphasises a correlative hostility between the warrior and ruler. This complementarity is explicitly drawn in Deleuze and Parnet's discussion of politics (D 141), where Clastres and Dumézil appear in the same passage concerning the nature of warfare, separated only by a single phrase mentioning the Africanist anthropologist Luc de Heusch's text *Le Roi ivre ou l'origine de l'État* (The Drunk King, or the Origin of the State]. On Deleuze and Guattari's use of Dumézil, see the chapter by Ron Bogue in the present volume.
24. Clastres, *Chronicle*, p. 57. For some reason, Auster renders Aché as Atchei. I have modified his translation throughout to reflect Clastres' usage.
25. Clastres, *Chronicle*, p. 65.
26. Ibid., p. 66.
27. Clastres, *Archeology*, p. 90.
28. Clastres, *Chronicles*, p. 193.
29. Ibid., p. 195.
30. Somewhat paradoxically, Deleuze and Guattari present Lévi-Strauss as the thinker to discover this point in *A Thousand Plateaus* (TP 433).

31. It is tempting to also infer the opposition, decisive in Kant's first *Critique*, of boundary (*Grenze*) and limit (*Schranke*) here.
32. While the analysis of the concept of threshold is all but exclusively a feature of *A Thousand Plateaus*, the play of the 'last' and the 'penultimate' is found elsewhere in Deleuze's work in relation to the alcoholic's last drink – in *Logic of Sense* (LS 159–60) and in the 'B as in "Boire"' section of the *Abécedaire* interviews (AZ).
33. Clastres, *Society against the State*, p. 185.
34. Ibid., p. 184.
35. Ibid., p. 186.
36. Clastres, *Archeology*, pp. 180–1.
37. Clastres, *Society against the State*, p. 185.
38. Clastres, *Archeology*, p. 137.
39. Clastres, *Chronicle*, p. 115, cited at AO 180.
40. Clastres, *Society against the State*, p. 186.
41. Clastres, *Archeology*, p. 208.
42. Ibid., p. 71. Clastres concludes this passage wryly insisting that we should 'remember this at sixty when demanding our retirement funds'.
43. Clastres, *Archeology*, p. 198.
44. Viveros de Castros, 'The Untimely Again', p. 13.
45. Clastres, *Archeology*, p. 193.
46. Clastres, *Society against the State*, p. 199.
47. Clastres, *Archeology*, p. 271.
48. Ibid., p. 195.
49. Ibid., p. 197.
50. Ibid., p. 198.
51. Ibid., p. 205.
52. For a more detailed discussion of Deleuze and Guattari's account of the economic facet of social formations and its relationship to debt, filiation and alliance, see Jon Roffe, 'Economic Systems and the Problematic Character of Price', in *Posthuman Ecologies Complexity and Process after Deleuze*, ed. Rosi Braidotti and Simone Bignall (London: Rowman Littlefield International, 2019), pp. 223–42. Debt is also a central category in the work of Eugene Holland: see both *Deleuze and Guattari's* Anti-Oedipus*: Introduction to Schizoanalysis* (New York: Routledge, 1999) and *Nomad Citizenship: Free-Market Communism and the Slow-Motion General Strike* (Minneapolis: University of Minnesota Press, 2011).
53. See Clastres, *Chronicle*, p. 202.
54. On this point, see Daniel W. Smith, 'Flow, Code and Stock: A Note on Deleuze's Political Philosophy', in *Essays on Deleuze* (Edinburgh: Edinburgh University Press, 2012), especially pp. 165–6.
55. The two key essays on this topic – 'Archeology of Violence' and 'Sorrows of the Savage Warrior' – were published in the inaugural issue of the

journal *Libre*, founded by Clastres with some of the former members of the *Socialism or Barbarism* collective, including Cornelius Castoriadis and Claude Lefort. The journal's second issue opens with Clastres's obituary. See Christian Delacampagne, 'Un ethnologue contre l'État', *L'Anti-autoritarisme en enthnologue*, Les Colloques ethnologiques de Bordeaux 2 (Bordeaux: Presse universitaire de Bordeaux, 1997), pp. 103–4.

56. Clastres, *Chronicles*, p. 161.
57. Viveros de Castros, 'The Untimely Again', p. 10.
58. Clastres, *Archeology*, p. 270.
59. Ibid., p. 256; cf. p. 270.
60. Clastres, *Chronicle*, p. 220.
61. Ibid., p. 222.
62. Ibid., p. 206.
63. Ibid., p. 229.
64. Lefort, *Writing*, p. 229.
65. Clastres, *Archeology*, pp. 178–9, translation modified.
66. Viveros de Castros, 'The Untimely Again', p. 38.
67. Pierre Birnbaum, 'Sur les origines de la domination politique. À propos d'Étienne de la Boétie et de Pierre Clastres', *Revue française de science politique* 27:1 (1977), pp. 5–21.
68. Clastres, *Archeology*, p. 230.
69. Ibid., p. 89.

Bibliography

Abadía, Oscar Moro and Palacio-Pérez, Eduardo. 'Rethinking the Structural Analysis of Palaeolithic Art: New Perspectives on Leroi-Gourhan's Structuralism'. *Cambridge Archaeological Journal* 25(3), August 2015, 657–72.

Adereth, M. *Commitment in Modern French Literature: A Brief Study of 'Littérature Engagée' in the works of Péguy, Aragon, and Sartre*. London: Victor Gollancz, 1967.

Adkins, Brent. 'What is a Literature of War? Kleist, Kant and Nomadology'. In Craig Lundy and Daniela Voss (eds), *On the Edges of Thought. Deleuze and post-Kantian philosophy*. Edinburgh: Edinburgh University Press, 2015, 105–22.

Allen, N. J. 'Debating Dumézil: Recent Studies in Comparative Mythology'. *Journal of the Anthropological Society of Oxford* 24, 1993.

Alquié, Ferdinand. 'Jean Wahl et la philosophie'. *Critique* 10, 1954, 519–23.

—. 'Jean Wahl'. *Les Études philosophiques* 1, 1975, 79–88.

Amrine, Frederick. 'The Music of the Organism: Uexküll, Merleau-Ponty, Zuckerkandl, and Deleuze as Goethan Ecologist in Search of a New Paradigm'. *Goethe Yearbook* XXII, 2015, 45–72.

Ansell Pearson, Keith. 'Affirmative Naturalism: Deleuze and Epicureanism'. *Cosmos and History* 10(2), 2014, 121–36.

Ansell Pearson, Keith and Protevi, John. 'Naturalism in the Continental Tradition'. In Kelly James Clark (ed.), *The Blackwell Companion to Naturalism*. Malden, MA: Wiley-Blackwell, forthcoming.

Artaud, Antonin. 'Letter to Andre Breton, 28 February 1947'. Trans. Yvonne Houlton. *Interstice* 2, 1996, 33–4.

—. 'Lettres à André Breton'. *L'Ephémère* 8, 1968, 3–25.

—. *Œuvres complètes*, 26 vols (of 30 prepared). Paris: Gallimard, 1976–.

—. *Selected Writings*. Ed. Susan Sontag and trans. Helen Weaver. Berkeley: University of California Press, 1988.

Audouze, Françoise. 'Leroi-Gourhan, a Philosopher of Technique and Evolution'. *Journal of Archaeological Research* 70(4), December 2002, 277–306.

Badiou, Alain. *Logiques des mondes*. Paris: Seuil, 2006. *Logics of Worlds: Being and Event II*. Trans. Alberto Toscano. London: Continuum, 2009.

Barabas, Renaud. 'Vie et extériorité: Le problème de la perception chez Ruyer'. *Les Études philosophiques* 80(1), 2007, 5–37.

Baugh, Bruce. *French Hegel: From Surrealism to Postmodernism*. New York and London: Routledge, 2003.

—. 'Transcendental Empiricism: Deleuze's Response to Hegel'. *Man and World* 25, 1992, 136–7.

Beckett, Samuel. *The Letters of Samuel Beckett, Volume 1*. Ed. George Craig, Martha Dow Fehsenfeld, Dan Gunn and Lois More Overbeck. Cambridge: Cambridge University Press, 2009.

Bednarek, Joanna. 'Logika sensu – najbardziej lacanowska z książek Deleuze'a?' *Praktyka Teoretyczna* 5, 2012, 33–48.

Bégoin, Jean. 'L'Anti-Œdipe ou la destruction envieuse du sein'. In *Les Chemins de l'anti-œdipe*. Ed. Edouard Privat. Toulouse: Bibliothèque de Psychologie Clinique, 1974, 139–59.

Benjamin, Walter. *The Correspondence of Walter Benjamin, 1910–1940*. Ed. G. Scholem and T. W. Adorno and trans. M. R. and E. M. Jacobson. Chicago: University of Chicago Press, 1994.

Bennett, Michael J. *Deleuze and Ancient Greek Physics: The Image of Nature*. London: Bloomsbury Academic, forthcoming.

—. 'Deleuze and Epicurean Philosophy: Atomic Speed and Swerve Speed'. *The Journal of French and Francophone Philosophy* 21:2 (2013), 131–57.

Bergson, Henri. *Creative Evolution*. Trans. Arthur Mitchell. Mineola, NY: Dover Publications, 1998.

—. *The Creative Mind: An Introduction to Metaphysics*. Trans. M. L. Andison. Mineola, NY: Dover Publications, 2007.

—. 'Life and Consciousness'. In *Mind-Energy*. Trans. H. Wildon Carr. London: Macmillan, 1920, 1–28.

—. *Matter and Memory*. Trans. N. M. Paul and W. S. Palmer. Mineola, NY: Dover Publications, 2004.

—. *Notice sur la vie et les œuvres de Félix Ravaisson-Mollien*. Paris: Firmin Didot, 1904. http://www.asmp.fr/travaux/notices/ravaisson_bergson.htm (last accessed 7/2/2016).

—. *Œuvres*. Paris: Presses universitaires de France, 1959.

Berressem, Hanjo. '*Incerto Tempore Incertisque Locis*: The Logic of the Clinamen and the Birth of Physics'. In Niran Abbas (ed.), *Mapping Michel Serres*. Ann Arbor: University of Michigan Press, 2005, 51–83.

Bianco, Giuseppe. *Après Bergson. Portrait de groupe avec philosophe*. Paris: Presses universitaires de France, 2015.

Birnbaum, Pierre. 'Sur les origines de la domination politique. À propos d'Étienne de la Boétie et de Pierre Clastres'. *Revue française de science politique* 27(1), 1977, 5–21.

Blanchot, Maurice, *Faux Pas*. Stanford: Stanford University Press, 2001.

—. *Le Livre à venir*. Paris: Gallimard, 1959.

Boer, Pim den, *History as a Profession: The Study of History in France, 1818–1914*. Princeton: Princeton University Press, 1998.
Bonta, Mark. 'Rhizome of Boehme and Deleuze: Esoteric Precurses of the God of Complexity'. *SubStance* 39:1, 2010, 62–75.
Bogue, Ron. 'Apology for Nomadology'. *Interventions* 6(2), 2004, 169–79.
—. *Deleuze on Cinema*. New York: Routledge, 2003.
—. *Deleuze on Literature*. New York: Routledge, 2003.
—. *Deleuze on Music, Painting, and the Arts*. New York: Routledge, 2003.
Bowden, Sean. 'An Anti-Positivist Conception of Problems: Deleuze, Bergson and the French Epistemological Tradition'. *Angelaki* 23(2), 2018, 45–63.
—. *The Priority of Events: Deleuze's* Logic of Sense. Edinburgh: Edinburgh University Press, 2011.
Boyer, Carl. *The History of the Calculus and Its Conceptual Development*. New York: Dover, 1959.
Brassier, Ray. *Nihil Unbound: Enlightenment and Extinction*. Basingstoke: Palgrave MacMillan, 2007.
Brentari, Carlo. *Jakob von Uexküll. The Discovery of the Umwelt between Biosemiotics and Theoretical Biology*. Trans. Catriona Graciet. Dordrecht, Heidelberg, New York and London: Springer, 2015.
Brunschvicg. Léon. *Les Étapes de la philosophie mathématique* [1912]. Paris: Blanchard, 1981.
—. *L'Expérience humaine et la causalité physique*. Paris: Alcan, 1922.
—. *Le Progrès de la conscience dans la philosophie occidentale*, 2 vols. Paris: Presses universitaires de France, 1928.
Buchanan, Brett. *Onto-Ethologies. The Animal Environments of Uexküll, Heidegger, Merleau-Ponty and Deleuze*. Albany: State University of New York Press, 2008.
Campbell, Donald T. 'Evolutionary Epistemology'. In Philip Schilpp (ed.), *The Philosophy of Karl Popper*. LaSalle: Open Court, 1974, 412–63.
Ciavolella, Riccardo. 'Alterpolitics or Altertopies: A Critique of Nomadology with Reference to West African Fulbe'. *Focaal*, Summer 2015, 23–36.
Cioran, Emil. *Le Mauvais Démiurge*. Paris: Gallimard, 1969. *The New Gods*. Trans. Richard Howard. New York: Quadrangle, 1974.
Clastres, Pierre. *The Archeology of Violence*. Trans. Jeanine Herman. New York: semiotext(e), 2010.
—. *Chronicle of the Guayaki Indians*. Trans. Paul Auster. New York: Zone Books, 1998.
—. *Entretien avec* L'Anti-Mythe. Paris: sens&tonka, 2012.
—. *Society against the State*. Trans. Robert Hurley and Abe Stein. New York: Zone Books, 1998.
Collett, Guillaume. *Psychoanalysis of Sense: Deleuze and the Lacanian School*. Edinburgh: Edinburgh University Press, 2016.

Cooper, Melinda. 'Vitesses de l'image, puissances de la pensée: la philosophie épicurienne revue par Deleuze et Guattari'. *French Studies* 56(1), 2002, 45–60.

Crease, Robert P. *World in the Balance: The Historic Quest for an Absolute System of Measurement*. New York: Norton, 2011.

Darwin, Charles. *The Descent of Man*, 2nd edn [1879]. London and New York: Penguin Classics, 2004.

David-Ménard, Monique. *Deleuze et la psychoanalyse*. Paris: Presses universitaires de France, 2005.

Davidson, Donald. *Essays on Actions and Events*, 2nd edn. Oxford: Oxford University Press, 2001.

—. *Truth, Language, and History*. Oxford: Oxford University Press, 2005.

Dawkins, Richard. *Climbing Mount Probable*. New York and London: W. W. Norton, 1996.

—. *The Extended Phenotype*. Oxford: Oxford University Press, 1982.

Dean, Mitchell. *Critical and Effective Histories: Foucault's Methods and Historical Sociology*. London and New York: Routledge, 1994.

Defert, Daniel and Donzelot, Jacques. 'La charnière des prisons'. *Le Magazine littéraire* 112–13, May 1976, 33–5.

Delacampagne, Christian. 'Un ethnologue contre l'État'. In *L'Anti-autoritarisme en enthnologue, Les Colloques ethnologiques de Bordeaux tome II*. Bordeaux: Presse universitaire de Bordeaux, 1997, 103–4.

Deleuze, Gilles. 'À quoi reconnaît-on le *structuralisme*'. In *Histoire de la philosophie VIII. Le XXe siècle*. Ed. François Châtelet. Paris: Hachette, 1973.

—. *Le Bergsonisme*. Paris: Presses universitaires de France, 1966. *Bergsonism*. Trans. Hugh Tomlinson and Barbara Habberjam. New York: Zone Books, 1988.

—. 'Bergson's Conception of Difference'. Trans. Melissa McMahon. In *The New Bergson*. Ed. John Mullarkey. Manchester: Manchester University Press, 1999, 42–65.

—. *Cinema 1: The Movement Image*. Trans. Hugh Tomlinson and Barbara Habberjam. Minneapolis: University of Minnesota Press, 1989.

—. *Cinema 2: The Time Image*. Trans. Hugh Tomlinson and Robert Galeta. Minneapolis: University of Minnesota Press, 1989.

—. 'Coldness and Cruelty'. In *Masochism*. Trans. Charles Stivale. New York: Zone Books, 1989.

—. 'Désir et plaisir'. *Le Magazine littéraire* 325, October 1994, 57–65.

—. *Deux regimes de fou*. Paris: Les Éditions de Minuit, 2003. *Two Regimes of Madness and Other Texts*. Trans. Michael Taormina. New York: semiotext(e), 2006.

—. *Différence et répétition*. Paris: Presses universitaires de France, 1968. *Difference and Repetition*. Trans. Paul Patton. New York: Columbia University Press, 1994.

—. 'Écrivain non: un nouveau cartographe'. *Critique* 343, December 1975, 1207–27.
—. *Empiricisme et subjectivité*. Paris: Presses universitaires de France, 1953. *Empiricism and Subjectivity*. Trans. Constantin Boundas. New York: Columbia University Press, 1991.
—. *Essays Critical and Clinical*. Trans. Daniel W. Smith and Michael A. Greco. Preface by Daniel W. Smith. Minneapolis: University of Minnesota Press, 1997.
—. *Foucault*. Paris: Les Éditions de Minuit, 1986. *Foucault*. Trans. Sean Hand. Minneapolis: University of Minnesota Press, 1988.
—. *Francis Bacon: Logique de la sensation*, 2 vols. Paris: Éditions de la difference, 1981. *Francis Bacon: The Logic of Sensation*. Translation of the first volume, Daniel W. Smith. London: Continuum Press, 2003.
—. 'L'homme, une existence douteuse'. *Le Nouvel Observateur* 81, 1–7 June 1966, 32–4.
—. *L'Île déserte et autres textes*. Paris: Les Éditions de Minuit, 2002. Ed. David Lapoujade. *Desert Islands and Other Texts*. Trans. Michael Taormina. New York: semiotext(e), 2004.
—. 'L'immanence: une vie ...'. *Philosophie* 47, September 1995, special issue on Deleuze, 3–7. *Pure Immanence: Essays on a life*. Trans. Anne Boymen and ed. John Rajchman. New York: Zone Books, 2001.
—. 'Le "Je me souviens" de Gilles Deleuze'. *Le Nouvel Observateur* 1619, 1995, 50–1.
—. *Kant's Critical Philosophy*. Trans. Hugh Tomlinson and Barbara Habberjam. London: Althone Press, 1983.
—. Lectures/Seminars. Available online at http://www.webdeleuze.com/php/sommaire.html
—. 'Lettre-préface de Gilles Deleuze'. In Jean-Clet Martin, *Variations: La Philosophie de Gilles Deleuze*. Paris: Payot, 1993.
—. *Logique du sens*. Paris: Les Éditions de Minuit, 1969. *The Logic of Sense*. Trans. Mark Lester and Charles Stivale. New York: Columbia University Press, 1990.
—. *Le Pli: Leibniz et le baroque*. Paris: Les Éditions de Minuit, 1988. *The Fold: Leibniz and the Baroque*. Trans. Tom Conley. Minneapolis: University of Minnesota Press, 1992.
—. *Masochism*. Trans. Jean McNeil. New York: Zone Books, 1989.
—. *Negotiations*. Trans. Martin Joughin. New York: Columbia University Press, 1995.
—. *Nietzsche et la philosophie*. Paris: Presses universitaires de France, 1965. *Nietzsche and Philosophy*. Trans. Hugh Tomlinson. New York: Columbia University Press, 1983.
—. 'Un nouvel archiviste'. *Critique* 274, March 1970, 195–209.
—. Online Seminars. Transcribed by Richard Pinhas. http://www.webdeleuze.fr/sommaire

—. *Périclès et Verdi: La philosophie de François Châtelet*. Paris: Les Éditions de Minuit, 1988.

—. 'Pierre Klossowski ou les corps-langage'. *Critique* 214, March 1965, 199–219.

—. 'Pour en finir avec le jugement'. *Critique et clinique*. Paris: Les Éditions de Minuit, 1994, 158–69.

—. *Proust and Signs*. Trans. Richard Howard. Minneapolis: University of Minnesota Press, 2000.

—. 'Raymond Roussel ou L'Horreur du vide'. *Arts* 933, October 23–9, 1963, 4.

—. 'The Schizophrenic and Language: Surface and Depths in Lewis Carroll and Antonin Artaud'. In *Textual Strategies*. Ed. and trans. Josué Harari. New York: Cornell University Press, 1979.

—. *Spinoza et le problème de l'expression*. Paris: Les Éditions de Minuit, 1968. *Expressionism in Philosophy: Spinoza*. Trans. Martin Joughin. New York: Zone Books, 1990.

—. *Spinoza: Practical Philosophy*. Trans. Robert Hurley. San Francisco: City Lights Books, 1988.

Deleuze, Gilles, and Foucault, Michel. 'Les intellectuels et le pouvoir: Entretien avec Michel Foucault'. *L'Arc* 49, 1972, 3–10.

—. 'Introduction générale aux *Œuvres philosophiques complètes de F. Nietzsche*'. In Michel Foucault, *Dits et écrits*, vol. 1. Paris: Gallimard, 1994, 561–4.

Deleuze, Gilles, and Guattari, Félix. *L'Anti-Oedipe*. Paris: Les Éditions de Minuit, 1972. *Anti-Oedipus: Capitalism and Schizophrenia*. Trans. Robert Hurley, Mark Seem and Helen Lane. New York: Viking Press, 1977.

—. 'Balance-sheet for "Desiring-Machines"'. In Félix Guattari, *Chaosophy: Texts and Interviews, 1972–1977*. Ed. Sylvère Lotringer, trans. David L. Sweet, Jarred Becker, and Taylor Adkins. New York: semiotext(e), 1992.

—. *Kafka: Pour une littérature mineure*. Paris: Les Éditions de Minuit, 1975. *Kafka: Towards a Minor Literature*. Trans. Dana Polan. Minneapolis: University of Minnesota Press, 1986.

—. *Mille plateaux*. Paris: Les Éditions de Minuit, 1980. *A Thousand Plateaus: Capitalism and Schizophrenia*. Trans. Brian Massumi. Minneapolis: University of Minnesota Press, 1987.

—. *Qu'est-ce que la philosophie?* Paris: Éditions de Minuit, 1991. *What is Philosophy?* Trans. Hugh Tomlinson and Graham Burchell. New York: Columbia University Press, 1994.

Deleuze, Gilles, and Parnet, Claire. *Dialogues* II. Trans. Hugh Tomlinson and Barbara Habberjam. New York: Columbia University Press, 1987.

—. *Deleuze from A to Z*. Trans. Charles Stivale. New York: semiotext(e), 2011.

Derrida, Jacques. *Of Grammatology*. Trans. Gayatri Chakravorty Spivak. Baltimore: Johns Hopkins University Press, 1977.
—. 'La parole soufflée'. In *L'Écriture et la différence*. Paris: Seuil, 1967, 253–92. *Writing and Difference*. Trans. Alan Bass. London: Routledge, 1978, 169–95.
Derrida, Jacques. *Le Toucher. Jean-Luc Nancy*. Paris: Galilée, 2000.
Descartes, René. *Meditations and Other Metaphysical Writings*. London: Penguin, 1998.
Dosse, François. *Gilles Deleuze et Félix Guattari, Biographie Croisée*. Paris: La Découverte, 2007. *Gilles Deleuze and Felix Guattari, Intersecting Lives*. Trans. Deborah Glassman. New York: Cambridge University Press, 2010.
—. *History of Structuralism, Vol. 1: The Rising Sign. 1945–1966*. Trans. Deborah Glassman. Minneapolis: University of Minnesota Press, 1997.
—. *History of Structuralism Volume 2, The Sign Sets, 1967–Present*. Trans. Deborah Glassman. Minneapolis: Minnesota University Press, 1997.
Dumézil, Georges. *Archaic Roman Religion*. Trans. Philip Krapp. Chicago: University of Chicago Press, 1970.
—. *Entretiens avec Didier Éribon*. Paris: Gallimard, 1987.
—. *Heur et malheur du guerrier: Aspects mythiques de la fonction guerrière chez les Indo-Européens*. Paris: Presses universitaires de France, 1969. *The Destiny of the Warrior*. Trans. Alf Hiltebeitel. Chicago: University of Chicago Press, 1970.
—. *Horace et les Curiaces*. Paris: Gallimard, 1942.
—. *L'Idéologue tripartie des Indo-Européens*, Collection Latomus, vol. 31. Brussels: Latomus, 1958.
—. *Mitra-Varuna: Essai sur deux représentations indo-européennes de la souveraineté*, 2nd edn. Paris: Gallimard, 1948. *Mitra-Varuna: An Essay on Two Indo-European Representations of Sovereignty*. Trans. Derek Coleman. New York: Zone Books, 1988.
—. *Mythe et épopée I: L'idéologie des trois fonctions dans les épopées des peuples indo-européens*. Paris: Gallimard, 1968.
—. *Mythe et épopée II* (part one). Paris: Gallimard, 1971. *The Stakes of the Warrior*, trans. David Weeks. Berkeley: University of California Press, 1983.
—. *Mythe et épopee III. Histoires romaines*. Paris: Gallimard, 1973.
—. *Mythes et dieux des Germains*. Paris: Ernest Leroux, 1939.
—. *Servius et la Fortune*. Paris: Gallimard, 1943.
—. *Le Troisième Souverain*. Paris: Maisonneuve, 1949.
Eliot, T. S. 'Views and Reviews: Journalist of Yesterday and Today'. *The New English Weekly*, 8 February 1940.
Eribon Didier. *Michel Foucault*. Trans. Betsy Wing. Cambridge, MA: Harvard University Press, 1991.

Epicurus. 'Letter to Herodotus'. In *Hellenistic Philosophy: Introductory Readings*. Ed. Brad Inwood and Lloyd P. Gerson. Indianapolis: Hackett Publishing, 1997.

—. 'Letter to Menoeceus'. In *Hellenistic Philosophy: Introductory Readings*. Ed. Brad Inwood and Lloyd P. Gerson. Indianapolis: Hackett Publishing, 1997.

—. 'Principal Doctrines'. In *Hellenistic Philosophy: Introductory Readings*. Ed. Brad Inwood and Lloyd P. Gerson. Indianapolis: Hackett Publishing, 1997.

Foucault, Michel. *L'Archéologie du savoir*. Paris: Gallimard, 1969. *The Archaeology of Knowledge*. Trans. A. M. Sheridan. London: Tavistock, 1972.

—. 'Ariane s'est pendu'. *Le Nouvel Observateur* 229, 31 March – 6 April 1969, 36–7.

—. *Dits et écrits. Tome III*. Ed. Daniel Defert, François Ewald and Jacques Lagrange. Paris: Gallimard, 1994.

—. *Essential Works of Foucault 1954–1984, Volume 1, Ethics*. Ed. Paul Rabinow and trans. Robert Hurley et al. New York: The New Press, 1997.

—. *Essential Works of Foucault 1954–1984, Volume 2: Aesthetics, Method and Epistemology*. Ed. James D. Faubion and trans. Robert Hurley et al. New York: New Press, 1998.

—. *Essential Works of Foucault 1954–1984, Volume 3: Power*. Ed. James Faubion and trans. Robert Hurley et al. New York: New Press, 2000.

—. 'La grande colère des faits'. *Le Nouvel Observateur* 652, 9–15 May 1977, 84–6.

—. 'La prose d'Actéon'. *La Nouvelle Revue française* 135, March 1964, 444–59.

—. *Security, Territory, Population: Lectures at the Collège de France 1977–1978*. Ed. Michel Senellart and trans. Graham Burchell. Basingstoke and New York: Palgrave Macmillan, 2007.

—. *Society Must be Defended: Lectures at the Collège de France 1975–1976*. Ed. Mauro Bertani and Alessandro Fontana, Trans. David Macey. Basingstoke and New York: Palgrave Macmillan, 2003.

—. 'Theatrum Philosophicum'. *Critique* 282, 1970, 885–908.

—. *The Use of Pleasure: The History of Sexuality Volume Two*. New York. Pantheon, 1985.

Freud, Sigmund. *Beyond Pleasure Principle*. New York: Norton & Company, 1961.

—. '*The Ego and the Id*, 1923'. In *The Freud Reader*. Ed. Peter Gay. New York: Norton & Company, 1989, 628–59

—. 'Three Essays on the Theory of Sexuality (1905)'. In Sigmund Freud, *The Standard Edition of the Complete Psychological Works of Sigmund Freud, Volume VII (1901–1905)*. Ed. and trans. James Strachey, in collaboration with Anna Freud, assisted by Alix Strachey and Alan Tyson. London: The Hogarth Press Ltd, 1953, 130–248.

Gandillac, Maurice, 'Jean Wahl'. *Annuaire de l'Association des anciens élèves de l'École normale supérieure*. Paris: ENS, 1975.

Garrett, Aaron V. *Meaning in Spinoza's Method*. Cambridge: Cambridge University Press, 2003.

Geyskens, Tomas. 'Painting as Hysteria: Deleuze on Bacon'. *Deleuze Studies* 2(2), 2008, 140–54.

Gilbert, Jeremy, and Goffey, Andrew. 'Control Societies: Notes for an Introduction'. *New Formations* 84/85, 2015, 5–19.

Giolito, Christophe. *Histoires de la philosophie avec Martial Gueroult*. Paris: L'Harmattan, 1999.

Gleick, James. *Faster: The Acceleration of Just About Everything*. New York: Vintage, 2000.

Glucksmann, André. *Les Maîtres Penseurs*. Paris: Grasset, 1977. *The Master Thinkers*. Trans Brian Pearce. New York: Harper & Row, 1980.

Goddard, Jean-Christophe. 'Henri Maldiney et Gilles Deleuze. La station rythmique de l'œuvre d'art'. *Revista filosófica de Coimbra* 33, 2008, 109–24.

Goethe, Johann Wolfgang von. *Theory of Colours*, trans. C. L. Eastlake. Cambridge, MA: MIT Press, 1970.

Goetz, Benoît. 'L'araignée, le lézard et la tique: Deleuze et Heidegger lecteurs de Uexküll'. *Le Portique* 20, 2007. https://leportique.revues.org/1364 (last accessed 8/9/2016).

—. *Violence et subjectivité: Derrida, Deleuze, Maldiney*. Paris: Vrin, 2008.

Goldschmidt, Victor. *Le Système stoïcien et l'idée de temps*. Paris: Vrin, 1953.

Goodall, Jane. *Artaud and the Gnostic Drama*. Oxford: Clarendon, 1994.

Goody, Jack. *The Interface between the Written and the Oral*. Cambridge: Cambridge University Press, 1987.

Gordon Colin (ed.). *Michel Foucault: Power/ Knowledge: Selected Interviews and Other Writings 1972–1977*. Hemel Hempstead: Harvester Wheatsheaf, 1980.

Gould, James L. and Grant, Carol. *Animal Architects: Building and the Evolution of Intelligence*. New York: Basic Books, 2012.

Gould, Stephen J. *Wonderful Life: The Burgess Shale and the Nature of History*. New York: W. W. Norton, 1990.

Grace, Wendy. '*Faux Amis*: Foucault and Deleuze on Sexuality and Desire'. *Critical Inquiry* 36, Autumn 2009, 52–75.

Grant, Iain Hamilton. *Philosophies of Nature after Schelling*. London and New York: Continuum, 2006.

Graves, Paul. 'My Strange Quest for Leroi-Gourhan: Structuralism's Unwitting Hero'. *Antiquity* 68(259), 1994, 438–41.

Guattari, Félix (ed.). *Trois milliards de pervers: Grand encyclopédie des homosexualités*. Paris: Recherches, 1973.
Gueroult, Martial. *Berkeley, quatre études sur la perception et sur Dieu*. Paris: Aubier-Montaigne, 1956.
—. *Descartes selon l'ordres des raisons*, 2 vols. Paris: Aubier, 1953. *Descartes' Philosophy According to the Order of Reasons*, 2 vols. Trans. Roger Ariew. Minneapolis: University of Minnesota Press, 1984/1985.
—. *Dianoématique, II: Philosophie de l'histoire de la philosophie*. Paris: Aubier-Montaigne, 1979.
—. *Dianoématique, I: Histoire de la histoire de la philosophie*, 3 vols. Paris: Aubier-Montaigne, 1979/1984/1988.
—. *Dynamique et métaphysique leibniziennes*. Paris: Les Belles Lettres, 1934.
—. *Étendue et psychologie chez Malebranche*. Paris: Les Belles Lettres, 1939.
—. 'The History of Philosophy as a Philosophical Problem'. *The Monist* 53(4), 1969, 563–87.
—. *L'Évolution et la structure de la doctrine de la science chez Fichte*. Paris: Les Belles Lettres, 1930.
—. *Leçon inaugurale*, faite le 4 décembre 1951, Collège de France, chaire d'histoire et de technologie des systèmes philosophiques. Nogent-le-rotrou: Daupeley-Gourverneur, 1952.
—. *Malebranche*, 3 vols. Paris: Aubier-Montaigne, 1955/1959.
—. *La Philosophie transcendantale de Salomon Maimon*. Paris: Alcan, 1929.
—. *Spinoza, I: Dieu*. Paris: Aubier-Montaigne, 1968.
—. *Spinoza, II: L'âme*. Paris: Aubier-Montaigne, 1974.
Hallward, Peter. *Out of this World: Deleuze and the Philosophy of Creation*. London and New York: Verso, 2006.
Hartmann, Nicolai. *Philosophie der Natur. Abriss der speziellen Kategorienlehre*. Berlin: de Gruyter, 1980[2].
Haute, Philippe van. *Against Adaptation*. New York: Other Press, 2001.
—. 'Lacan Reads Klein: Some Remarks on the Body in Psychoanalytic Thought'. *Philosophy Today* 55, 2008, 54–62.
Haute, P. van and Geyskens, T. *Confusion of Tongues. The Primacy of Sexuality in Freud, Ferenczi and Laplanche*. New York: Other Press, 2004.
—. *From Death Instinct to Attachment Theory: The Primacy of the Child in Freud, Klein, and Hermann*. New York: Other Press, 2007.
Havelock, Eric A. *Preface to Plato*. Cambridge, MA: Harvard University Press, 1963.
Hayden, Patrick. 'Gilles Deleuze and Naturalism: A Convergence with Ecological Theory and Politics'. *Environmental Ethics* 19(2), 1998, 185–204.

Hedley, Douglas. *Coleridge, Philosophy and Religion: Aids to Reflection and the Mirror of the Spirit*. Cambridge: Cambridge University Press, 2004.

Hegel, G. W. F. *Ästhetik*. Berlin: Aufbau Verlag, 1955.

—. *Phenomenology of Spirit*. Trans. A. V. Miller. Oxford: Oxford University Press, 1977.

Hendlin, Yogi H. 'Multiplicity and *Welt*'. *Sign Systems Studies* 44(1/2), 2016, 94–110.

Hoffmeyer, Jesper. *Biosemiotics: An Examination into the Signs of Life and the Life of Signs*. Scranton: University of Scranton Press, 2009.

Holland, Eugene. *Deleuze and Guattari's* Anti-Oedipus*: Introduction to Schizoanalysis*. New York: Routledge, 1999.

—. *Nomad Citizenship: Free-Market Communism and the Slow-Motion General Strike*. Minneapolis: University of Minnesota Press, 2011.

Holloway, Ralph. 'Culture, a Human Domain'. *Current Anthropology* 10, 1969, 395–412.

Holmes, Brooke. 'Deleuze, Lucretius, and the Simulacrum of Naturalism'. In Brooke Holmes and W. H. Shearin (eds), *Dynamic Reading: Studies in the Reception of Epicureanism*. New York: Oxford University Press, 2012, 316–42.

Hughes, Joe. 'Ground, Transcendence and Method in Deleuze's Fichte'. In *At the Edges of Thought: Deleuze and Post-Kantian Philosophy*. Ed. Craig Lundy and Daniela Voss. Edinburgh: Edinburgh University Press, 2015, 146–67.

Ingold, Tim. 'The Temporality of the Landscape'. In *The Perception of the Environment: Essays on Livelihood, Dwelling, and Skill*. London: Routledge, 2000, 189–208.

—. '"Tools for the Hand, Language for the Face": An Appreciation of Leroi-Gourhan's *Gesture and Speech*'. *Studies in History and Philosophy of Biological and Biomedical Sciences* 30(4), 1999, 411–53.

Ionescu, Vlad. 'The Rigorous and the Vague: Aesthetics and Art History in Riegl, Wölfflin and Worringer'. *Journal of Art Historiography* 9(9), 2013, 1–24.

Isaacs, Susan. 'The Nature and Function of Phantasy'. In Melanie Klein et al. (eds), *Developments in Psycho-Analysis*. London: Hogarth Press, 1952, 67–121.

James, William. *A Pluralistic Universe*. Cambridge, MA and London: Harvard University Press, 1977.

—. *Talks to Teachers on Psychology, and to Students on Some of Life's Ideals*. New York: Henry Holt and Company, 1899.

—. *La Volonté de croire*. Trans. Loÿs Moulin. Paris: Flammarion, 1916.

—. *The Will to Believe and Other Essays in Popular Philosophy*. New York and London: Longmans, Green, 1907.

—. *The Writings of William James: A Comprehensive Edition*. Ed. John

J. McDermott. Chicago and London: The University of Chicago Press, 1977.

Janicaud, Dominique. *Ravaisson et la métaphysique. Une généalogie du spiritualisme française*. Paris: Vrin, 1997.

Johnson, Ryan J. 'Another Use of the Concept of the Simulacrum: Deleuze, Lucretius and the Practical Critique of Demystification'. *Deleuze Studies* 8(1), 2014, 70–93.

Jung, Carl. *Collected Papers on Analytical Psychology*. Trans. Constance E. Long. London: Baillière, Tindall & Co., 1916.

Kant, Immanuel. *Critique of Pure Reason*. Trans. Norman Kemp Smith. London: Macmillan, 1990.

Kelly, Kevin. *What Technology Wants*. New York: Penguin, 2010.

Kelly, Mark. 'Discipline is Control: Foucault contra Deleuze'. *New Formations* 84–5, 2015, 148–62.

Kerslake, Christian. *Deleuze and the Unconscious*. London: Continuum, 2007.

Klee, Paul. *Notebooks*, vol. 1. Trans. Ralph Mannheim. New York: Wittenborn Art Books, 1961.

Klein, Melanie. *The Psychoanalysis of Children*. London: Vintage, 1997.

—. *The Selected Melanie Klein*. Ed. Juliet Mitchell. New York: The Free Press, 1986.

Klein, Melanie et al. (eds). *Developments in Psycho-Analysis*. London: Hogarth, 1952.

Kristeva, Julia. *Melanie Klein*. Trans. Ross Guberman. New York: Cambridge University Press, 2001.

Leclerc, Stéphan (ed.). *Aux sources de la pensée de Gilles Deleuze*. Mons: Sils Maria, 2005.

Lacan, Jacques. *Écrits I*. Paris: Seuil, 1966.

—. *Écrits II*, Paris: Seuil, 1966.

—. 'Some Reflections on the Ego'. In *International Journal Psycho-Analysis* 34, 1953, 11–17.

Lapoujade, David. 'From Transcendental Empiricism to Worker Nomadism: William James'. *Pli* 9, 2000, 190–9.

Laruelle, François. *En tant qu'un*. Paris: Aubier, 1991.

Lefort, Claude. *Writing: The Political Test*. Ed. and trans. David Ames Curtis. Durham, NC: Duke University Press, 2000.

Leibniz, G. W. F. *Opuscules et fragments inédits de Leibniz*, ed. Louis Couturat. Paris: Félix Alcan, 1903.

Lemmonier, Pierre. 'Leroi-Gourhan: Ethnologue des techniques'. *Nouvelles de l'archéologie* 48/49, 1992, 13–17.

Leroi-Gourhan, André. *Évolution et techniques*, vol. 1, *L'Homme et la matière*. Paris: Albin Michel, 1943.

—. *Évolution et techniques*, vol. 2, *Milieu et techniques*. Paris: Albin Michel, 1945.

—. *Gesture and Speech*. Trans. Anna Bostock Berger. Cambridge, MA: MIT Press, 1993.

—. *The Hunters of Prehistory*. Trans. Claire Jacobson. New York: Atheneum, 1989.

—. 'Les fouilles d'Arcy-sur-Cure (Yvonne)'. *Gallia préhistoire* 4, 1961, 1–16.

—. *I piu' antichi artisti d'Europe*. Milan: Jaca Book, 1980. *The Dawn of European Art: An Introduction to Palaeolithic Cave Painting*. Trans. Sara Champion. Cambridge: Cambridge University Press, 1982.

—. *Méchanique vivante: Le crâne des vertébrés du poisson à l'homme*. Paris: Fayard, 1983.

—. *Pages oubliées sur le Japon*. Grenoble: Jérôme Millon, 2004.

—. *Pincevent: Campement magdalénien de chasseurs de Rennes*. Paris: Ministère de la Culture, 1984.

—. *Préhistoire de l'art occidental: L'art et les grandes civilisations*. Paris: Lucien Mazenod, 1965. *Treasures of Prehistoric Art*. Trans. Norbert Guterman. New York: Harry N. Abrams, 1967.

Leroi-Gourhan, André and Brézillon, Michel, *Fouilles de Pincevent: Essai d'analyse ethnographique d'un habitat magdalénien*, 2 vols. Paris: Éditions du CNRS, 1983.

—. 'L'habitation magdalenienne no. 1 de Pincevent près Montereau (Seine-et-marne)'. *Gallia préhistoire* 9, 1966, 263–363.

Leroi-Gourhan, André and Leroi-Gourhan, Arlette, 'Chronologies des grottes d'Arcy-sur-Cure (Yonne)'. *Gallia préhistoire* 7, 1967, 1–64.

Levinas, Emmanuel. *Outside the Subject*. Stanford: Stanford University Press, 1993.

Lewontin, Richard. *The Triple Helix: Gene, Organism and Environment*. Cambridge, MA: Harvard University Press, 2000.

Littleton, C. Scott. *The New Comparative Mythology: An Anthropological Assessment of the Theories of Georges Dumézil*, 3rd edn. Berkeley: University of California Press, 1982.

Lundy, Craig. 'Deleuze's Untimely: Uses and Abuses in the Appropriation of Nietzsche'. In *Deleuze and History*. Ed. Jeffrey Bell and Claire Colebrook. Edinburgh: Edinburgh University Press, 2009, 188–205.

—. *History and Becoming: Deleuze's Philosophy of Creativity*. Edinburgh: Edinburgh University Press, 2012.

Kapp, Ernst. *Grundlinien einer Philosophie der Technik: Zur Entstehungsgeschichte der Kultur aus neuen Gesichtspunkten*. Braunschweig: Verlag George Westermann, 1877. *Principes d'une philosophie de la technique*. Trans. Grégoire Chamayou. Paris: Vrin, 2007.

Keylor, William R. *Academy and Community: The Foundation of the French Historical Profession*. Cambridge, MA: Harvard University Press, 1975.

Kimball, Roger. 'Charles Péguy'. *The New Criterion* 36(10), 2001, 15.

Kleist, Heinrich von. *An Abyss Deep Enough. Letters of Heinrich von Kleist.* Ed. and trans. P. B. Miller. New York: E. P. Dutton, 1982.

—. *Heinrich von Kleist. Five Plays.* Ed. and trans. Martin Greenberg. New Haven and London: Yale University Press, 1988.

—. *The Marquise of O-.* Ed. and trans. R. Stokes. London: Hesperus, 2003.

—. *Penthesilea.* Trans. J. Agee. New York: HarperCollins, 1998.

—. *Selected Prose of Heinrich von Kleist.* Ed. and trans. P. Wortsman. New York: Archipelago books, 2010.

—. *Three Plays. Prince Friedrich von Homberg, The Broken Pitcher, Ordeal by Fire.* Trans. Noel Clark. London: Oberon Books, 2000.

Latour, Bruno. 'Charles Péguy: Time, Space, and *le Monde Moderne*'. *New Literary History* 46(1), 2015, 43–5.

—.'Trains of Thought: Piaget, Formalism and the Fifth Dimension'. *Common Knowledge* 6(3), 1997, 170–91.

Le Rider, Jacques. *Nietzsche en France: De la fin du XIXe siècle au temps présent.* Paris: Presses universitaires de France, 1999.

Lipps, Theodor. *Ästhetik. Psychologie des Schönen und der Kunst.* Hamburg: Voss, 1903.

Lorenz, Konrad. *Referat über J. v. Üxküll.* Unpublished transcription by Hilde Fürnsinn. Lorenz-Archive of the KLI Institute for Evolution and Cognition Research of Altenberg, Austria, 1948.

Lucretius. *On the Nature of Things*, trans. W. H. D. Rouse and Martin F. Smith. Cambridge, MA: Harvard University Press, 2006.

Macey, David. *The Lives of Michel Foucault.* New York: Pantheon, 1994

McGrath, Sean J. *The Dark Ground of Spirit: Schelling and the Unconscious.* London: Routledge, 2012.

—. 'The Psychology of Productive Dissociation'. *Comparative and Continental Philosophy* 6:1, 2014, 35–48.

McLuhan, Marshall. *Understanding Media: The Extensions of Man*, critical edition. Ed. W. Terrence Gordon. Berkeley: Ginko Press, 2013.

Madelrieux, Stéphane. 'Pluralism without Pragmatism: Deleuze and the Ambiguities of the French Reception of James'. In Sean Bowden, Simone Bignall and Paul Patton (eds), *Deleuze and Pragmatism.* New York and London: Routledge, 2015.

Malafouris, Lambros. *How Things Shape the Mind: A Theory of Material Engagement.* Cambridge, MA: MIT Press, 2013.

Maldiney, Henri. *Regard Parole Espace.* Lausanne: L'Âge d'Homme, 1973

—. *Regard Parole Espace.* Paris: Éditions du Cerf, 2012.

Mancuso, Stefano and Viola, Allessandra. *Brilliant Green: The Surprising History and Science of Plant Intelligence.* Trans. Joan Benham. Washington, DC: Island Press, 2015.

Mann, Thomas. *The Marquise of O- & Other Stories*, ed. T. Greenberg. London: Faber & Faber, 1960.

Manuel-Barnay, Sylvie. 'Charles Péguy and Prophecy'. *History of European Ideas* 40(6), 2014, 777–87.

Marx, Karl. *Capital: A Critique of Political Economy*, vol. 1. Trans. Ben Fawkes. London: Penguin, 1990.

Matthews, Bruce. *Schelling's Organic Form of Philosophy: Life as the Schema of Freedom*. Albany: State University of New York Press, 2011.

Mehigan, Tim. 'Kleist, Hume, Kant and the 'Thing in Itself''. In B. Fischer (ed.), *A Companion to the Works of Heinrich von Kleist*. Rochester: Camden House, 2003, 165–88.

Merleau-Ponty, Maurice. *Phenomenology of Perception*. Trans. Colin Smith. London: Routledge, 1962.

Miller, Christopher. 'The Postidentitarian Predicament in the Footnotes of *A Thousand Plateaus*: Nomadology, Anthropology, and Authority'. *Diacritics* 23(3), 1993, 6–35.

Miller, Dean. A. 'Georges Dumézil: Theories, Critiques and Theoretical Extension'. *Religion* 30, 2000, 27–40.

Miller, James. *The Passion of Michel Foucault*. New York: Doubleday, 1993.

Montebello, Pierre. *Deleuze: La passion de la pensée*. Paris: Vrin, 2008.

Morar, Nicolae and Gracieuse, Majorie. 'Against the Incompatibility Thesis: A Rather Different Reading of the Desire-Pleasure Problem'. In Nicolae Morar, Thomas Nail and Daniel W. Smith (eds), *Between Deleuze and Foucault*. Edinburgh: Edinburgh University Press, 2106, 232–46.

Nealon, Jeffrey. 'Control'. In Leonard Lawlor and John Nale (eds), *The Cambridge Foucault Lexicon*. Cambridge: Cambridge University Press, 2014, 84.

Nedoh, B. and Zevnik, A. (eds). *Deleuze and Lacan: A Disjunctive Synthesis*, Edinburgh: Edinburgh University Press, 2017.

Nietzsche, Friedrich. *The Genealogy of Morals*. Trans. Walter Kauffmann. New York: Viking, 1967.

—. *The Will to Power*. Trans. Walter Kaufmann and R. J. Hollingdale. New York: Random House, 1967.

Obbink, Dirk. 'Lucretius and the Herculaneum Library'. In Stuart Gillespie and Philip Hardie (eds), *The Cambridge Companion to Lucretius*. New York: Cambridge University Press, 2007, 33–40.

Ong, Walter J. *Orality and Literacy: The Technologizing of the Word*. London and New York: Routledge, 1982.

Ortigues, Edmond. *Le Discours et le symbole*. Paris: Aubier, 1962.

Owens, Jill. 'The Book of Paul Auster'. *Powell's City of Books*, 24 January 2007, available at http://www.powells.com/post/interviews/the-book-of-paul-auster (last accessed 19/12/2016).

Panofsky, Erwin. 'Abbot Suger of Saint Denis'. In *Meaning in the Visual Arts*. Garden City, NY: Doubleday Anchor Books, 1955, 126–31.

Patton, Paul. 'From Resistance to Government: Foucault's Lectures 1976–1979'. In C. Falzon, T. O'Leary and J. Sawicki (eds), *A Companion to Foucault*. Oxford: Blackwell, 2013, 172–88.

Peden, Knox. *Spinoza Contra Phenomenology: French Rationalism from Cavaillès to Deleuze*, Stanford: Stanford University Press, 2014.

—. 'Donald Davidson's "Spinozistic Extravagance"'. *Critical Horizons* 18, 2017, 347–58.

Péguy, Charles. 'Un économiste socialiste, M. Léon Walras'. *Revue socialiste* XXV, 1897, 174–86.

—. *Clio*, Paris: Gallimard, 1932.

—. *Œuvres en prose complètes*, vol. 2. Ed. Robert Burac. Paris: Gallimard, 1988.

—. *Œuvres en prose complètes*, vol. 3. Ed. Robert Burac. Paris: Gallimard, 1992.

—. *Temporal and Eternal*. Trans. Alexandre Dru. Indianapolis: Liberty Fund, 2001.

Pelegrin, Jacques. 'A Framework for Analyzing Prehistoric Stone Tool Manufacture and a tentative Application to Some Early Stone Industries'. In A. Berthelet and J. Chavaillon. *The Use of Tools by Humans and Non-Human Primates*. Oxford: Clarendon Press, 1993, 302–14.

Pieron, Julien. 'Monadologie et/ou constructivisme? Heidegger, Deleuze, Uexküll'. *Bulletin d'analyse phénoménologique* 6(2), 2010, 86–117.

Pilkington, A. E. *Bergson and His Influence: A Reassessment*. Cambridge: Cambridge University Press, 1976.

Pinkard, Terry. *Hegel: A Biography*. Cambridge: Cambridge University Press, 2000.

Popper, Karl. *Objective Knowledge: An Evolutionary Approach*, rev. edn. Oxford: Oxford University Press, 1972.

Privat, Edouard (ed.). *Les Chemins de l'anti-œdipe*. Toulouse: Bibliothèque de psychologie clinique, 1974.

Protevi, John. 'Review: Peter Hallward, Out of this World: Deleuze and the Philosophy of Creation'. *Notre Dame Philosophical Reviews* 3 August 2007, https://ndpr.nd.edu/news/23058–out-of-this-world-deleuze-and-the-philosophy-of-creation (last accessed 19/1/2015).

Proust, Marcel. *In Search of Lost Time (Volumes 1–6)*. Trans. C. K. Scott Moncrieff. London: Vintage, 1996.

Razac, Olivier. *Avec Foucault, Après Foucault: Disséquer la société de contrôle*. Paris: L'Harmattan 2008.

Renan, Ernest. *The Future of Science: Ideas of 1848*. Trans. Albert D. Vandam. London: Chapman & Hall, 1891.

Rey, Jean-François. *À dessein de soi. Introduction à la philosophie d'Henri Maldiney*. Argenteuil: Le Cercle herméneutique, 2014.

Riegl, Aloïs. *Die Entstehung der Barockkunst in Rom. Vorlesungen aus 1901–1902*. Vienna: Kunstverlag Anton Schroll, 1923.

—. *Historische Grammatik der bildenden Künste. Vorlesungen von 1897–1899*. Cologne: Böhlaus, 1966.

—. *Das holländische Gruppenporträt*. Vienna: Druck und Verlag der Österreichischen Staatsdrukerei, 1931.

—. *Spätrömische Kunstindustrie*. Vienna: Österreichische Staatsdruckerei, 1927.

Roe, Glenn. H. *The Passion of Charles Péguy: Literature, Modernity, and the Crisis of Historicism*. Oxford: Oxford University Press, 2014.

Roffe, Jon. 'Economic Systems and the Problematic Character of Price'. In Rosi Braidotti and Simone Bignall (eds), *Posthuman Ecologies: Complexity and Process after Deleuze*. London: Rowman Littlefield International, forthcoming.

—. 'Error, Illusion, Deception: Deleuze against James'. In Sean Bowden, Simone Bignall and Paul Patton (eds), *Deleuze and Pragmatism*. New York and London: Routledge, 2015, 73–88.

Rose, Steven. *The Chemistry of Life*, 4th edn. London: Penguin, 1999.

Rosset, Clément. *L'Objet singulier*. Paris: Minuit, 1989.

—. *Le Réel: Traité de l'idiotie*. Paris: Éditions de Minuit, 1977.

—. 'Sécheresse de Deleuze'. *L'Arc* 49, 1972. Reprinted in *Gilles Deleuze*. Ed. Catherine Clément. Paris: Éditions Inculte, 2005, 219–25.

Rothenberg, David, *Hand's End: Technology and the Limits of Nature*. Berkeley: University of California Press, 1995.

Ruyer, Raymond. *L'Animal, l'homme, la function symbolique*. Paris: Gallimard, 1964.

—. 'Du vital au psychique'. In *Valeur philosophique de la psychologie*. Paris: Presses universitaires de France, 1951.

—. *L'Hominescence*. Paris: Éditions Le Pommier, 2001.

—. 'Le paradoxe de l'amibe et la psychologie'. *Journal de psychologie normale et pathologique* July–December 1938, 472–92.

Scheer, Edward. 'I Artaud BWO: The Uses of Artaud's *To Have Done with the Judgement of God*'. In Laura Cull (ed.), *Deleuze and Performance*. Edinburgh: Edinburgh University Press, 2009, 37–53.

Schelling, F. W. J. 'Ideas on a Philosophy of Nature as an Introduction to this Science'. Trans. Priscilla Hayden-Roy. In *Philosophy of German Idealism*. Ed. Ernst Behler. The German Library, vol. 23. New York: Continuum, 1987.

—. *Philosophical Inquiries into the Essence of Human Freedom*. Trans. Jeff Love and Johannes Schmidt. Albany: State University of New York Press, 2006.

—. *Philosophie der Offenbarung 1841/1842 (Paulus Nachschrift)*. Ed. Manfred Frank Frankfurt am Main: Suhrkamp, 1977.

Schmaltz, Tad M. '*PanzerCartesianer*: The Descartes of Martial Gueroult's *Descartes selon l'ordre des raisons*'. *Journal of the History of Philosophy* 52(1), 2014, 1–13.

Schneider, Robert. *Schellings und Hegels schwabische Geistesahnen.* Würzburg: Tiltsch, 1938.

Schmitt, Hans. A. *Charles Péguy: The Decline of an Idealist.* Louisiana State University Press, 1967.

Schrift, Alan D. *Twentieth-Century French Philosophy: Key Themes and Thinkers.* Malden, MA: Wiley-Blackwell, 2006.

Schuster, Aaron. *The Trouble with Pleasure.* Cambridge, MA: MIT Press, 2016.

Sedley, David. 'Epicureanism in the Roman Republic'. In James Warren (ed.), *The Cambridge Companion to Epicureanism.* New York: Cambridge University Press, 2009, 29–45.

Sergent, Bernard. 'Georges Dumézil'. Trans. Chet Wiener, available online https://greekromanworld.wordpress.com/2013/05/023/georges-dumezil.

Serres, Michel. *The Birth of Physics.* Trans. Jack Hawkes. Manchester: Clinamen Press, 2000.

—. *L'Incandescent.* Paris: Éditions Le Pommier, 2003.

—. *Rameaux.* Paris: Éditions Le Pommier, 2004.

Servais, Y. *Charles Péguy: The Pursuit of Salvation.* London: Newman Press, 1953.

Simondon, Gilbert. *L'Individu et sa genèse physico-biologique.* Paris: Presses universitaires de France, 1964.

Sinclair, Mark. 'Embodiment: Conceptions of the Lived-Body from Maine de Biran to Bergson'. In Alison Stone (ed.), *The Edinburgh Critical History of Nineteenth-Century Philosophy.* Edinburgh: Edinburgh University Press, 2011.

Skinner, Quentin. *Visions of Politics, I: Regarding Method.* Cambridge: Cambridge University Press, 2002.

Smith, Arthur David, 'Spinoza, Gueroult, and Substance'. *Philosophy and Phenomenological Research* 88(3), May 2014, 655–88

Smith, Daniel W. 'Deleuze, Hegel, and the Post-Kantian Tradition'. *Philosophy Today* 44: Supplement, 2000, 119–31.

—. 'Flow, Code and Stock: A Note on Deleuze's Political Philosophy'. In *Essays on Deleuze.* Edinburgh: Edinburgh University Press, 2012, 160–72.

Speer, Andreas. 'Beyond Art and Beauty. In Search of the Object of Philosophical Aesthetics'. *International Journal of Philosophical Studies* 8(1), 2000, 74–88.

—. 'Medieval Aesthetics'. In *The Oxford Handbook of Medieval Philosophy.* Ed. John Marenbon. Oxford: Oxford University Press, 2012, 661–84.

Spinoza, Benedict. *The Ethics.* Trans. R. H. M. Elwes. New York: Dover Publications, 1955.

Steigler, Bernard. *Technics and Time 1: The Fault of Epimetheus.* Trans. Richard Beardsworth and George Collins. Stanford: Stanford University Press, 1998.

Straus, Erwin. *The Primary World of Senses: A Vindication of Sensory Experience*. Trans. Jacob Needleman. London: Free Press, 1963.
Świątkowski, Piotrek. *Deleuze and Desire*. Leuven: Leuven University Press, 2015.
Sylvester, David. *The Brutality of Fact: Interviews with Francis Bacon*, 3rd edn expanded. New York: Thames & Hudson, 1963.
Terray, Emmanuel. 'Une nouvelle anthropologie politique?'. *L'Homme* 110, April–June 1989, 5–29.
Tomlinson, Gary. *A Million Years of Music: The Emergence of Human Modernity*. New York: Zone Books, 2016.
Toscano, Alberto. 'The Intolerable Inquiry: The Documents of the *Groupe d'information sur les prisons*'. *Viewpoint Magazine* 3, 2013. https://viewpointmag.com/2013/09/30/issue-3–workers-inquiry/
—. *The Theatre of Production: Philosophy and Individuation between Kant and Deleuze*. Basingstoke: Palgrave Macmillan, 2006.
Uexküll, Jakob von. *Bedeutungslehre*. Leipzig: Verlag von J. A. Barth, 1940.
—. *A Foray into the Worlds of Animals and Humans with A Theory of Meaning*, Trans. Joseph D. O'Neil. Minneapolis: University of Minneapolis Press, 2010.
—. *Mondes animaux et monde humain, suivi de Théorie de la signification*. Trans. Philippe Muller. Paris: Denöel, 1965.
—. *Streifzüge durch die Umwelten von Tieren und Menschen: Ein Bilderbuch unsichtbarer Welten. Bedeutungslehre*. Hamburg: Rowohlt, 1956.
—. 'Das Subjekt als Träger des Lebens'. *Die neue Rundschau* 23, 1912, 99–107.
—. *Theoretische Biologie. 2. gänzlich neu bearbeitete Auflage*. Berlin: Springer, 1928.
—. 'Die Umwelt'. *Die neue Rundschau* 21, 1910, 638–49.
—. *Umwelt und Innenwelt der Tiere*. Berlin: Springer, 1909.
—. *Der unsterbliche Geist in der Natur*. Hamburg: Wegner, 1938.
—. 'Wie gestaltet das Leben ein Subjekt'. *Die neue Rundschau* 23, 1912, 1082–91.
—. 'Wirkungen und Gegenwirkungen im Subjekt'. *Die neue Rundschau* 23, 1912, 1399–1406.
Uexküll, Jakob von and Kriszat, Georg. *Streifzüge durch die Umwelten von Tieren und Menschen: Ein Bilderbuch unsichtbarer Welten*. Berlin: Verlag von Julius Springer, 1934.
Uhlmann, Anthony. 'Expression and Affect in Kleist, Beckett and Deleuze'. In Laura Cull (ed.), *Deleuze and Performance*. Edinburgh: Edinburgh University Press, 2009, 54–70.
Vater, Michael. 'Reconfiguring Identity in Schelling's *Würzburg System*'. In Lore Hühn, Paul Ziche and Philipp Schwab (eds), *Schelling-Studies*, vol. 2. Freiburg im Breisgau and Munich: Verlag Karl Alber, 2014.
Villani, Arnaud. *La Guêpe et l'orchidée*. Paris: Benin, 1999.

Villiers, Marjorie. *Charles Péguy: A Study in Integrity*. New York: Harper & Row, 1965.

Vivieros de Castros, Eduardo. *Cannibal Metaphysics: For a Post-Structural Anthropology*. Trans. Peter Skafish. Minneapolis: Univocal Press, 2014.

—. 'The Untimely Again'. In *The Archeology of Violence*. Trans. Jeanine Herman. New York: semiotext(e), 2010, 9–51.

Voss, Daniela. *Conditions of Thought: Deleuze and the Transcendental Ideas*. Edinburgh: Edinburgh University Press, 2013.

Wahl, Jean. *L'Avant-dernière pensée de Nietzsche*. Paris: Centre de documentation universitaire, 1961.

—. *Human Existence and Transcendence*. Trans. and ed. William C. Hackett. Notre Dame: University of Notre Dame Press, 2016.

—. 'Nietzsche et la philosophie'. *Revue de métaphysique et de morale* 68(3), 1963, 352–79.

—. *La Pensée philosophique de Nietzsche des années 1885–1888*. Paris: Centre de documentation universitaire, 1959.

—. *The Pluralist Philosophies of England and America*. Trans. Fred Rothwell. London: Open Court, 1925.

—. *Transcendence and the Concrete: Selected Writings*. Ed. Alan D. Schrift and Ian Alexander Moore. New York: Fordham University Press, 2017.

—. *Vers le concret*. Paris: Vrin, 1932.

Weeks, Andrew. *Boehme: An Intellectual Biography of the Seventeenth-Century Philosopher and Mystic*. Albany: State University of New York Press, 1991.

Whitehead Alfred N. *Process and Reality*. Toronto: The Macmillan Company, 1929.

Widder, Nathan. 'From Negation to Disjunction in a World of Simulacra: Deleuze and Melanie Klein'. *Deleuze Studies* 3(2), 2009, 207–31.

Wiesing, Lambert. *Die Sichtbarkeit des Bildes. Geschichte und Perspektiven der formalen Ästhetik*. Reinbek: Rowohlt Taschenbuch, 1997.

Williams, James. 'A. N. Whitehead'. In Ed. Graham Jones and Jon Roffe (eds), *Deleuze's Philosophical Lineage*. Edinburgh: Edinburgh University Press, 2009, 282–99.

—. *Gilles Deleuze's Logic of Sense: A Critical Introduction and Guide*. Edinburgh: Edinburgh University Press, 2008.

Wilson, E. O. *The Insect Societies*. Cambridge, MA: Harvard University Press, 1971.

Wilson, E. O. and Holldobler, Bert. *The Ants*. Cambridge, MA: Harvard University Press, 1990.

Wirth, Jason. *The Conspiracy of Life: Meditations on Schelling and His Time*. Albany: State University of New York Press, 2003.

—. 'Introduction'. In Jason Wirth (ed.), *Schelling Now: Contemporary Readings*. Bloomington and Indianapolis: Indiana University Press, 2005.

—. *Schelling's Practice of the Wild: Time, Art, Imagination*. Albany: State University of New York Press, 2015.

Worringer, Wilhelm. *Abstraktion und Einfühlung. Ein Beitrag zur Stilpsychologie*. Munich: Fink, 2007.

—. *Abstraction and Empathy. A Contribution to the Psychology of Style*. Trans. Michael Bullock. New York: International Universities Press, 1953.

—. *Fragen und Gegenfragen. Schriften zum Kunstproblem*. Munich: Piper, 1956.

Wynn, Thomas. *The Evolution of Spatial Competence*. Urbana: University of Illinois Press, 1989.

Zafiropoulos, Markos. *Lacan et Lévi-Strauss, ou le retour à Freud 1951–1957*. Paris: Presses universitaires de France, 2003.

Zamberlin, Mary F. *Rhizosphere: Gilles Deleuze and the 'Minor' American Writings of William James, W. E .B. Du Bois, Gertrude Stein, Jean Toomer, and William Faulkner*. New York and London: Routledge, 2006.

Žižek, Slavoj. *Organs without Bodies*. London: Routledge, 2004.

Zerner, Henri. 'L'histoire de l'art d'Aloïs Riegl. Un formalisme tactique'. *Critique* August–September 1975, 941–52.

Zourabichvili, François. *Deleuze: A Philosophy of the Event, together with The Vocabulary of Deleuze*. Trans. Kieran Aarons. Edinburgh: Edinburgh University Press, 2012.

Notes on the Contributors

Michael J. Bennett is Faculty Fellow in the Humanities at the University of King's College, Canada. He is the author of *Deleuze and Ancient Greek Physics: The Image of Nature* (Bloomsbury, 2017) and co-editor of *Deleuze and Evolutionary Theory* (Edinburgh University Press, forthcoming). He publishes in the areas of twentieth-century European philosophy, the philosophy of biology, and the history of philosophy.

Ronald Bogue is Distinguished Research Professor Emeritus of Comparative Literature at the University of Georgia. His books include *Deleuze and Guattari* (Routledge, 1989), *Deleuze on Literature* (Routledge, 2003), *Deleuze on Cinema* (Routledge, 2003), *Deleuze on Music, Painting, and the Arts* (Routledge, 2003), *Deleuze's Wake: Tributes and Tributaries* (SUNY Press, 2004), *Deleuze's Way: Essays in Transverse Ethics and Aesthetics* (Routledge, 2007), *Deleuzian Fabulation and the Scars of History* (2010) and *Thinking with Deleuze* (Edinburgh University Press, 2019).

Sean Bowden is Senior Lecturer in Philosophy at Deakin University, Australia. He is the author of *The Priority of Events: Deleuze's* Logic of Sense (Edinburgh University Press, 2011) and the co-editor of *Deleuze and Pragmatism* (Routledge 2015, with Simone Bignall and Paul Patton) and *Badiou and Philosophy* (Edinburgh University Press, 2012, with Simon Duffy). His work has appeared in the *European Journal of Philosophy*, *Angelaki*, *Critical Horizons*, *Journal of Speculative Philosophy*, *Deleuze Studies*, *Parrhesia* and elsewhere.

Carlo Brentari is Research Fellow at the Department of Humanities of the University of Trento (Italy). In 2002 he obtained a doctorate in philosophy at the Karl-Franzens-Universität of Graz (Austria). His main research fields are the German philosophical anthropology of the twentieth century, the ethology of Konrad Lorenz, modern and contemporary theoretical biologyand, in particular, the work of Jakob von Uexküll. His current research is devoted to the ontology of nature developed by the Latvian-German philosopher Nicolai Hartmann.

Kyla Bruff is a PhD candidate in the Department of Philosophy at Memorial University. Her work primarily investigates the metaphysical commitments of political positions, particularly in classical German philosophy. Kyla speaks and works in English, French and German. Many of her publications track the interactions and resonances between nineteenth- and twentieth-century German and French philosophy. She is Managing Editor of *Kabiri*, Treasurer of the North American Schelling Society and Co-Director of For a New Earth. Her doctoral dissertation is on the relation between Schelling and Adorno, and is supervised by Dr Sean McGrath.

Vlad Ionescu is a post-doctoral researcher at the Faculty of Architecture and Arts, Hasselt University, Belgium. He has read philosophy at the KU Leuven where he defended his doctoral thesis entitled *Touch and See: Image Analysis in Aloïs Riegl, Heinrich Wölfflin and Wilhelm Worringer* (2012). Since then, he has published on art and architectural theory in *Architectural Histories*, *The Journal of Art Historiography*, *Deleuze Studies*, *Image and Narrative Cultural Politics*, *ARS* and in various edited volumes. He is the author of *Applied Arts, Implied Art. Craftsmanship and Technology in the Age of Art Industry* (A&S Books, 2016) and *Pneumatology: An Inquiry into the Representation of Wind, Air, and Breath* (ASP Editions, 2017) and the co-translator of the Leuven University Press series *Jean-François Lyotard. Writings on Contemporary Art and Artists.*

Graham Jones is a Lecturer in Creative Writing, Literary Studies and Media and Communications at Federation University, Australia and the author of *Lyotard Reframed* (I. B. Tauris, 2013), and co-editor of *Acinemas: Lyotard's Philosophy of Film* (Edinburgh University Press, 2017) and *Sensorium: Aesthetics, Art, Life* (Cambridge Scholars, 2007). He was the co-founder and original convenor of the Australasian Society for Continental Philosophy. His current research interests concern French poststructuralist philosophy, avant-garde art and cybernetics.

Craig Lundy is a Senior Lecturer in Social Theory at Nottingham Trent University. He is the author of *Deleuze's Bergsonism* (2018) and *History and Becoming: Deleuze's Philosophy of Creativity* (2012) and co-editor with Daniela Voss of *At the Edges of Thought: Deleuze and Post-Kantian Philosophy* (2015), all published with Edinburgh University Press.

Paul Patton is Scientia Professor of Philosophy at the University of New South Wales in Sydney, Australia. He is the author of *Deleuze and the Political* (Routledge, 2000), *Deleuzian Concepts: Philosophy, Colonization, Politics* (Stanford University Press, 2010), and numerous articles and book chapters on Deleuze, Foucault and a variety of topics in contemporary social and political philosophy.

Knox Peden is Gerry Higgins Lecturer in the History of Philosophy at the University of Melbourne. He is the author of *Spinoza Contra Phenomenology: French Rationalism from Cavaillès to Deleuze* (Stanford University Press, 2014) and the co-editor, with Peter Hallward, of a two-volume work devoted to the *Cahiers pour l'analyse* (Verso, 2012). His writings have also appeared in *Modern Intellectual History*, *History of European Ideas*, *History & Theory* and *Intellectual History Review*.

Jon Roffe teaches philosophy at the Melbourne School of Continental Philosophy. The co-editor of a number of volumes on twentieth-century and contemporary French thought, he is the author of *Badiou's Deleuze* (Acumen, 2012), *Abstract Market Theory* (Palgrave, 2015), *Gilles Deleuze's* Empiricism and Subjectivity (Edinburgh University Press, 2016) and the forthcoming two-volume *Works of Gilles Deleuze* (re-press); he is also the co-author of *Lacan Deleuze Badiou* (Edinburgh University Press, 2014) and *Practising with Deleuze* (Edinburgh University Press, 2017). His latest book is *Seduce or Die* (Surpllus, 2019), a collection of aphorisms.

Edward Scheer is Head of School of Art and Design at the University of New South Wales, Australia. He is author, co-author and editor of numerous books in the area of performance and new media including, most recently, *New Media Dramaturgy* (Palgrave, 2017, with Peter Eckersall and Helena Grehan and William Yang) and *Stories of Love and Death* (New South Press, 2016, with Helena Grehan). He was President of PSi, *Performance Studies International* (2007–11) and a member of the Australian Research Council College of Experts (2013–15).

Daniel W. Smith is Professor of Philosophy at Purdue University. He is the author of *Essays on Deleuze* (Edinburgh University Press, 2012) and editor of the *Cambridge Companion to Deleuze* (2012, with Henry Somers Hall); *Deleuze and Ethics* (2011, with Nathan Jun) and *Gilles Deleuze: Image and Text* (2009, with Eugene W. Holland and Charles J. Stivale). He is also the translator, from the French, of books by Gilles Deleuze, Pierre Klossowski, Isabelle Stengers and Michel Serres.

Piotrek Świątkowski is a Senior Lecturer in International Economics at Rotterdam University of Applied Sciences and an independent researcher in philosophy. He is the author of *Deleuze and Desire* (Leuven University Press, 2015).

Kamini Vellodi is Lecturer in Contemporary Art Theory and Practice at Edinburgh College of Art, University of Edinburgh. She is the author of *Tintoretto's Difference: Deleuze, Diagrammatics and Art History* (Bloomsbury, 2018), and has published widely on Continental philosophy of art, the philosophy of art history and sixteenth-century visual art.

Index

Printed and bound by PG in the USA